The Theory and Practice of Personnel Management

The Theory and Practice of Personnel Management

MAURICE W. CUMING
M.A. (Wales), F.I.P.M.

Education Officer, Institute of Health Service Administrators. Formerly, Senior Tutor in Personnel Management, King's Fund College

THIRD EDITION

Revised reprint

HEINEMANN : LONDON

William Heinemann Ltd
15 Queen St, Mayfair, London W1X 8BE

LONDON   MELBOURNE   TORONTO
JOHANNESBURG   AUCKLAND

Made and printed in Great Britain
by Butler & Tanner Ltd, Frome and London

For
EIRA

Preface

Why a third edition of this book?

Taking the traditional functions of personnel management as being Employment, Training, Remuneration, Industrial Relations and Welfare — then the simple answer is that earlier texts are now dated. Since the second edition of *The Theory and Practice of Personnel Management* was published in 1972, all these main aspects of personnel management have undergone significant developments: for example, through the Employment and Training Act 1973; the abolition of statutory prices and incomes policies; dramatic changes in industrial relations law; and new policies, legislation, and research reports affecting job satisfaction, occupational health and safety at work. Altogether, a score or more new activities or policy statements, emanating from central government and professional bodies, have appeared during the past three years, each of which has represented a step forward towards enlightened staff management which in turn contributes to the over-riding aim of organizational efficiency.

Most of these developments have been peculiar to the personnel management scene in Britain, so there is no reference to them in books published in America. My objective, then, has been to make available to British personnel managers and students a comprehensive and up-to-date text which analyses proven good policy and practice in their professional work.

M.W.C.

Postscript The opportunity to reprint has enabled much of the information and statistics contained in the text to be further updated, and corrections to be made to slight errors which readers have kindly brought to my attention.

M.W.C., 1977

Acknowledgments

I am most grateful to Frank Reeves, Director of the King's Fund College, and to my employer, King Edward's Hospital Fund for London, for their own example of enlightened personnel policy in granting me 'sabbaticals'— both in 1967 to write the original work, and in 1972 to produce the second edition. My thanks also to Mrs. A. Gilbert who typed the many changes necessary in this third edition.

May I also express my sincere thanks to all the individuals and organizations who so readily granted permission to use references and quotations. The final chapter grew from a concept of Management Audit developed by my former colleague Tony Dale.

M.W.C.

Contents

         Page

Preface   vii

Acknowledgments   viii

1 The Personnel Management Function   1

Definitions—The scope of personnel management—Historical development—Theories on organization—Justification—Advisory role—The individual and personnel management—The behavioural sciences

2 Personnel Policy   21

Principles—Main policy statements: Employment, Training, Wages and Salaries, Labour Relations, Welfare—Practical examples—Publishing personnel policies—Creating policies: consultation and explanation—Future enlightenment?

3 Motivation   32

Why man works—Research into behaviour at work—Job satisfaction and frustration—Effective leadership—Individual personality—Work group sanctions—Group dynamics

4 The Employment Function   52

Manpower planning—Local employment intelligence—Recruitment procedure—Job requisitions—Job analysis—Sources of labour supply—Advertising Jobs—Dealing with applications—References

5 Selection of Staff   76

The interview—Panel interviews—Selection tests—Group selection techniques—Validation

6 Aspects of Employment—Transfer, Promotion, Termination   88

The Contracts of Employment Act, 1972—Transfers of staff—Staff promotion—Termination of employment—Redundancy—The Redundancy Payments Act, 1965

7 Special Categories of the Labour Force   101

Married women—Part-time workers—Older people—Disabled workers Immigrant workers—Race Relations Act, 1968

8 Staff Assessment   120

Theory—Purposes—Procedure—Content of report forms—The second
stage: discussion of reports—A positive contribution from the subordinate—Follow-up—Criticisms of reports on staff—Group assessments—Assessment centres

9 Management by Objectives   145

Applying the technique—Unit improvement plan—The formula for
development—Conclusion

10 The Training Function   159

Legislation—Industrial Training Boards—The Government's direct
role—Induction training—Job training—Programmed instruction—
Apprenticeships—Retraining older workers

11 Training Supervisors and Managers   175

Supervisory training—Management development—The circuit scheme
—Training personnel managers—Evaluation of training

12 Wages and Salaries—The National Scene   190

Collective bargaining—Factors in negotiating wages—Government
intervention—Attempts at a national wages policy—Success or failure?
The way ahead—Long-term wage agreements—Problems of low pay—
The Equal Pay Act and the Sex Discrimination Act

13 Wages and Salaries—The Individual and Productivity   213

Differentials—Incentives—Job evaluation—Merit-rating—Suggestion
schemes—Profit-sharing—Salaries—Productivity bargains

14 The Framework of Industrial Relations   233

Traditional structure—Disputes machinery—The problems faced by
the Donovan Commission—The two systems—The Trade Union and
Labour Relations Acts, 1974 and 1976—Code of Industrial Relations
Practice—Institutions

15 Labour Relations at the Workplace   254

Shop stewards—Workshop rule—Joint consultation—'The reform of
collective bargaining at plant and company level'—Trade unionism
among white-collar workers—The Employment Protection Act, 1975—
Conclusion

16 Communications   279

The process of communicating—What to communicate—How to communicate—The art of persuasion—Measuring success in communicating

17 Problems of Morale   292

Definition of morale—Discipline—Democracy in industry—Dealing
with individual staff problems—Absenteeism—Labour turnover—
Mergers and take-overs

18 Working Conditions, Welfare, and Status   310

Physical environment—Hours of work—Welfare—Staff-worker status

19 Health and Safety   326

The Factories Act, 1961—The Offices, Shops, and Railway Premises Act,
1963—Occupational Health Services—Safety of workers—The Health
and Safety at Work Act, 1974

20 Administering the Personnel Function   339

Structure—The department budget—Introducing personnel management—Help from outside organizations—Department of Employment
services—Management consultants—Professional associations and
voluntary organizations—Reception and security—The records section

21 Human Asset Accounting   358

Techniques—Practical applications—Accountancy and personnel
management

22 Auditing the Personnel Management Function   365

Techniques for managing total labour resources: Getting the best from
individuals

Appendix A: Addresses of Organizations   375

Appendix B: The Bullock Committee Report on Industrial   375
            Democracy

Index   377

1 The Personnel Management Function

DEFINITIONS

'To obtain and retain employees', or its Anglo-Saxon version—'To get and keep workers'—is as good a nutshell definition of personnel management as any.

Most people who work in organizations large enough to have a specialist personnel officer regard him, in the first place, as the man to whom they applied for their jobs. His prime task is *to recruit* the number of employees of suitable calibre required to meet his organization's needs. Having got them, he is concerned to keep them happy so that they will want to stay. The personnel officer must see to it that each employee is properly *trained* to cope with the demands of his job; otherwise he will feel inadequate, become increasingly frustrated, and eventually leave. He will not be happy if his *wages and working conditions* are unsatisfactory: if he feels his pay is unjust, or if hours of work, holidays or the physical environment around him are not what they should be—again he will try to improve on them elsewhere. Disputes that are not settled quickly will upset the delicate balance of *labour relations*. Changes introduced by management without prior consultation to obtain the views of all staff affected will have the same effect. Finally, most industrial communities have now developed a tradition of catering for the *welfare* of employees: helping them in times of need, for example, with sickness benefits and pension schemes, offering guidance with domestic problems, and providing social facilities for leisure hours.

All these activities together amount to an organization's attempt to maintain a stable labour force and to stimulate the efforts of its members in a positive manner. To expand the 'snap' definition which opened this chapter, then, *personnel management is concerned with obtaining the best possible staff for an organization and, having got them, looking after them so that they will want to stay and give of their best to their jobs.*

In 1963 the Institute of Personnel Management celebrated its Golden Jubilee, and took the opportunity to publish an 'official' definition:

'Personnel management is a responsibility of all those who manage people as well as being a description of the work of those who are employed as specialists. It is that part of management which is concerned with people at work and with their relationships within an enterprise. It applies not only to industry and commerce but to all fields of employment.

'Personnel management aims to achieve both efficiency and justice, neither of which can be pursued successfully without the other. It seeks to bring together and develop into an effective organization the men and women who make up an enterprise enabling each to make his own best contribution to its success both as an individual and as a member of a working group. It seeks to provide fair terms and conditions of employment and satisfying work for those employed.'

The first paragraph applies directly to small businesses or to those larger organizations, particularly in the public sector, where specialist personnel departments have not yet been established. It also makes the point from the outset that personnel management is an advisory function, seeking to give practical help to line managers, but in no way detracting from their ultimate responsibility for controlling their subordinates.

The second paragraph of the definition contains a number of key words or phrases. 'Efficiency' bluntly indicates the need to judge the personnel function in the same terms as every other management activity—does it contribute to the profitability of the business? To draw an analogy: as the number of legal problems arising from its business grows, a firm will ask itself 'will it pay to employ a solicitor full time, or should we continue to buy legal advice from outside?' The same sort of question, but in a wider sphere, should be answered about the specialization of personnel management, before a board of directors can be convinced of its effectiveness in economic terms. 'Justice', as applied to staff matters, simply demands that all employees should be treated fairly and consistently; it also surely implies that policy towards staff should be progressive, steadily improving as workers' motivation is better understood and the climate of industrial opinion becomes more and more enlightened.

The phrases 'effective organization' and 'working groups' underline this need for management understanding of worker motivation. Few people work in splendid isolation as backroom boffins; most of us are members of teams, and the human problems of our ever-changing relationships with each other are of fundamental importance to the personnel specialist. For instance, the first-line supervisor may grow increasingly apprehensive about the erosion of some of his traditional tasks by the proffered advice of work study officers, production planners, quality inspectors, and even personnel managers.

But as well as concern with techniques and practices and with the development of the right team spirit, the personnel manager must constantly be conscious that he is dealing with individual human beings, each with his own dignity to safeguard. Every employee questions the impact of management activity from a personal point of view, and the reaction of individuals should be anticipated before decisions or changes are made affecting them. Running throughout any formal study of the practice of personnel management, therefore, must be a fundamental regard for *human relationships* and *communications*.

THE SCOPE OF PERSONNEL MANAGEMENT

By no means can all the functions listed below be found in every personnel department up and down the country, but they do cover the range of tasks seen in many commercial and industrial organizations where personnel management has been established as a speciality for some time:

1. EMPLOYMENT

Manpower planning.

Preparation of job descriptions.

Contact with and development of all potential sources of labour supply.

Interviewing applicants for jobs; engaging labour; transfers; promotions; dismissals.

Maintenance of employee records and control statistics.

Application of the organization's terms and conditions of employment; hours of work; overtime.

Grading of employees.

Legislation concerning employment.

2. TRAINING AND EDUCATION

Induction and job training of all new entrants; follow-up of their progress.

Provision of instructors and training officers.

Development of potential supervisors and managers.

Encouraging further education through day continuation schools, technical colleges, and correspondence courses.

Arranging programmes of visitors for works tours.

Provision of a library.

Meeting legal requirements.

3. WAGES AND SALARIES

Maintenance of the organization's wage and salary structure, while observing Government pay policy.

Job evaluation—control of differential rates of pay.

Measurements of individual performance—incentives, merit-rating (usually with work study experts).

Running a suggestions scheme.

Efficiency agreements and productivity bargaining.

4. INDUSTRIAL RELATIONS

Publishing and interpreting the organization's personnel policy.

Negotiating with trade unions, through a recognized procedure for dealing with workplace grievances.

Providing joint consultative machinery—works councils, joint production committees, for example.

Publishing a staff magazine; controlling notice boards and information bulletins.

Representing the organization in outside negotiations affecting its staff.

5. WELFARE SERVICES AND SAFETY

Employee amenities—canteen, benevolent club, savings schemes.

Superannuation; long-service grants.

Legal aid; consultations about individual personal or domestic problems.

Assistance with accommodation and transport difficulties.

Provision of social and recreational facilities.

Application of provisions of the Health and Safety at Work, etc., Act; contact with Inspectorate.

Occupational health service—medical examination of employees, keeping health records, and visiting sick absentees.

Accident prevention; safety education.

HISTORICAL DEVELOPMENT

The origins of personnel management can be found wherever enlightened employers have tried over the years to improve the lot of their workers. The activities of such men as the Duke of Bridgewater, Lord Shaftesbury, and Wedgewood are well known; by the mid-nineteenth century, Courtaulds had something approaching a guaranteed minimum wage scheme for their workers. Robert Owen (1771–1858) is best remembered for his trade union activities, but he also incurred the wrath of his business partners by spending some of their profits on improving the working and living conditions of his labour force at New Lanark. Perhaps his most enduring memorial, however, are the principles of management that he pioneered—particularly the right of all his employees, however low in the hierarchy, to see him personally on any matter concerning their welfare. This right of access to the highest authority is still not freely available to industrial workers, 150 years after Robert Owen's insistence upon it in his woollen mills.

Social change developed apace towards the end of the nineteenth century. The Education Act of 1870 resulted in the growth of a literate working class, which in turn became much more receptive of the ideas of trade unions and their activities in improving working conditions. Religious motives inspired the remarkable social work of employers like Rowntree and Cadbury, whose own workers benefited directly, of course.

The emphasis on the provision of welfare facilities grew, marked in 1913 by the formation of the Welfare Workers Association; in 1916 this became the Central Association of Welfare Workers, in 1924 the Institute of Industrial Welfare Workers, and after other changes in name, the Institute of Personnel Management in 1946. A large number of welfare workers, mainly female, were appointed during the years of the First World War, particularly in munitions factories. Their theoretical aim was to try to bring closer together the clashing interests of employers and workers; in practice, their efforts concentrated on making working conditions more congenial, experimenting with fringe benefits, and providing social amenities for leisure hours. Employers split away to form their own organization in 1919: this was the Industrial Welfare Society, which changed its name to The Industrial Society in 1965. Its original aims were to foster the exchange of ideas and information about welfare policies and techniques, but these have long since been broadened to cover the whole field of personnel management.

The *welfare* phase was a period of time, then, when deliberate efforts were made to create the ideal factory, in which the physical environment was perfect in terms of cleanliness, temperature, and lighting, and where worthwhile leisure pursuits were offered to workers in their spare time.

A marked reaction to this sort of paternalism soon developed. Workers always question the unsolicited provision of costly welfare facilities; most of them would prefer to have the money in their weekly pay packets instead. Inevitably, too, paternalism means influencing the private lives of workers: it is wishful thinking for an employer to consider his labour force as a family, motivated by the care he shows for their welfare. Lavish amenities might attract some types of employees to an organization in the first place, but they will not act as incentives for them to stay; more profound psychological needs must be satisfied to achieve this.

During the nineteen-twenties and thirties, Great Britain, in common with most industrial nations, went through long years of economic depression. Inevitably this caused a cutting back on non-essentials in industry, and many welfare departments were closed. The whole climate of economic opinion was negative; by and large, employers adopted a casual approach to labour, hiring and firing almost at will, and accepting no responsibilities towards their employees other than those required by law. For their part, workers feared insecurity so much that they were only too ready to accept whatever jobs and conditions were offered; in such circumstances, trade unions could be nothing else but on the defensive.

Efforts by the Government and progressive employers to overcome the Depression led to the emergence of the second main phase in the development of personnel management—the *scientific management* phase. The building of trading estates up and down the country and the expansion of light engineering factories depended largely on their owners' appreciation of the advantages of maintaining stable labour forces. The protagonists of scientific management argued in favour of clearly defined organization structures, each job within them being precisely described. The employees filling these jobs should be carefully selected, given appropriate training, and be provided with an environment conducive to efficient working. Even the economies of high wages, directly influencing labour stability, came to be realized.

These developments were accompanied by research projects controlled by industrial psychologists who aimed to improve selection tests and training methods, and investigated aspects of working conditions, for example, those causing fatigue and boredom. They particularly concerned themselves with worker motivation, seeking to understand men's reasons for working and the factors influencing their morale, in order to devise effective incentives to stimulate them to greater efforts. The result of all this activity was that personnel management became increasingly accepted during the nineteen-thirties as being able to offer a positive service to industry and commerce in terms of profitability.

Government recognition came with the Second World War, which brought about the third stage of development—the *industrial relations* phase. During the war, the cry was for continually increased production to meet the demands of the war effort. The emphasis was on co-operation— 'we must all pull together to win': management and trade unions were asked to forget the acrimony of the Depression years and combine their energies to win the war. The growth of factory joint consultation, particularly the establishment of joint production committees designed to tap workers' ideas for improving efficiency, was symptomatic of this concept. The Government encouraged the appointment of personnel officers throughout industry, and sponsored crash training programmes for these specialists at universities. A Personnel Management Advisory Service was created, attached to the Ministry of Labour; this still exists and any employer can call on the services of an officer from the Department of Employment's Advisory, Conciliation and Arbitration Service for advice about his staffing problems. Clearly, this demand for co-operation has remained with us: the need to export more to improve our balance of payments, and the need to increase productivity to improve our standard of living—both are familiar invocations, and both emphasize overcoming the 'them-and-us' mentality in industry. If we all produce more, we will all benefit.

Thus there has been nothing altruistic about the ways in which personnel management has developed. Innovations have tended to be based on the assumption that what is good for the individual is good for the organization as well. Each step forward can be seen as an investment to enhance the contribution, and thus the value, of the labour force, with the ultimate aim of enabling each individual to see that his interests and those of the organization for which he works are the same.

To a large extent, political and economic events have determined the rapid expansion of personnel management activities since the war. Successive governments in Great Britain have pursued a policy of full employment, and, apart from regional imbalances, have been largely successful in doing so. Anti-inflationary measures, taken to counter world-wide trends of rising prices, have adversely affected this situation in recent years, but available labour is still fully employed in most parts of the country. Managements' efforts at getting the best return from its labour force has therefore led to a fourth phase in the development of personnel management—that of *manpower planning*: on one hand, trying to deploy the total labour resources available to an organization in the most efficient manner; and, on the other, getting the best from each individual by developing to the full whatever potential he has to be trained for bigger and better jobs.

On the national scale this has involved economic planning, with measures to encourage industry to move to those regions with the highest unemployment, and to persuade labour to move from contracting to expanding industries. At the level of the individual firm, the concept of manpower planning involves techniques of assessing the suitability of employees in their present jobs, and devising training programmes to develop their potential to meet estimated future staff requirements. More and more, too, the participation of the individual is demanded. He is encouraged to play a positive part in the staff assessment procedures which determine the pattern of his future career; and there is much more concern being shown for immediate improvements in performance, for example by applying the technique of management by objectives.

In recent years there has also been a considerable increase in Government 'intervention' across the whole range of personnel management activity, aimed both at securing continuous growth in the country's economy and at developing a greater sense of social justice throughout the nation. There has been decisive, though not always successful, action taken on such matters as improving employment and training facilities, prices and incomes policies, attempts to control industrial relations, offer better protection to individual workers in employment, and improve working conditions and accident prevention.

Nothing emerges more clearly from this sketch of the history of personnel management than the increasing emphasis on the word 'management' in the phrase. Much of the work of a personnel department has always been routine in nature, applying established policies and procedures, well understood by the line managers being advised, to solve the sort of staff problems that crop up day by day in any business. Necessary as it is, this type of activity is basically clerical or administrative in nature; for example, the provision of personnel records, recruitment services, wage and salary administration, and welfare facilities. But the personnel specialist has, in addition, a much more dynamic role to play in the efficient management of his organization. He must be able to advise how present staff and labour resources can be adapted to meet future requirements. To draw a medical analogy, his function should be that of diagnosing the problems inherent in the current situation, and then prescribing the action that must be taken for his organization to move from the here-and-now to its forecasted desirable future position. This function is obviously much more creative than any form of routine administration.

THEORIES ON ORGANIZATION

Parallel with these developments in the procedures and practices of personnel management have been changes in that branch of management theory concerned with explaining the social organization of industry.

The *classical school*, largely influenced by the principles of scientific management, saw any organization as being firmly directed by one central authority within it, supreme and unquestionable. Organization charts made clear this unity of direction, illustrated the concepts of division of labour and span of control, and defined the lines of command. These followed the military pattern, which also set the tone for a code of employee behaviour based on loyalty and discipline—each individual willingly doing what was expected of him and not doing things which might harm the organization. Management's leadership task was to create conditions that would foster this loyalty among staff; there could be no opposition between management and worker representatives, and both must pull together to eliminate possible areas of conflict. Since efficiency depended on the clear exercise of qualities of personal leadership, the prerogative of management to manage must be kept intact; for example, the payment of high wages was seen both as a long-term economy and as an indication that negotiations with trade unions were unnecessary. The classical view of loyalty to the authority controlling the organization thus also implied that there should be no interference with its members from any outside body whether trade union, professional association, or government agency.

The *human relations school* saw authority as an attribute requiring acceptance by subordinates, rather than something that they gave up to management. Mayo's research at the Hawthorne Works of the General Electric Company in Chicago had proved that informal leaders emerge in working groups, and that each of these groups is likely to develop its own goals and standards of behaviour which may well be opposed to those of the official organization. Conflict was seen not as a symptom of the technical incompetence of management, but as a weakness in the social skills of individual leaders resulting in breakdowns in communications between management and workers.

Modern *system theory* sees each organization as a complete whole, influenced by its formal and informal structure, external conditions, technological factors, and the individual personalities of its employees. The concept of *role expectations* is a product of this theory—people at work like their relationships with each other to be predictable, otherwise they feel uncomfortable or under strain. Role conflict occurs when an individual is subjected to pressures from different sources and cannot comply with them all; or when the demands of his role in one group are not compatible with demands made of him in another group. Role ambiguity occurs when a person does not fully understand his job nor the expectations that other people have of his role. Both role conflict and role ambiguity cause the individuals affected to feel anxious, which in turn generates stress within the organization, thus making it less effective. Members of working groups cast their fellows and superiors in roles that are prescribed by their own expectations; and there is great pressure, because of the desire for predictability, for these roles to remain stable. Hence the reason why it is so difficult to make social changes, even in times of rapid technological advance.

Joan Woodward* has also proved that the technology of an industry demands certain forms of organization if a business is to be successful. Particular human relations difficulties emerge according to the type of technology concerned. In factories making motor cars, the manufacturing

* *Industrial Organization: Theory and Practice*, by Joan Woodward (Oxford University Press, 1965).

system means that large groups of employees work under conditions of strain and pressure, determined by the speed of the production line, with each supervisor in charge of a large number of workers; in other technologies, for example oil and chemical processing, production arrangements are such that workers are much less harassed and each supervisor has many fewer workers to control. The more leisurely atmosphere in the latter case means that staff problems which arise can be solved more readily. Where the technology is such that change inevitably takes a long time, the chances are better for reaching amicable solutions to the problems usually associated with the introduction of change. Miss Woodward's conclusions clearly show that when creating organization structures, and in trying to stabilize relationships between staff, considerable attention must be paid to the technological demands of the industry or service concerned.

Analysing the historical development of organizational theory has led Alan Fox* to plead for management to adopt a new frame of reference in the field of labour relations, based on an acceptance of the fact that organizations are composed of individuals and groups with some interests in common but with others in conflict. Managers should stop yearning for teams, families or 'happy ships', and face the reality of work-group interests that conflict, quite legitimately, with their own. 'The test of success here is how far management seeks honestly to understand the causes of work-group attitudes and policies, and why they are different from those of management. Failure lies in lacking the patience to find out, in refusing to take seriously the problems of those whose work and life experience is different from one's own, and in dismissing their policies as merely stupid, short-sighted or selfish. There must be a recognition that the legitimacy of unions rests not on the misdeeds of (other) managers, but on a socially preferred method of shared decision-making on labour matters. Given that "loyalty" is not an appropriate measure of behaviour in a contractual, impersonal employment relationship, it follows that a man can be aggressive in defence of his or his fellows' rights and still be a valuable employee. Management's job is that of engineering the highest level of reconciliation among the divergent interests of their divided, pluralistic realm.'

Exhortation has, so far, failed to achieve this state of affairs, and coercion is clearly impractical. What have emerged in recent years, under the guise of productivity bargaining, are attempts to effect structural change through negotiation. Such bargaining illustrates that some aspects of structure which management is seeking to change are positively valued

*'Managerial Ideology and Labour Relations', by Alan Fox, *British Journal of Industrial Relations*, page 375, Nov. 1966.

by employees, and they will be strongly defended unless a sufficient *quid pro quo* is offered in exchange.

JUSTIFICATION

How, in this development of theory and practice, has the personnel manager emerged as a specialist? What peculiar contribution does he make to the efficiency of an organization?

The primary justification, as with any other appointment, must be in terms of business efficiency. The salaries and wages costs of most organizations form a substantial part of total expenditure, in many service industries rising higher than 75 per cent. Capital is also invested in buildings to accommodate these staff and to furnish their rooms; senior staff are provided with assistants and with secretarial and clerical help. The overall concern of personnel management is to make sure that these huge investments are put to the best use.

This cannot be done without regard to fundamental concepts of human relations. Clearly no organization can operate efficiently unless its staff are content with what is offered them as human beings by way of job satisfaction, prospects, and working conditions. The personnel specialist's task is to identify the needs of employees in these areas, recognize what it is about his organization that fulfils these needs or frustrates them, and be able to advise departmental managers on actions that will promote this fulfilment or remove the frustrations. Heads of departments basically have technical responsibilities; the personnel specialist's job is to explain to them reasons for social behaviour which may not be obvious. Why, for example, are decisions that are technically and economically sound sometimes met by seemingly irrational resistance by subordinates? What emotional factors are at play when this sort of thing happens? Offering advice to clarify such situations is a task that demands an expert who has been trained to perceive the ways in which individuals and groups interact within an organization, and who can convey his understanding in practical terms to departmental heads who are too preoccupied with their technical activities to have time to consider the social system of the workplace as a whole.

It would clearly be too much to expect the personnel manager to practise all the behavioural sciences—psychology, anthropology, sociology, and others—but his training should be such that he can make intelligent use of the conclusions reached by such scientists.

ADVISORY ROLE

The role of the personnel manager has been tagged as acting as 'the social conscience of an organization', and it is clear that, as such, he is in a position to contribute considerably to the state of its staff morale. But it is important that this contribution is understood as being of an advisory nature: executive decisions must finally be taken by the line managers to whom advice is offered.

'Line' management can perhaps most readily be understood in terms of military organization, which imposes a clear line of command from the most senior officer down to the private soldier. Line managers are held fully accountable for the results achieved and everything else that happens in their departments; they are given orders from above and carry them out, often by passing on instructions to their own subordinates.

The personnel specialist, on the other hand, is a 'staff' or 'functional' manager, offering an expert service of advice to line managers to help them perform their jobs. Other examples are the legal officer, cost accountant, or work study officer—together with the personnel manager, all these specialists advise, assist, and service line managers, but have no direct authority over them or their staff. They work with senior colleagues through ideas, relying mainly on persuasion. Of course, to the extent that the personnel specialist's ideas are useful, timely, and generally acceptable, line managers will come to ask for his advice and will take it when given. When such advice is consistently put into effect, there is inevitably some blurring of the distinction between 'executive authority' and 'functional advice', but in such circumstances this is a welcome situation rather than one that should be resisted.

Nevertheless, in the last resort, it must be abundantly clear to everyone working in an organization that final authority rests in the hands of the chief executive. Otherwise the personnel manager could well find himself caught in a dilemma when some issue is raised where he personally feels that the viewpoint of his management colleagues is wrong. Such problems sometimes arise over individual cases of fair treatment, for example where promotion is concerned or hours of work of some employees are changed; the personnel manager could well find himself faced with a clash between the decisions of general management and his own view of the right thing to do.

In fact, difficulties of this nature only occur where executive powers are ascribed to the personnel specialist, and when he is put into the position of having to arbitrate between management and employees. This sort of situation simply should not be allowed to develop. The chief executive must retain ultimate control and there should be no blurring of line management's responsibilities by even a partial transfer of executive authority to a specialist adviser; otherwise there is a risk of contradictory policies emerging.

The Commission on Industrial Relations fully analysed the role of the personnel specialist in a report* published in 1973, suggesting the following considerations as an aid to the evolution of constructive management relationships. Firstly, both personnel and line managers need the authority to carry out their respective functions. The line manager is necessarily responsible for industrial relations (defined as embracing the broad range of all employment policies) in his particular area of operations; and he needs freedom to manage his plant, department, or section effectively within agreed policies and with access to specialist advice. The personnel manager should help by supplying expert knowledge and skill and by monitoring the consistent execution of personnel policies and programmes throughout the organization. He needs the backing of top management and must establish the authority which comes from giving sound advice.

Constant cross-consultation and collaboration between line and personnel managers makes both more effective. Line managers should be involved in formulating personnel policies and plans. 'The personnel manager is an integral part of the management team, and whatever his position in their hierarchy should be consulted and be able to influence all decisions where there are human implications.' The relationship between the two is likely to be constructive, however, only if there are clearly defined personnel policies which enable all managers to work towards the same objectives. Ultimately management's responsibility for good personnel practices is collective.

THE INDIVIDUAL AND PERSONNEL MANAGEMENT

Personnel policies and the techniques of personnel management all imply 'something being done' by an organization to or for its employees. But, if the personnel specialist is to carry out a creative role, it must be part of his day-to-day working philosophy to have regard for those employees as individual human beings. He must be able to view the other side of the coin and be aware that everyone working in this organization may constantly be asking—'in all the actions taken by my superiors under the guise of personnel management, what are the things that really matter most to me personally?' The answer to this question can perhaps simply be summarized as *knowledge* and *recognition*.

*C.I.R. Report No. 34, *The Role of Management in Industrial Relations* (H.M.S.O.).

In the first place, an individual needs to know what his job is, what his conditions of employment are, and how his work fits into the general activity going on around him. This seems so obvious as hardly to be worth stating, and yet there is evidence of such an obscurity about job definitions that it is a wonder how some organizations achieve any degree of efficiency at all. Maier and Hoffman's research* into job perception at the University of Michigan showed that of 222 managerial pairs, only eighteen agreed what the junior partner's duties were precisely. Fifteen of the present author's own students, carrying out their first job analysis exercises, each interviewed a hospital employee of supervisory grade. When these analyses were then checked with the supervisors' own bosses, there was not one single case of the subordinate's description of his job coinciding with his superior's understanding of it.

This whole area of expectation becomes even more confused when senior staff move around. For example, some managers seem unable to delegate authority to their subordinates, while others delegate extensively; when a boss changes from the former type of person to the latter, subordinate staff are sometimes placed in untenable positions, to the extent of feeling that their boss is giving them more work to do simply to make his own life easier. All this because no attempt has been made to clarify what is expected of subordinates in the performance of their duties, and what exactly their relationships to each other and with senior and junior staff should be.

Every employee, then, has the right to know what his job is, what results are expected of him, the standards by which his performance is measured, and what authority he has to take decisions on his own initiative. In turn, this should clarify his relationship with his superior—for surely, once expectations are clear, most people ask nothing more than to be left to get on with the job. In other words, few people like bosses who continually breathe down their necks—they much prefer them to be unobtrusive, but available to give help when asked.

Furthermore, this may now help to identify the individual's requirements for further training. His manager should know what standards of performance he expects: watching a subordinate work day by day will enable him to spot if he is falling short of those standards and try to do something, by way of additional training, to close the gap. The vast majority of training should take place in this way on the job; attendances at outside courses are infrequent events, and managers need to show much more courage and integrity in recognizing their personal responsibilities towards subordinates.

* *Superior–Subordinate Communication in Management*, by Norman R. F. Maier and others (A.M.A. Research Study No. 52; New York, 1961).

Individuals, too, look for recognition. We all like to be told when we are doing well; most of us choose to have our errors or shortcomings pointed out as well, especially if this is accompanied by positive advice about corrective action. The appraisal of staff by their seniors is a controversial subject, however, and its best-known forms are being replaced by the management-by-objectives technique which, in the event, demands the active participation of each individual employee in improving his own performance (*see* Chapter 9). Obviously, recognition must take tangible forms if employees are to be satisfied in the long term, and most individuals are ambitious for promotion and more pay. More frequent informal recognition is also important: on the one hand, a word of praise or the confidence that a boss clearly shows in a subordinate; on the other, the 'rocket' for a mistake. Both have a profound effect on the individual's attitude towards his boss and hence the organization for which he works, and on the status that he holds in the eyes of other staff.

Thus all the functions of personnel management must be looked at from the point of view of each individual employee's expectations. This approach helps to show how interdependent they are, for all these expectations must be realized if employees are to achieve efficient and improving results. Turning back to the techniques of personnel management to illustrate this point, an enlightened promotion policy, with an appropriate salary structure linked to it, will be of little use if the initial recruitment procedures are such that poor-calibre men are selected in the first place.

THE BEHAVIOURAL SCIENCES

Particularly relevant to the development of personnel management during the past few decades has been the research work carried out by behavioural scientists—sociologists, anthropologists, occupational psychologists, for example—aimed at developing techniques which will enable managers to obtain the best results from their labour forces. If any one common theme has emerged, it is surely that the concern which Alan Fox expresses about reconciling conflict in industry will only be relieved by methods designed to ensure the maximum participation of all employees in resolving the problems which affect them at work.

Historically, the development of the behavioural sciences must be set against the emergence of Western society's way of life. For the dominance of the consumer inevitably means conditioning the labour force to expect mainly economic satisfactions from work; only the higher-status professional groups are allowed to see any real meaning in their work. Admittedly, workers and trade unions are currently demanding more from the working situation than in the past; but although these requests some-times touch on interesting work and job satisfaction, more commonly they take the form of demands for a greater part in decision-making and parti-cipation in management processes.

Against this background, the social organization of the workplace may be analysed as a network of roles determined by the technology of the industry concerned, organizational objectives, methods of work control through sanctions, status factors and communications. As Alan Fox* points out, authority is based on legitimacy, so one of management's main tasks is to get workplace systems accepted as legitimate by their organiza-tion's employees. In a democratic setting, management can function suc-cessfully only so long as decisions are upheld by shared values on organ-izational objectives and methods of achieving them. It is this importance of shared values which poses a dilemma in modern industry, for the aspira-tions of individuals and groups of workers must also be taken into account; pressure is constantly growing from unions for improvements in the re-wards and satisfaction which people seek from work, and for greater influence on employers through participation in decision-making.

At the same time, it is also clear that there is no single technique guaran-teed to be the panacea for all ills; every organization has its peculiar features and needs, and the multiplicity of available techniques must be examined with those in mind. Nor have the experts yet finalized a 'chicken-and-egg' controversy about some of their more important conclusions. For example, the human relations school insists that the factors involved in motivation (*see* Chapter 3) are highly significant in determining the structure of relationships within organizations, and hence their efficiency. In simpler words, treating people right has no altruistic purposes: it pays off economically. On the other hand, there is a body of research which supports the opposite view—that the chain of causation is one in which the economic and technical efficiency of an organization determines the pattern of relationships and styles of behaviour revealed by its employees.

In the event, the philosophical question must also be raised—will we ever achieve ultimate truths in management? For instance, in analysing styles of management, Douglas McGregor's Theory X and Theory Y (*see* page 145) carry overtones of general approval for the latter approach. By the same token, the equally famous Blake–Mouton grid† presents a model of managerial commitment and training techniques aimed at developing 9,9 managers who achieve production through mature inter-personal rela-

---

* *A Sociology of Work in Industry*, by Alan Fox (Collier-Macmillan, 1971).
† *The Managerial Grid*, by R. R. Blake and J. S. Mouton (Gulf Publishing Co., 1965).

tionships which are integrated with the purposes of the organization: thus

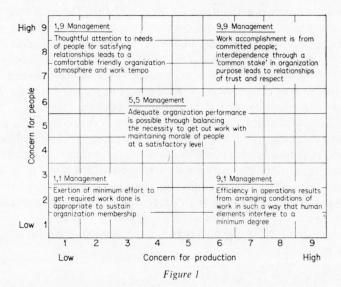

High 9	1,9 Management			9,9 Management	
	Thoughtful attention to needs of people for satisfying relationships leads to a comfortable friendly organization atmosphere and work tempo			Work accomplishment is from committed people; interdependence through a 'common stake' in organization purpose leads to relationships of trust and respect	

Figure 1

Another view came with Reddin's analysis* of managerial styles, in which he discards the concept that any one style is universally desirable. While accepting relationships-orientation and task-orientation as the basic directions of management activity, Reddin argues that flexibility is essential for effectiveness: that is, managers must be prepared to use different styles in different situations. Among all the approaches possible, there is no one general best fit: if the style used is appropriate to the situation, it will be effective; if it is inappropriate, the situation will be handled ineffectively.

McGregor's work calls for a rather fuller comment; for in addition to the profound influence which his Theory X and Theory Y proposition has had on management thinking, he developed other basic ideas which collectively assert that long-term progress in staff management will come only with a better understanding of the behavioural sciences. Thus he analysed† the standards of performance achieved by an individual at work as being a function of the relationships between the personal characteristics of that individual (including his knowledge, skills, motivation, and attitudes) and certain aspects of his working environment (including the nature of his job, its rewards, and the leadership he receives):

$$P = f(I_{abc} \ldots E_{123} \ldots)$$

* *Managerial Effectiveness*, by W. J. Reddin (McGraw-Hill, 1970).
† *The Professional Manager*, by Douglas McGregor (McGraw-Hill, 1967).

The relationships among these variables are many and complex; behavioural scientists are concerned with helping managers reach precise and quantitative statements about them. Linked with this, Theory Y postulates that management strategy should be aimed at creating conditions which enable each individual to achieve his own goals best by directing his efforts towards organizational goals. Tactically, this is very demanding of management, who have to agree acceptable performance standards with subordinates, secure commitment to clear targets for improvement, build mutual trust and support, and maintain open communications.

In effect, McGregor's research resulted in a new value system for management. One example is his view on the management of differences, rejecting all the traditional methods of resolving conflict—divide and rule, suppressing disputes, majority voting, and even arbitration—in favour of a strategy of working through differences as a means of achieving innovation, commitment to the decisions reached, and a strengthening of relationships between the members of a working group.

The main problems* to which behavioural scientists have directed their attention have included:

1. Problems of structuring work and authority.
2. Understanding the motivation of people at work, incentives, and job satisfaction.
3. The causes of frustration and conflict in the workplace.
4. The leadership role of managers in optimising employees' performance.
5. The development of better training techniques.
6. Communications systems.
7. The impact of the physical and social environment on employees' health, attitudes, and working efficiency.
8. Methods of introducing changes to effect organizational improvement, especially those involving employee participation.

In general, the intertwining of the behavioural sciences and personnel management has been concerned with 'tools', concepts and methods of tackling new problems. As regards the former, for example, psychologists have provided tests of specific capacities to help in staff selection; in turn, the results achieved, linked with those of other tests, have helped to develop the theoretical framework of mental ability and skills: (thus theory and practice advance step by step). Rewards, especially incentive schemes, and analyses of informal organization† are examples of concepts emerging

---

* Many of these are analysed in detail in later chapters.

† *cf.* the Donovan Commission Report.

from personnel practice, while typical of the new problems currently being tackled are those of organizational design and career development.

At the same time, the limitations of the techniques must be recognized. Few, if any, purport to apply to a broad canvas; most scientific progress is on a small scale and step by step: so it is with advances in the behavioural sciences. It has also been proved that the best results are likely to be obtained not by importing consultants with prepared packages of ready solutions, but by involving an organization's own representatives and personnel staff in the decisions taken about which behavioural science techniques to use, and in running and monitoring the programme then put into practice. Trade union representatives especially need to be won. over, for there is always the fear that any new or unusual approach may exploit their members.

Thus the behavioural and social sciences provide an ideological basis for many of the most recent developments in the practice of personnel management. Psychology has offered many techniques; sociology has investigated organizational design; social psychology has contributed performance assessment and career planning; manpower planning techniques are inter-disciplinary. 'The subject most potentially fruitful today for the personnel manager goes by the title of "Organisational Behaviour", which attempts to explore the interface between the organization and its environment.' In this context,* Professor Cherns advances the happy thought that to the extent that leadership in an organization passed to the sector which is trying to cope with that organization's area of maximum uncertainty, the immediate future of the personnel specialist seems assured.

This new general approach, better known as *Organisational Development*, has been defined† as—'The process of planning and implementing changes in an organization through the application of the behavioural sciences with the objective of strengthening human processes and so improving the functioning of the organization in the achievement of its objectives.' Thus planning means making changes in a deliberate manner, and involves applying behavioural science knowledge in the initial diagnosis of problems, planning and executing the necessary changes, and finally evaluating their results. Organizational development in this sense means a continuous process of movement, from a static situation where staff perhaps inherently resist change, to a climate which promotes it so that the organization becomes readily adaptive. If change is seen as a continuing activity in this way, then the organization will be better equipped to survive and grow in a rapidly changing environment.

* 'Personnel Management and the Social Sciences', by Professor A. Cherns, *Personnel Review*, Vol. 1, Spring 1972, page 10.
† H. S. Gill and D. R. Tranfield in *Personnel Management*, April 1973.

FURTHER READING

Practice of Personnel Management, The, by David Barber (I.P.M., 1970).
Personnel Management 1913–63, by M. M. Niven (I.P.M., 1967).
The Role of Management in Industrial Relations, C.I.R., Report No. 34 (H.M.S.O., 1973).
A Sociology of Work in Industry, by Alan Fox (Collier-Macmillan, 1971).
Personnel Management in Context, by Anne Crichton (Batsford, 1968).

2 Personnel Policy

PRINCIPLES

The policy of an organization is a clear-cut statement of its aims and objectives, setting out what is to be achieved. Looking at this definition negatively, its significance can perhaps be brought out thus. That policy is *not* the writing of a plan or programme: it is concerned with what is to be done rather than how to do it. *Nor* is policy a summary of what has happened in the past, presented as a report. Above all, policy statements are *not* vague, waffly documents—they must be clear and precise.

Policies are needed for the whole range of an organization's activities, of course: production, financial, marketing, exporting, plant maintenance, and public relations are examples. But the preparation of personnel policies, and their subsequent publication generally or to a limited list of senior staff, seems to arouse much more controversy than the others. Nevertheless, it is generally acknowledged that where policies are not widely known throughout an organization, there is inevitably a reluctance on the part of senior staff to delegate authority. In turn, this means that the confidence of junior managers is not developed in the ways it can be when they are given clear policy statements to guide their daily activities at work. The job of top management is essentially creative in nature and should concentrate on major long-term aspects of the business. But where the use of policies is lacking in the over-centralized manner described above, then this task may become overladen with the heavy burden of having to settle many of the individual grievances and problems that crop up day by day but which, from the point of view of business efficiency, should usually be settled at a much lower level of authority.

To some extent, the personnel policies of any organization will always be determined by factors outside its control—by the nature of the society in which it exists, Government action, political pressures, local culture, and business ethics. We in Western civilization observe *Christian ideals*, which have achieved their maximum impact on social service during the twentieth century. The humanitarian content of the Sermon on the Mount is inescapable, and we profess concern about the economic abuses of our affluent society both in our own country and abroad. Of course, even in its limited industrial context, this is an enormous subject, beset with accusations of sharp practice levelled at management and unions alike. Charge and counter-charge are easily made. For example, any victimization on the part of management or strike action by unions can be called un-Christian, because they are aggressive in nature; but the answer that, in an imperfect world, we all have the right to defend our own interests, is shattering in its simplicity.

Against this ethical background there are certain *principles* which must be observed in formulating the *main personnel policies*. These may be expressed initially in terms of the five main areas of personnel management activity, but they must then be elaborated in the form of a number of *subsidiary policies* under each heading. In turn, associated with all these headings will be certain *rules* and *regulations* to ease the interpretation and application of policy by junior managers who rely on documentary guidance when dealing with particular kinds of problems or when taking decisions in repetitive situations.

The three main principles upon which personnel policies in British industry, commerce, and public service are based acknowledge:

1. That all employees should be treated with *justice*, under a 'code of fair play' which means having regard for equity, that no favouritism or antagonism should be shown towards individuals, and that there should be consistency in treatment between all employees and over periods of time.

2. That the *needs* of employees must be *recognized*, particularly their desires for job satisfaction, for knowledge of what is going on within the organization, and for consultation before changes affecting them take place.

3. That a business will function better *democratically* rather than autocratically; success is much more likely if the co-operation of employees is sought in achieving objectives than by trying to coerce them to these ends with the use of authority.

The personnel manager has a direct part to play in ensuring that these principles are applied in practice. To look on them merely as expressions of good intentions is not sufficient; they must be reflected in the policy statements which will be used as guides to decision-taking. This is clearly a much more satisfactory situation than desperately trying to remember, each time a problem crops up, what previous decisions exist by way of precedent.

MAIN POLICY STATEMENTS

Once the principles upon which personnel policies are based have been generally accepted, the next step is to prepare the actual policies for the five main areas of the personnel function. These must be clear-cut and precisely written, so that everyone in the organization knows exactly what are its aims concerning its employees.

Here is an example of a policy statement in each of the main areas, as they might apply to a large company in private industry.

1. EMPLOYMENT POLICY

To obtain suitably qualified and experienced personnel, and to enable them to derive satisfaction from employment by offering them attractive wages, good working conditions, security, and opportunities for promotion.

2. TRAINING POLICY

To provide adequate training facilities to enable each employee to learn to do his job effectively and to prepare himself for promotion.

3. WAGES AND SALARY POLICY

To pay wages and salaries that compare favourably with other firms locally, within a structure that has due regard for recognized differentials and individual ability.

4. LABOUR RELATIONS POLICY

To operate adequate procedures for dealing with all disputes and grievances quickly and to make every effort to improve relations between management and employees through joint consultation.

5. WELFARE POLICY

To safeguard the health and safety of all employees, and to provide such welfare and social amenities as are sincerely desired by employees and are mutually beneficial to them and the company.

No matter how precise these main statements are, each covers such a wide area that they must be supplemented by subsidiary policies under more specific headings. To some extent these will inevitably reflect local circumstances and economic pressures; it is likely, for example, that their content will take a more generous form in areas of over-full employment compared with places where labour is plentiful. It is difficult to generalize, therefore, but taking account of the principles and main statements set out above, policies for these subsidiary headings might include the following.

EMPLOYMENT

EXAMPLES

(*a*) *Manpower planning:* The company's recruitment and staff development programmes will be based on forecasts of its future labour requirements, projected five years ahead, and kept under constant review.

(*b*) *Job descriptions:* These will be written for all vacant posts and will be supplied to candidates. Staff charged with filling posts will be given job specifications.

(*c*) *Recruitment methods:* The recruitment process will be supervised by personnel department staff who have been fully trained in selection techniques, and who will advise on the methods appropriate to the type and seniority of the job concerned.

LIST OF OTHER HEADINGS

(*d*) Staff transfers.

(*e*) Promotion policies.

(*f*) Termination of employment.

(*g*) Redundancy policy.

(*h*) Employment of special categories of labour; for example, married women, disabled workers, and the aged.

(*Note:* Policies for these headings are discussed in later chapters.)

TRAINING

EXAMPLES

(*a*) *Induction:* All new employees will be helped to settle in their jobs by receiving instruction in the company's organization, policies, and working practices.

(*b*) *Operator:* All employees will be given full training in the skills, methods, and equipment used in their jobs.

LIST OF OTHER HEADINGS

(*c*) Apprenticeships.

(*d*) Staff assessment.

(*e*) Foremanship (for potential and experienced supervisors).

(*f*) Management development.

WAGES AND SALARIES

EXAMPLES

(*a*) *Basic payments:* These will be made according to national agreements, with local adjustments as negotiated, and current Government policy.

(*b*) *Differentials:* Payment for jobs will take into account such differences as the effort and skill required, the responsibilities involved, and the unpleasantness of working conditions.

LIST OF OTHER HEADINGS

(*c*) Rewarding individual performance.
(*d*) Job evaluation.
(*e*) Merit-rating.
(*f*) Use of financial incentives.
(g) Efficiency agreements.

LABOUR RELATIONS

EXAMPLES

(*a*) *Communications:* All employees of the organization will be kept fully informed of company policies and plans for the future.

(*b*) *Joint consultation:* No changes concerning working arrangements or conditions will be decided until the views of staff concerned have been obtained.

(*c*) *Grievances and disputes:* All these will be dealt with by management quickly; they must not be allowed to drag on and thus damage the co-operative spirit established over the years.

LIST OF OTHER HEADINGS

(*d*) Attitude towards membership of trade unions.
(*e*) Recognition and training of worker representatives.
(*f*) Negotiating procedure.
(g) Worker participation at board level.

WELFARE

EXAMPLES

(*a*) *Occupational health:* It is mutually beneficial to the company and employees to ensure that the physical capacity of all staff matches the requirements of their jobs. Services covering initial and periodic medical examinations, for the treatment of accidents and sudden illness of staff, and the prevention of occupational diseases, will therefore be provided.

(*b*) *Safety:* All possible measures, from specialist education to investigation, will be taken to prevent accidents: joint consultation on the subject is essential.

(*c*) *Personal problems:* All employees may look to their departmental heads, and through them to the personnel department, for help with personal or domestic problems.

LIST OF OTHER HEADINGS

(*d*) Pension plans.

(*e*) Sickness benefit schemes.

(*f*) Transport arrangements for employees reaching and leaving work.

(*g*) Help with accommodation difficulties.

(*h*) Financial help.

(*i*) Canteens.

(*j*) Sports clubs, leisure, and social activities.

These policy statements will need to be further elaborated in some cases by rules and regulations which must be observed by all staff affected. The distinction between these various types of procedure can perhaps best be made clear by the means of an illustration, this time taken from the public sector, concerning salaries and wages.

1. The appropriate *principle* is obviously that of justice—a fair payment for a fair day's work.
2. *The main policy* statement might be: 'to pay salaries and wages according to scales laid down nationally in Whitley Council agreements for all grades of staff and all jobs within those grades.'
3. The *subsidiary policies* will deal with such matters as differentials and incentives, where relevant.
4. An example of a *rule* would be that any increase in salary can only be awarded to an individual if his job is regraded to a higher level.
5. This rule would then be followed by certain *regulations* for putting it into effect. One of these might be that, to obtain a regrading of his job, any individual must submit his case in writing to the Management Committee or Council.

PUBLISHING PERSONNEL POLICIES

There has always been controversy among personnel managers about the extent to which policies should be made known throughout an organization. Indeed, some feel that the dangers inherent are so great that the policies should not even be written down—but this all leads to the centralized or personalized view of management activity previously criticized. That there are dangers and problems in theory cannot be denied, but if safeguards are taken against these, then the practical advantages of publishing personnel policies far outweigh the potential snags.

The basic difficulty is that of trying to ensure precise definition of the policies. This is essentially a problem of communications, of overcoming the semantic barrier so that all senior staff share a common understanding of the language used in describing human situations. As individuals, they are, of course, themselves subject to the organization's policies and, human nature being as it is, they may make their own reservations or feel personal resistance in interpreting and applying policy. The personnel manager's advisory work must therefore embrace the conflicts which his line-manager colleagues may feel exist between their own personal objectives and those of the organization.

Other alleged dangers include those of—entering a type of contract with employees from which management could not withdraw, even though circumstances may change considerably; the impossibility of writing policies to cover the whole range of likely staff problems; and the fact that the rigidity of policy statements may restrict management discretion to deal sympathetically with individual cases. In practice, these fears simply prescribe the care that must be taken when writing policy, rather than amounting to a case against its publication at all. The same thoroughness in preparation must be shown as when drawing up any legal document relating to the company's activities. By definition, policy statements indicate the general lines of action; their wording should be flexible enough to cover all possible problems and changing circumstances, and to allow scope for the exercise of judgment on the part of management in interpreting them. In an entirely different field, the Wireless and Telegraphy Act, 1906, provided an excellent example of flexible policy writing: only four pages long, it required no amendment until 1959, although radio and television were not in use until many years after its original enactment.

Having refuted the theoretical drawbacks in this way, it is abundantly clear that a published statement of personnel policies has many practical benefits. The type of action necessary to achieve the organization's objectives is specified, and thus serves to clarify management thinking on personnel problems. Co-operation and teamwork are encouraged by the fact that decision-making will now be uniform and consistent between departments and over periods of time. Policy statements help in the delegation and decentralization of authority, and consequently they are useful aids when training supervisors and developing managers. As far as staff as a whole are concerned, policies reflect the interest taken in them by employers and show their goodwill. The 'rules of the game' which govern employee behaviour at work are clearly conveyed in this way, too, thus helping in induction and job training. Generally, morale will tend to be high throughout an organization when everyone is aware that any labour relations problems will be tackled in a fair and consistent manner.

In any event, minimum standards of personnel policy are increasingly imposed by legislation: the Contracts of Employment Act, Redundancy Payments Acts, Race Relations Act, and Equal Pay Act are all examples. Bearing in mind the principles already set out for personnel policies, it ill-behoves professional personnel managers to associate themselves with any of the efforts which, it is alleged, have been made to circumvent various aspects of these statutes because of their potential threat to profits. The personnel manager should, in fact, represent the social conscience of his organization.

FUTURE ENLIGHTENMENT?

Largely dictated by the increasing challenge of economic conditions, the policies of employers towards their staff have become more and more progressive over the years. The main improvements in the future will be those intended to encourage employees to give of their best in their jobs, by removing the frustrations that affect morale and performance at the moment.

Taking a wider view, personnel policies must always reflect current adjustments to the conflict which inevitably occurs over fundamentals throughout all industry. Peaceful conditions are a prerequisite to efficient performance. Yet, industrial peace is not compatible with the desire of organizations to be autonomous nor with the rights of individuals to pursue their own interests. Policy statements must therefore be made with the goal of securing a balance between peace and autonomy. They must also be concerned with the economic progress of the organization and higher standards of living for its members, overcoming the resistance to improvements which develops if they involve changes that can only be made at a high cost. This is very much the context of today's industrial society, where automation and mechanization increasingly dominate the lives of employees. There are no universal solutions to such problems, but policy can be presented in such a way as to ease the necessary adjustments to changing conditions.

Sociologists see Western civilization moving into a 'post-industrial' state of society, which will have several predictable characteristics. *Per capita* incomes will be high. Employment will become concentrated in the service area: already manufacturing employment in the U.K. is declining and more than half of the working population is employed in the service sector. Leisure time will be increased as working hours become shorter. Values are likely to change rapidly as regards work, authority, the place of women in the working community, and the power and accountability of large organizations. Growing concern will be shown for the quality of life and the conservation of resources and environments. These are the pressures to which personnel policies must respond if manpower requirements are to be met, and if adequate commitment to the overall purposes of an organization is to be ensured.

Increasing concern is being shown for the 'quality of life' in the working situation; this not only affects standards of living and economic security, but extends to an acceptance that each individual has the right to a satisfying job in congenial surroundings, opportunities for the full development of his abilities, and a voice in decisions which affect him. Society also reflects a general concern about the power wielded by large organizations and constantly searches for balancing influences, such as joint consultative machinery, worker members of boards, and consumer associations. Authority and conforming to conventions tend to be rejected. Status systems, distinguishing between 'staff' and labour are also disappearing; productivity bargains have given 'staff' conditions to all employees in many organizations, removing such differences as existed in conditions of work, security of employment and fringe benefits. Finally, there is more and more legislation bringing pressure to bear against discrimination on grounds of colour, creed, and sex.

'The current concern with manpower planning reflects a realisation that provision must be made for the future development of human organisations in the context of rapid environmental change ... As society moves towards the post-industrial era new tasks and challenges will present themselves and the scope of personnel work will become wider than ever before: organisational development in its broadest sense will emerge as the primary task of the personnel function. To face this challenge will call for a new "technology" of personnel management—knowledge of a broadly sociological kind about society and the process of social change: techniques of organisation analysis and the diagnosis of sources of organisational stress and conflict: and skills in implementing change.'*

Britain's entry into the European Economic Community, seen in the general context of the aims of the Treaty of Rome—to harmonize the economic, employment, and social policies of all member countries—has considerable implications for the development of all aspects of personnel management in this country in the near future. In fact, the Treaty is quite precise in calling for action on employment matters, vocational training, pay and working conditions, industrial relations, and employees' welfare.

* 'Personnel Policy in a Changing Society', by P. Sadler, *Personnel Management*, April 1974, page 29.

How long it will take to confirm all these plans in practice remains to be seen; the other European countries are much more used to a legalistic approach than the British are, and our trade unions have often shown great resistance to any domestic attempts to curtail their bargaining freedom through the statute book.

As far as the employment function is concerned, the main provisions concern the free movement of labour between member countries, with E.E.C. workers being granted the same working conditions as nationals in each other's territories. Work permits are no longer required, but residence permits will be needed by those staying in Britain for longer than six months. By the same token, workers from this country may seek employment in any of the other E.E.C. countries, and will receive treatment equal to their own nationals as regards employment service facilities in finding suitable jobs, pay and working conditions, trade union rights, vocational training and retraining facilities, social security, and access to housing and property. A Community worker also has the right to be joined by the members of his immediate family.

Training is covered by the provisions of the European Social Fund, set up to help where the employment situation is likely to be affected directly by the policies or actions of the Community, or where there is a clear need for common action to secure a better balance between the supply of, and the demand for, labour. The fund is intended to meet up to 50 per cent of the costs incurred in approved government training and resettlement schemes—thus making employment easier and increasing the geographical and occupational mobility of workers. Retraining, special aid to the disabled, and help for the disadvantaged in entering the labour market are all included. Other special funds provide the same sort of facilities for workers leaving coalmining, steel works or agriculture. There is also a Community-wide vocational training policy, designed to contribute to the harmonious development both of the national economies and of the Common Market.

On the wages front, the hope is that continued economic growth, despite current inflation, will perpetuate the levelling upwards of wages and salaries, so that real incomes will go on rising. Cross-frontier joint action by trade unions may be expected to press for parity with the highest existing rates of pay. Equal pay for equal work between men and women is also official E.E.C. policy. The harmonization of holiday arrangements will benefit British workers: their European counterparts all have longer periods of annual leave and more public holidays. Holiday bonuses are also common.

The Law plays a a much greater part in industrial relations in Europe than in Britain—directly affecting trade union and workers' rights, negotiating procedures, consultation and communications processes, redundancy and job security. British unions tend to resist such controls, of course, as interfering with their bargaining freedom. The European Company Statute of 1970 has resulted in directives about two-tier management structures, with worker participation on the supervisory board, in all organizations with over 500 employees. The U.K. is the only West European country where works councils are not mandatory, so 'harmonization' may lead to their wider adoption here; certainly their aims—to promote co-operation, to encourage productivity, and to consider the effects of management decisions on workers—are commendable.

3 Motivation

WHY MAN WORKS

Concern with motivation has been apparent since the early work of industrial psychologists and their investigations of the commonsense belief that nobody can stimulate anyone else to work unless he knows how that person is motivated and to what incentives he will respond. What then are the reasons why man works?

His prime motive is economic, to obtain the resources to meet his physiological needs and support a family, ideally in ever-increasing comfort. Ambition therefore plays a part, in the sense of the desire to get on and acquire more of the good things in life. But ambition is essentially a personal matter and is conditioned to some extent by environment. Thus an individual's job preferences are important—for example, he may prefer a low-paid job where he is left to his own devices, away from the noise and strain of the main production area; or, if he is caught up in a redundancy situation, merely retaining his job may become the height of his ambition. This last point adds security of employment to the list, again an aspect of the economic motive, for security means steady pay over a long period of time.

The second main motive concerns man's social needs, which have wide ramifications. He wants to feel that he belongs, that he is accepted by his fellows, and that his work has some importance. This is clearly associated with a desire for companionship, but also has a negative aspect in that he must accept work as a social obligation unless he wishes to be rejected by the community around him. Burlinghame wrote in the seventeenth century —'Work is the source of man's most basic satisfactions, it is his social catalyst—the purveyor *par excellence* of his status and prestige among his fellows'.*

This desire for social status is linked with the need for self-realization. The teachings of many psychologists, such as Jung and Adler, centre around the belief that the supreme goal of man is to fulfil himself as a unique individual, according to his own innate potential and within the

* Quoted by J. A. C. Brown, *Social Psychology of Industry* (Penguin, 1964), page 282.

limits of reality. The factors about a job which meet this need are those which challenge his abilities, stretch him in achieving his aspirations, and place him in a position of responsibility in the eyes of his workmates and the neighbours among whom he lives. Self-fulfilment is also dependent in some measure on the degree of specialized training received, which, for example, inspires some men to go on working at their jobs long after it becomes unnecessary in economic terms. Lengthy, meticulous training nurtures the feeling that if a job is worth doing, it is worth doing well. Many types of craftsmen, technicians, and professional men cannot be thinking all the time about the money they are earning, nor for that matter about the good they may be doing mankind; they find it much more satisfactory to concentrate on the work they have been highly

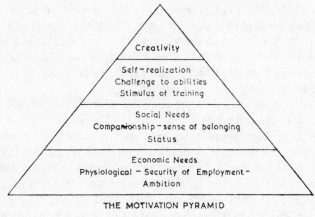

THE MOTIVATION PYRAMID

Figure 2

trained to do. If, in addition to all this, they can actually be creative, so much the better; but most people in modern civilization are so taken up by the struggle to satisfy their more basic needs that few aspire to this summit of achievement.

Probably the majority of people are most often partially satisfied and partially unsatisfied in all their wants. Even so, it is clear that links forging total motivation form a recognizable hierarchy; those at the base of the pyramid must be satisfied first before those ranged further up can be given much consideration (Figure 2). These facts are important to the personnel manager, for they indicate that as needs become satisfied, they can no longer be taken account of when designing incentives. Sights must then be set higher, and as they rise there must be fuller awareness of employees' reaction against drudgery and routine and their demands instead for jobs which offer interesting work and a chance to get on.

RESEARCH INTO BEHAVIOUR AT WORK

Industrial psychologists and industrial sociologists have played a great part in the development of personnel management by applying the findings of their research work to problems of business administration. To distinguish between them, psychologists are concerned with the behaviour of individuals, while sociologists emphasize group behaviour; both study how people behave, what the relationship is between human behaviour and the working environment, and why people behave as they do. Their ultimate aim may be defined as trying to bring together all knowledge about managing people into one discipline, establishing the universals of the management process, and advocating management tools for general application. Comparing present practice with such an aim highlights the extent to which behavioural sciences are still in their infancy.

The earlier investigators in these fields are criticized today for having looked at isolated factors in the working situation, with little attempt to measure their relationships with other variables in the environment. Practising managers thus often found their results to be academic and of no relevance to their own particular problems.

Not that everyone failed in the challenge to establish 'principles' that would hold true regardless of time and place. The details of Elton Mayo's experiments at Hawthorne have been well documented. In the relay assembly room he proved how closely the production and social functions of management are linked. Dramatic improvements in productivity were effected because the workers involved changed their attitudes towards the organization when their co-operation was asked for and they were thus made to feel important. Their consciousness of being a group with a clear purpose, both as regards production and in helping to solve a management problem, meant that they achieved stability and satisfied their needs for belonging. Mayo even found that the mere fact that research work was being carried out improved workers' morale and their relationships with management. Then in the bank wiring room, he demonstrated the realities of group behaviour, with its own leadership, informal organization, social norms, code of conduct, and restrictions on output. He pointed out the futility of trying to break up these groups—rather management should act positively, planning for group cohesion so that everyone worked towards the same objectives. Later, in the aircraft industry in 1943, he was able to paint a profile of the good supervisor which has influenced foremanship training ever since.

As well as this type of basic research, the behavioural scientist carries out applied research on immediate industrial problems or may work as a consultant, advising particular clients and helping them to implement changes.

Success in these approaches counts more than anything else in ensuring his acceptability to practising managers, which is so essential if he is to get their continuous co-operation in future research.

A more recent example of involvement in this way can be seen in the work of Dr. Elliott Jaques* at the Glacier Metal Company. One of his projects sought to determine the optimum size of a work group, taking account of the working environment as a whole. He concluded that it should be a mutual-acquaintance group, its size controlled by the rule that its members should be able to recognize one another and greet each other by name. Groups of about fifty in number were considered to be the right size for operational purposes, and the entire factory was reorganized on this basis. The major responsibility of the leader of each group was defined as being to build up group cohesion. This particular firm, under its managing director, Wilfred Brown,† was prepared to pioneer in this courageous manner because it put human factors first, believing such a course of action to be sound business practice.

Jaques's work serves also to illustrate the change that has been taking place in industrial psychology. This is a movement away from investigating single factors in the working situation to concentrate more and more on the large organization. Organizational psychology studies the individual in the organization—how he affects its behaviour and how it affects his. Organizations are treated as systems made up of dynamically related parts: the individual cannot be understood apart from his social context, nor can this be understood without reference to its technical setting.

Research of this nature has resulted in a body of principles about industrial behaviour that influences current personnel management practices enormously. These are:

1. Normal workers desire association with groups where they find security and recognition.
2. Workers' satisfactions are expressed mainly in terms of how they regard their social status in the firm. Such considerations cause far more labour trouble than wage demands.
3. Complaints are not necessarily based on fact—they may be merely symptoms of much more deep-seated disturbances. Giving people the opportunity to talk and air their grievances can boost morale considerably.
4. Management problems of absenteeism, high labour turnover, inefficiency, and poor morale all reduce to the single problem of how to deal with primary group life, for the greatest cohesion can be obtained by building up from small face-to-face groups.

* Now Professor of Sociology at Brunel University.
† Now Lord Brown.

5. The first-line supervisor is more important in determining the morale of a work group than any other single factor.

6. The most effective supervisor is 'employee-orientated', being sensitive to their needs and giving priority in his work to motivate them positively.

7. 'Flat' organizations with as few levels of authority as possible develop more initiative and greater responsibility in supervisors and managers than the 'tall' type.

8. Clearly defining responsibilities, and granting appropriate authority, reduces misunderstanding and increases efficiency between groups.

9. Similarly, open communication systems throughout an organization reduce the risk of misunderstanding and conflict.

10. Changes in the social environment which affect the people working in an organization are most accepted when these same people are allowed to participate in making the relevant decisions.

Putting these principles into practice requires a courageous team of well-informed managers who have the ability to adapt theoretical concepts to the peculiar requirements of their own businesses, and to do so in such a way that production, selling, and financial arrangements are not disrupted by having to meet the social needs of the organization.

Behavioural scientists will go on providing theories, research findings, analytical concepts, and models—all of which are of great value in the development of a science of management. It is the duty of personnel specialists to keep abreast of all this activity, to pick out what is useful to their own work, adapt relevant ideas, and generally integrate the knowledge gained from behavioural scientists into the practice of management. Last but not least, they must look ahead and be willing to promote further research into those areas which are of special significance to them.

JOB SATISFACTION AND FRUSTRATION

The job of the personnel manager has already been described in Chapter 1 as being centred around people's needs while working in the organization; he must first of all recognize what these needs are and then identify the ways in which work in that organization promotes or frustrates their fulfilment. He can then direct his efforts towards methods of furthering job satisfaction or removing the frustrations.

This is a subject, for once, which is perhaps best tackled with a negative approach. Satisfaction is clearly in large measure the obverse of frustration, but the latter reveals easily detected symptoms which form a ready starting point for management action. Frustration is the result of tensions arising in a workplace through dissatisfaction with the jobs concerned, the physical conditions, or the people working there. It has an obvious link with low morale: if the state of morale is indicated by people's willingness to work, then their frustration is shown by an unwillingness to work. The more precise symptoms are:

1. Low level of production or poor quality of service, both reflected by the number of complaints received from customers.
2. High rates of absenteeism and labour turnover.
3. Bad time-keeping and generally lax discipline.
4. Poor industrial relations, shown by the record of grievances, disputes, and strikes.

Symptoms must have causes, of course, and these can usually be traced to:

1. 'Square pegs in round holes' as a result of the placement of people in jobs to which they are not suited.
2. Anxiety, due to inability to perform the job adequately; the ill-matching of people to jobs is often aggravated by not giving them precise job descriptions to clarify what they should be doing, and by lack of training to do the work properly.
3. Ineffectiveness of leadership: supervision too close or lacking; discipline too lax or too harsh; refusal to delegate; delays in reaching decisions; poor communications, particularly regarding changes likely to affect employees; general inability to obtain group cohesion.
4. Lack of recognition of individuals and their capacities to take on more responsible work; this, in turn, is often reflected in the absence of promotion opportunities and in the 'interference' of specialists in what people consider to be their main tasks.
5. Working conditions—employees will accept unpleasant conditions where these are unavoidable, and this will have no deleterious effect on morale; but they will not work willingly if they are conscious that conditions are unnecessarily poor and that management appears to be doing nothing about them.

Providing remedies for these causes is largely the subject-matter of the practice of personnel management which follows in detail in subsequent chapters. First concern must be for the structure of the organization, with all jobs in it precisely defined so that everyone knows his responsibilities and sees a clear ladder of promotion between jobs. Secondly, there must be an enquiry into the quality of supervisors and managers, particularly in those departments that show all the symptoms of low morale. Effective action must then be taken to improve matters, along lines which should be set out in a comprehensive personnel policy statement.

Removing the causes of job frustration will go a long way towards promoting job satisfaction, and there is no need to repeat comments already made. Taking a positive approach to creating satisfaction, however, perhaps the overall aim should be to try to get all employees to understand, accept, and identify themselves with the objectives of the organization, thus building up a sense of corporate pride. Proper induction of newcomers; effective communications and presentation of information; joint consultation and encouragement of the techniques of participative management; appraisal of the efforts of individuals and offering them scope for development; and, not least, adequate financial rewards—these are all examples of the detailed steps that would help to achieve this aim.

Possibly the best known research study of motivation is that of Herzberg* *et al*, who surveyed groups of engineers and accountants. Many similar studies have since been conducted, with different categories of workpeople, their basis an analysis of individuals happy in their work, and others who were unhappy.

The following list of motivating factors emerges:

1. sense of achievement;
2. recognition of achievements by superiors;
3. being given responsibility;
4. times of advancement and promotion;
5. awareness of prospects for further growth;
6. when work is interesting.

On the other hand, demotivating incidents can be attributed to:

1. poor features of an organization's policies or administrative procedures;
2. poor quality of supervision;
3. difficult relationships between staff;
4. anxieties about salary, security, or status;
5. the impact of the job on the personal life of the individual concerned.

One important concept emerging from such surveys is that all the motivating factors relate to the content of jobs, while the demotivating factors concern the context in which the jobs are performed. The fact that the former is within the immediate control of superiors clearly indicates that all managers can rightly be expected to have a positive impact in

* Herzberg, Mausner and Snyderman, *The Motivation to Work* (New York: Wiley, 1959).

.stimulating their staff. That the causes of dissatisfaction lie more outside their control does not, however, mean that they are absolved from the responsibility of removing any frustrating influences: rather, it demands that they work harder at doing so.

Analysing job satisfaction means looking at the individual's needs at work and the extent to which they are being met. But this must be done realistically, and set against the pressures and restraints which bear on the organization itself and which may prevent it from providing maximum job satisfaction. Thus job satisfaction must be considered in two ways:* first, in terms of the fit between what an organization requires of its employees and what the employees are seeking from the firm; secondly, in terms of what the employee is seeking from the firm and what he is receiving. This may be represented diagramatically thus:

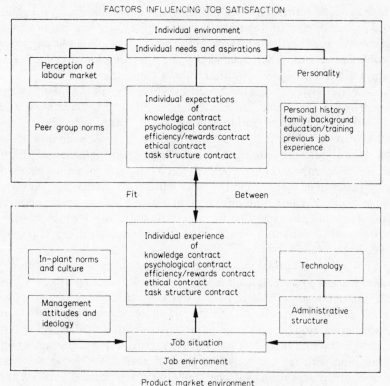

FACTORS INFLUENCING JOB SATISFACTION

Figure 3

* 'Job Satisfaction: a Method of Analysis', by Enid Mumford, *Personnel Review*, Spring 1972.

Modern behavioural science theory propounds that employees throughout an organization will feel committed to their work if they are offered opportunities for personal development by extending their capacities and responsibilities, backed with positive managerial support and understanding. If work is made more satisfying for individual employees, then an atmosphere can be created which will lead to greater flexibility in introducing necessary changes, which will enable human resources to be used more effectively, and will thus improve productivity.

Attempts to increase satisfaction with clerical work provide many interesting case studies of efforts to tackle problems of labour wastage, absenteeism, and the recruitment of staff for what is commonly regarded as dull, repetitive work with little room for the use of initiative or responsibility. Pay is always an important factor in such situations, of course; but in times of persistent government controls over wage increases, it cannot be seen alone as a long-term motivator. Employers must consider many other factors in trying to retain their existing staff and attract new employees at a time of acute shortage of people with clerical skills. In addition, young people are generally better educated and they develop ever-increasing expectations and higher aspirations about their jobs.

Since the Civil Service is the largest employer of clerical workers in Britain, it is appropriate to describe one of its experiments* in creating greater job interest. It must be borne in mind, at the outset, that Civil Service work differs from that in commerce in three ways: there are no production lines; the basic level of intelligence of staff is generally high (clerical officers are recruited with five G.C.E. 'O' levels); and the loyalty of employees tends to be better than average. On the other hand, there are special problems: the principle of equity is all-important and leaves little room for personal discretion, which increases the difficulty of finding areas in which job satisfaction can be enhanced; the existing staff grading structure also tends to be inflexible.

Against this background, a provincial office of one government ministry was examined by a small team from the Civil Service Department's own job satisfaction unit. Taking twenty-one civil servants, consisting of an executive officer, four clerical officers and sixteen clerical assistants as an experimental group, the unit set about restructuring their working patterns. At all stages there was full participation with the department concerned and with representatives of the staff themselves. Brain-storming sessions and close liaison with local staff associations formed a crucial part of the unit's work, together with attitude surveys, surveys of age, experience and education, and studies of work-flow.

* Reported in 'Three Studies in Improving Clerical Work', by Jon Blair, *Personnel Management*, February 1974, page 32.

In the restructuring of the twenty-one staff, the unit moved from what a C.S.D. spokesman called 'the clerical factory', to group working. They were organized into four groups of four clerical assistants, each headed by a clerical officer, with the executive officer in overall charge. This satisfied the stringent security and cross-checking regulations of the department concerned, provided variety of work for the staff, and a more pleasing geographic organization of the immediate working environment by breaking up the long rows of desks. In addition, because the experiment took place side by side with the traditional working arrangement, it was possible to compare the two ways of working. The staff expressed greatly increased satisfaction as a result of the new system.

All C.S.D. experiments incorporate the notion that group working is more satisfying, and also possibly more satisfactory and productive managerially speaking, than the established flow work systems. There is an attempt where possible to utilize further the civil service tradition of personalization of work. This is not only to fulfil job satisfaction criteria, but because it is believed that where members of the public have contact with civil servants it is in everyone's interests that they know with whom they are dealing.

Finally, where possible, the experimenters try to offer more responsibility to individual members of staff. Thus people who used to draft letters and then submit them for approval to supervisors should be able to write their own correspondence with the discretion to refer items of difficulty to supervisory staff. In addition, there is room for greater use of initiative in determining staffing levels, working out overtime schedules, and in other quasi-managerial functions. It is also found that a group imposes its own discipline more realistically and stringently than when rules and regulations are imposed from outside.

EFFECTIVE LEADERSHIP

A leader is the sort of person who can motivate a group of people to achieve its tasks and maintain team unity throughout the process. This sort of definition has emerged literally after years of debate and research, much of it obscured by misconceptions and half-truths. The original popular assumption was that the desirable qualities of a leader could be listed. Unfortunately, no two authorities ever seemed able to agree precisely on such lists. The problem of this approach is that it ignores the situation in which the leader acts; the village idiot is hardly likely to possess much by way of 'leadership qualities', yet he might very well take over leadership of a group of hikers lost in fog on the local moors. In fact, this example points to the concept which subsequently developed, that leadership is a function of the situation, and that the professional or technical knowledge required in the situation pushes the leader forward. But this again seems to be based on a false assumption, that leadership can be passed from hand to hand within the same group as the occasion demands. In any event, it is undeniable that there is a general area of competence not related to expert knowledge (which the 'qualities investigators' were trying to identify). From the U.S.A. then came the 'group' approach: since leadership exists largely to ensure that the common needs of the group are satisfied, then the functions necessary to achieve this can be shared by its members. This idea completely excludes the previous concepts of leadership qualities and professional competence, but its argument in favour of shared responsibility surely wrongly assumes that leadership means the same as authoritarianism.

'Functional leadership' has developed from these earlier analyses, concentrating on what the leader actually does. It too is based on the assumption that the group shares common areas of need:

1. To get certain tasks done, which presumably is the reason why the group was created in the first place; its members will become dissatisfied if the tasks cannot be completed.
2. To be held together as a working team and motivated as such (the need for 'group cohesion').
3. Each individual member of the group has personal needs that must be satisfied through his work.

The leader must be constantly aware of the interdependence of these three factors (Figure 4). If tasks cannot be achieved, morale will fall; members will tend to blame each other or quarrel, thus disrupting the group

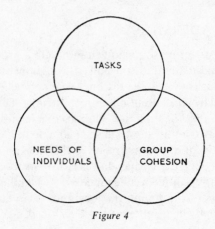

Figure 4

cohesion, and they will become individually dissatisfied because their needs for status are not being met.

The role of the leader therefore demands that he must do certain things:

1. Explain the group's tasks to it.
2. Plan how these tasks might be achieved.
3. Set the standards of performance required.
4. Maintain morale and encourage the group.
5. Keep an eye on its individual members.

The extent to which these functions can be shared with the members of the group is also important. If the leader announces his decisions in an autocratic manner, then the time taken to carry them out is likely to be longer than if they were discussed with the group members first so that they fully understood the decisions (Figure 5). The actual amount of participation by the members of the group will in fact depend on some of the aspects already mentioned—how much technical knowledge they have of the problem and such factors in the situation as the amount of time available, for example.

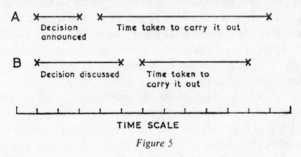

Figure 5

In all these ways, then, the functional approach concentrates on what the leader does, rather than trying to analyse what he is. In particular, he must concern himself with maintaining good relations with his subordinates, each of whom should be given a clear understanding of where he stands in the estimation of his group leader. The sting of criticism can be avoided if the group leader makes a habit of discussing each member's work with him regularly, assessing progress, praising strong points, and discussing weaknesses. Such techniques can rightly be considered as being non-financial incentives, stimulating subordinates on to greater efforts. Where practical, elements of competition may be introduced—competing against one's own previous best performance, against standards set by other staff or rival departments, or against target times. All these can help individuals to develop through having to extend themselves to meet some form of challenge and thus gain in prestige when successful.

This raises another of the very real problems that senior managers in large organizations have to face. There is in any managerial hierarchy a system of protocol designed to control the methods by which the 'bright young men' can get past the block of their immediate superiors and tell senior people of their ideas. Such a regimen clearly has disadvantages: orderly systems there must be, but a rule such as 'not seeing the man below without the knowledge of the man between' is nothing more than red tape. How can top managers be sure that, below the level of their own subordinates, there are not some really valuable younger managers whose abilities are not being fully used?

There must be some sort of mechanism to expose the talent at lower levels. 'Ginger groups' such as work study and operational research teams which report direct to the top can pass information upwards which might otherwise not be obtained. Unfortunately this gains the teams concerned the reputation of being spies, which makes their own work more difficult and puts their information sources on the defensive. The most effective method, perhaps, consists of several minor administrative practices: to encourage departmental heads to bring their deputies to meetings; to persuade them to set up their own working parties; to use internal courses as a means of eliciting ideas and criticisms, particularly across departmental boundaries. These are all open and recognized methods, built into the regular chain of executive action, by which three rather than two levels of management are brought into frequent contact.

The group leader should also be willing to delegate to subordinates, especially to the younger members so that they can develop their potential. Delegation is a process whereby a manager entrusts a subordinate with the authority to perform a defined task and requires him to be accountable for it. Effective delegation is a finely balanced technique: it does not mean giving a man a task and then breathing down his neck to make sure it is done properly; nor does it mean allocating work and leaving subordinates to get on with it as best they can. The important thing with delegation is that the leader should grant freedom to act, thus showing that he has confidence in his subordinates. The person to whom a task has been allotted should be allowed to carry it out in his own way and not necessarily in accordance with the traditional methods used in his department or by his group leader. He must feel that he is not only responsible for his action but also trusted. The control which a manager exercises over delegated tasks is inherent throughout the process. At the outset he must provide subordinates with proper job descriptions, see to it that they are adequately trained and are fully briefed on what he wants done—in all these ways ensuring that tasks are approached in ways likely to achieve the desired results. Then while they are actually working at their tasks there must be a system of control through personal observation, reporting back, and consultation.

The leader who takes this functional approach relies heavily on his own personality and capacity for directing and controlling others. The 'technical' leader, on the other hand, is followed because of his superior knowledge or because he has the services of expert advisers at his command: by exploiting this expertise he is able to help the group decide what common action must be taken. There is a third type—the 'institutional' leader—who relies on a position in the recognized system of discipline, as in the Armed Forces, the Church, or the nursing profession. Authority is here more easily asserted and the right to order and control more quickly acknowledged; at the same time the respect of subordinates is often more apparent for a position and its status than for any personal qualities its holder may seem to possess.

It is also true to say, even of this latter institutional type of situation, that both formal and informal leaders usually emerge in all working groups. The formal leader is appointed by authority and should have recognized terms of reference within his sphere of competence. An informal leader represents a group in a manner which fosters its interests, and his behaviour will depend very much on its attitudes. He will reflect the claims and views of the group, and initiate acts of leadership; in this respect, it is conceivable that in different situations the role of informal leader may switch from one person to another. The prestige of the informal leader allows him to rub shoulders on equal terms with other group leaders. Unfortunately, a group may elect him because of his good fellowship rather than his efficiency, and this can lead to trouble.

Switching finally to the other side of the coin, what is it that individual members of working groups want from their leaders? Much has been implied already in explaining the leadership role. The individual wants the requirements of his job made clear to him, and wants to be kept informed of his superior's assessment of his performance. He expects to be treated fairly and justly, of course, seeing no favours shown to one man or another. He wants his superior to be accessible and always ready to listen and be helpful. Where a subordinate has authority delegated to him, he looks to the group leader to back him up in his decisions and actions. He hopes that his leader can inspire loyalty to the group and set standards of behaviour, largely by his own example of hard work and integrity. He must also try to understand the personal characteristics of his superior, because he cannot feel really secure until he has established a good personal contact with him; this is often difficult in authoritarian types of organization, where the status of the superior's post may obscure the personality of the man or woman holding it.

INDIVIDUAL PERSONALITY

Man is a perpetually wanting animal, new needs emerging as old ones are satisfied, a never-ending process from cradle to grave. His behaviour in life is entirely governed by the circle of hereditary or environmental influences creating needs within him and his taking action to fulfil those needs. Fulfilment removes the original cause of the needs he feels, as illustrated in Figure 6. Always a person's behaviour can be questioned—what is the motive for that behaviour, and what caused that motive to develop in the first place?

The adjustment that man makes between his particular motivation, his ability to achieve the goals implied, and the limitations placed on his drives by his environment and opportunities, is reflected in his *personality*. This is the quality that distinguishes him from every other man, whether it makes

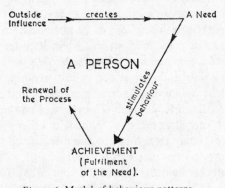

Figure 6. Model of behaviour patterns

him outstanding among his fellows or draws little attention from them. Both hereditary characteristics and the environment in which he lives affect a man's personality and attitudes. Intelligence is inborn, and temperament is largely controlled by the endocrine systems of the body, which in turn depends on the state of a person's health. The basic forms of motivation—for food, shelter, sex, parenthood—are also inborn, as are certain aptitudes to be mechanical, good at languages, or artistic, for example. Considerable evidence has been gathered to show that physique has a direct bearing on personality; thus the short, stocky-built type of man tends to be sociable and emotional.

Much or little can be made of these inborn characteristics by the way a person is brought up. His family and the environment in which he lives will cause his development to be channelled along lines which prescribe conformity with adult conventions. These differ throughout the world, qualities that are much admired by one race being considered repulsive by others. All sorts of physical, social, and emotional events will have their impacts and help to expand or stultify a person's potential. Acceptable behaviour on all occasions results in society regarding a man as having an adjusted personality.

The normal pattern of personality development throughout life is well understood. Parental control and school instruction instil a sense of values and social obligations early on, so that we in Great Britain, for instance, learn to repress natural aggressiveness and respect other people's feelings and their property, and accept a measure of responsibility for their welfare. We are taught to value privacy, have great regard for intelligence, and admire certain types of physical beauty. Then in adolescence, rebellion against parental control emerges as emotional needs change. We accept middle age as the best time of life: natural drives for a home and family, a pleasant job with status, the struggle for success—all have largely been accomplished (or, at least, disillusionment has not yet set in). Old age, on the other hand, is not a happy time: there is too much dependence on younger people, and this, in small family units, is often over-burdensome.

Throughout this process of growth we are developing *attitudes*—towards authority, religion, types of people, work, leisure, and a host of other things. Everything that happens is viewed in the light of experience, and judgments and behaviour modified accordingly. It is important for the personnel manager to appreciate that once an attitude is firmly established, it is not easily changed. Thus many people would prefer to change their jobs rather than their attitudes, seeking an environment where they feel at ease and need make the least personal adjustments. In this way it is possible to become blinkered from any further experiences, to reject any opinions that conflict with one's own, and end up with attitudes firmly entrenched as prejudices. These always tend to indicate insecurity or lack of intellectual ability on the part of the person concerned. On the other hand, someone who is confident, perhaps because his life is already successful, will risk meeting new challenges and will change and develop his attitudes throughout his life.

WORK GROUP SANCTIONS

The individual at his place of work is judged not only in terms of his own personality and attitudes, however, but also by the way he adapts to the general working situation and, in particular, his ability to work with other people. Except for the rare backroom boffin, all workers are members of formal and informal social groups.

The personnel manager must accept this as a fact of life and advise on ways of encouraging the efficiency of these groups: positive measures can be taken to strengthen their bonds, which will improve the social climate of the organization and hence raise productivity. In the first place, the prevention of strain or disturbances can be tackled from the outset, by taking care to allocate newcomers to groups where they seem likely to fit in. Thus objective selection, proper induction, and the practice of participative management are all designed to ease contact with fellow-workers and supervisors, and enable quick adjustment to the discipline and atmosphere of the organization. The actual formation of groups can be fostered, and the effectiveness of existing groups improved, by such measures as training courses, joint consultative committees, or by sponsoring leisure-time clubs. Where there are signs of disruption in group relationships, then management must take corrective action to eliminate it (cf. Elton Mayo's work).

This presupposes an understanding of the ways in which group patterns of behaviour and values are established, maintained, and transmitted. In fact, these are determined by *sanctions* – formal or informal rewards and penalties designed to channel behaviour in certain directions, ranging from smiles and frowns at one end of the scale to fines, suspension, and dismissal at the other end. It is precisely because smiles of encouragement and frowns of disapproval are important that group discipline can be achieved: through them, in particular, newcomers are taught how to conform to group values without recourse to the more serious penalties.

In any large organization, three main types of sanction can be seen in operation:

1. Management sanctions—applied to enforce discipline and control quality of work: 'carrots' such as bonuses and promotion, and 'sticks' like suspension or dismissal.
2. Union sanctions, which have two forms—
   (*a*) Those aimed at enforcing trade union discipline over members whose behaviour seems likely to bring their union into disrepute or to disrupt the unity of workers' interests: reprimands, fines, and expulsion have varying degrees of impact, while such social pressures as 'sending to Coventry' have a tremendous psychological effect.
   (*b*) Those applied against management to make them keep to negotiated agreements: they tend to run counter to management's own sanctions, of course, and are largely aimed at defending union members against disciplinary action.
3. Work-group sanctions: these are enforced by workers directly in three ways—
   (*a*) Against management for breaking unwritten rules not covered by formal agreements.

(*b*) Against their unions for actions regarded as officious or inefficient.

(*c*) Against their fellow-workers to uphold approved patterns of conduct within each group.

The differences between these main types of sanctions are closely related to the sort of behaviour which management or trade union members seek to encourage. Management's incentives are intended to pick out the individual with initiative and start him on the promotion ladder, thus rising above his fellows; but trade union and work-group sanctions are designed to foster loyalty to the group and to resist management's efforts to set workers in competition with each other. The threat of loss of the social life associated with primary work groups is the most powerful sanction for conformity. The man who becomes a foreman may be made to feel that he has switched to the other side and can no longer be trusted with knowledge of the activities of the group to which he previously belonged. Newcomers to groups, especially youngsters, become indoctrinated with group ideas without even realizing that this is happening, often reaching what they think are their own decisions when in fact they are responding to group influence. One group value that they are commonly taught is disapproval of the promotion-seeker, which suggests that men who do accept promotion tend to reject work-group pressures and values; for this very reason, they may be unable to interpret to top management the real nature of worker attitudes.

Group arrangements are among the most important causes of job satisfaction, absenteeism, and labour turnover. They are particularly important when the work is dangerous or stressful. An optimum design* for working groups suggests that they should be small (five or six in membership), cohesive, co-operative teams, able to take decisions about their own affairs.

But how can these conditions be brought about? To a limited extent, groups will emerge with their own leaders and norms, whether or not planned by management. If very large groups are created, they will divide up into smaller groups; if leaders are not appointed, they will emerge informally; group norms will develop to influence the methods and rate of work. Official arrangements may thus be considerably distorted, with subsequent changes in communications channels and even in incentive systems.

However, all this is true only up to a point, and with highly technical processes, consultants have been able to devise effective new group arrangements. One example is the Tavistock study of Longwall coal-mining, the starting point of which was a working group of forty-one miners,

* 'Working in Groups', by Michael Argyle, *New Society*, 26 October 1972, page 221.

divided into three shifts, who never met, doing cutting, filling, and stone-work. Since these three interdependent groups never met, there was a loss of cohesiveness and co-operation. Great improvements were achieved by restructuring the men into three different types of groups, each containing all three skills: output then rose by 51 per cent. Co-operative motivation has its own advantages, and must necessarily be fostered when jobs are complementary to one another.

Other group problems could not be solved without similar changes in technology. Long assembly lines are an example, for this kind of work produces a very low level of job satisfaction. Making lines shorter, or changing their shape into squares so that workers face each other and inter-act more easily, are proven simple solutions. So is the Volvo (Sweden) experience of scrapping the assembly line altogether and having small groups of workers responsible for constructing the entire car.

Group norms are developed about most matters relating to the group's main activities. Most important are norms about the work, including output restrictions and the elaborate deceptions which go with them, and conventions about how the work should be done. There are norms which de-termine attitudes towards management and unions, and others concerned with social activity—humour, practical jokes, gossip, clothes, appearance, and private slang, the meaning of which may be known only to members of the group. Some norms are created to deal with the external problems of the group (the work and its environment), and others with its internal problems (survival as a harmonious social group). Once developed, the norms are imposed on new members who may conform initially only under pressure, but who usually then come to accept the group's pattern of behaviour. In certain circumstances this pattern may facilitate the communication of new ideas, but some norms may also have the effect of making groups conservative in outlook and resistant to change.

GROUP DYNAMICS

The study of group behaviour has become more and more sophisticated over the years, culminating in the technique of *group dynamics*, which describes what happens within and between groups when working at tasks. It has been defined as 'the examination of the inter-acting intellectual and emotional activity of human beings endeavouring to relate to one another co-operatively whilst preserving their personal identity and individual aspirations'.* The aim of such studies clearly is to try to increase the effectiveness of groups in achieving objectives.

* *Personnel Management and Working Groups*, by Anne Crichton (I.P.M., 1962), page 9.

People who lack confidence in themselves as individuals or in their groups, who fear they are of little standing in their groups, who expect others of more ability or status to take the lead, who feel they have no great stake in a group problem or its outcome, who resist change or fail to see the need for it, who feel no need to understand others: such people find it difficult to share fully in group activities. Helping them by offering opportunities to discuss their personal feelings in a constructive way, so that increasing awareness can be achieved—this is the special concern of experts in group dynamics. The word 'experts' needs to be stressed, as it is essential that specialists, preferably qualified psychologists, should apply the training techniques involved rather than amateurs who happen to be interested in the subject.

The best-known of these techniques is the so-called 'T-group'—a group of people formed with the task of considering how small face-to-face groups work by looking at the behaviour of their own group. The early stages are often frightening to many people who want a clearly defined discussion so that they and the other group members will not get hurt too much. But experience shows that, although some members feel status-conscious at the outset, barriers do come down quickly as the group members settle to talk about why they feel and behave as they do. Over a period of time, the group builds its own identity and becomes intent on examining its methods of reaching agreement about values. In doing so, it discovers personal motivations through studying internal relationships within the group, and it is claimed that the whole conspectus of the interaction of individual personalities influenced by wider group pressures becomes clearer.

Specific benefits from T-group training have been listed thus:*

1. Receiving communications: more effort to understand, attentive listening.
2. Relational facility: co-operative, easier to deal with.
3. Awareness of human behaviour: more analytic of others' actions, clearer perception of people.
4. Sensitivity to group behaviour: more conscious of group processes.
5. Increased sensitivity to others' feelings.
6. Acceptance of other people: more considerate and patient.
7. Tolerant of new information: less dogmatic, more willing to receive suggestions.

Observers generally agree on the types of change seen: improved skills in diagnosing individual and group behaviour, clearer communication, greater tolerance and consideration, and greater action skill and flexibility.

* 'The Impact of T-Groups on Managerial Behaviour', by I. Mangham and C. L. Cooper, *The Journal of Management Studies*, February 1969.

4 The Employment Function

MANPOWER PLANNING

'Obtaining the best staff for an organization' is the prime function of the personnel manager's task, but before he sets about filling individual jobs, he should consider the overall management problem of making the best use of available resources. *Manpower planning* is concerned basically with budgeting for the best use of labour resources, just as the management accountant budgets for the best use of financial resources. It aims to 'maintain and improve the ability of the organization to achieve corporate objectives, through the development of strategies designed to enhance the contribution of manpower at all times in the foreseeable future'.*

NATIONAL MANPOWER POLICY

Looking at the national economy as a whole, the key word in any manpower policy is 'redeployment', covering problems of overmanning and the movement of workers, both from declining to expanding industries and from inefficient to efficient firms within an industry. Nor can people be allowed to work below their capacities because of inadequate training or skill, or because of restrictive practices by management or unions. To achieve growth targets specified for the national economy, there must be large movements of labour between industries and within industries, and ever more rapid changes in working methods to meet the demands of technological developments. In other words, effective redeployment includes all measures designed to ensure the movement of labour into more productive work. Of prime importance in this is the requirement that those affected by such changes must be helped to adapt to them.

First, much more comprehensive information must be gathered about the demand for and supply of skilled labour: the National Economic Development Council, the regional Economic Development Committees, the Industrial Training Boards, and the Government itself must co-operate to produce such information. 'This will then be used to assess training

Manpower Planning, by Gareth Stainer (Heinemann, 1971), page 3.

needs, to guide companies considering the establishment of new plants in the various regions, and to help an efficient redeployment of labour. The ideal is that with any redundancy notification to a worker should also be a notification of the new jobs available to him.'*

Further specific actions involved in manpower planning at a national level include:

1. Lump-sum payments to redundant workers.
2. Earnings-related unemployment benefits.
3. Help provided for workers moving to new areas.
4. Modernization of the employment service provided by the Department of Employment.
5. Expansion of Government Training Centres (Skillcentres) eventually to provide 100,000 places annually for training in some 50 skills.
6. The creation of industrial training boards in all major sectors of industry, now covering three-quarters of the total working population.
7. Helping married women and older workers, who wish to do so, to take or remain in paid employment; employers are encouraged to adopt flexible attitudes towards working conditions, especially hours, in order to utilize these particular categories of labour.
8. Overall Government policy to improve employment prospects in development areas and industries which need more labour. Measures include, for example, the building of advance factories, capital grants, and regional employment premiums which offer continuing subsidies to manufacturing firms who expand within the development areas.
9. Since unemployment has become a major problem, job creation, work experience and job release programmes have been introduced.

All these activities should be based on an initial fundamental productivity study of all sectors of the national economy, designed to establish the present rate of economic performance of manpower in different industries and at different places within those industries. Identifying where high productivity already exists will help to make Government targets for future economic growth much more realistic. It will also enable labour forecasts based on economic trends to be made more accurately: that is, the numbers required, both by skills and by location.

WITHIN EACH FIRM

Whatever effect these measures may have in achieving national productivity targets, the individual personnel manager must obviously be concerned mainly with his own organization's labour problems. The skeleton of a firm's manpower plan can be sketched as in Figure 7.

* *The National Plan*, Cmd. 2764, page 11 (H.M.S.O., 1965).

The present situation must be analysed in terms of the structure of the organization and the competence of the people working for it. An organization chart will show what their jobs are and the lines of promotion between them. For effective planning, however, more detail is required, and full job descriptions must be prepared evaluating the relative significance of all the jobs listed. The suitability of the existing staff in carrying out their jobs must then be assessed, with some form of rating to enable comparison

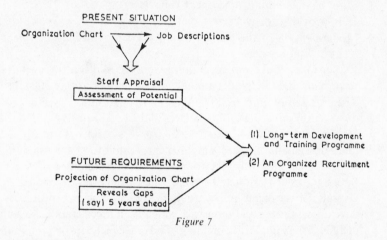

Figure 7

with the requirements of the different jobs previously described. In particular, the assessment must include a method of identifying those individuals who appear to have potential for development on to bigger and better jobs in the future.

An estimate of future staff changes and requirements must then be made, based on three main sources of information:

1. Knowledge of the age structure of the present staff, and what is likely to happen by way of retirements.
2. Natural wastage—labour turnover statistics should enable a forecast to be made of the numbers of present staff likely to leave during the period under review.
3. The proposed expansion or contraction of the business activities of the organization—based on market research findings, likely technological advances, and anticipation of the prospects of competitors.

Once the comparison between future requirements and present resources has been made, the personnel manager can then devise a long-term training and development programme to prepare for promotion those staff who have been assessed as having the necessary potential. The changing nature of the jobs themselves, apart from any consideration of promotion, can also be catered for in such a scheme of training. Finally, any remaining gaps foreseen will have to be filled by recruitment from outside; but with adequate warning, at least this can be properly phased, rather than the personnel manager finding himself faced with vacancies occurring unexpectedly.

Clearly, the more precise the information available, the greater the probability that manpower plans will be accurate. But, in practice, they are subject to many imponderable factors, some completely outside an organization's control. For example, occasional comment in the popular press about the future state of labour supply and its effect on the national economy almost always ignores the impact that further development in automation, education and training, the merging of firms, and productivity bargains might have on production figures in the meantime. Other imponderables include general technological advances, population movements, the human acceptance of or resistance to change, and the quality of leadership and its impact on morale. The environment, then, is uncertain, and so are the people whose activities are being planned. Manpower plans must therefore be accepted as being continuous, under constant review, and ever-changing. Since they concern people, they must also be negotiable—with the T.U.C. and C.B.I. at national level, with works committees at local level.

As far as possible, however, the imponderables should be taken into account by the personnel department in preparing its manpower plans. Obviously there must be a *precise statement of the organization's objectives* to start with, in order to calculate the size of the labour force required to meet them. From the outset, too, managers and supervisors at all levels must be given a clear *understanding of the need for a manpower plan in detail.*

Having said this, there is initially a great need for much more *information* than is usually at present available to the planners; fortunately the increasing computerization of personnel records and control statistics may aid this process. As far as *existing manpower* is concerned, the planners must know everything about the size and composition of their organization's labour force, rates of turnover and absenteeism, the cost of overtime, recruitment difficulties, anticipated results of training activities, and the types of changes in jobs that go on week by week. Comparisons of performance can then be made—inter-firm, industrially, and nationally.

Relevant information that should be collected about the *external environment* would cover local provision of housing and public works; social plans and trends, including sickness, retirement, unemployment; reductions in hours of work, and longer holidays; and industrial development schemes.

Then, in looking at *labour supply*, its availability would be compared with other areas, as would its distribution in terms of age, skills, membership of trade unions, and sex (including part-time and full-time married women workers). The difficulties of obtaining labour can be measured and expressed as the average length of time taken to fill jobs of varying types of skill and levels of seniority. A forecast must also be made of the *pace of technological change*, particularly the speed with which capital investment is enabling equipment to replace labour.

The whole range of this planning activity will be new to many personnel managers, and will be found to be very demanding. It is truly a managerial task; in no way can such planning become merely a repetitive process, with information being applied to a standard formula; rather it means forecasting, taking action, receiving control information, and constantly adjusting decisions and correcting forecasts to meet an ever-changing situation. The importance of thoroughly developed *communications* in all this cannot be over-emphasized. The planners must be able to obtain the most comprehensive information about manpower locally, industrially, and nationally; they must also be able to present this data to the management team throughout their organization in ways which enable its significance to be fully appreciated.

It may well be that manpower forecasts for about three to seven years ahead are the most meaningful, and that this will therefore be the optimum period for planners to concern themselves with. Little can be done to influence the size or structure of the labour force, nationally or locally, in much under three years; and the further one looks ahead, the greater become the imponderables, especially technological change—who can tell whether machines will do all the work in twenty years time, leaving man to lead a life of leisure?

Stainer* has analysed the strategies involved in manpower planning thus:

'1. the collection, maintenance, and interpretation of relevant information about manpower;

2. periodic reports of manpower objectives, requirements and actual employment, and of other characteristics of the resource;

3. the development of procedures and techniques which will enable all requirements for different types of manpower (including those for new capital projects) to be determined over a wide range of periods in the light of known corporate objectives; and the modification of these objectives where they make unrealizable demands for manpower;

4. the development of measures of manpower utilization as part of the

*op. cit., pages 3–4.

process of establishing forecasts of manpower requirements, coupled if possible with independent validation;

5. the use, where appropriate, of techniques designed to result in more effective allocation of work, as a means of improving manpower utilization;

6. research into factors (which may be technological, social, or individual) which limit the contribution that individuals or groups can make to the organization, with the aim of removing or modifying such limitations;

7. the development and use of methods of economic evaluation of manpower which adequately reflect its characteristics as income generator and cost, and hence improve the quality of decisions affecting the resource;

8. the assessment of availability, acquisition, promotion, and retention, in the light of the forecast requirements of the organization, of individuals whom it has been established are likely to perform well;

9. the analysis of the dynamic processes of recruitment, promotion, and loss to which an organization is subject, and the control both of

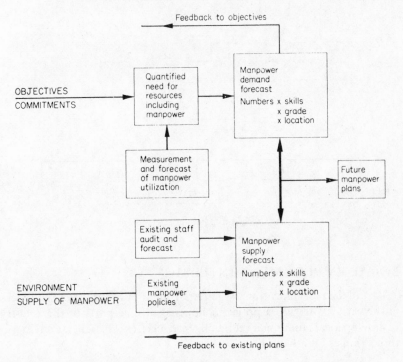

Figure 8. The Manpower Planning Process in Post Office Telecommunications.

these processes and of the organizational structure; so that as far as possible the maximum performance of individuals and groups is encouraged without excessive cost.'

The manpower planning process used by Post Office Telecommunications is illustrated above (Figure 8), and is followed by another diagram which sets out a general approach to company manpower planning (Figure 9).

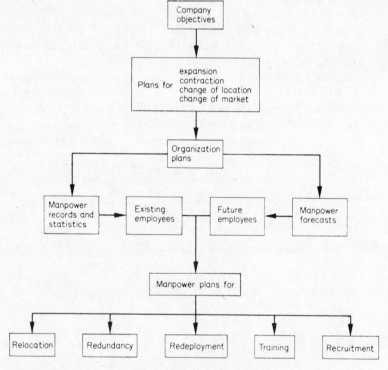

Figure 9. Company Manpower Planning Process.

LOCAL EMPLOYMENT INTELLIGENCE

Part of the reorganization of the Department of Employment's services in the early 1970s was a project conducted in nine parts of the country to develop local labour market intelligence services. The scheme envisaged three kinds of innovation:

1. An extension of the range of information recorded in local offices.

2. More positive involvement of employers, for example, through more frequent visits and more systematic discussion.
3. Regular bulletins to circulate important information.

The records to be maintained were determined by the managers of the nine local employment offices, and include: background information on such things as local transport, housing, educational, and training facilities; data on the industrial structure of the area—the main industries and firms, analyses of employees by industries, occupations and age, expansions and redundancies; and data on employment activity—entry into employment of young people, proportion of women in employment, travel-to-work patterns, and figures on placings, vacancies, and unemployment.

For their part, employers have taken great interest in the visits paid by their local employment office managers, and appreciated their defined purpose of obtaining and discussing information on changes in labour requirements. In many areas, while acknowledging the confidentiality of data about individual firms, it has been possible to make available fairly reliable information on changes for up to a year ahead. Published bulletins have included outlines of important developments likely to affect prospects in the area and appraisals of the effect on the labour market to be expected from them; advance information about skilled workers due to become available for employment as the result of closures; analyses of workers registered for employment in a particular industry; and notices about new training courses. For purposes of local comparison, national data on labour turnover, absenteeism, rates of participation of women in employment, and average earnings have been provided.

Two practical examples* will illustrate how employers' decisions have been facilitated by reference to local labour market intelligence. One concerns an area where there are several very large clothing firms. In the course of his round of visits to these, the area employment office manager discovered that almost all of them had accepted greatly increased orders, which would require the employment of extra machinists. Each firm's needs, in fact, were relatively modest and, on their own, might have been easily met; so that none of the firms was expecting any difficulty. But the total picture was that a substantial shortage was inevitable. When this situation came to be fully appreciated, the employers concerned came to the opinion that they could train the extra workers themselves, provided that they could be sure that the women recruited were suitable for the work, and, particularly, that they would not be worried by the speed of the high-power sewing machines they were to use—a major cause of trainee wastage in the past. As a result, a series of 14 four-week courses

* *Department of Employment Gazette*, October 1974, page 893.

was arranged at a local college, with the limited objectives of familiarizing women and girls with the sort of machine they would work with, and identifying those who lacked the necessary flair. Sufficient workers eventually joined the labour force to meet all the firms' needs.

In the second case, a food manufacturing firm was planning on an extra production line, to be staffed, in the traditional manner, mainly by female labour. But data in the local labour market intelligence bulletin led the factory manager to look more closely at the prospects of obtaining suitable women workers. The bulletin had analysed the current supply, and by reference to future expected demands by other firms in the area had predicted a growing shortage of women and girls. At the same time it was shown that there was likely to be a surplus of young men suitable for training for semi-skilled production jobs. On the strength of this the factory manager adopted the deliberate policy of recruiting boys to fill production line jobs, reducing the intake of women. The firm benefited from the better level of manning that was achieved and was able to reduce labour turnover. At the same time it contributed to a reduction of unemployment among young men in the local community.

Not that the provision of labour market intelligence is all that new. Many labour office managers have constructed files of useful data, beyond those figures required for their day-to-day work. The intention of the nine-area project was to discover how the collection and dissemination of such information could be efficiently broadened and made more systematic. That said, much information of value to employers is already available for all local areas on request.

RECRUITMENT PROCEDURE

The basic problem of recruitment is knowing what staff are required and where to get them. This simple statement outlines the procedure that must be followed when trying to select a candidate for any responsible post:

1. Assuming the organization tries to conduct its recruitment in an orderly manner, the procedure will be based on a forecast of manpower requirements as far ahead as possible.
2. The departmental head will submit to the personnel manager a requisition for the staff he requires at the appropriate time.
3. The job concerned will then be fully analysed, to prepare two documents—
   (a) A *job description*, a copy of which will be sent to all applicants.
   (b) A *personnel specification*, for use by the selectors in conjunction with the job description.

4. All likely sources of recruitment must be notified of the vacancy, and advertisements placed where necessary.
5. Applications will begin to flow in, by telephone, letter or personal calls. The methods for dealing with these will largely depend on the urgency of filling the vacancy. If the procedure has been well planned beforehand, there should be time to ask all candidates to complete an application form and for these to be considered together before going on to the next stage.
6. This will be to interview the candidates. Where there are a large number of them, it may be necessary to do this in two stages, with preliminary interviews held initially in order to make up a short-list for the final interviews and selection later. But when there are only a few candidates, the short-list is virtually settled for the selectors. The successful candidate is then usually chosen after the final interviews.
7. References are normally taken up chronologically, either just before or just after the interviews. The former applies generally in public services when references are obtained for all the candidates on the list for final interview. In private industry, the common practice is to make reference enquiries only about the successful candidate after he has been offered the job; the offer is conditional upon his references proving satisfactory, but this method is considered necessary to avoid jeopardizing that person's existing job.
8. The contract of employment must be completed, and suitably worded letters sent to the unsuccessful candidates.
9. Before the new employee starts, proper reception arrangements must be made for his arrival, and an induction programme prepared. Subsequently, some method of follow-up should be observed after three or four weeks to see how he is settling. Further brief checks should be made from time to time, not least as one way of evaluating the selection decision taken and the success of the methods used.

JOB REQUISITIONS

Job requisitions are intended to give the recruitment officer enough information about each job to enable him to fill it. They may be presented in an informal manner, verbally by telephone or even during a chance meeting between a departmental head and the personnel officer; or there may be rules insisting on the completion of a requisition form. Whichever method is used, requests should be as detailed as possible, listing the duties of the job, the conditions of employment, and the qualifications, experience, and personal qualities required of candidates. High-level approval is usually needed if the job is additional to the existing labour force rather than a direct replacement for someone leaving.

Linked with the job analysis that follows, the recruitment officer's aim should be to gather sufficient information about the job to be able to answer any questions that candidates may put to him. Hence the advantage of the more formal approach, using a form like the one shown in Figure 10, to make sure that all the points are in fact covered.

JOB ANALYSIS

[In order to avoid the confusion and ambiguity of some of the terminology associated with this technique, the following definitions have been agreed

REQUISITION FOR STAFF

Staff or Hourly: ....

Location: ....

Job Title:

Date required to start :

Department ....

Details of Duties

Promotion Opportunities : ....

PERSON REQUIRED

Preferred Age ....   Sex ....

Education & Professional Qualifications	Practical Experience required

Special Qualities (physical, personal, etc) ....

EMPLOYMENT CONDITIONS   ....

Rate of Pay	Hours	Shifts	Holidays	Pension

Addition to existing staff ? .... Addition approved by ....

Requisitioned by .... (Dept.head) Date ....

FOR USE BY PERSONNEL DEPT.

Name of person engaged : ....

Date started : ....

Source of recruitment

Figure 10

between the Department of Employment and the industrial training boards. The general use of these definitions would have obvious advantages:

Job description: a broad statement of the purpose, scope, duties, and responsibilities of a particular 'job'.

Job analysis: the process of examining a 'job' to identify its component parts and the circumstances in which it is performed. The detail and approach may vary according to the purpose for which the job is being analysed: for example, vocational guidance, personnel selection, training, equipment design.

Job specification: a product of 'job analysis'—a detailed statement of the physical and mental activities involved in the 'job' and, when relevant, of social and physical environmental matters. The specification is usually expressed in terms of 'behaviour'—in other words what the worker does, what knowledge he uses in doing it, the judgments he makes and the factors he takes into account when making them.

Personnel specification: an interpretation of the 'job specification' in terms of the kind of person suitable for the job. The characteristics are often set out on the lines of the N.I.I.P. 'Seven-Point Plan'.]

Job analysis is a technique which has been evolved to study the detailed content of a job and all the relevant factors that influence it. It has wide applications in many aspects of personnel management, one of which is recruitment.

But before continuing with this main theme, let us examine the technique generally and its other *main uses* in the personnel manager's work:

1. In *filling jobs:* whether by internal transfer or promotion or by recruitment from outside, it is essential to have a detailed description of the vacant job, supplemented by a specification of the sort of person who could do it satisfactorily. Also used for *appraisal.*

2. In devising *training programmes:* the need is to know what skills and knowledge are required to perform particular jobs well, and to make an appreciation of the training necessary to acquire such skills and knowledge.

3. In establishing *rates of pay:* here the emphasis is different, being placed on assessing the relative factors of jobs—how difficult, unpleasant, important they are, for example—and putting wage or salary values to them. In large organizations, it is clearly impossible to have separate rates for each individual, so the vast range must be reduced by placing jobs in grades or categories. Classifying them in this way means closely examining how they resemble or differ from each other, for the overall purpose is to reduce the number of categories to the smallest possible.

4. In *eliminating accidents*: the technique is readily adapted to investigating the hazards contained in jobs as a preliminary to devising methods of eliminating them.

5. In *reorganization*, made necessary in times of growth, contraction, mergers or amalgamation, or whenever the existing organizational structure is seen as a handicap to efficiency. Once again the emphasis is different, for here the analyst is seeking the purpose of all the tasks carried out in the organization and their relationship to each other.

Gathering all this information is a long and tedious task, and one suspects that this is the main reason why so few large employers maintain up-to-date analyses of the jobs in their organizations. Yet it must be apparent that if such detailed information is required to carry out the five functions just listed, no personnel manager is going to be able to operate efficiently unless he conscientiously acquires it by applying the technique of job analysis. Its tedium is perhaps best relieved in practice by carrying out analyses as opportunities present themselves—for example, when a job falls vacant, when its salary scale is being reviewed, or when improvement targets are being set for the person doing it. The personnel manager can thus 'kill two birds with one stone', and it is surprising how quickly he can build up a complete file about jobs. He will also more readily obtain the co-operation of departmental heads in this way, for they will be able to see the relevance of the technique to their own problems.

With a routine or repetitive manual job, the analysis may be carried out simply by watching the person doing it at work. But, of course, many jobs comprise tasks which are not repeated at regular intervals or which involve a great deal of mental work that cannot be seen; in such cases observation must be supplemented by interviews and discussions with the people doing these jobs.

The sources for information about jobs are clearly supervisors and the workers actually doing them, but both have their drawbacks. The former can be surprisingly ill-informed about the detailed content of subordinates' jobs, since it is difficult for them to notice or grasp all the numerous imperceptible changes that happen to jobs in a large department over a period of time. On the other hand, the person doing a job quite naturally tends to 'puff it up', placing greater emphasis on its important aspects and playing down the more tedious, routine side so that the investigator may be left with a false impression. On balance, it is probably better practice to interview the holder of the job first, and then check the information obtained with his superior; if any marked differences of opinion emerge, the job should be discussed with them together until a common understanding is reached.

Most people tend to be very sensitive about their jobs, and the fact that these are going to be analysed may cause considerable apprehension. It is essential, therefore, to gain their confidence in the first place and maintain it throughout the exercise. Gaining it is largely a matter of the job analyst fully explaining what he is going to do, the methods he will be using, and what the purpose behind his activities is. He can maintain this confidence only by the thoroughness of his investigation, while paying due regard to the normal work of the department which must continue while he is there. Nothing is more likely to mar people's confidence than if he has to return two or three times to each job because he overlooked certain points on the first occasion.

Finally, confidence must be consolidated by staff seeing that the purpose originally explained to them is in fact achieved: if, for example, office staff are asked to co-operate in devising a clerical training programme, but nothing subsequently happens about it, then they are hardly likely to respond when their help is sought again.

If comparison between jobs is to be possible, then the analyst must use the same framework throughout his investigations. This should cover the following points:

1. INITIAL REQUIREMENTS

(*a*) What a person must bring to his job by way of aptitudes, educational achievement, training, and previous experience.

(*b*) What training will be given to any newcomer to that particular job.

2. DUTIES AND RESPONSIBILITIES

(*a*) Physical aspects: what movements are actually carried out when doing the job, and the amount of effort involved; this should include a statement of disqualifications (for example, candidates for some police forces cannot be under 5 ft 8 in. in height).

(*b*) Mental effort: the degree of intelligence involved in the work.

(*c*) Whether the job is routine in nature, or demands the use of initiative.

(*d*) An assessment of the difficulty of the job: what its agreeable and disagreeable features are; what the causes and consequences of failure are.

(*e*) Responsibilities: for controlling other staff, for materials, equipment, and cash.

3. ENVIRONMENT AND CONDITIONS OF EMPLOYMENT

(*a*) Physical surroundings: indoor or outdoor, temperature, humidity, noisiness, dirtiness.

(*b*) Accident hazards inherent in the job.

(*c*) The form of wage payment, and frequency of its review.

(*d*) Other conditions: hours, shifts, superannuation, sickness benefits, holidays.

(*e*) The prospects of advancement.

(*f*) The provision of employee services: canteens, social clubs, protective clothing, for example.

4. THE SOCIAL BACKGROUND

(*a*) The size of the department.

(*b*) Whether the job means isolation from other people or membership of a working team.

(*c*) The sort of people with whom the job means contact: senior management, fellow-workers, outside representatives, the public.

(*d*) The amount of supervision received.

(*e*) An assessment of the status of the job.

In working through such a check-list, the analyst must beware of being unduly influenced by the personality and qualifications of whoever happens to be doing the job at that particular time. Rather, he must be conscious of the demands the job may make on any man performing it. It must be clearly realized, therefore, that there is a distinction between the ideal and the minimum for satisfactory performance: the latter can be described as 'essential' requirements and the former as 'desirable' in any subsequent specification.

Job analysis, then, is a tool of management aimed at eliciting the detailed information so necessary if staff problems are to be dealt with satisfactorily. Viewed in this perspective it is a problem-solving device, and as soon as a programme of job analysis has been carried out management must check that the problems concerned have in fact been solved: for example, that rates of pay are more equitable, or that a departmental reorganization is resulting in higher productivity. Otherwise the programme must be revised and tried again, or some new approach adopted.

Returning now to recruitment procedure—once a job has been analysed, the information is readily available to prepare a *job description* listing the duties involved in the job and setting out the conditions of employment. Each candidate should be supplied with a copy, so that he has sufficient information to decide whether to pursue his application. The selectors would be given copies too, and they should also receive a *personnel specification* which will present an 'identi-kit' of the sort of person considered suitable for the job available. Again a form should be used for this purpose, as in Figure 11, so that selectors become used to having this information presented in a uniform manner.

JOB SPECIFICATION FORM. | Job Title

Age Preferred/ Limits	Sex	Married/ Single	Qualifications
			Essential :
			Desirable :

Previous Experience.

Essential :

Desirable :

ABILITIES REQUIRED

Notes on degree of ability required and the situations in which it would be used.

Intelligence	
Speech	
Writing	
Numeracy	
Administration	
Social	
Initiative	
Ambition	

General comments on personality required, appearance, manner, etc:

Home circumstances likely to affect ability to perform the job:

Figure 11

SOURCES OF LABOUR SUPPLY

The techniques described so far have been concerned with knowing what staff are required; the second part of the recruitment problem is where to get them. There are many potential sources of labour supply, and it is most important that the personnel manager should maintain the right sort of contact with each of these and regularly review their effectiveness. Some of the most widely used are official agencies, directly concerned with employment:

1. Local Employment Offices and Job Centres of the Department of Employment: a service both to employers looking for labour and to the individual worker looking for a job. The usefulness of this service generally depends on the state of the market in a particular area—good in those regions where unemployment is high, but not very helpful, especially as regards skilled men, in areas where there is virtually no unemployment. In addition to specialized branches, a Professional and Executive Recruitment Service is operated throughout the country, offering, as the name implies, an employment service for men and women seeking professional, technical, or managerial posts.
2. Career Advisory Offices offer the same type of facilities for young people finding their first jobs.
3. Schools, Technical Colleges, and Universities—most of these have members of staff with special responsibilities for helping students to find suitable jobs: careers masters at most schools, and University Appointments Officers engaged full-time on this activity, for example.
4. Private Employment Bureaux—licensed by local authorities in many large towns, where they usually offer specialized services for secretarial, clerical, nursing, catering, and domestic workers.
5. Ex-Service Organizations and some police forces have resettlement offices which sponsor candidates for employment, having knowledge available about their previous experience and records of behaviour. In London, an Over Forty-Five's Association exists to help the older man or woman to find work.

A major point needs to be stressed about all these local agencies. Each area may have several hundred potential employers competing for the labour available, and the individual personnel manager thus has to make a special effort to get his voice heard. This can best be done by maintaining close personal contact with such people as the manager of the local Employment Office, Careers Advisory Officers, careers masters at local schools, and the bureau proprietors. Every day these people probably receive dozens of letters or phone-calls notifying them of available jobs. Faced with so many enquiries, they will naturally call to mind those employers who have appreciated the importance of a personal, friendly relationship, and who have invited them along to see something of the work carried out in their factories or offices (and, indeed, entertained them properly at the same time). Regular, personal contact of this sort is the most certain method of ensuring a fair share of the best available labour.

Continuing with the sources of supply:

6. Trade Unions and Professional Bodies often maintain registers of unemployed members or offer an appointments service. Where industrial relations are good, trade unions can sometimes produce
   reliable men, but in areas of over-full employment this is rarely a
   fruitful source. On the other hand, the appointments service of a professional association can be extremely useful to the closed membership of that profession. The Institute of Personnel Management, for
   example, runs one, details being circulated twice monthly with the
   Institute's publications *Personnel Management* and *Digest*, subscribed
   to by all members.

7. Personal recommendations by existing staff—in many ways the most
   satisfactory source of labour supply. An employer can usually rely on
   workers who have been in his service for a long time, and they in turn
   respect him. They will not recommend relatives or friends for jobs
   lightly, because if such people prove to be bad employees, then this
   would reflect as much on the recommender as on the 'duds'. Some
   firms positively encourage this method of recruitment by offering
   financial rewards. One example was as follows:

Workers get £25 Bonuses for Recruits

Black and Decker, makers of portable electric tools, are paying
out £25 to each of 118 of their workers who has recruited a new
employee for the factory at Harmondsworth, Middlesex. The
company now has a waiting list of 40.

The personal recommendation scheme was introduced last
September to help recruitment in an area with one of the lowest
unemployment rates in the country.

The firm said yesterday that it would not have reached its target
without the scheme. The company has 1600 workers, an increase
of 400 in the past 12 months.

Every worker who introduces a new employee receives a £5
cash payment and four similar payments at 3-monthly intervals
as long as both employees stay with the company.

It can clearly be a much more successful method of recruitment
than a repetitive series of advertisements in local papers which, in
such areas as the one just mentioned, seem to produce very few
suitable applicants.

8. The 'Circular Letter'—also used where local press advertising seems to have little impact, possibly when it is suspected that the types of labour sought do not even read the local papers. These letters or brochures can easily be delivered to every household in a neighbourhood, through the normal postal service, delivery agencies, or even by boy scouts in 'bob-a-job' week. They tell the local community what jobs are available, explain conditions of employment, and can highlight any attractive features of the work (just as a press advertisement would, but with the added assurance that they will be read by someone in every house). One large dairy company in London used this method when the reorganization of its services created a demand for more milk roundsmen; in this case the 'letters' were delivered to each house with the bottles by their milkmen. One large hospital spent £96 on a similar campaign and recruited thirteen new employees as a result; in the previous month an expenditure of nearly twice that figure on local press advertisements achieved no success at all.

ADVERTISING JOBS

In addition to all the methods mentioned above, advertising vacancies in national and local newspapers, trade and professional journals is consistently undertaken by most employers. This can be a very expensive business, especially display advertisements for senior staff in the national papers, and it is therefore essential that the personnel manager should be sure that the best results are being obtained for the money spent.

It is important to grasp, at the outset, what the purpose of an advertisement is. This is to *attract applications*. The sifting of those that are suitable comes later—there should be no attempt to build it into the advertisement as such. The text should be written so that it contains all the information about a job likely to interest the candidate—its title, to whom responsible, outline of duties, qualifications and experience required, conditions of employment, salary, fringe benefits, any particularly attractive features about the job (which distinguish it from other similar jobs), and the name and address of the firm. Including the telephone number makes it easier for people to apply, especially if application forms have to be sent for first: it requires much less effort to make a phone-call than to write a letter. The wording must be carefully devised and should avoid such vague phrases as 'appealing to men with initiative' or 'strong personalities'—who among the readers will believe he does not possess these qualities? A model that most organizations could well emulate is the advertisement of the Glacier Metal Company reproduced in Figure 12.

Figure 12

Where vacancies could involve promotion within an organization, they should be advertised internally first, and any subsequent press advertisement should mention that this step has been taken. The embarrassment of receiving an application from one of its own employees can thus be avoided, although this sometimes happens when a Box Number is used instead of giving the firm's name. This practice is very controversial, but the reasons why a firm wishes to keep its name secret rarely reflect any credit on the quality of its management. In practice, a Box Number seems to be used mainly when a replacement is sought for an unsatisfactory senior employee who would then be sacked (but if no one is found, he is allowed to continue). The personnel manager who places such an advertisement must face up to the fact that he is automatically excluding a large proportion of possible applicants who will not send letters containing personal information to an unknown address. To some extent these difficulties can be overcome by using a double-envelope system. The candidate writes out his application and seals it in an envelope; he then lists the companies he would not wish to see his letter, and inserts this, together with the sealed letter of application, in a second letter. The newspaper's executive responsible for Box Number replies can then take the appropriate action.

Because of the great expense of advertising, it is imperative to keep records of the response to each insertion, analysing both the number of replies and their quality. It will often be found, for example, that advertising in a professional journal produces the best results, because men of high calibre will look there first when they want to change their jobs, rather than hunt through pages and pages of the national newspapers. This control information can have a dramatic effect on advertising costs when first introduced, quickly eliminating those papers and journals which yield a poor return.

DEALING WITH APPLICATIONS

All the relevant sources of recruitment having been notified and the job advertised if necessary, applications should now start to arrive. What form should these take: should candidates be asked to write a letter of application, or should they all fill in the same application form? A clear understanding of the purpose of applications and their role in recruitment procedure as a whole should provide the answer to this question. In fact, applications serve three purposes:

1. To enable an initial 'weeding-out' of unsuitable candidates.
2. To act as a frame of reference for the interview which follows, when particular points can be checked and elaboration sought.
3. To form the basis for the personal record file of the successful applicant.

These purposes surely argue the merits of candidates using the same application form, so that they can all be considered and interviewed from a basis of exactly comparable information. The protagonists of the letter of application urge that its layout and content indicate something about the candidate's abilities; this is questionable, since the recipient can never be sure that the candidate has himself designed the layout of his application. Again, is this the right time to try to analyse the candidate's abilities—is it not far better to wait until he appears for his interview? The most significant argument against letters of application, however, is that the contents of each tend to be so different. Some people feel conciseness is what is required, others that they must be expansive; almost all leave out important facts or gloss over (with relief?) parts of their career that do not stand too close inspection or which may have little bearing on the vacancy in hand.

None of these drawbacks exist with application forms, which can ask for all the information pertinent to the job. This is no plea for a standard form to be used throughout an organization (there is really no need for a £9,000 p.a. senior executive to be asked about his shorthand and typing speeds, but it commonly happens). The ideal, which should certainly be practised for senior posts, would be to design a separate application form for each appointment, aimed exclusively at obtaining from candidates the information directly relevant to that job. Thus, for example, although some

EMPLOYMENT HISTORY

Name and Address of Previous Employers	Dates		Job Title and Summary of Duties	Reasons for Leaving
	From	To		

Figure 13

parts of a building firm's application form could be common to all applicants, different information would be sought from an architect compared with an accountant. Surely, with so much at stake for the prospective employer and the candidates, it is not asking too much for this extra effort to be put into the recruitment procedure.

Those parts of the application form which could be common include:

1. Personal details—name, address, age, married/single, nationality.
2. Education and qualifications.
3. Health—registered disabled?
4. Spare-time interests.
5. Length of notice to be given.
6. Names of referees.
7. Record of previous employment, leading up to the present job, set out perhaps in the manner of Figure 13.

Additional information may then be obtained by way of the candidate's personal assessment of his own experience and abilities. The relevant aspects of the job are listed on the application form and he indicates how much knowledge or experience he thinks he has of each. Thus the list for an Employment Officer post might start:

Experience	1	2	3	4	
Job Analysis					1 = No knowledge or experience
Writing Job Descriptions					
Writing Job Specifications					2 = General background knowledge
Interviewing—Operatives					
Interviewing—Executive Staff					3 = Reasonable practical experience
Use of Selection Tests					
Use of Group Selection Procedures etc. etc. etc.					4 = Very well informed, with long experience

REFERENCES

References come into the picture at this stage of the procedure, although many candidates in private industry will probably ask for their present employer not to be approached until later. Only occasionally are candidates told to submit open references or testimonials with their applications; in fact, little attention seems to be paid to them when they are unsolicited, and for this reason many firms refuse to give testimonials to employees leaving them, except possibly when they are emigrating.

On the other hand, most employers both in private industry and the public service do ask for references from previous employers. These enquiries usually take one of two forms:

(a) A normal business letter (which will be answered in like manner), outlining the job for which the candidate has applied, and asking the previous employer's opinion of his suitability for it.

(b) An enquiry form, with spaces in which the job and application details can be filled, followed by a number of specific questions, for example:

Are the facts given by the candidate about his employment with you correct?

If not, will you please supply accurate information?

What were the dates on which he started and left your employment?

What were his actual duties?

Why did he leave you?

Is he, in your opinion, sober/honest/dependable?

But, no matter how detailed the enquiry, the value of the information thus acquired is discounted by many personnel specialists. It is argued, for example, that so much depends on interpretation and this, in turn, on knowing the person who writes the reference, that expressions of opinion about character are worthless. There are legal complications, too, about putting bad references on paper, apart from the natural reluctance of most people to write so ill of the candidate concerned that inevitably he will not get the job (although to some extent these situations can be overcome in practice by phone-calls or even visits to discuss a reference with the prospective employer).

Generally speaking, these criticisms are valid, so that the usefulness of references is little more than a means of checking that the factual information provided by the candidate about his previous jobs is correct; if not, then he must be asked to account satisfactorily for any discrepancies before his appointment is confirmed. In the public services, where staff move between authorities as a matter of normal career progression, it is much more likely that the officers called upon to write references will know each other, for example, town clerks or hospital consultants; apart from this personal knowledge there are also closer bonds of professional integrity between such staff than can possibly be the case in private industry. More reliance can perhaps be placed on references in these circumstances.

FURTHER READING

Job Analysis, by H. E. Roff and T. E. Watson (I.P.M., 1967).

Recruitment and Selection in a Fully Employed Economy, by R. A. Denerley and P. R. Plumbley (I.P.M., 1968).

Aspects of Manpower Planning, edited by D. J. Bartholomew and B. R. Morris for the Manpower Society (English University Press, 1971).

Towards a Comprehensive Manpower Policy, Manpower Services Commission, 1976.

5 Selection of Staff

Once applications have been received (and references where appropriate) they have to be sifted to decide which candidates will be interviewed. This process demands great care, matching the information provided against the personnel specification, for when a large number of people have applied there is always the possibility of excluding better candidates than those who manage to secure an interview. This is partly a matter of the time and expense an employer is prepared to incur to get the best man, weighing this against the seniority or importance of the job. If he is going to recruit a man in his mid-forties and pay him an average of £5,000 p.a. until he retires, this represents an investment of £100,000 and he may feel justified in giving preliminary interviews to as many as thirty seemingly good applicants out of a hundred enquiries received. He must in effect decide on a budget for the cost of each appointment to be made.

THE INTERVIEW

Interviews are carried out in many ways: by the departmental manager in small firms, by a personnel officer with technical assistance, by panels of senior executives sitting together, by large committees in some of the public services, and by variations and combinations of all these.

Whatever the form, the three purposes of interviewing remain the same, and if only these were fully appreciated by people charged with responsibility for filling jobs, many of the complaints so frequently heard about the ways in which candidates are treated at interviews would disappear. The purposes are:

1. To enable the employer to obtain enough information about the candidate to decide his suitability for the job in question.
2. To give the candidate all relevant information about the job and the organization.
3. The public relations aspect of leaving the candidate with the feeling that he has had a 'fair crack of the whip'.

The first function has been the constant study of specialists in selection for many years and much has been done to perfect methods of getting information from candidates. But the second purpose has been comparatively neglected. Job descriptions may have been sent to candidates, and these may be expanded verbally at the interview, but far too often candidates are not shown the actual place or office where they will be working, nor do they see anything of the people with whom they will work—both vital ingredients in job satisfaction and morale. A group of my own management students once found this to be a significant factor in labour turnover.* Some 300 people in managerial or supervisory posts were questioned, more than half of whom at some stage in their careers had left jobs within a short time of starting (eighteen months). Of these, nearly three-quarters said that one of the factors which caused their rapid departure was disappointment with the way the job turned out compared with how it had originally been explained to them. There was little suggestion of their having been deliberately misinformed, more that they were not given as much information as they might have been, and particularly that no opportunity was allowed for them to see the physical conditions nor become acquainted with their future colleagues.

If the third purpose is kept continually in mind, it will greatly influence the manner in which any interview is conducted. For a candidate to feel that he has been fairly treated, he must be given the chance to ask any questions he wishes, and these should be answered; some of them may seem trivial to the interviewer, but they may be very important to the candidate. An employer's ultimate aim should be to send an unsuccessful applicant away genuinely sorry that he has not got the job, because it seemed such a good firm to work for. As it is, employers seem quite oblivious to the amount of goodwill they lose in a local community as the result of bad interviewing practices.

The first impression that a candidate gains of an organization is most important. Thus his written application should be individually acknowledged, rather than by a cyclostyled note, and reception staff should be properly trained to deal with personal callers seeking employment, helping them to fill in application forms if necessary.

When an appointment has been made for an interview, punctuality is of the essence, as with any other business engagement. If candidates are early or some delay is unavoidable, then a comfortable waiting room should be available, with up-to-date magazines to look at (including company literature), and with toilet facilities adjacent. The basic physical requirements for the interview itself are a private room, preferably without a telephone, and freedom from interruptions. There is much to be said in favour

* Survey carried out by Diploma of Management Studies Group at the Medway College of Technology, summer 1962 (unpublished).

of furnishing this room informally, say with easy chairs around a coffee table, as many people find interviews across a desk to be intimidating.

Most managers would hotly reject any suggestion that they cannot conduct good interviews, because they see this particular ability as a reflection of how well they can handle people, get them to talk freely, and make judgments on their personalities. Yet interviewing demands skills in which few senior managers have been properly trained. To start with, these skills can be improved by adopting a systematic approach: staff selection is not simply a matter of dropping everything else for a few minutes to chat with the candidates for a job.

Probably the best-known system is the *Seven-Point Plan*,* which is an attempt to list the items that must be considered in any comprehensive investigation of a person's occupational assets and liabilities. The need for the preparation of a full job description and specification has already been stressed, and the first application of the plan lies in doing this under the seven headings from which the technique takes its name:

1. PHYSICAL MAKE-UP

What does the job demand in the way of general health, strength, appearance, manner, voice?

2. ATTAINMENTS

What does it demand by way of general education, specialized training, and previous experience?

3. GENERAL INTELLIGENCE

What level is required to do the job (*a*) satisfactorily, (*b*) well?

4. SPECIAL APTITUDES

Does the job involve any special dexterity—manual, verbal, musical, artistic, etc.?

5. INTERESTS

How far does the job require a special interest in, for example, outdoor life, being with other people, artistic expression? Are any hobbies likely to be relevant?

* *The Seven-Point Plan*, N.I.I.P. Paper No. 1, was written by Professor Alec Rodger and is published by the National Institute of Industrial Psychology, 14 Welbeck Street, London, W1N 8DR, by whose permission this extract is here reproduced.

6. DISPOSITION

Does the job call for any of the following qualities—leadership, accept-ability to others, reliability, sense of responsibility, self-reliance?

7. CIRCUMSTANCES

How will the pay, prestige, status of job affect the worker's private life?

Having thus evolved the job's requirements, the selector will attempt to link these and the differences shown between the candidates, in order to find the best 'match'. The assessment of candidates should therefore also be carried out under the same headings:

1. PHYSICAL MAKE-UP

Has the candidate any defects of health or physique that may be of occupational importance? How agreeable are his appearance, bearing, and speech?

2. ATTAINMENTS

What type of education has he had, and how well has he done educa-tionally? What occupational training and experience has he had already, and how well has he done in his previous jobs?

3. GENERAL INTELLIGENCE

How much intelligence can he display and does he ordinarily display? (This may be assessed by testing.)

4. SPECIAL APTITUDES

Has he any marked mechanical aptitude? manual dexterity? verbal facility? artistic or musical ability? (Again, may be found by tests.)

5. INTERESTS

To what extent are his interests intellectual? practical–constructional? physical–active? social? artistic?

6. DISPOSITION

How acceptable does he make himself to other people? Does he influence others? Is he steady and dependable? Is he self-reliant?

7. CIRCUMSTANCES

What are his domestic circumstances? How large a family? Does he own his house? Is he willing to travel?

Using this plan conscientiously is an excellent discipline for anyone new to interviewing, as it so clearly assists the process of matching the candidate and the job requirements. With experience, the interviewer may learn to take a number of short cuts and can be less formal in his approach. Even so, he should still use some sort of plan, not in the sense of following a stereotyped sequence (because an interview should always be allowed to develop naturally), but rather as a means of checking that all the required information has in fact been obtained.

Some preparation is necessary before the candidate actually arrives. The interviewer should carefully study his application and try to memorize the more important personal details supplied. This is not only good manners, but it also leaves the interviewer free during their discussion to concentrate on his main task of assessing the candidate. His initial approach should be friendly and designed to put the candidate at ease so that he behaves in a normal manner: this is perhaps best done by starting on some subject of mutual interest, which is often revealed in the candidate's application.

The interviewer should follow certain well-established rules during his time with the candidate:

1. He must appear interested throughout, and not seem merely to be going through an irksome routine (it is not always easy to concentrate towards the end of a tiring day).
2. He should do the minimum amount of talking himself, encouraging the candidate to speak freely, but without dwelling too long on irrelevancies. Ideally he could say to the candidate, 'Now tell me all about yourself' and, providing he sticks to the point, speak no more until the end. In practice, of course, he will have to interject occasional questions to get more information or change the subject from time to time.
3. The questions that he does ask should be phrased so that they are easily understood, but cannot just be answered 'yes' or 'no'. Nor should they be leading questions which, by their content or voice inflexion when putting them, suggest the answer likely to score.
4. The interviewer must remain detached. There should be no question of obtruding his own personality into the exchanges in order to create an impression; he should not express opinions about episodes in the candidate's career, let alone censure him. Nor should he offer unasked for advice, except possibly to an occasional youngster who obviously needs vocational guidance.
5. He should be aware of his own prejudices, and allow for them and any predilections he has to generalize, to believe stereotypes, or to be swayed by 'halo effects'. Stereotyping describes a form of bias

which arises from the tendency to attribute wide-spread cultural beliefs about groups of people to individuals, such as 'all red-heads are hot-tempered'; alleged national characteristics, for example, over-look the obvious differences between individuals—'all Germans are hard-working'. Halo effects result from favourable conclusions being reached about an individual, stemming from just one particular trait which he possesses. For example, a good attendance or time-keeping record will often result in that person being generally viewed as some-one who produces a lot of work of high quality; a likeable person is often judged to be more intelligent than someone who is disagreeable.

6. The interviewer must also beware of superficial first impressions and hasty decisions. One study* of a series of fifteen-minute interviews showed that the average 'decision time' was under four minutes. In such cases the interviewer could produce little better results than de-cisions based solely on an application form. It also means that the interviewer seeks to confirm his early impressions by means of the emphasis he places on particular parts of the interview; and he may consciously reduce the possibility of non-congruent information emerging by his very choice of the subject-areas explored.

7. Notes of fact may be taken during the interview, with the candidate's agreement. But notes concerning the interviewer's assessment of the candidate should be written after the latter has left the room and there is no possibility of his seeing them. Certainly recent research† has proved conclusively that it is important to keep notes if inter-viewers wish to recall information accurately. One experiment in-volved forty managers watching a video-taped interview, and then answering twenty straightforward factual questions about it. The average score was only ten, and the best results were obtained by those managers who followed their normal practice of keeping notes.

8. There can be no hard and fast rules about the length of time an inter-view takes; so much depends on the candidate, the type and seniority of the job, and the methods used, that it can vary from ten minutes to a couple of days. With experience, an interviewer will learn to gauge how much time he needs for each type of applicant.

9. Perhaps the overriding consideration is to be as thorough as possible. In particular, there should be no reluctance, for whatever reason, to examine closely any areas of doubt about a candidate's career. A new

---

* *See* 'Summary of Research on the Selection Interview Since 1964', by O. R. Wright, *Personnel Psychology*, Vol. 22, 1969, page 394.

† 'Improvements in the Selection Interviews', by R. E. Carlson *et al*, in *Personnel Journal*, 1971, page 268.

job is a vitally important event, likely to affect a man's life and have
some direct impact on a firm's affairs for many years to come. There
must therefore be no evasion of responsibility and the questioning
must be exhaustive. Naturally, too, a candidate will try to put himself
in the best light, slanting his answers to impress his audience (on
occasions, even telling lies). Where he suspects this is happening, the
interviewer must probe and cross-check as much as he can.

Interviews of likely candidates are usually started by a personnel
officer; he may then pass them on to the departmental head concerned, or
they may interview candidates together. Whichever method is used, the
personnel officer's advisory role must always be kept in mind and the
departmental head's decision accepted as final. This responsibility is clear,
and removes any likelihood of the personnel department being blamed
later if candidates turn out disappointingly. It also has the advantage of
allowing the departmental manager to show the candidate something of
the place and the conditions under which he will be working.

The main qualification of a good interviewer is his ability to establish an
empathy with a candidate, 'becoming one' with him. This presupposes that
he has done his homework and thoroughly knows the job and anything
else about the organization likely to interest the candidate. The interviewer himself needs to be intelligent, well adjusted, emotionally mature so
that he stays unshockable, and well aware of his own biases and prejudices.
Good health and freedom from strain or fatigue are also essential.

PANEL INTERVIEWS

Many of our public services are run by elected councils or management
committees appointed by appropriate Ministers. One of their major responsibilities is the selection of their senior officers, administrative and
technical, and usually interviewing panels (sometimes twenty or thirty
strong) are formed for this purpose. Councils and committees are frequently criticized as amateurs in an increasingly professional world, and
this is very apparent as far as staff selection is concerned: it is a task for
which very few members have ever received any training at all. The consequence is that most senior officers in local government and health service
administration (two of the largest employers of labour in the U.K.) can
relate numerous selection 'atrocities' within their personal experience.

Is there anything, then, to be said in favour of this system which, by law,
must be carried out in this way? The trouble is, of course, that some public
authorities still do not employ specialist personnel officers, so there is no
expert in selection methods available anyhow. In this case, perhaps it is

better to have a panel—at least the members can prompt each other and hope to cover the whole field of enquiry between them. And since the filling of senior posts is so often a matter of promotion as well, this method offers some guarantee of objectivity and fairness.

But there are serious disadvantages. One which increases as the number on the selection committee grows is the difficulty of putting each candidate at his ease. How can he be expected to relax and behave naturally, as he would in the job if appointed, when he sits on a solitary chair surrounded by a large group of people all of whom may be complete strangers to him? Apart from their effect on the candidate's nerves, large committees often become confused in their procedure: important aspects of candidates' experience are overlooked, questions are repeated, and members sometimes seem more intent on impressing each other than considering the candidate.

If selection panels are to be used, they should follow a more constructive pattern. Their size should be limited to a maximum of six, each of whom should be properly introduced to the candidates in turn. They should agree areas of questioning between them so that there is no repetition or 'hogging' of the time by individual members. Above all, they should carry out the necessary preparation by studying the job descriptions and specifications issued beforehand, and try to acquire some training in the methods of finding out if candidates possess the qualities needed to do the jobs successfully.

SELECTION TESTS

Most employers take their decisions about whom to select for a job when the interview stage of the recruitment procedure has been concluded. An increasing number, however, seek further evidence before making up their minds, by asking candidates to take a number of tests which have been devised to try to measure certain aspects of an individual's total personality in an objective and accurate manner. The main types are:

1. Intelligence tests, of general mental capacity.
2. Special aptitude tests of particular talents.
3. Proficiency or trade tests in particular fields, for example, typing, or reproducing the main elements of a work task.
4. Tests which explore certain aspects of personality.

Intelligence tests can give a useful general indication of a candidate's mental calibre, thus helping to assess if he is likely to be bright enough to meet the demands the job in question would make on him. Spearman's work on measuring intelligence is well known: he explained what he called the 'g' factor thus—'we are divided by schooling and experience and we differ in our aptitudes, but below this we share a deeper basis of common ability.' Clearly, any reliable measure of 'g' can be of great help to a recruiting officer.

Special *aptitude tests* are widely used in giving vocational guidance when considering school leavers for certain types of apprenticeships, or when someone is seeking an entirely new type of employment (for example, computer programming). All sorts of aptitudes can be tested—mathematical, mechanical, practical–constructional, musical, for example—and here again these tests can be useful in many ways, not least in cutting down the wastage from expensive training programmes for young people.

Proficiency and trade tests are perhaps the most straightforward, since basically they test ability to do the work involved. Thus if a job demands a certain level of ability in calculating, a 'maths. exam.' can easily be devised to find out if a candidate is good enough. Similarly, shorthand and typing tests are commonly given to applicants for secretarial work. Sometimes only part of the job, its 'key factors', can be tested: this calls for specialist advice to ensure that these factors are a fair test of competence, and that they are properly standardized and scored. Security of the tests is another problem; their content needs to be changed from time to time to prevent local candidates passing on knowledge of the tests.

Personality tests are intended to measure such aspects as emotional stability, social attitudes, and various traits of character. There are two main types—the *questionnaire* and the *projective*. The first simply asks a series of questions: unfortunately some candidates seem to find it easy to anticipate what answers score best and it then becomes necessary to complicate the process by building in some form of lie-detector. The most famous example of the second or projective type is the Rorschach ink-blot test—but many selection experts reject the basic concept that any one test can reveal a complete character study, which is the claim made. Long training and great skill is required in interpreting the results of such tests, and even then there is little evidence that any more useful information is obtained than from the interview or from other simpler, less costly methods. Personality tests for specific vocations (for example, salesmen) can also be a waste of time and effort: the simple truth is that different people succeed for different reasons and a man is just as likely to sell large quantities because customers feel sorry for him as he would if he had an expansive, charming personality. Many of the tests that have been advocated over the years are suspect, both as regards the qualifications of their inventors and the psychological validity of the tests themselves. Nothing can overemphasize the potential danger of such tools in the hands of people with power over others' careers. For this very reason, many candidates for managerial jobs, aware of the controversy that rages about these tests, are extremely reluctant to undergo them.

In a paper given at the 1972 I.P.M. Conference, Roger Holdsworth, one-time Head of Selection Guidance at the National Institute of Industrial Psychology, summed up thus:

'My own sad conclusions, after 14 years' reading, scientific study, and practical work in personnel selection, are that we are still very hard put to make predictions better than chance about occupational success based on personality judgements. The accuracy often claimed for such predictions is mainly illusory, and many of the reported research studies in this field contain glaring errors and are quite misleading ... In the long term, personality measurement will rely on objective tests based on psycho-physiological discoveries. In the short term, however, as far as personnel selection is concerned, we should make more use of situation tests. Enough is known for leaderless group discussions and in-basket exercises to be devised with good chances of success.'

Intelligence, aptitude, and proficiency tests can provide useful additional information in an objective manner about certain abilities which are perhaps difficult to discover by interviewing alone. The best claim for personality tests seems to be as a catalyst before the interview; once a man has been told the results of such tests, he seems much more prepared to let his hair down and discuss his character traits than if the interviewer had questioned him directly. Validity and reliability are the key considerations about all tests—'where valid instruments exist, one should measure rather than make far less reliable interview estimates ... Performance on certain tests is positively correlated with success in certain jobs. It is, of course, interesting to speculate on the reasons for these correlations, but the predictive value of these tests is justification enough for their use.'*
But it is the unease that people feel about these inexplicable correlations that makes tests the subject of so much controversy. Personnel managers responsible for advising on recruitment and promotion should use any means of objective measurement available, but where limitations are known to exist, tests must be very carefully chosen, properly administered, accurately scored, and sensibly interpreted.

GROUP SELECTION TECHNIQUES

In the case of senior appointments, or where a number of candidates have to be considered for one vacancy, still more information can be

* Letter to *The Financial Times*, 4 April 1966, from Mackenzie Davey, chairman of a firm of management consultants.

obtained by giving them a task to carry out as a group and observing how they react to each other. The point about this technique is that people in senior posts spend a good deal of their time thinking up ideas and then trying to persuade their colleagues to agree with them. It is very difficult to judge a candidate's ability to succeed in this vital role merely by interviewing him, but group selection methods can give some indication of how each candidate is likely to get on with other people.

The standard method can be described quite simply as putting a small group of candidates into action together, observed by a panel of selectors. This panel should be small, with not more than four members, experienced men of good judgment who have been properly trained to know what they are looking for and how to find it. The group of candidates should be about six in number, so that adequate time can be allowed for each person to contribute to the discussions: these should take place without interruption from the selectors. The setting in which the group works should be comfortable and as informal as possible; seating at a round table is a sound practice, for there is then no obvious chairman.

Actual procedure can vary considerably, from direct discussions on general subjects or problems put to the group by the selectors, through to complicated prepared briefs for 'committee sessions' when each candidate in turn acts as chairman or advocate of his own ideas for solving a particular problem. (This latter method is used in the three-day Method B technique of the Civil Service Selection Board.)

While these discussions are going on, the selectors are observing the intellectual and social skills of the candidates and the attitudes of mind they display. Afterwards, the panel will analyse the effort made by each individual—the number and quality of his contributions to the discussion, whether they were well expressed, to the point, and positive. Above all, they will consider what influence he had had on the group, the extent to which he had dominated it, whether he helped it to achieve its task or prevented it from doing so, and the ways in which he made his criticisms and received any directed at him. His intellectual skill would be reflected by the evidence he gives of thinking logically, clearly, and in a flexible manner. Evidence of social skills will be seen in his relationships with other members of the group, if he is tactful in what he says, and if his own personality makes an impact. In the group discussions something of his attitudes and approach to life should be detected: whether, for example, he tends to be positive and constructive or negative and critical. Finally, certain other elements of his personality—initiative, self-confidence, and dependability —might also be revealed.

The important thing to remember about the group selection method is that it is but one way of providing additional information about candidates. It is not a substitute for any other aspect of the selection procedure; the evidence it produces must be added to and compared with that derived from other sources. Summing up, in fact all types of selection tests and group observation techniques can have some value in helping to determine a candidate's abilities, assess his disposition, and evaluate his attitudes; but they should all be applied by well-trained staff. Improperly used they can be a waste of time and the results can be downright misleading.

VALIDATION

Following up the success achieved by candidates appointed under a recrvitment procedure is essential if the effectiveness of that procedure is to be kept under review. Selection is essentially a prediction, and it is not easy to prove how good predictions are. Usually one person is chosen from a group of candidates—even if he does turn out well, how can the selector ever be sure that one of the rejected members of the group would not have done better? How can success in a job be measured, anyhow? Is it a matter of visible results achieved, an assessment by a superior, a personal feeling of satisfaction, salary progression—or some combination of all these factors?

There can therefore be no strictly scientific measure to validate a recruitment procedure. Nevertheless a great deal can be learned from both successes and failures if proper records are kept. In practice, the latter approach might well be the more fruitful, studying the reasons for failure and the sequence of events which finally indicated that a person had failed. If evidence then emerges of some shortcoming in the selection methods used, corrective action can be taken. None of this can be done, however, unless follow-up is planned from the outset with an efficient system for keeping the necessary records.

If the interviewer is asked from the outset to predict the applicant's likely success in performing the various component tasks of the job being filled, then these records will enable feedback to be quite specific. Such an approach, rather than trying to assess overall suitability, will mean that the interviewer's own achievements and failures can be more readily identified. It has another advantage in forming the first step in the successful candidate's career development programme. For once the 'whole job' concept of suitability is rejected, and recognition given to the fact that very few candidates ever start as perfect matches with job requirements, then selection can also be seen as beginning the process of defining training needs.

FURTHER READING

The Skills of Interviewing, by Elizabeth Sidney and Margaret Brown (Tavistock Publications, 1961).

6 Aspects of Employment— Transfer, Promotion, Termination

THE CONTRACTS OF EMPLOYMENT ACT, 1972

The first main provision, in Section 1 of the Act, gives both employers and employees rights of minimum periods of notice to terminate employment. The following periods obtain for employees: if they have been employed for more than thirteen weeks but less than two years, they must receive at least one week's notice; more than two years but less than five years' employment entitles them to two weeks' notice; more than five years but less than ten years, four weeks' notice; between ten and fifteen years, six weeks' notice; and over fifteen years' employment, eight weeks' notice. Section 2 sets out employees' rights concerning minimum payments that must be made to them during these periods of notice, and these payments must now be linked with the provisions of the Redundancy Payments Act.

Section 4 obliges employers to give employees written particulars of their main terms of employment. The contract or agreement between them must name the parties, state the date when the employment begins, and set out:

1. The rate of pay, or the method of calculating it.
2. The intervals (monthly, weekly, etc.) at which remuneration is paid.
3. Conditions relating to hours of work.
4. Conditions relating to holidays and holiday pay, payments when absent through sickness or injury, and provision for pensions.
5. Length of notice to be given and received for termination of employment.
6. The date on which a fixed-term contract is to end.
7. Information about the calculation of accrued holiday pay due on the termination of employment.
8. The employee's right to belong to a trade union.
9. To whom the employee can apply for redress of any grievance relating to his employment.

Industrial tribunals are empowered to hear complaints relating to any alleged breach by either party of the contract of employment.

Experience in putting Section 4 of the Contracts of Employment Act into practice has varied. It is sometimes difficult to incorporate all conditions relevant to a person's job in a single letter. For this reason, many employers send a much shorter letter, simply confirming the engagement and briefly welcoming the newcomer; a separate document is then enclosed setting out terms of employment. Another method is for an employment handbook to be used to explain conditions common to all staff. For management and executive appointments, most organizations get their legal departments to draw up a full-length contract; special conditions may have to be agreed for such staff, and perhaps an undertaking about the organization's trade and manufacturing secrets signed (sometimes including the Officials Secrets Act, for example in the aircraft industry). Apprentices are generally employed under the strict provisions of their indentures which specify the obligations of both firm and apprentice to each other.

It is still to be hoped that most employers view this legislation for what it is—a statement of their minimum responsibilities. The clarification of terms of employment can help to improve relationships between management and workers in many ways, provided they both recognize obligations towards each other under the Act as well as accepting the improved rights it introduced. The longer periods of notice should also bring about a greater feeling of security; but, again, if the provisions of the Act are taken only as minima, and this sense of security strengthened even further by local initiative, the result could be much more willingness on the part of workers to accept changes and new methods.

TRANSFERS OF STAFF

In the previous Chapter the problems of filling jobs by outside recruitment were analysed. They may also be filled, of course, by the internal transfer or promotion of existing employees.

Transfers from one job to another may be temporary or permanent, but in any event they will call for a certain amount of management control by the personnel department. First the transfer request itself must be dealt with: this may come from the worker concerned, from his supervisor, from the head of another department, or may be made necessary by rises or falls in trading activity which have an impact on the organization as a whole. The way a transfer request is handled often calls for considerable tact and diplomacy. If it is made as a result of a minor difference of opinion between a worker and his supervisor, the best initial approach may be to try to patch up the difference. If a transfer proves inevitable, then the search for a suitable alternative job must start, and this must be undertaken in a manner that will calm any suspicion the receiving supervisor may have that he is being asked to take someone who is a trouble-maker, a poor workman, or who has otherwise been disagreeable in his previous department. Very often there are financial difficulties about making transfers, too: when the new job carries the same rate of pay (which is what the word 'transfer' implies) there is no problem; but if it carries a lower rate, then the person transferred sees it as a demotion. It is clearly no solution to maintain his previous rate in these circumstances, as this will only cause trouble between him and those workers in his new department who are doing similar work. Resolving such differences calls for great powers of persuasion on the personnel manager's part, and also makes follow-up of the transferred employee necessary to check the success of his diplomacy.

When the transfer request emanates from the employee himself, it is usually because he wants to broaden his experience by working elsewhere or because he does not like the work, the place where he has to do it, or the people he has to work with. From a departmental head's point of view such a transfer request can be a confounded nuisance, especially when he has gone to great lengths to train his team of workers up to a level where they operate well together and are producing good results: he now has to face the prospect of seeing part of his efforts destroyed. This dilemma serves to emphasize the importance of senior executives maintaining close contact with supervisors and their subordinates. Managers must try to be constantly aware of people's feelings towards their jobs, so that personal antipathies in the workplace are never allowed to develop to the point where someone asks to be transferred elsewhere. At the same time, it must be recognized that change is the natural state of affairs in industry, and that it is abnormal for a working situation to remain static. If this is accepted, then managers will see that it would be foolish to obstruct transfers of their staff made necessary by these changes. Indeed, healthy relations between management and employees will mean that transfers can be made with goodwill on both sides, since those affected will appreciate their firm's problems and difficulties.

Finally, *job rotation* is a form of staff transfer which is commonly used for training purposes. Its success is partly due to the fact that the need to learn is so obvious when the trainee is deliberately put into an unfamiliar situation. Even so, it is a method about which there is considerable controversy. It may be a good means of introducing youngsters into business life, but is it efficient at more senior levels? For example, technically qualified men of high ability are often prepared for general management by placing them for short periods in various commercial departments. But how much benefit derives from an unqualified man actually working in a specialist department for a few months? Since he can rarely make any constructive contribution, he will be more a hindrance than a help, and it is clearly wasteful that his own technical ability should be squandered simply looking over other experts' shoulders. Are there not better methods—training courses, or even just a carefully prepared book list—to enable him to appreciate the various branches of general management? Apart from these considerations, it is obviously bad for morale if the staff of specialist departments regard the trainee as a 'high flyer' patently being given opportunities for promotion which they feel are being denied to them.

STAFF PROMOTION

The management of an organization should always make every effort to provide opportunities for their subordinates to obtain promotion, as personal advancement is undoubtedly one of the best inducements for people to stay with an employer. While it is not necessarily good practice to fill every vacancy in this way and never bring in 'new blood', it is very encouraging for employees to see that the best jobs do not go to outsiders very often. An organization's promotion policy might well be that, other things being equal, it will give preference to internal candidates for senior posts, and that it will advertise all vacancies involving promotion within the organization before placing them in the press.

Another aspect of policy is whether promotion should be based on seniority or merit. If the former, able younger men are likely to become impatient about 'waiting-for-dead-men's-shoes' and will leave to look for better prospects elsewhere. In the long run, this may mean that an organization comes to be managed by second-rate people who have stayed, possibly because they are not of sufficient calibre to make a move. On the other hand, the use of merit alone can cause difficulties; for example, unions often distrust the sincerity of management mainly because the measures of ability used by many supervisors in identifying merit are open to question and give rise to charges of favouritism. Such allegations can only be refuted by managers showing that they have evolved effective controls to recognize merit objectively. Nevertheless, seniority cannot be ignored; although it is no substitute for competence in the job, it can be used as a deciding factor when all other things are equal.

Unfortunately, it has truly been said that the best way to avoid promotion is to be good at your job. In trying to implement an internal promotion policy, often the most difficult task is to get a departmental head to agree to part with a promising subordinate: he is naturally reluctant to lose a good man and resistant to the idea of having to train a successor. That the personnel manager must be able to persuade him to overcome these feelings is obvious, for once an employee has an inkling that he is in the running for promotion he will become very disgruntled if he finds his way barred by his present departmental head; and if resistance to training new men were allowed to prevail, then the whole policy of promotion from within would be stultified. The process of persuasion can be greatly helped, however, if the personnel manager is able to produce a satisfactory replacement for the promoted man with as little delay as possible.

Promotion usually means several things to the person concerned: higher status, both at work and in the community outside; more pay; perhaps the substitution of greater job security and fringe benefits for direct financial incentives; and a more senior position, from which he should be able to render a better return to his organization. For this last reason, if no other, a comprehensive promotion programme* should be evolved, covering these details:

1. The relative significance of jobs must be established by means of techniques (already described) of the analysis, description, and classification of jobs; this must result in the lines of promotion between jobs becoming clear.
2. A method of assessing the potential of staff for promotion must be introduced, rating individuals against the job requirements already specified.
3. Whenever a senior position falls vacant a decision has to be taken whether it would be better to fill it internally or to go outside to recruit someone with different experience, a broader outlook, and a fresh mind. Bearing in mind the cost of training a newcomer into the firm's methods, and the dismay that its present employees may feel at being passed over, external recruitment would seem to be justified only if there is no obvious candidate within the firm.
4. The question of training for promotion must be resolved. The sensible answer surely is for firms to plan ahead as far as possible and send employees on supervisory and management training schemes in advance of promotion. Those selected will then feel that their firm is taking an interest in their careers, and they will be ready to step into gaps as they appear.

Some large organizations tackle the problem presented when numerous internal candidates are available by using the administrative device of a *promotion board*. This may carry out two functions: deciding who is

* *See* also discussion of a company's manpower planning programme in Chapter 1, page 14.

eligible for promotion by means of a series of tests and interviews, and trying to select the right men for actual vacancies. The composition of such a board may be flexible, but it should be small, with perhaps only the works manager and the personnel manager as permanent members; where a particular vacancy is being considered, they could then be joined by the head of the department concerned and the manager of the candidate's department. The same members of the board should also interview outside candidates if that step is taken.

Such a board would be guided in its task by the promotion policy of the organization. Certain aspects of it—external recruitment or internal promotion, seniority or merit—depend on 'other things being equal'. Making them so largely depends on operating a programme such as that just explained, for success means that the organization will benefit by having several internal candidates available when positions fall vacant. Even so, being realistic, it is unlikely that all members of an organization will support its promotion policy, no matter how carefully it has been prepared. Discontent will inevitably exist among those who do not progress in their careers; such employees will be left with feelings of personal inadequacy, which the experienced personnel manager must expect to become rationalized into grievances against the methods by which their more fortunate fellows were selected.

TERMINATION OF EMPLOYMENT

Termination of employment may take one of three forms: lay-off or suspension, discharge by the employer, or resignation by the employee. Lay-offs and suspensions are temporary in nature and represent actions by the employer, usually taken in the hope of re-employing the workers involved in the near future. Lay-offs are occasioned by lack of work, as when bad weather prevents outside building activity: those laid off are then recalled when work becomes available again. Suspensions are usually imposed for breaking rules and regulations and last a fixed short period of time.

Until appreciation of the principles of scientific management* was driven home by the post-war reality of full employment, it was regarded as the sole prerogative of management to hire and fire labour. This concept is accepted as being both unethical and impractical in industry today, so that workers are now protected against arbitrary discharge.

A legal definition of the reasons sufficient to justify the fair dismissal of an employee, originally set out in the Industrial Relations Act, was repeated in the Trade Union and Labour Relations Act, 1974:

* *See* Chapter 1, page 6.

1. relating to the capability or qualifications of the employee for performing work of the kind which he was employed to do; thus if he is persistently sick, or is struck off a relevant professional society's list of members, he may be fairly dismissed; so would a driver who lost his driving licence;
2. relating to the conduct of the employee: dangerous 'skylarking', for example; or even dishonest activities outside work may warrant a fair dismissal;
3. that the employee was redundant;
4. other substantial reasons, taking into account the circumstances surrounding them.

On the other hand, the Act specifies a number of cases where dismissals may be unfair, relating to employees' rights to join unions, redundancy, strikes, and lockouts.

The procedures involved in terminating an individual's employment must, above all, be designed to ensure fairness. The views expressed by the 1967 report of the Committee on Dismissal Procedures were affirmed in the Code of Industrial Relations Practice, and subsequently reinforced in the Department of Employment's publication 'In Working Order: a Study of Industrial Discipline'.* The guidance on good practice which these reports contain starts with the suggestion that a written copy of relevant procedures should be handed to each employee so that he is fully aware of all disciplinary rules and the circumstances which may lead to suspension or dismissal. If these procedures are mutually agreed in the first place, as a result of joint consultation between management and worker representatives, then the whole process may achieve the aim of promoting self-discipline. The emphasis then falls on preventing breaches of agreed rules, rather than on sanctions imposed after the event.

No employee whose work is considered to be unsatisfactory should be dismissed without being given a fair warning and a chance to improve. Nor should he be dismissed for the first breach of discipline, except in the case of gross misconduct. An oral warning should be given; if there is then a repetition or more serious misconduct, a written warning, setting out the circumstances, should be recorded. A final written warning may then follow before subsequent suspension or dismissal.

Thus no decision on termination should be taken hastily or without regard to the full facts. The employee concerned must be given the opportunity to state his views on the matter, helped by his trade union representative, if he wishes. The decision itself should not rest solely in the hands of that employee's superior; it will best be taken in consultation with the

* Manpower Paper No. 6 (H.M.S.O., 1973).

personnel department, by a line manager at least one stage up in the hierarchy above the immediate supervisor.

In the event, the reasons for the dismissal must be stated clearly and frankly. There should be a right of appeal, if possible to a level of management not yet involved, and then even to an independent arbitrator if the parties so desire. Senior managers brought into the issue in this manner must obviously try to rid their minds of bias or any misplaced belief in a duty to support junior managers irrespective of the merits of the case. It is important that such an appeals procedure works quickly and without unnecessary formality. Experience shows, in fact, that when these guidelines are observed, very few appeals succeed. The ultimate value of such procedures therefore lies in their effect in ensuring that no-one is dismissed without very good reasons.*

When an employee himself resigns, important management action should follow in the form of an exit interview to try to find the real reasons why he is leaving. These reasons may well reflect on the efficiency of the organization's management and lead to a review of its policies and practices on pay, training, promotion, working conditions, and the quality of supervision. One fundamental aspect of policy about resignations that must be settled is the lengths to which a firm is prepared to go in order to dissuade someone from leaving. This question frequently arises when a person has been expensively trained or when he has knowledge of secrets or working methods that his firm might be anxious to keep from competitors. Should the salary promised by his prospective new employer be matched or improved upon? If so, what will be the reaction of his present colleagues doing similar work—can all-round increases be justified?

The arrangements that have to be made when an employee leaves are quite complicated and the personnel manager needs to insist upon receiving full information from departmental heads about intending departures, so that the right procedure can be followed. Assuming that attempts to persuade an employee to stay are unsuccessful, an exit interview should be arranged. Apart from this, a certain amount of paper work is involved, notifying the details of the departure to such people as the wages clerk, pension fund officer, social club secretary, and security officer, so that they can have everything ready at the time he leaves. The departmental head should be asked to complete a leaving report, assessing the employee's performance while working for him, which is then filed for future reference purposes. The key question on this form might well be—'Would you re-employ this man in your department: if not, why not?'

* Current thinking is consolidated in the A.C.A.S. Code of Practice, *Disciplinary Practice and Procedures.*

REDUNDANCY

Industrial development and economic changes involve risks such that no organization can unconditionally guarantee security of employment to its workers. But at the same time, if a sense of loyalty is expected from these workers, a firm must in return show a sense of responsibility towards them in times of uncertainty as well as when conditions are stable. Anxiety can be greatly diminished at such times if agreement is reached beforehand on a policy designed to keep redundancies to a minimum and to mitigate their impact on the individual. Redundancy means having a labour force surplus to productive capacity. It is a situation that arises usually as a result of a marked fall in demand for a firm's products or because the reorganization of working practices or capital investment in new equipment reduces the number of workers required. When this happens, the conflict that inevitably occurs over which employees should lose their jobs underlines the need to have a carefully prepared policy ready to implement.

When trying to formulate such a policy, trade unions and the workers they represent usually emphasize seniority and length of service—'last in, first out'. For their part, management naturally prefer to consider efficiency and argue that quality of workmanship must be the main factor: their logic is that an efficient staff will allow the organization to maintain its competitive power, thus reducing the likelihood of further redundancies and enabling them to expand the labour force again as soon as economic conditions improve. In fact, these opposing views can be integrated in a policy statement such as this:

> Management will tell workers and their trade union representatives of any redundancies in advance, will consult* with them on methods of dealing with the situation, and undertake that, other things being equal, length of service will be taken into account.

Such a policy demands that each employee be assessed as to his qualities of workmanship before length of service is considered, and clearly must embrace the labour force as a whole, not just that of the few departments which may happen to be directly affected. This assessment should be an exercise in joint consultation between management, supervisors, and shop stewards, aimed not at choosing those to be dismissed but at grading the abilities of men they all know well.

If threatened redundancy seems likely to be only temporary in nature, as when demand fluctuates seasonally, then the best practice may be to create some sort of reserve fund so that good workers can be retained; the firm will not then have to face the prospect of recruiting inferior workers

---

* Such consultation is now a legal requirement, since the Employment Protection Act, 1975.

later when demand revives. The earnings of the men retained would be made up to their previous average level from this fund, as long as they were prepared in the meantime to do work other than their normal jobs, for example, maintenance tasks or labouring.

A number of other measures can be taken to keep redundancies to a minimum:

1. Marketing policy can be reviewed, including the possibility of an increased selling effort at lower prices.
2. All recruitment can be stopped (except where this may lead to increased sales), thus allowing natural wastage to account for some of the surplus jobs.
3. Part-time working, sub-contracted work, and overtime should all be cut as much as possible.
4. Work-sharing and short-time working should be allowed wherever practical, although both should be recognized as uneconomical and must therefore be limited in extent and duration.
5. Some workers likely to be redundant can be transferred to other sections or plants within the organization and provided with facilities for retraining.

If the redundancy is permanent, with no prospect of re-employment, the longest possible notice should be given and the organization should do its best to help employees find alternative work. Executives in the personnel department itself can help initially by contacting their opposite numbers in other local firms to tell them of the types and skills of employees being made redundant and to find out if there are any vacancies available. These men should then be allowed time off with pay to attend interviews for new jobs. Similarly, facilities should be offered to the staff of the local employment exchange to come to the firm's premises during working hours to meet the men concerned and interview them, as a preliminary to finding them new jobs before their period of notice expires.

Another aspect of the problem that could be settled by joint consultation is the method of dealing with certain special categories of labour, in particular, older workers, married women, foreign workers, and shop stewards.*

Normally the first people to be asked to leave are those workers who

---

* The *Ministry of Labour Gazette*, February 1963, published a survey of redundancy policies in 371 firms in private industry. The results as regards order of dismissal show that 40 per cent rely on a combination of lack of seniority and least efficiency; 40 per cent state the categories of workers to be dismissed first, for example, married women, part-time workers; most of the remaining firms rely solely on lack of seniority, and a few rely solely on the least efficient.

have carried on beyond the statutory retiring age. Looking at seniority from a different angle, too, it might be possible to bring forward the departure of those who are nearing the retirement age, although this could only be done by offering financial compensation or if they were otherwise eligible for pensions. This seems a just step to take if it allows a larger number of younger men, who usually have more pressing domestic responsibilities, to stay. Where pensions are not available, however, the opposite view can be put with some force—that the younger men should go first because they will find it easier to get other jobs than the older employees.

Married women are usually well up on the list of those to be made redundant. In fact, when their husbands are working there are obvious economic reasons why many unions argue that they should be the first to leave: they certainly should be discharged before men whose families are wholly dependent on their employment. A very serious social problem arises in the case of immigrant workers: although there may be little objection to their being offered jobs when labour is short, the common attitude is that they should be made redundant before local labour. Thus the worker's country of origin becomes a factor in the redundancy situation. In fact, in all three of these cases there are elements introduced over and above the normal controversy between seniority and efficiency, and it is in clarifying policy on such points that joint consultation can prove its strength or weakness.

The position of shop stewards is a problem in itself, and many industrial disputes have been caused by their dismissal or transfer through redundancy. The whole procedure must clearly allow for no favourites; yet at the same time the steward is the workers' chosen representative, and they will react strongly if there is any suspicion that he is being victimized for having served their cause. If he is dismissed or transferred, their choice is being diverted and they are forced to elect another official. It therefore does seem reasonable to make an exception here and allow shop stewards to continue in their jobs for the duration of their union appointments.

Much of the procedure outlined above relies heavily on joint consultation for its successful implementation. But even where the practice of this technique is so advanced that workers can share in deciding policy of this nature, final decisions must remain in the hands of management, who, more than ever in such a serious situation as redundancy, must be conscious of their overall responsibility for the firm's efficiency. Nevertheless, to avoid all charges of injustice, management could further demonstrate its goodwill by submitting the names of those to be dismissed to union representatives for comment or even to try to get their agreement. 'Comment' would give them the chance to suggest other names, with reasons for these alternatives; 'agreement' would assure everyone concerned that the selection had been carried out strictly according to the negotiated policy.

Most of the nationalized industries have redundancy policies, the provisions of which tend to be rather more generous than in private firms. Examples are:

1. Consultation: in the electricity industry at least twelve months' warning must be given about the closure of a power station.
2. Transfers of staff: assistance is given, where appropriate, to cover travelling expenses, house removal costs, and temporary accommodation.
3. Guarantees of former earnings: the railways give full pay for five years to employees who are downgraded because of redundancy.

Lowest seniority is usually the guide to selection for redundancy in the nationalized industries. Weekly payments are made to those affected, usually two-thirds of standard pay for a normal week, less unemployment benefits—for as long as forty weeks in the case of railway workshop employees. A redundant miner with over ten years' service is paid an immediate pension if he is over sixty, as well as receiving a lump-sum payment.

THE REDUNDANCY PAYMENTS ACT, 1965

Most individual organizations with progressive redundancy policies included provisions for severance pay to help soften the initial impact of possible unemployment. The need for such provisions was lessened by the 1965 Act which stipulated that all employees with a minimum period of two years' service are entitled to lump-sum payments if their jobs cease to exist, as follows:

$1\frac{1}{2}$ weeks' pay for each year of service between ages 41 and 65 (60 for women);

1 week for years between 22 and 40;

$\frac{1}{2}$ week for years between 18 and 21.

Thus the scheme provides payments, based on a combination of length of service, age, and normal pay when dismissed, which are intended to compensate a worker for his loss of job expectations and to encourage him to move. The wage-related unemployment benefit scheme, subsequently introduced under the National Insurance Act, 1966, is intended to cushion any unemployment before he finds a new job.

The cost of payments is met partly from a Redundancy Fund, financed by employers' contributions of 6p per week for men and 3p for women, collected with their national insurance contributions. Employers who make lump-sum compensation payments may claim a 50 per cent rebate from the fund (Redundancy Rebates Act, 1969). Employees do not have to pay tax on their redundancy pay, nor do they lose any subsequent unemployment benefits. Any disputes about entitlement to redundancy payments or about claims for rebate from the fund are settled by industrial tribunals established under the Industrial Training Act, 1964. In 1966, the first full year of operation, 137,208 payments to redundant workers were made, totalling nearly £26½ million; nearly 6,000 appeals were heard by industrial tribunals, almost all of which were by workers seeking to establish their entitlement to a payment or the correct amount payable. By comparison, in the quarter July–September 1976, payments made under the 1965 and 1969 Acts totalled £42·8 million: £23 million was borne by the Fund, the rest by employers. The number of payments was 68,518.

7 Special Categories of the Labour Force

The slow rate of natural growth in the working population during the 1970s and 1980s is a cause of considerable concern for manpower planners and personnel managers.

GREAT BRITAIN: ACTIVE LABOUR FORCE PROJECTION
(*thousands*)

Year	Total	Male	Female	Female Married
1975	25,098	15,841	9,257	6,219
1976	25,164	15,833	9,331	6,327
1977	25,267	15,845	9,422	6,439
1978	25,395	15,867	9,528	6,562
1979	25,540	15,900	9,640	6,690
1980	25,653	15,936	9,717	6,792
1981	25,839	16,005	9,834	6,909
1986	26,659	16,330	10,329	7,521
1991	27,028	16,532	10,496	7,920

[Source— *Department of Employment Gazette*, April 1974]

Over this sixteen-year period, then, the total working population will grow by only 7·7 per cent, less than ½ per cent per annum. The female population at work will rise rather more quickly, by 13·3 per cent during the period. Most significant, however, is the growth of 27·3 per cent in the total number of married women working: in 1972, 64 per cent of females at work were married; by 1991 this will have risen to nearly 79 per cent.

Organizations currently facing labour shortages, therefore, can hardly afford to sit back and hope these will go away of their own accord. Management must take positive manpower planning steps to try to increase the size of the labour forces available locally, to train their employees in order that they may produce more, and to utilize their skills to the maximum.

Certain categories of the labour force present their own problems, and tackling these will go some way towards improving the effectiveness of total labour resources. The peculiar difficulties of school-leavers and other young people are so bound up with training that this aspect will be left until Chapter 10. But apart from these youngsters, all three approaches mentioned above relate directly to the employment of married women and disabled people and, to a lesser extent, to the problems of elderly workers.

MARRIED WOMEN

Management action to make the employment of married women more effective involves:

1. Persuading more of them to take jobs, because they are the largest remaining untapped source of labour supply.
2. A new attitude towards training them for skilled jobs (there is a marked reluctance to do so at the moment).
3. The need to recall and make greater use of the skills these women acquired before leaving work after marriage.

It is interesting to reflect here on the role of the personnel manager in advising departmental heads about patterns of staff behaviour. Many common assumptions about the alleged unreliability of married women employees as regards attendance, time-keeping, sickness, and labour turnover have been questioned and proved wrong by recent surveys. Obviously much depends on whether the women have small children, and some firms insure themselves against possible unreliability by not recruiting women with young families. The fact remains that as far as regular work habits are concerned, the record of married women is generally as good as, if not better than, single women. Older women can also be relied on to bring a steadying influence to their jobs, and skills and training from previous employment may well include such characteristics as the ability to deal with the public, operate complex machinery, and supervise junior staff. Thus, while married women will always try to adjust their employment to meet their domestic requirements, those employers who help them to do so will reap the benefits of dependable service.

The personnel specialist should also be able to capitalize on what is known about the motivation of married women in working, in order to attract them into his firm's employment. To start with, the fact that the majority of part-time workers are over thirty-five indicates that financial considerations rather than domestic circumstances determine whether a woman will look for full-time or part-time jobs. There may be economic pressures which force young married mothers to work full-time when no part-time jobs are available, but older women, whose husbands are at the peak of their earnings, can afford to be much more selective. Thus, although the financial motive is always present, only in a small proportion of cases during early years of marriage does actual necessity seem to be involved. The majority look on their work more as a means of obtaining higher standards of living for their families—buying better furniture for the home, running a car, taking holidays abroad, for example. The psychological uplift of not having to be 'careful' over money and the desire for personal independence are other relevant aspects of the financial motive. The desire for companionship is very important, especially to those women who find themselves left alone all day after being used to looking after children. The routine of housework and shopping can become very depressing in such circumstances, and they particularly enjoy the prospect of being kept young by going back to work with a friendly crowd of younger people. In any case, married women today have much more time on their hands than their mothers, and certainly their grandmothers, had; the days of very large families have disappeared so that, whereas a mother spent some fifteen years nursing her own babies at the turn of the century, this has now fallen to an average of only four years.

In theory, personnel policies should always reflect equal conditions for all staff, with no special treatment for particular groups. Nevertheless, conditions of supply and demand in the labour market inevitably mean that concessions must be made when necessary to obtain the required amount of labour. In practice, these concessions usually take the form of:

1. Shorter hours or longer lunch-breaks to allow family shopping to be done; a retail shop is sometimes provided on the premises.
2. Unpaid leave of absence for domestic reasons, such as children's illness or husband's holidays.
3. Fitting hours in with husband's shifts whenever possible.

There is a negative side to this subject as well, for many organizations place certain restrictions on the employment conditions of married women: making them the first to be declared redundant, not considering them for promotion, excluding them from pension schemes and sickness benefits (especially if part-time), and in some cases giving them only temporary status. Some of these policies need to be changed if a realistic attitude is to be taken towards employing married women.

There can be little doubt that a large proportion of married women are under-employed. The vast majority of them in manufacturing industries, for instance, work in unskilled jobs so that, as well as having lower rates of pay than men to start with, very few have any prospects of getting into the skilled or better-paid occupations. It is common practice for firms to try to place married women in 'odd jobs' away from the main stream of production, where their assumed irregularity of attendance will make itself least felt; apart from the falseness of this assumption, it means that many women are offered jobs far below their level of ability.* Similarly, the reluctance of many organizations to offer training to those women seeking a second career after the age of about thirty-five means that they too will be working below their natural capacities.

Skill is one thing, responsibility another. Although many married women resent the humdrum nature of their work and would like something more challenging, they do not on the whole want to be supervisors and thus add further responsibilities to their domestic commitments. If they possess any organizing talents, they prefer to use them at home where their sense of status and security are centred. Above all, they do not want to take their work home with them, which a supervisor with problems often has to do. Nor is there much financial incentive to accept promotion, for supervisors do not usually get piece-rates or the chance to earn more money before holidays or at Christmastime. There is also a marked reluctance to move above friends whose companionship was one of the main reasons for coming back to work in the first place. Even so, many managers recognize particular qualities in married women as supervisors—experience of life, maturity, and tolerance, for example, plus the ability to handle other married women and recognize excuses for what they are. To draw on these skills in the future, however, may very well mean offering much more realistic financial incentives at supervisory level, further concessions as regards hours, and a more elaborate structure of deputy or relief supervisors to cover times of family crisis.

But recruiting more married women, whether to the usual type of job offered or as supervisors, will only partly depend on the attitude of employers. Much will naturally depend on the readiness of married women to come forward in sufficiently large numbers, and this, in turn, will be influenced by the financial inducements offered, and by the availability of public and private services such as nurseries and crèches. Government action will be necessary here—by amending the existing factory legislation where necessary, and particularly in providing local facilities for mothers with young children which will enable them to go out to work while successfully coping with their domestic responsibilities. An important amenity that any employer might himself provide, if he feels convinced that he will thereby recruit staff who would not otherwise come to him, is a day nursery to look after employees' children during working hours. The costs of establishing, equipping, and staffing such a unit must be carefully considered by management beforehand, in relation to the number of new

* Since the Sex Discrimination Act 1975, women may not be discriminated against because they are married.

employees likely to be recruited, and any decision should be based on these factors:

1. How many married women with children are actually available for employment (information from local employment offices).
2. How much competition there is from other employers for this type of labour; the possibility of combining with any of them to provide a nursery.
3. What facilities are already available in local-authority and private nurseries in the area.
4. The costs involved in providing accommodation and facilities to the standards required by the Department of Health.
5. The extent to which these costs can be offset by charging mothers who place their children in the nurseries.
6. The net expected gain in staff.

There still remains, of course, some social resistance to solving problems of labour shortage by recruiting married women. Opponents point out the increasing incidence of split homes, divorce, neglected children, and juvenile delinquency. Public opinion therefore needs to be educated about the inescapable economic facts of labour supply; social attitudes will change when it is seen that there is really no alternative to the employment of married women that will meet the size of our national labour requirements.

The personnel manager or his welfare assistants have a direct role to play in easing the adjustment of married women to the working situation, by appreciating their difficulties and problems and by helping to solve them. More and more General Practitioners in the community are protesting about the 'working-wife syndrome'—the increasing number of patients who present themselves near the stage of nervous and emotional collapse, asking for some sort of tonic to remove their irritability, tiredness, headaches, insomnia, and indigestion. 'The usual story is: get up at 7 a.m. or earlier; do some rapid housework, including breakfast for the family; leave home at 8 a.m.; work all day—often standing all the time—shopping in the lunch break or on the way home; and return home to a bleak house with unmade beds, breakfast dishes unwashed, at about 6 p.m. The evening is spent in catching up on neglected housework and the weekend in washing, shopping, cleaning, and mending. . . . The cause of this syndrome is sheer overwork. The attempt to run a home—especially if there are children—and yet spend 8–10 hours a day away from the home doing another job is almost impossible.'*

* Letter in *The Lancet*, 5 February 1966, from Dr. J. F. Hanratty.

The need for welfare officers to be available to give friendly advice to women who show signs of reaching this state is obvious. It is partly a matter of providing services and making concessions over working conditions, as already described, but fundamentally calls for acceptance of the fact that married women must be allowed to put their families first. For example, when a woman returns after a few days off work, she should not be subjected to a nerve-racking inquisition with threats of dismissal included for good measure; rather she needs an understanding discussion of her domestic problem. Financial advice should be made available for young married couples, too, so that they do not come to rely so heavily on the wife's income that her absence from work can cause a family economic crisis over hire-purchase debts.

PART-TIME WORKERS

On the whole, married women are reluctant to work overtime and indeed can often afford to be choosy about the hours they actually do work. Many organizations have responded to this situation by arranging special shifts for part-time workers or even deciding tasks individually with married women for the hours when they are available. Again this is a matter of facing up to the economic facts of life and accepting the inevitable; but there is a much stronger feeling of making the best of a bad job, for part-timers are generally regarded as unreliable in attendance, time-keeping, and turnover. Most firms employ them only because full-time labour is not available or because demand for their products fluctuates. There is no doubt that it is more expensive to employ part-time staff. As there must be more of them to obtain an output equivalent to full-time workers, administrative and training costs are higher and so are overheads; full insurance contributions must be paid for the larger number of workers involved; costly machinery tends to stand idle for a greater proportion of the time and highly rented accommodation may also be empty. On the other hand, there are certain advantages: when labour is acutely short, part-timers are usually readily available in the numbers required; and they can more easily be made redundant when the labour force has to be cut. The best method of organizing their efforts seems to be in using them on jobs which lie outside the main flow of production, or by employing them together on special evening shifts, thus keeping production going after the full-time staff have left for the day.

But here again there is scope for greater flexibility in approach. Do not present attitudes create the very atmosphere which causes part-time workers to feel that they are resented and that their contributions to production are minimal? The 'take-it-or-leave-it' confrontation about hours, offers of the lowest-paid routine jobs despite past good experience, the wariness of young supervisors when faced by this wealth of experience—all are attitudes that need to be overcome if the most effective use is to be made of part-time workers. Why promote a younger person prematurely rather than have two older part-time women sharing the control of a department? Why not resolve the hours problem by interviewing husband and wife together and discussing a satisfactory solution to any mutual difficulties that appear to exist?

The significance of all these problems about the employment of married women is that they are all likely to become more acute. Full employment, growing affluence, and the numerical preponderance of men in the marriageable age groups are all factors forcing down the age at which women marry and thus increasing the proportion of married women in the working population. The national economy cannot do without these women at work, and employers must move away from the position of regarding their employment simply as an expedient while labour shortages continue. A much more positive approach is required; traditional attitudes towards working conditions must be reappraised and made more flexible, so that married women will be given better opportunities to pull their full weight.

OLDER PEOPLE

With higher standards of living, improved health, and better medical services, people stay fitter for work much longer. The average age of the working population has increased steadily over the past two decades, and now that so much concern is being shown for making the most effective use of available manpower, a great deal more needs to be done in tackling the problems of all those people who, because of their age, meet with special difficulties in obtaining or retaining jobs.

The time at which these difficulties arise varies with the individual, the area where he lives, and his occupation, and depends not only on his physical and mental ability but on the nature of the work, the attitudes of his employer and workmates, and the state of the local labour market. Although knowledge about the processes of ageing is still very incomplete, it is well established that a feeling of continued usefulness has great psychological benefits. In later middle age, most people try to move away from jobs which make severe demands on them for speed, agility, or sustained heavy muscular effort. They are quite capable of doing work which requires less effort, of course, and can offer positive advantages in some types of jobs, for example, those requiring accuracy and attention to detail, and those in which judgment based on experience is called for. Some skilled workers also make very good instructors for young craftsmen. The qualities that older people generally bring to their work, such as regularity of time-keeping and conscientiousness, must not be overlooked.

The National Advisory Committee on the Employment of the Older Worker found that 60 per cent of employed persons preferred to stay on at work when they reached pensionable age. Their reasons were mainly financial, but also because they feel fit enough and want to carry on working, even when they have enough money to be able to retire. Main reasons for retirement are ill-health or lack of opportunities to continue working: employers tend to give the latter as a reason for enforcing retirements rather than dismissing people for inefficiency or incapacity for work.

The difficulties of employing older people are varied and complex. Individual mental and physical shortcomings may prevent them from doing many types of jobs that call for quick reflexes. Often there is marked resistance from younger workers to their continued employment, because they may block promotional opportunities. The phrase 'too old at forty' still has some significance, although with continued high employment levels there is a noticeable tendency for age limits in staff advertisements to be extended. The cost of providing pensions rises according to age when joining a superannuation scheme. Most of this financial burden falls on the employer's shoulders, which is a sound reason for not engaging an undue proportion of staff above middle age; again, many pension funds exclude the entry of men and women above a specified age (sometimes as low as fifty). In a redundancy situation, it is common practice for pensioners and those nearing retirement to be discharged first, in order to preserve the security of young employees with family responsibilities. Sometimes the age structure of an organization becomes unbalanced in relation to future work requirements, and firms have been known to retire older workers compulsorily to inject some younger blood into the organization.

Professional and executive jobs tend to be the most stable, but older people who lose such posts often find it difficult to get other work. Some go into premature retirement if they can afford to; some have to take employment which makes little use of their professional abilities; some find only part-time jobs. Others have to change not only their employment late in life, but also their profession: for example, regular servicemen of the armed forces. Such people can only rarely offer experience worth much to a prospective employer and in most cases they are philosophical about the inevitable reduction in pay and status, especially if there are some prospects of improvement once experience has been gained. Direct help is given by the Civil Service, which offers some posts, without age limits, in both clerical and executive grades for competition by ex-regular members of the Forces. Specialized employment bureaux have been created to help, too.

The Ex-Officers' Association, the Regular Forces Employment Association, and the Over Forty-Five's Association are the best known, and there have been examples of professional men banding together to provide their own self-help service in finding new jobs. Even the psychology of the problem has been tackled in the attempt to change employers' attitudes. The National Advisory Council strongly recommends that phrases like 'the normal age of retirement' should be replaced by 'the *minimum* pensionable age', thus directing the employers' attention away from the concept of statutory retirement.

Much wider publicity needs to be given to all these problems of employing older people, in the hope that pressure of public opinion will itself help to break down long-established traditions and prejudices held throughout industry. As a boost to these efforts, in 1966 the National Joint Advisory Council approved proposals put forward by the Ministry of Labour to try to improve the situation and agreed to co-operate in persuading employers to accept these ideas:

1. Full use of the older worker can go a long way to ease the general labour shortage, thus reducing the inflationary pressures on the economy and on the individual firm.
2. Older workers can be expected to respond favourably to an attempt by an employer to make special arrangements for their continued employment.
3. The situation may vary from industry to industry and even between individuals, but in general the productiveness of older workers is not less than younger workers when employed on familiar work in suitable conditions.
4. Some quite simple modifications are often all that are necessary to adapt working conditions to suit older workers.
5. Adjustment of working hours may be helpful. Part-time jobs may attract older workers who would not be willing or able to take full-time employment.

The Council approved other action to be taken in support of the campaign:

1. Some review of the effect of statutory and other arrangements concerning retirement pensions, redundancy payments, and similar matters.
2. Greater use of training in Government Training Centres and Employment Rehabilitation Centres.
3. More special arrangements to be made by firms for employing and training older workers.

4. A new initiative by local offices of the Department of Employment in placing older workers by intensified activity and a more sophisticated approach.

Finally, many employers do their best to give practical help and advice to their employees as they near retirement. The actual burden of work in the late years can be eased by transfer to lighter duties or by shortening hours to allow travel that misses the discomfort of rush hours. The very last stage of their training can take the form of courses run by local technical colleges intended to prepare for the transition to retirement and the leisure it brings, and the employees concerned can be put in touch with many clubs and other agencies which will help them to occupy their time.

DISABLED WORKERS

A disabled person is one who suffers from some physical or mental impediment on a permanent basis. In April 1976* there were 543,064 workers registered as disabled; at the end of that year some 76,045 of these were unemployed and 11,446 too severely disabled to be able to work. Certainly these numbers are large enough to demand careful consideration of how to use this type of labour most effectively as one means of improving national productivity.

The basic intention when offering employment to someone who is disabled is to help him to rehabilitate himself to a normal life. But finding suitable jobs for handicapped people has to be approached in two ways—from the points of view of both the individual concerned and the group with whom he will be working. In practice, the first need is to give him the opportunity of training to do a job which is within his capacity. The members of the group about to receive him must also be educated so that they have some insight into his problems. The average working group seems to find little difficulty in making the necessary adjustment, but it can be a matter of fine balance: if people are too kind to the disabled man and want to help him when he really does not need it, or if they make him an object of pity, they may eventually cause him to become too dependent and lose his self-respect.

The problems of disabled workers were originally tackled by voluntary agencies, but these have long since been extended by legislation and other state action:

1. Disabled Persons (Employment) Acts, 1944.
2. National Insurance Act, 1946, which provides for benefits for those unable to work.

* *Department of Employment Gazette*, November 1976.

3. National Insurance (Industrial Injuries) Act, 1946, covers benefits and pensions for men injured or contracting prescribed diseases at work.
4. National Health Service Act, 1946, of course, provides for actual treatment and for surgical appliances where necessary.
5. National Assistance Act, 1948, contains provisions for the welfare of people who are permanently disabled.
6. Royal warrants and grants which provide pensions for ex-regular members of the Armed Forces, Merchant Marine, and civilians injured during the war.

The most significant of these statutes is the Disabled Persons Employment Act. Employers engaged upon Government contracts are bound to employ a percentage of Registered Disabled Persons within the meaning of the Act (at present 3 per cent). Compliance with their quota regulations entitles employers to inclusion in a National Roll of Employers who may tender for Government contracts and they may advertise the fact on their letter-heading by the display of a badge. Unreasonable failure to comply can result in the removal of the firm's name from the National Roll, and the consequent withdrawal of contracts. Provision is also made for the Secretary of State to designate jobs to be filled only by disabled persons, and employers must have a permit before giving such jobs to normal men. So far, two jobs have been designated—car-park attendant and electric-lift operator. The names of disabled workers are placed on the register for five years, although people usually register only if they want to take advantage of the financial provision and often do not bother to re-register at the end of this period.

Men and women with extreme disabilities can be offered work in sheltered workshops, run by such organizations as Remploy Ltd. These represent an attempt to compromise with the mixed motives of people who are unable to face the world at large but do not want charity, who need to feel that they are giving of their best and being paid fairly for it. However, it is sound psychology to insist that people protected in this sheltered environment should transfer to normal work as soon as possible. Those who are unable to do so, the chronically disabled, can sometimes be found work at home: for example, making poppies for the British Legion.

Most people returning to work after prolonged absence due to sickness or injury face difficulties. Some return too early and are unable to meet the demands of their previous job. Some stay away too long because of doubts about whether they could cope with the work. A few firms have their own rehabilitation arrangements which are instrumental in getting their own sick or injured men back to work. This often calls for ingenuity on the part of supervisors in adapting methods and machinery to assist rehabilitation. Some workers who cannot manage their old jobs or who have lost their confidence may be transferred to work that requires less effort or concentration. Far too often, however, the net result of these good intentions is that the worker concerned is resettled into a more simple or less responsible job, which amounts to a downgrading and loss of expectations if not an actual reduction in earnings.

The considerate attitude of employers would best be channelled along lines of sending workers who are in this unfortunate position for retraining in new skills. Much more should be known about the role of the Department of Employment's Rehabilitation Centres in this respect; in particular, greater publicity about them should be directed at employers who all too often seem quite unaware of their existence. There are now twenty-five of these units spread throughout the country, capable of providing training courses for some 14,000 people annually. Some units offer residential accommodation, the others can find lodgings for their 'students' if necessary. The average length of the courses undertaken is about eight weeks. The great majority of cases are referred from hospitals or by General Practitioners on completion of medical treatment. Most of the rest are spotted at local employment exchanges and are considered likely to benefit from such courses of retraining even though some of them have no permanent disabilities.

The scope of the courses is intentionally wide, in order to help as many people as possible. They encompass:

1. Those who need special help, subsequent to medical treatment, to adapt themselves to return to work or to find the most suitable job.
2. Those who find the stress of their present jobs too much for them.
3. Those who have become unemployed because of industrial change, especially older workers.

Each person's training is designed to meet his individual needs and there is no set syllabus. Courses are planned and controlled by a case conference, the composition of which clearly indicates the care given to these problems. Its members are the rehabilitation officer in charge of the unit, a doctor, an occupational psychologist, a social worker, a technical man in charge of workshops, and a resettlement officer who is in contact with local employment exchanges for subsequent placement purposes.

The basic aim is to simulate the environment and conditions which the rehabilitated worker will meet when he returns to normal employment. So the workshops are given a factory atmosphere and the trainees are engaged on genuine production work sub-contracted from Government departments and local firms. This covers a wide variety of semi-skilled activities and machine operating, but craft training can also be offered at other government training centres.

Thus experts are used—vocational guidance from occupational psychologists and practical assistance from workshop supervisors who are craftsmen selected for their ability to help people—to improve the disabled person's physical capacity, restore his confidence, and enable him to find out what work is most suitable for him. At the end of the course, the case conference discusses a report with him, and this is sent off to the employment exchange in his home area where it is hoped he can be found a job along the lines recommended.

It seems that this rehabilitation service could help many more workers than it actually does, especially since the directing staff are prepared to gear any individual's programme towards his employer's requirements or the potential openings available on his return to work. The benefits clearly are mutual: workers return to gainful employment in a manner which uses their skills and abilities to the highest possible degree, and employers are helped to use their labour force to best advantage, particularly by reducing the length of absence on long-term sickness.

A review of the Department of Employment's disablement resettlement service was started in 1972, with several objectives. Bearing in mind the costs and benefits involved, the overall aim has been to consider whether the existing disablement resettlement service should be broadened so as to include other disadvantaged people with special employment problems, such as those who suffer periods of mental illness. On the other hand, things could be left as they were, with efforts concentrated on improving that existing service, especially its resettlement aspects. Attention has also been given to the need for more sophisticated and professional assessment facilities, and for better arrangements for the follow-up of those recently resettled in employment.

IMMIGRANT WORKERS

The situation in Great Britain today is that immigrant workers in the public services and on the factory floor are making substantial contributions, especially in areas of high employment. Some half-million are already in employment, supporting wives and children totalling about the same number. They work largely in the unskilled, more unpleasant, and less well-paid jobs that British workers tend to avoid; skilled employment is difficult to get, mainly because their previous experience is usually of too general a nature to meet the demands of highly specialized workshops in this country.

The rate of immigration has its own history of controversy: in 1955 there were about 40,000 immigrants, this figure rising rapidly until early 1962 when the rate was running at nearly 150,000 per annum. Since the Commonwealth Immigrants Act, 1962, entries have been stabilized at 42,000 per annum. The purpose of the Act was primarily to introduce a system of quantitative control of labour from abroad. This was to be exercised over three types of potential employee:

> *Category A.* Those named persons who have a definite job to come to.
> *Category B.* Those who have qualifications or skills of particular value in Great Britain.
> *Category C.* Those who want to come to look for work (a numerical limit has been imposed, subject to periodic review).

The ideal, as far as immigration itself is concerned, is to have Category A arrangements in effect as far as possible. Firms which have overseas subsidiaries can use their foreign staff to carry out local recruitment for them and send the nominated personnel to Britain. Employers not in this fortunate position should press for closer links between our Department of Employment and corresponding departments in the Commonwealth countries, to try to make the Category A procedure work this way. Obviously, if employers are going to rely on recruiters in the countries of origin selecting on their behalf, they must be prepared to send out very full and clear job descriptions and job specifications in the first place. The anxiety of the selectors in these countries to build good reputations should help to overcome the unease that most employers feel about taking on immigrant labour unseen. One good example of special arrangements being made is the case of the London Transport Executive and the Barbados Government, which undertakes to supply a fixed number of recruits periodically to meet the Executive's great staff needs.

Recruitment of immigrant workers in this country is often as the result of personal recommendation. There is also a marked tendency for 'one-man' employment agencies to spring up—an individual acting as a recruiting agent and receiving a fee in return from each worker placed in a job. This smacks of the evils of sub-contracted labour systems, but could only be countered by legislation to insist that all recruitment be carried out through employment exchanges or registered bureaux. If the best use is to be made of the abilities they bring, great trouble must be taken by the exchanges' and bureaux' interviewers in giving immigrants advice about openings for jobs and opportunities for training. Such staff themselves require special training if they are not to find this task too troublesome or forget their responsibilities when faced with the chance of placing immigrant workers quickly. They must also be willing to help with actual applications, as many immigrants are unable to fill in forms.

RACE RELATIONS ACT, 1968

This Act was passed to try to solve the problems encountered by coloured immigrants in the spheres of housing, employment and the provision of goods and services. In the matter of discrimination, it introduces a code that includes clauses relating to employment, trade unions and employers' associations, advertisements and notices. The Act declares that a person discriminates against another if on the grounds of colour, race or national origins he treats that person less favourably than he would treat others.

The following acts by an employer are made unlawful, if they involve discrimination:

1. refusal of work to a qualified person;
2. refusal of the same terms of employment, conditions of work, or opportunities for training or promotion as the employer makes available to other persons employed in the same circumstances;
3. dismissing a person in circumstances in which other persons employed on the same type of work would not be dismissed.

Acts of discrimination made unlawful when committed by employers or workers' organizations are (1) refusing admission to membership on the same terms as other applicants; (2) refusing a member the same benefits as other members; (3) refusing to take the same action on his behalf as on behalf of other members; and (4) expelling him.

The procedure for enforcing the Act goes through three stages—investigation of complaints, conciliation, and then legal proceedings. Complaints have to be made directly or through the Race Relations Board or local Conciliation Committees to the Secretary of State for Employment, who has then to refer them to a suitable body for investigation, otherwise to the Board. There are regulations about the making of enquiries, steps to secure a settlement of differences, reports to the Secretary of State, and notification to the parties of their right to have the complaints further investigated. Only after this procedure has been exhausted may proceedings be brought, and no person or body other than the Race Relations Board may institute such proceedings.

Of course, doubts have been expressed frequently as to whether race relations can be improved by means of legislation. Social attitudes are the key factor: if the 1968 Act can produce an atmosphere in which racial prejudice comes eventually to be regarded as anti-social, that will be the measure of its success. The achievement of this aim is certainly helped by the emphasis placed on conciliation. All industries were invited to set up investigation machinery (or use existing joint bodies for this purpose), and some fifty different industrial organizations, affecting about 7,000,000 workers, have responded.

In the first year the Act was in force, 819 employment complaints were made—313 related to non-engagement, 254 to dismissal, and 173 to terms and conditions—but in only 5 per cent of these cases were there findings of discrimination.

By 1972 the total number of complaints had fallen to 427; 190 of these were about recruitment, 145 about dismissal, and 92 about terms and conditions. In fact, the Board's annual reports comment on the weakness of the complaints machinery and suggest that the Act be strengthened to secure action from employers that ensures equal opportunity. 'The threat of further legislation may lead to voluntary action, but one cannot be optimistic when employers have not recognized that it is a matter of self-interest to recruit, train, and promote the best man or woman regardless of race, colour, ethnic, or national original.'*

In practice, the Act has also played a part in clearing up some misunderstandings over the employment of workers of different races. For instance, the fears of many employers that their customers would not like to be served by coloured shop assistants have proved largely groundless. Where shop-floor opposition has been encountered, the hands of both employers and unions have been strengthened by the fact that discrimination is illegal. Much more effort is being made to provide English classes for immigrants, who, after all, usually have twenty to forty years' working life ahead of them. The racial balance provision of the Act has served to arrest the undesirable development of particular sections of factories or particular occupations coming to be identified with one racial group.

Legislation of this nature must clearly be followed up by organizational policy statements. The I.P.M. has suggested a code of practice for personnel managers, neatly termed *affirmative action*.† 'Discrimination in employment leads to a waste in manpower. Thus a company must be certain that equal employment opportunities exist in practice before it can be satisfied that it is making the best use of its human resources. Exhortation is not enough. Specific orders must be given to check that active steps are being taken to recruit, train and promote suitable members of coloured and other minority groups. The concept of control, too, is just as applicable to this affirmative action programme as to any other policy or plan: so periodic checks and reviews should be carried out to determine that it is being practised.'

Perhaps the general position leaves too much to the initiative of the

* *After four years*, by E. Burney and D. Wainwright (Runnymede Trust, Trust, 1972), page 10.

† *Race Relations in Employment* (I.P.M. policy statement, November 1969).

immigrant: to transport himself here, find accommodation, go from firm to firm before eventually finding a job, and then settle in as best he can. A much more positive approach is required from employers, and there is need for a strong lead over personnel policies, with much greater publicity for the principles and practices of the progressive minority. More preparation for life in Britain could be made in countries of origin, explaining British customs, social services, and such things as P.A.Y.E. Perhaps the British Council could play a part here, in view of the lack of local teaching resources. On the other hand, a firm itself can help by becoming better informed about the countries from which it recruits workers—some of the overseas graduate students living locally could be asked to give talks about their home territories to works committees or on training courses. If firms are going to take on Category A recruits, employment procedures need to be improved, especially the preparation of job descriptions and job specifications, in order to be able to rely on overseas labour departments in selecting the people to send. Because of the drastic change in environment, immigrant workers need a special induction procedure and some extra attention during the early days to ease the transition. Immigrants should be encouraged to join trade unions; as members, they are better protected by the liberal ideas of most unions' leadership. Personnel specialists must concern themselves with the social problems of these employees, and direct them to the state and voluntary agencies which exist in the community to help them.

Prejudice is rampant, of course, among both management and workers, with many stereotypes held concerning all immigrants, about such things as their intelligence, reliability, laziness, cleanliness, and the amount of supervision required. This is particularly unfortunate in the case of young coloured workers, many of whom were born, brought up, and educated in Britain. They thus have the right to expect equality of opportunity and for their skills and abilities to be developed and used to the full. The growing size of the problem can be seen from these figures in Birmingham:

In 1965, 3 per cent of all school leavers were children of immigrants.
In 1972, 6 per cent of all school leavers were children of immigrants.
In 1977, 15 per cent of all school leavers will be children of immigrants.

Undoubtedly the greatest single factor contributing to prejudice is the language problem. It is very difficult to make acceptable social contacts at work or in the community unless people can converse clearly together. The natural reserve of the Englishman makes him appear aloof to people who cannot speak English well—and this is the way that stereotypes are formed. The language problem also makes life difficult for supervisors: they seldom have time to learn how to handle men who find difficulty in understanding instructions and who often have different temperaments from their fellow white workers.

Employers of immigrant labour have had to learn how to cope with racial, national, and religious groups. For example, Cadbury's found trouble in employing girls from different West Indian islands in the same work groups (St. Kitts and Jamaica have a traditional feud) and so they are kept separate. Some employers avoid friction by recruiting only one nationality. Different welfare provisions are also needed, especially for Asian workers, to cater for their particular eating, clothing, and toilet habits, which can cause serious friction if not carefully observed.*

A particular problem which has emerged in recent years is that concerning promotion and the immigrant. The fully integrated labour force is not simply one which appreciates wages, benefits, and job security. The research findings of behavioural scientists about status, loyalty, and access to opportunities for advancement apply as much to immigrants as to British employees. Nothing illustrates this more clearly than promotion policies, for a keen practical distinction can be drawn between non-discrimination and equality of opportunity.

All the evidence seems to suggest a lack of carefully thought-out policies and a failure to recognize that new types of workers demand new policies, procedures, and skills. One solution which does not work is that of confining promotions to departments which very largely or wholly employ immigrant staff. The pursuit of such a 'promotion-by-necessity' policy continues segregation in practice, and does nothing to help other workers accept and respect immigrants as equals or as capable of holding authority.

There is something of a 'vicious circle of self-fulfilling prophecy'† about the situation. First-line management form a stereotype of the immigrants' inability, for whatever reasons, to do certain jobs, and this is reinforced by open hostility among some white workers. In the past some immigrants may have been badly selected for upgrading, or may have been given a rough ride by their British fellow-workers. All these factors accumulate to dissuade immigrants from seeking promotion to jobs which existing supervisors do not believe they can do and white workers do not want them to do. The overall result can only be one of wasted potential which creates negative attitudes, and which the immigrants themselves see as being unjust. They do have special needs and difficulties, and it is not enough to give them training in groups dominated by British super-

---

* All these initial impressions were confirmed in the Department of Employment report 'TAKE 7' (H.M.S.O., 1972).

† 'Promotion and the Immigrant' by Tony Jupp, *Personnel Management*, April 1974, page 36.

visors operating traditional attitudes and patterns of behaviour at work. A willingness to rethink policy along more positive lines is essential; in turn, its application must be carefully monitored by senior management.

Measures to strengthen the law against racial discrimination are contained in the Race Relations Act, 1976. Discrimination is re-defined to include nationality and other unjustifiable conditions which are discriminating in effect. The employment provisions of the Act include: recruitment of new employees; the treatment of existing employees as regards promotion, training, transfer and dismissal; and discrimination against contract workers, by trade unions and employers' associations, by employment agencies, and in the granting of licences and other qualifications needed for carrying on a particular trade or occupation. Exceptionally, employers may provide training confined to members of a particular racial group to help fit them for work in which they have recently been under-represented. They will also be able to encourage members of such a group to take advantage of opportunities for doing work in which comparatively few members of that group are represented.

A powerful new Commission for Racial Equality has been established, replacing the former Race Relations Board, with the overall aims of the elimination of racial discrimination and the promotion of racial equality and good race relations. Its powers of investigation and enforcement are similar to those of the Equal Opportunities Commission, although in the employment field most individual complaints will continue to be made directly to industrial tribunals.

8 Staff Assessment

Experienced managers generally agree that in the past there has been a lack of precision about efforts to make the optimum use of staff and labour resources, compared with the much more meticulous attention paid to the material and financial resources of an organization. Clearly, every firm is anxious to find good supervisors and managers, and most of them would acknowledge that it is more important to their future growth that such staff should come from within their own ranks rather than be recruited from outside. Apart from general techniques and practices, there is, too, the fundamental concern of personnel management for getting the best out of each individual working in an organization. Yet the procedures for achieving these dual aims of securing growth and fulfilling employees' potential are haphazard and leave much to be desired. Many managers feel instinctively that they carry dead-wood in their departments, but seem unable to do anything about it. The fact that employment in the public services, in particular, carries a high degree of security of employment prompts many administrators to complain that they have to put up with staff whose shortcomings are well known, but for which, again, there are no remedies.

THEORY

The theory of the role played by each individual in an organization is quite clear-cut, and is most simply explained in terms of a diagram (*see* Figure 14).

The objectives of the organization will determine its structure in the first place. For example, if a manufacturing company intends to export most of its products, its structure will be different from what it would be had it decided to concentrate on distribution direct to retailers in this country. Another good example is our National Health Service. The act of 1946 laid down that the nation's health requirements would be met by General Practitioners, hospitals, and local health authorities: hence the previous tripartite structure, with the need for close co-operation between each branch. Had the specification been couched in more general terms, a system of area

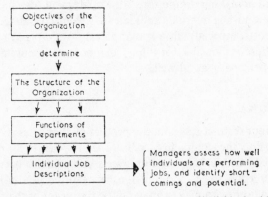

Figure 14. The organization and the performance of individuals within it

health authorities might have emerged instead, thus avoiding any problems of co-ordination. (This pattern was adopted in 1974).

Any large organization must be sub-divided into departments and sections, all with their own defined contributions to make towards achieving the purpose of the organization as a whole. Each department then splits down to separate tasks that have to be carried out, and these, too, must be precisely described. At this basic level, it surely then emerges as a clear responsibility of the departmental manager to assess how well the individuals allocated to these tasks are performing, to identify and correct their shortcomings, and to report on their potential for advancement to bigger and better jobs within the organization. It should be emphasized from the outset that this is a continuous responsibility, not simply a matter of formal reports at particular points in time.

PURPOSES

Thus the overall purpose of a staff assessment scheme is to improve the efficiency of an organization by trying to get the best out of the individuals working for it. Within this concept, staff assessments are used in practice for four other specific purposes:

1. Salary reviews—as a means of measuring how much of an increase one employee should be awarded in comparison with his fellows: (some personnel managers believe that salary reviews should be kept separate from performance appraisals, however).
2. The development and training of individuals—to fulfil the potential or correct the shortcomings revealed by their reports.
3. Planning job rotation—the movement of staff to broaden their experience.

4. As an aid in making promotions—the assessments can provide useful information when internal candidates are being considered for vacant senior posts, especially in a geographically widespread organization where those responsible for filling such posts may not know the candidates personally at all well.

PROCEDURE

There are four distinct stages in the process of staff assessment. All employers who apply the technique carry out the first, that of a written report prepared at fixed intervals by an employee's immediate supervisor. Many go on to the second stage—a discussion between the person reported on and a senior officer, who may or may not be the writer of the report. Very few, however, seem to make much attempt to take the third step, and obtain some sort of positive contribution to the process from the employee reported on. Finally, no assessment scheme can be successful unless it is completed by a careful follow-up of the recommendations made about each individual.

There are a number of well-known hurdles to be overcome if reports are to be written effectively. The first is that of ensuring that the writers are objective: clearly it is important that they should be so, and avoid any personal friendliness or antagonism that they may feel towards particular subordinates. The danger of overmarking is very real, especially when it is known that the subordinate concerned is nearing consideration for promotion; but it is obviously unfair to everyone involved—the person himself, his competitors for promotion who may have been marked realistically, and those more senior managers who are faced with the responsibility of making the actual promotion.

The best safeguards against subjectivity seem to lie in the actual design of the form itself. The more detailed this can be made, the more demanding will writers find it. Provision should also be made for the reports to be reviewed, and commented on by more senior executives: by the writer's own boss certainly, and if possible (as in the Civil Service) by his boss, too. The original reporter, knowing that his best efforts are subject to this close perusal and comment, will feel under considerable pressure to meet the required standards of objectivity.

The second problem to be tackled is that of securing uniformity of assessment among the report writers. This is very difficult where an organization has numerous units in different parts of the country or may even be international in its operations. Undoubtedly, the best way to deal with this is by arranging training sessions for reporting officers, when instructions can be given verbally and any difficulties discussed fully on the spot. The inclusion of a case study in such sessions, asking those attending to assess an imaginary employee, is very useful. When the results are correlated and analysed, individuals become well aware of their own tendencies to be harsh or lenient in making their assessment, and can correct these when preparing actual reports. Experienced personnel managers have concluded, in fact, that highly capable managers tend to mark harshly, while those of less ability are over-generous (believing that good reports on the staff in their departments will redound to their own credit).

The difficulty of ensuring a common understanding of the meaning of the questions contained in the form, and what is required in completing it, can also be overcome to a large extent in these training sessions. One simple exercise to emphasize the reality of this semantic problem is to ask the group to rank in order, 1–14, the following words, commonly used in assessing staff:

> *adequate, average, competent, excellent, exceptional, fair, good, inadequate, indifferent, ordinary, poor, reasonable, satisfactory, superior*

The subsequent process of ironing-out individual disagreements about the shades of meaning of these words reinforces the lesson that assessors must give very careful and objective thought to what they write.

In addition to the training session, comprehensive guidance notes must be issued to everyone taking part in the assessment scheme, giving precise instructions about its purposes and the way in which the report forms should be completed.

CONTENT OF REPORT FORMS

Personal details of the employee reported on will appear first, with his job title, and the length of time he has spent in his present post. This may seem to be stating the obvious, but it can be more important than appears at first sight. It will show how long his superior, writing the report, has known him and his work. If this has been only a short time, he may have to reserve his judgment; if it has been for many years, he would clearly know his work better than anyone else in the organization.

The report aims at assessing the employee's performance in his job during the period (usually a year) immediately preceding it. It is important to be quite clear what the job actually is, and the second part of the form should therefore be a brief job description, outlining the main duties undertaken. There is abundant evidence (*see* Chapter 1, page 14) that departmental managers do not know the jobs of their subordinates in precise detail, so this part of the form might well be filled in by the employee being reported on; at the very least, it should be the subject of consultation and agreement between the two people involved. Special note should be made of any changes in duties since the last report, and any new qualifications obtained could also be added here.

The main part of the report then follows, assessing his effectiveness in performing the job that has been described. This is normally done under a number of headings, as in the examples appended, often in the manner of a graded scale of marks, supplemented with comments giving evidence for the grades awarded. His various attributes are summarized in a general assessment, together with some sort of 'pen-picture' to describe his personality and attitude of mind towards his job and the organization.

The assessor must then give his opinion about the employee's suitability for promotion, including the level of the job to which he might aspire and an indication of when promotion might be given. The safest guideline here, as with the writing of references, is for the assessor to consider if he himself would welcome the man concerned if he were to be promoted to a senior post in his own department.

To ensure that positive action is taken about an employee's shortcomings, a separate note should be made of these.

Then the main 'action section' should follow, clearly specifying what must be done, either to fulfil the potential that he shows or to correct his deficiencies; this might include personal guidance by senior executives or specialists, a change of duties within the organization's provisions for job rotation, or attendance at particular training courses.

The form will be signed by the assessor and passed on to his superior for any additional comment and counter-signature, thus ensuring that reports are seen by an executive at least one level removed from the staff under review.

Finally, the report form should contain a section for notes on follow-up, in which entries can be made to show how and when the recommendations for action are carried out. The assessment procedure as it affects any individual should not be regarded as 'closed' until these notes on action are added.

When the forms are counter-signed, they are usually sent to a central personnel records section. One particular advantage claimed for doing this is that the personnel manager can readily pick out those staff whose reports indicate potential for the future, and who would therefore benefit from training in supervisory and management skills. Such training can then be properly planned on an individual basis.

In summary, the content of a staff assessment form may be illustrated as in Figure 15.

Most space on the report form is usually taken up by the assessment of

CONTENT OF
STAFF ASSESSMENT FORM

1. Personal details.
   Job title—time spent in that job.
2. Job description:
   including changes in duties since last report.
   Any new qualification obtained.
3. Assessment of performance.

Headings.	Comment column:
. . . .	giving evidence for
. . . .	the grades awarded.
. . . .	

4. Overall assessment.
   Pen-picture of personal qualities and attitudes.
5. Suitability for promotion:
   level to which he might aspire;
   when promotion might be given.
6. Notes on present deficiencies.
7. Action to be taken:
   to fulfil potential shown;
   or to correct deficiencies.
8. Signed—by writer of report.
9. Comments and counter-signature of the report-writer's superior.
10. Follow-up—to record how and when the recommendations for action
    were carried out.

Figure 15

the employee's performance of his job. Present practice is for this to be done under a number of headings, such as: *knowledge of the job; judgment; initiative; management and supervision; output; expression on paper; figure work*. In turn, these headings are frequently qualified by explanations or key-words intended to direct the thoughts of the assessors along the lines intended, in a uniform manner. Thus:

Output—effectiveness, speed, reliability, diligence.
Expression on paper—intelligibility, precision, style, cogency, lucidity, conciseness.

In practice, some sort of design compromise usually appears in the layout of forms. The job assessment is asked for under headings, with a graded scale, but a comments column appears at the side of each graded assessment. Where this is so, it is important that this column be used freely, and it should therefore have its own appropriate heading. The simple word 'Remarks' is itself too general to guarantee the desired informative comment; far better for it to read—'Remarks—in explanation of the grade awarded,' and the assessor is then forced to weigh his judgments carefully.

Two specimens of report forms follow in Figures 16 and 17, which provide actual examples of current practice. One is used by the Esso Companies* to review the performance of their executive staff, and clearly compares favourably with the views expressed in this Chapter. The second has a more limited application, being designed specifically to record the progress made by apprentices and other young people throughout their training programmes.

However thorough may be the training sessions arranged to prepare managers for writing reports about their staff, caution dictates that they should also be given comprehensive *guidance notes* to remind them about the purposes of the assessment scheme, its rules, and the correct approach to their responsibilities towards their staff.

Here is a typical list of such reminders as they affect the written report part of the process:

1. This report is required as a means of assessing present performance in the job, for planning each individual's career development, to pick staff for particular types of training and job rotation, and to help in selecting suitable applicants for promotion.
2. The immediate superior of the person reported on should write his report.
3. The job description, on which the report is based, should be prepared in consultation with the person reported on, to ensure that it is an agreed outline of his basic duties and responsibilities.
4. Where space for 'Remarks' is provided on the form, this should be used freely to explain the grades awarded.
5. These grades should reflect actual performance, and where this has been affected by special circumstances (e.g. ill-health or unfortunate domestic events), separate notes to this effect should be added in the 'Remarks' columns.

---

* The *review form* only is illustrated here. The most detailed *guiding instructions*, some ten pages in length, accompany the forms to help managers responsible for staff reviews.

6. The report deals with the employee's performance during the preceding twelve months only. There should, therefore, be no looking back to previous reports, nor should duplicate copies of this report be kept.

7. All reports are strictly confidential; their contents must not be disclosed to nor discussed with anyone not concerned with them in the course of his official work.

8. Each report should normally be commented on and countersigned by a departmental manager or some other appropriate executive senior to the person who writes it.

9. Every executive who has the duty of writing reports is reminded, above all, that he has a continuous responsibility to keep his subordinates informed of his opinions about the ways they perform their jobs: this should cover both good as well as unsatisfactory performance. No 'below average' grading should ever be recorded under any heading without the subordinate concerned having previously been told verbally of his deficiency and thus having been given the opportunity to correct it.

THE SECOND STAGE—DISCUSSION OF REPORTS

Most staff assessment schemes provide that, when the written report has been completed, it should be discussed with the person it concerns. This discussion might take place between him and his immediate superior, or the departmental manager himself might inform him of its content. In some of the nationalized industries a panel of senior officers is formed for this purpose.

The extent to which the discussion is based on the written report varies widely in practice. In some cases, it seems to play no part at all; in others, the 'main highlights' are mentioned, or only those aspects which have caused adverse comment; and at the other extreme, the person concerned is sometimes given the report to read and signs an acknowledgment that he accepts its contents.

The important thing to realize is that these discussions are essential in any assessment scheme which is used as part of a promotion selection procedure. If employees do not know what is being written in their annual reports, and at the same time are repeatedly unsuccessful in their efforts to gain promotion, then clearly they will come to view the whole assessment process with the utmost suspicion, and it will fail in its overall purpose of trying to get the best out of individuals in their jobs. It should also be realized that these discussions have a particular importance at certain stages in the development of each person's career:

1. After he has occupied any new post for about eighteen months, when he has had time to decide if it is turning out right for his career.

ESSO COMPANIES   **STRICTLY CONFIDENTIAL**
UNITED KINGDOM AND IRELAND

STAFF PERFORMANCE
REVIEW

Date of Review.................

SURNAME:...................................... CHRISTIAN NAME(S): ....

....

POSITION: .... DEPT/LOCATION: ....

DATE APPOINTED TO PRESENT

  POSITION: ....

DATE OF BIRTH: .... DATE JOINED COMPANY: ....

PERIOD COVERED BY THIS REVIEW: FROM.................TO ....

DATE OF LAST REVIEW: ....

1st REVIEWER:
NAME .... POSITION ....

DATE APPOINTED .... SIGNATURE ....

2nd REVIEWER:
NAME .... POSITION ....

DATE APPOINTED .... SIGNATURE ....

DIRECTIONS

A. Before completing this form study the Guiding Instructions carefully.
B. Assess the qualities and performance of this employee considering the questions listed under each of the five headings: 1. MENTAL ALERTNESS. II. PERSONALITY, III. JOB PERFORMANCE, IV. ADMINISTRATIVE ABILITY, V. LEADERSHIP. The questions are intended to assist you in forming your judgment of the employee. They should indicate training needs. The lines after the questions provide space for notes or comments which might assist when planning the interview, when recording your judgments under Sections VII and VIII, or when making plans for training or development under Section IX.
C. Check the column 'D' opposite those questions where in your opinion, there are weaknesses and where development or training is indicated for the employee to improve his present job performance, or to prepare himself for future positions.
D. If Sections IV and V ('Administrative Ability' and 'Leadership') do not apply for this particular position, you need not select one of the blocks in these sections, although you are expected to note this fact under 'Comments'. You can still answer any of the individual questions in such cases, paying particular attention to the need for training.
NOTE: Pages 2 and 3 are designed to serve as Work Sheets to assist you in completing Sections VII, VIII and IX.

Figure 16. Esso report form

DESCRIPTION OF GRADINGS

ADEQUATE. Level of productivity and general effectiveness meets **the standards for this position.** Quality and quantity of output are satisfactory. Minor weaknesses can be improved by training but work is substantially sound. Loyalty and reliability are sound and predictable. Only an ordinary amount of explanation and follow-up are required. A 'solid' type of performance.

MORE THAN ADEQUATE. Calibre of performance and level of effectiveness definitely superior to that described in 'adequate'. Zeal, effort, ambition and attitude superior. Abilities and leadership recognized by colleagues. Weaknesses, in relation to strengths, are few and insignificant.

OUTSTANDING. Performance and effectiveness are excellent. Employee has a potential for higher or wider responsibilities. If, however, he has reached his 'ceiling', his achievements are still clearly exceptional and never mediocre. Work requires minimum of review.

BARELY ADEQUATE. Effectiveness and productivity are below the standard required by the job, but not so low as to be considered as 'Inadequate'. Employee may be rather slow in reactions; his ability to plan his work or to use imagination may be somewhat lacking, or he may have other similar weaknesses that could be overcome by training, self-development or by closer supervision. Might be better fitted for a different job.

UNPROVED. Employee has not had an opportunity to demonstrate his abilities to a degree where a supervisor's judgment would be valid.

---

1. MENTAL ALERTNESS   The ability to learn quickly, develop a retentive memory, solve problems with imagination and vision, and to try out new ideas and procedures

		D
1. Does he learn facts quickly?	....	
2. Does he have a retentive memory?	....	
3. Is he keen to acquire new ideas?	....	
4. Does he solve problems accurately?	....	
5. Does he solve problems quickly?	....	
6. Is he quick to detect inaccuracies?	....	

OUTSTANDING	UNPROVED	BARELY ADEQUATE	ADEQUATE	MORE THAN ADEQUATE
☐	☐	☐	☐	☐

COMMENTS:

Figure 16 (contd.). Esso report form (page 2)

II. PERSONALITY The sum total of habits, traits and emotional qualities which affect one's relationship with others. | D |

1. Is he tolerant of others? ....
2. Is he tactful? ....
3. Is he reasonably self-confident? ....
4. Are his appearance and manner acceptable? ....
5. Is he relatively calm in emergencies? ....
6. Is he open-minded? ....
7. Is he easily distracted? ....
8. Has he the courage of his convictions? ....
9. Does he have drive and energy? ....

ADEQUATE	OUTSTANDING	MORE THAN ADEQUATE	UNPROVED	BARELY ADEQUATE
☐	☐	☐	☐	☐

COMMENTS:

III. JOB PERFORMANCE Work output and the degree to which knowledge, training and experience are applied to produce the desired results on time. | D |

1. Is the quality of work satisfactory? ....
2. Is the volume of work satisfactory? ....
3. Is he cost conscious? ....
4. Does he maintain communication? ....
5. Is he accurate in routine matters? ....
6. Does he produce results on time? ....
7. Does he have the required job knowledge? ....

MORE THAN ADEQUATE	ADEQUATE	UNPROVED	OUTSTANDING	BARELY ADEQUATE
☐	☐	☐	☐	☐

COMMENTS:

Figure 16 (contd.). Esso report form (pages 2–3)

IV. ADMINISTRATIVE ABILITY

The ability to delegate responsibility with corresponding authority, to plan effectively, to distinguish between major and minor issues and co-ordinate the work of others.

	D

1. Are his decisions sound?
2. Does he make decisions promptly?
3. Does he plan his own work successfully?
4. Is he successful in organizing and co-ordinating the work of others?
5. Does he delegate responsibility with corresponding authority?
6. Does he become absorbed in too much detail?
7. Does he express himself clearly, both orally and in writing?

UNPROVED	BARELY ADEQUATE	OUTSTANDING	ADEQUATE	MORE THAN ADEQUATE
☐	☐	☐	☐	☐

COMMENTS:

V. LEADERSHIP

The ability to win the respect and loyalty of others and to guide them in developing good team-work

	D

1. Do his colleagues respect him? ....
2. Does he stimulate team-work? ....
3. Is he objective in judging others? ....
4. Does he take initiative when required? ....
5. Does he have good work relationships? ....
6. Is he dependable? ....

MORE THAN ADEQUATE	ADEQUATE	BARELY ADEQUATE	UNPROVED	OUTSTANDING
☐	☐	☐	☐	☐

COMMENTS:

Figure 16 (contd.). Esso report form (page 3)

VI. SPECIAL COMMENTS

Include any other information which is important in assessing this employee's performance, e.g. character, interests, special abilities, health, family considerations, training and educational courses taken on own initiative, etc.

VII. SUMMARY OF EFFECTIVENESS IN PRESENT POSITION

	UNPROVED	OUTSTANDING	MORE THAN ADEQUATE	BARELY ADEQUATE	ADEQUATE
Assessment by 1st Reviewer	☐	☐	☐	☐	☐
Assessment by 2nd Reviewer	☐	☐	☐	☐	☐

COMMENTS: (Indicate the employee's greatest assets and weaknesses in this position. Make special note if the employee's performance is falling far below the accepted standards.)

VIII. PROMOTABILITY

Specify the next likely promotion(s) ....

	READY NOW	NOT QUITE READY	FAR FROM READY	PROMOTION NOT FORESEEN	UNDETERMINED
Assessment by 1st Reviewer	☐	☐	☐	☐	☐
Assessment by 2nd Reviewer	☐	☐	☐	☐	☐

INDICATE IF EXCEPTIONAL PROMISE IS SHEWN ....

COMMENTS:

IX. PLANS FOR DEVELOPMENT

What training or development is recommended to enable this employee to become more efficient in his present position or to carry wider or higher responsibilities? Be specific and practical.

Figure 16 (contd.). Esso report form (page 4)

X. INTERVIEW REPORT

Include employee's reactions to this interview. Evaluate last year's training.

Date of interview:........................... Conducted by: ....

XI. MANAGERIAL COMMENTS

Signed: ....

Figure 16 (contd.). Esso report form (page 4)

[Figure 17, the apprentice report form, will be found overleaf.]

REPORT ON TRAINEES

(This includes Technical Staff Trainees, Craft Apprentices and all other young employees under training, where appropriate)

Name: .... Date of birth: ....
Date commenced apprenticeship or training: ....
Date due to end apprenticeship or training: ....

Type of Trainee or employee: ......
District or Dept.: ....

| TO

1. IMMEDIATE SUPERVISOR'S REPORT (Covering period...............)

Consider here the work done and the *aid* given—*not the trainee.*

Quality of Work produced (finish—accuracy)	Top quality work, usually unaided *Above accepted standards with occasional aid* **Satisfactory standard with some assistance** *Correction often needed to reach satisfactory standard* Excessive correction necessary to avoid scrap	☐ ☐ ☐ ☐ ☐
Speed of working (under good discipline)	High enough to cause surprise *Compares favourably with adult average* **Acceptable though less than adult average** *Low enough to attract some attention, though not slacking* Painfully low	☐ ☐ ☐ ☐ ☐

Consider here the *trainee*—not the work produced.
Consider him as he is *now* (Do not consider his age).
Consider him with *all* the similar Trainees you have known.

Attitude to supervision (discipline)	Unusually co-operative and helpful *Noticeably pleasant and willing* **Not noticeably different from the general run of trainees** *Requires correction rather too often (discipline irksome)*	☐ ☐ ☐

Category	Descriptions	Grades
Attitude to fellow employees (teamwork)	*Noticeable, sometimes, for good team spirit* **Not noticeably different from the general run of trainees** *Noticeably slow to mix and occasionally 'odd man out'* Thinks only of himself: sometimes difficult or cause of friction	☐ ☐ ☐ ☐
Initiative and alertness	Enquiring, resourceful and quick in trying to solve problems *Tries to tackle difficulties himself and often grasps a point at once* **Not noticeably different from the general run of trainees** *Too often asks where he could think it out for himself* Seldom thinks: waits to be told	☐ ☐ ☐ ☐
Reliability (sense of responsibility)	Can be given some special jobs without fear of costly failure *Usually careful: requires but little attention* **Not noticeably different from the general run of trainees** *Sometimes careless or forgetful: needs some extra supervision* Generally careless and often irresponsible	☐ ☐ ☐ ☐
Punctuality and time-keeping	Always early to start—never stops work before time *Wastes very little time—very rarely late* **Not noticeably different from the general run of trainees** *Occasionally late or stops work early* Often late or stops work early	☐ ☐ ☐ ☐
Special aptitudes (if any)	**Special limitations** (if any)	

Date:.................. Signature of Immediate Supervisor ....POSITION

Figure 17

Ratings: It will be found that if a large number of trainees were correctly assessed on these scales 4/10 of the total would be in the 'average' or medium grade, 2/10 in each of the grades immediately above and below the average, and 1/10 in the highest and lowest grades. In order to keep this in mind the form has been designed to emphasize the average grade. In general if you don't notice a trainee much he probably deserves this grade. If you do notice him he probably deserves one of the other grades—if he is particularly good or bad (i.e. one in ten) he deserves the top or bottom grade. If he is noticeable to the extent of being two in ten, he deserves the intermediate grade above or below average.

2. At about thirty, when he wonders if he has made sufficient progress in his job, for he is now at the age when he must do something about it.
3. At the age of forty when he wonders if he should carry on with the same firm for the next twenty-five years until he retires; if not, it may be 'now or never' as regards changing his job.

Most large organizations now readily accept the need to deal with the progress of staff by means of these frank discussions. Yet there is much evidence that this is done badly by many heads of departments who feel uncomfortable at the very intimate contact forced on them by the process, when their normal day-to-day relationships with subordinates may be based on personal friendships in a fairly free-and-easy atmosphere. In 1963 Kay Rowe* surveyed the practice of six firms and 1,440 assessment forms, and found that appraisers are reluctant to make frank assessments in the first place, and are even more reluctant to interview their staff subsequently. Her conclusions were that lack of frankness, embarrassment, the view that 'we all have to live together, so it doesn't do to be too down on people', are all factors which inhibit discussions on job performance between staff and their superiors, causing them to become generalized, glib, and evasive, so that they often achieve very little.

Apart from the embarrassment of the departmental manager in this situation, there is another very real problem from the employee's point of view. Up to this point he has been in the dark: he knows nothing of what his report contains until he faces his boss across a desk and is told something of its contents. Is it fair to expect anything constructive to emerge as a result? The initiative is entirely in the manager's hands—his subordinate may mumble some appreciative or defensive remarks, go away, discuss what was said with his wife that evening, sleep on it, and then kick himself the following morning for not having reacted in an entirely different manner. But the opportunity has gone, at least until the same unsatisfactory process is repeated in a year's time.

Depending on the purpose of the assessment, various attempts have been made to overcome this difficulty. For instance, one procedure involves issuing the report form in triplicate in the first place: the departmental heads makes his assessment on one; he hands the second to the subordinate concerned who makes his own self-assessment; they then come together to discuss their respective findings, and complete the final, third copy between them. The purpose of this procedure is the further training of the individual under review, however, with a guarantee to honour the recommendations that the manager–subordinate pair jointly agree.

Another precise analysis of the effectiveness of job appraisal reviews was reported by the Behavioural Sciences Research Division of the Civil

* 'Appraisal of Appraisals', *Journal of Management Studies*, March 1964.

Service Department.* A survey of appraisal interviews given to 252 officers in one government department again revealed that the handling of negative performance feedback is fraught with anxiety and difficulties, and therefore tends to be avoided. At the same time, it was abundantly clear that those interviews in which discussion of the interviewee's deficiencies took place were the most effective in producing positive results in terms of the number of post-appraisal recommendations for action and the proportion of officers who felt that such interviews increased their sense of job satisfaction. They were also the appraisals to which the interviewees responded most favourably; most of them welcomed a full, frank discussion of their performance at work and saw this as the most useful function of the whole process.

The survey revealed the most common fault to be, predictably, that of interviewers talking too much. This is highly significant because training courses on appraisal techniques usually advocate the 'problem-solving' approach which encourages the subordinate officer to do most of the talking, the interviewer's main purpose being to help him to think his own way through job problems and provide solutions for them. This approach contrasts wih the traditional 'tell and sell' style of the superior who tells his subordinate what he thinks of his performance and what he should do to improve it (the interviewee thus having little say in the matter).

A series of rating scales, assessed by the interviewees who took part in this study, give an indication of the good and bad points of technique. The table below summarizes the results and speaks for itself: for ease of presentation, the responses for each item have been condensed into just two categories.

'Tell and sell' style	Percentages		'Problem-solving' style
1 The interviewer did nearly all the talking in the interview	54	46	I did most of the talking in the interview
2 The interviewer seemed wholly concerned with assessing my work performance over the last year	50	50	The interviewer seemed chiefly interested in improving my work performance in the year ahead
3 I took the line of least resistance when criticized	23	77	I discussed the assessments with the interviewer when I did not agree with him

*'An Evaluation Study of Job Appraisal Reviews', by C. A. Fletcher, *Management Services in Government*, November 1973, pages 188–195.

'Tell and sell' style		Percentages		'Problem-solving' style
4 The interviewer did not allow me to offer my viewpoint on the way I coped with the job	6		94	The interviewer allowed me to put forward my own views on how I coped with the job
5 The interviewer seemed to have made up his mind about things before the interview started	28		72	I got the impression that the interviewer was willing to change his views on things in the light of what I said
6 Almost all the ideas for getting round job difficulties came from the interviewer	45		55	I provided most of the solutions to the problems we discussed
7 The interviewer made no attempt to understand my feelings about the job	11		89	The interviewer made every attempt to understand the way I felt about the job
8 The interviewer did not appear to be paying attention when I was speaking	6		94	The interviewer listened most attentively whenever I spoke
9 The interviewer did not invite me to put forward any ideas or suggestions about the job	14		86	The interviewer continually pressed me for *my* ideas and suggestions about the job
10 The interviewer did not really make my own thoughts about my job any clearer	38		62	The interviewer helped me clarify my own thoughts and ideas about the work

A POSITIVE CONTRIBUTION FROM THE SUBORDINATE

No matter how good staff procedures and practices of personnel management may appear on paper, the concern of each member of an organization's staff is always: 'how does this affect me as an individual?' A deliberate attempt must be made to improve the present methods of appraisal discussions to enable staff reported on to play a positive role in the process. The integration of the views of the boss and his subordinates is essential if assessments are to be accepted as forming part of a staff development programme; without full consultation and discussion with subordinates, the results will smack of manipulating people to the organization's ends rather than constructive staff management.

The best way of getting something worthwhile from these discussions is to persuade departmental heads to regard them as presenting opportunities rather than as unpleasant chores. This will undoubtedly call for some fundamental rethinking on the part of those managers who have been brought up in the belief that the demands of their organizations and the needs of the people working in them compete with each other. In emergencies staff know that more is expected of them; they seem somehow to be inspired to rise to these challenges and co-operate to get the job done. The worker who mutters 'If I were boss for a day, I would show them', or his mates who rush off when the hooter sounds to dig their gardens or paint their homes, may seem oversimplified examples. But they nevertheless illustrate the point that hard, demanding work both spurs people on to high performance and is a major source of satisfaction for a whole range of human needs. This concept points to a tremendous unrealized potential for greater organizational effectiveness.

Why then are so few managers able to use the full capacities of their staff to increase productivity by expanding their contributions to their jobs? Surely it is largely because they concentrate on what is wrong, on solving problems and overcoming obstacles, rather than on where they want to go and the prospects of getting there through the fuller use of the individual talents of their staff.

Contrast the conventional form of staff attitude surveys with the opportunity presented by a properly conducted appraisal discussion in which the employee plays a positive role. At present, the former concerns itself with finding out how 'happy' staff are, if they are 'proud' to work for their employer, whether their fringe benefits are to their liking, and if their bosses treat them in a kindly manner—all stemming from the basic assumption that work is nasty, and that management's task is to make other things pleasant by way of compensation. Replace this with the contrary assumption (proved by the way they respond to crises) that staff in fact have both the capacity and the desire to increase their productivity. The appraisal discussion then presents the opportunity to strive for improvement by posing questions such as these to each individual:

1. Do you fully understand your job? Are there any aspects you wish to be made clearer?
2. What parts of your present job do you do best?
3. Could any changes be made in your job which might result in improved performance? (Consider work-load, equipment used, financial resources available, ability of juniors, help from seniors, and physical environment.)
4. Have you any skills, knowledge or aptitudes which could be made better use of in the organization?

5. What are your career plans? How do you propose achieving your ambitions in terms of further training and broader experience?

There would be an obvious advantage to staff being given the chance to think about these points beforehand—so they could well be set out as a printed questionnaire and handed to the employee a few days before his assessment discussion.* Prepared with the answers to these questions, each individual can make a positive contribution at this discussion, while his management superior can seize any opportunity that presents itself to link operational needs of his department with its employees' readiness to increase their output. Peter Drucker, whose own 'manager's letter't is another variation of this effort to get subordinates more positively involved in their own personal development, summed up the concept thus in an address to the Industrial Society in April 1964:

'Look for strength in your people and load that strength. Never be concerned with what people cannot do but with what they can, and give them that to do.'

FOLLOW-UP

Whatever form the assessment takes, the long-term success of any scheme will depend on the effectiveness of follow-up. Everyone involved in the assessment process is concerned here—the personnel manager, the departmental head, the report writer, and the employee himself.

The personnel manager's responsibility lies mainly in the actual administration of the scheme. In large organizations, for example, he will have to arrange the timing of reports, region by region, or department by department; obviously he will not want several thousand reports arriving on his desk on the same day. Correct phasing will even out the work-load, and also enable the action recommended, in terms of training courses or job rotation, to be spread throughout the year.

The departmental manager also plays a key role, for it is his duty to direct and control the ways in which his executive staff assess their subordinates. If he merely accepts the reports submitted to him uncritically, then the assessors in their turn will give less consideration to what they write and become increasingly careless in this aspect of their work. For their part, the assessors will be most concerned with what they see in terms of results and appreciation of their views. Nothing is more certain to frustrate them and lead to carelessness in the preparation of reports than to

* For example, the *pre-interview preparation form* of the Distillers Co., Ltd.
† *The Practice of Management* (Heinemann, 1969), page 127.

see that their assessments appear to carry little weight when promotions are being considered or training programmes developed.

The remaining element essential for success is that the assessment scheme must have the confidence of all staff who are subject to annual reports. This, too, is most readily secured and consolidated by the results that flow from the assessments, when staff see that the promised action is being taken to change their duties, to train them in some new aspect of their work, or that they are being considered for promotion. Frank discussions about their progress and deficiencies may raise high hopes for the future; these hopes must never be dashed because of lack of follow-up.

CRITICISMS OF REPORTS ON STAFF

Staff appraisal schemes have been applied to the problems of executive development for many years, dating, for example, in the British Civil Service from 1910. Some organizations are well satisfied with the results obtained, while others are currently experimenting with new schemes in their efforts to improve methods of personnel control. Even so, the development of the technique of *management by objectives* has undoubtedly sprung from well-founded criticisms of the conventional type of staff appraisal.

Although the procedure, and the guidance notes that go with it, may emphasize that it is performance of the job that is being assessed, there is, in the event, still a great deal of subjective opinion too much concerned with personality aspects, seemingly trying to measure the employee against the standards of some mythical ideal manager. Secondly, it so often happens that the recommended action includes job rotation and, more especially, training courses outside the organization. All such recommendations tend to evade the responsibility of individual managers to give personal guidance to their subordinates. They should not be allowed thus to abdicate their duty to develop their own staff and hand over the complexities of executive training to a specialized personnel department. On the contrary, they must be made to appreciate that this is essentially a job-centred function which can only properly be fulfilled by line managers.

The so called 'crown-prince complex' also inevitably emerges from a system in which the central personnel manager reads through all assessments of staff in order to pick out those with the best potential for development. But concentration on these, and on such people as graduate trainees (of whom there is always a high turnover, in any case), must mean some neglect of all the other staff who also need guidance to improve their job performance. Indeed it is alleged that existing staff assessment schemes place far too much emphasis on the whole question of promotion, instead of being a means of getting staff to do their present jobs better and thus naturally outgrow them.

The final major criticism concerns the use of a graded scale to assess various attributes of each individual. Most of these scales have a middle grade, representing average or standard performance. The difficulty of ensuring uniform marking by managers throughout a widespread organization has already been mentioned, and this assessment of average performance makes the point. What does 'average' mean in this context? It cannot be the standard that each manager personally expects, because these would obviously differ. Can it be a measure of comparison with a number of people whom a manager has already known in the assessed employee's post? Again experience may vary, even though the net is cast more widely. What about factors such as age? Should special allowances be made if the holder of a post is much younger than normal, or should the attitude be that he is being paid the rate for the job and must therefore measure up to it? Even with the most detailed report forms, comprehensive training sessions and precise guidance notes, it still remains very doubtful if all these difficulties in ensuring uniform practice in working can be overcome.

GROUP ASSESSMENTS

One system that has been developed to try to overcome the dangers of the subjective approach involves assessments being made by a group of appraisers working together. This group would consist of the immediate superior, possibly his boss, and two or three other managers who know something of the man being reviewed and the quality of his work.

The personnel department plays a direct role in this process by providing the last member of the group. Where top managerial staff are being assessed, the personnel manager himself, or his colleague in charge of management development, might take part; with lower levels of staff, a personnel officer attached to the local unit will join the assessment group. The function of this personnel department representative is to act as 'appraisal co-ordinator', taking no active part in the actual appraisal, but being responsible for seeing that it is carried out in a thorough and comprehensive manner. This check is necessary because, although the final assessment will include much the same information as the conventional staff assessment form, the actual discussion between the group of appraisers is informal. At its close, he is responsible for writing the assessment report, summarizing what the four or five appraisers have concluded.

This method clearly decreases the likelihood of any personal bias in favour of or against the person being assessed, and it is claimed that a balanced judgment is reached by virtue of the number of managers taking part. The presence of the co-ordinator greatly helps to secure the desired uniformity of assessment throughout an organization.

ASSESSMENT CENTRES

Still rather unfamiliar, but growing in terms of the number of organizations using them to appraise staff performance, are assessment centres. Rooted in the War Office Selection Board methods of the Second World War, which were designed for officer selection, assessment centres provide a broad approach to the identification of managerial potential among existing staff. They involve the multiple assessment of several individuals by a group of trained assessors using a variety of techniques such as games, simulations, problem-solving exercises, tests, and group discussions.

The purposes, like other forms of appraisal, are concerned with the assessment of potential and the identification of the development needs of individuals. Typical of the approach is this statement from the briefing letter sent by one company to participants in the scheme—'It is important to understand that the major purpose of the assessment centre is to allow a group of tutors (senior company managers) to assess the nature of your potential for development. The methods and final results will be discussed openly with you. The centre should also provide you with an opportunity to review your present abilities and to consider your future career—it can therefore be a helpful and worthwhile experience for you.'*

One strong claim for the usefulness of this approach is at supervisory level, where it is considered to be virtually impossible to predict accurately management potential from current performance in non-supervisory positions. The assessment centre, in fact, provides the opportunity to observe an individual's performance in a number of situations which simulate a variety of realistic supervisory problems. Normal practice is for the participants to be selected initially by their immediate superiors, who obviously consider that they have the potential for promotion to a higher level

Assessors are usually line managers two levels above the participants: they are thus people who should have a thorough knowledge of the jobs for which the participants are being assessed. Sometimes consultant psychologists become involved when psychological tests form part of the programme. Assessors require preliminary training, of course, in order to become familiar with all the exercises used and to obtain practice in the observation methods.

* *Performance Appraisal in Perspective*, by D. Gill, B. Ungerson, and M. Thakur (I.P.M., 1973).

The culmination of the assessment is a final report compiled from information drawn from several sources: the tutors' assessment of the participants based on test results and observation of his performance in the activities at the centre; the participant's own assessment of himself; and the assessments of participants by other participants. The report may also suggest how the participant's skills and abilities can best be used within the organization.

An interview is then held when one of the assessors discusses all the details of the report with the participant. If there is general agreement with the assessment, the tutor and participant discuss ways in which any strengths that have been identified can be used, in terms of future roles and activities which the participant might successfully carry out. Emphasis is placed on considering the things he can do well and deciding how these things can be built on. Where there is disagreement, the tutor must try to find the reasons for the differences of view: if it persists, a note of the discussion is included in the report. A copy of the final report is sent to each participant, before it is sent to his immediate boss.

The advantages claimed for this approach follow logically. Apart from achieving the purposes originally stated, substantial staff relations benefits are claimed, in that this form of assessment appears to be an open, objective, and fair way of assessing potential and making promotion decisions. Assessors develop skills in observations and evaluation, hence deeper self-awareness; one company has described assessment centres as 'the best method of management training we have yet discovered'.* The method helps to overcome the problem of the employee who suffers from bias on the part of his superior. Finally, it can act as a motivator, the participant returning to his normal work with a realistic self-assessment and a plan for his own development.

FURTHER READING

Performance Appraisal in Management, by M. R. Williams (Heinemann, 1972).
Staff Appraisal, by G. A. Randell, P. Packard, R. Shaw, and A. Slater (I.P.M., 1972).
Appraisal for Staff Development: a Public Sector Study, by Ronald Wraith (R.I.P.A., 1975).

*ibid.

9 Management by Objectives

Management by objectives is the best example of participative management—the ultimate acknowledgment of the fact that the most positive effect on morale can be obtained by allowing staff to share in management decisions which affect their destinies. The philosophy behind the technique can be traced back to Plato's concept of man's inherent desire to strive for 'excellence'—a quality which we most readily associate perhaps with saints, musicians, or artists, but also an obvious attribute of leadership and the good manager. It calls for a steady self-discipline, rigorous standards, an abhorence of mediocrity, and refusal to accept the second-best: challenging the manager's personal skills and his integrity in seeking the best for its own sake.

The best-known exponent of the theories of human behaviour from which the practical concept of management by objectives has developed was Douglas M. McGregor.* The basis of his argument, expanded in his famous Theories X and Y, is that past understanding of the nature of man is in many ways incorrect and that, under proper conditions, unimagined resources of creative human energy could become available within the organizational setting.

Theory X states that the central principle of organization is that of control and direction through the exercise of authority, with these premises:

1. The average human being has an inherent dislike of work and will avoid it if he can.
2. Because of this human characteristic of dislike of work, most people must be coerced, controlled, directed, threatened with punishment, to get them to put forth adequate effort toward the achievement of organizational objectives.
3. The average human being prefers to be directed, wishes to avoid responsibility, has relatively little ambition, wants security above all.

With Theory Y, the central principle is that of integration—the creation

* *The Human Side of Enterprise*, by Douglas M. McGregor. Copyright 1960. Used by permission of McGraw-Hill Book Company.

of conditions such that staff can achieve their own goals *best* by directing their efforts towards the success of their organization. The premises are:

1. Work is as natural as play or rest. Depending upon *controllable conditions*, it may be a source of satisfaction (and will be voluntarily performed) or a source of revulsion (and will be avoided if possible).
2. External control and punishment are not the only means for achieving effort. Man will exercise self-direction and self-control in the service of objectives to which he is committed.
3. Personal satisfaction can be the direct product of effort directed toward organizational objectives.
4. Most people, under proper conditions, learn not only to accept but to seek responsibility. Avoidance of responsibility, lack of ambition, and emphasis on security are generally *consequences of experience, not inherent human characteristics*.
5. The capacity to exercise creativity in solving problems is widely, not narrowly, distributed in the population. But under modern working conditions, the intellectual potential of the average human being is only partially utilized.

The technique of management by objectives can most simply be seen as the application of Douglas McGregor's Theory Y in practical terms, seeking as it does to make a deliberate attempt to link improvement in managerial competence with the satisfaction of individual personal needs. This calls for a four-fold approach:

1. Clarification of the broad requirements of each job.
2. Establishing specific targets for defined periods of time.
3. The management process during these target periods, and the help given by superiors.
4. Appraisal of the results at the end of the target period.

This strategy must be based on a very clear understanding of what the words 'target' or 'objective' means in a business situation. It is axiomatic that unless you know where you are going, you will not get there. So in the first place an objective implies moving forward or making progress; but to do this, a manager must fully appreciate where he is moving from (the present position), where he is moving to (desirable results), and by when he is required to get there. The second implication about setting objectives is that they will involve changes, and naturally these are intended to be for the better. So the overall aim of the technique, then, may be described as taking action to obtain improvement in the measurable results being achieved throughout an organization.

A business is primarily concerned with its affairs today, with seeing that all is going well at the moment. But it must also have a clear vision of its future, set out in terms of objectives at all levels—for the Board itself, for subordinate formations, for operational units, and for the individual managers working within these units. All these objectives should appear in writing, clearly stating the present situation and future aims in the utmost detail. Objectives are useless unless they are broken down into statements of the *precise actions* that must be taken to achieve *specified results* within a *given period of time* by *individual members* of staff.

APPLYING THE TECHNIQUE

Just as work study and O & M specialists have studied factory and office workers in the past, so the work of managers will now be studied by staff teams, the members of which must obviously be knowledgeable about management by objectives and must also be skilled job analysts. These teams will want to deal with an entire operating unit at a time, starting with the production departments (where the 'real work' of the business is carried out) and moving to the service sections later.

Within each unit, the advisory team will apply a four-step procedure:

1. Identification of the 'key result' areas of the business, i.e. those in which positive results must be obtained if it is to succeed.
2. Analysis of the work of every executive in these areas—carried out by the holder of the job himself, advised by one of the team's analysts.
3. This produces a performance improvement guide which the executive, his boss, and the analyst will discuss together, until agreement is reached between them on specific targets for improvement.
4. Since time limits will have been set for the achievement of these objectives, performance reviews must be carried out when the due dates arrive, to decide whether or not the desired results have been obtained, and why, and to formulate new objectives for the next period.

Having decided in which production unit the management-by-objectives team is to work, the process starts by means of a series of meetings between its head and the team in order to resolve clearly what the key areas of the unit's activities are, and how results in these areas can be precisely measured. A lengthy list of these might emerge, examples being: profitability, the manufacturing programme, utilization of machine capacity, quality of the product and customers' complaints, and the level of productivity of operatives. There are four main aspects of business activity which can be used to identify the key result areas of the work of any department or of any individual's job. These are—the *quantity* of work done, its *quality*, the *time* taken for activities to be completed, and the *cost* involved in all this.

Having identified these key result areas, three questions must then be asked:

1. What particular problems are associated with each area?
2. How are acceptable standards of performance defined and measured?
3. Who is responsible for initiating action in each of these areas?

When the management activities associated with the unit have been established in this way, and are commonly understood, the tasks of each executive (say, foremen upwards) can be analysed. This should be aimed at producing a guide document which is very different from the job description mentioned in Chapter 4, being essentially concerned with providing a framework for improvements in performance. The initial documentation for this can be a single foolscap sheet of paper, divided into four columns, as shown in Figure 18.

Key Result Areas of the Job	Targets for Each Area	Control Information Required	Review notes— Lessons learned From working methods. Follow - up.

Figure 18. Guide to performance improvement

The first column will list a number of aspects of the job where any improvement in results will clearly contribute to the achievement of the objectives to be specified: obvious examples are rate of production, control of costs, wastage rates, quality of goods, and productivity of employees. For each of the points listed, the executive concerned, in discussion with the analyst, should then be able to suggest targets, representing improvements in performance which he himself feels confident of being able to achieve. There can be no generalizations here: each target must be quantitative and measurable in terms of business results. Thus 'to reduce scrap' is too vague an objective; it must be expressed in precise terms, such as, 'to achieve a 10 per cent reduction in scrap rates in my department within the next three months'. Of course, control information must be made available to each individual taking part in this procedure, so that he can monitor his progress towards achieving his objectives; for example, if one of his objectives concerns improving quality control, then he has the right to ask to be supplied with information about amounts of items rejected at the inspection stage and the number and nature of customers' complaints. The last column has a variety of uses: notes can be kept for future reference about the success or failure of the particular methods used in trying to achieve objectives; further training needs of the individual concerned can be identified; and any obstacles preventing objectives from being reached should be noted, especially if they are beyond his control and require action by more senior management to remove them.

When this analysis is finished and the guide sheet completed, it must be fully discussed by the employee concerned with his boss, both advised again by the analyst. The most important aim of this discussion is to reach agreement on a number of clear objectives for the executive concerned, with time limits for their realization, together with notes on any additional training or assistance from other senior staff he may need in order to achieve them. Further meetings may then be necessary to make a detailed analysis of the steps which must be taken to realize each objective.

A specimen sheet has been part completed by way of a specific example: it is for a recruitment officer and is presented as Figure 19.

The departmental manager must, of course, maintain a control system to remind him of the review dates for each of these objectives. All that is necessary here is a simple bar chart (Figure 20), listing his subordinates, their targets, and the dates by which the targets should be achieved.

Each review is based on the simple question—has he, or has he not, reached this objective? If he has, the next stage is to look again at this particular key result area and consider if its performance standards can be raised even further; otherwise, the 'achieved objective' becomes the normal standard of performance for that task. If the target has not been achieved, this is no occasion for recriminations; rather, it calls for a detailed consideration of all factors which prevented its realization, and how these might now be overcome. In these ways the review process throws up new targets for the next period of time, again specifying precise objectives in terms of business results, what assistance will be required from more senior managers, and what additional training is needed to improve the employee's ability to meet these new demands.

The introduction of the management-by-objectives technique into an organization in practice may call for a certain amount of strategy. No

Key Result Areas	Targets	Control Information	Remarks
1. Maintaining labour force at full strength.	(a) Special campaign to recruit 20 additional married women operatives within the next 2 months. (b) Organize a day nursery in the factory grounds, to open within the next 6 months.	(a) Info. on availability from employment office Weekly returns on recruitment and labour turnover. (b) Local authority regulations. No. of mothers using it? No. of mothers recruited because of it? Weekly cost statement.	Read available literature on problems of employing married women. Watch for supervisors' prejudices?
2. Time taken to fill vacancies.	Average to be reduced from 3 weeks to 2 weeks within the next 6 months. (a) Standard job requisition procedure to be introduced within the next month. (b) Start new applications procedure within the next month, encouraging personal visits or phone-calls.	Time taken to fill each vacancy to be recorded. Effect on appointments diary.	Organize reception staff to be able to deal with callers.
3. Cost of recruitment services.	Reduce advertising costs by 25% within the next 3 months.	Record of response received to all advertisements placed in press and journals.	

N.B. Further notes might appear in Remarks Column at the end of each target period.

Figure 19. Part of a performance improvement guide for a recruitment officer

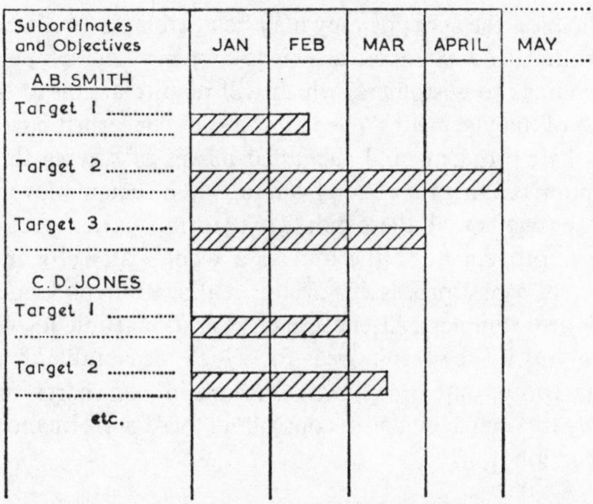

Subordinates and Objectives	JAN	FEB	MAR	APRIL	MAY
A.B. SMITH					
Target 1	////////				
Target 2	//////////////////////////				
Target 3	////////////////////				
C.D. JONES					
Target 1	////////////////				
Target 2	////////////////				
etc.					

Figure 20. Bar-chart: control of objectives

matter how much each individual participates in agreeing his own objectives, and no matter what reassurances may be given about not achieving them, there may still remain some fear of failure, for it is difficult to remove entirely the traditional concepts of punishment for not reaching targets. It is essential, then, to gain people's confidence in the technique at the initial stages. This can perhaps best be done by setting fairly easy targets at the outset, so that staff will soon lose any apprehension they may feel about the demands of this new approach to management. In fact, the experience of organizations already using the technique shows that in the initial stages only about half of the objectives set are actually achieved. The main reason is that, human nature being as it is, staff devote most energy to those areas in which they enjoy their work, tending to neglect the more unpleasant or difficult areas and miss targets set in these as a result. Of course, as time goes on and the easier objectives are achieved, then those which are more difficult can no longer be avoided.

UNIT IMPROVEMENT PLAN

A logical refinement of the process of preparing individual improvement guides is to build in a system of suggestions for overall organizational improvement. While his job is being analysed, each executive can be asked to indicate any problems or obstacles which he believes to be impeding his efforts to improve his performance and achieve his objectives. These may be internal to his own department and he may be able to suggest action to deal with them on the spot; or they may be attributed to other sections of the organization (for example, drawings arriving late, or delays in dispatching products to customers) which will require action to be taken by higher levels of management. When all the staff concerned have thus commented on their problems and suggested means of solving them, a large number of points calling for action from top management may well emerge. Indeed, taken together, all these points may form a pattern from which objectives for improvement of the unit as a whole can be defined (the reorganization of work processes, or the reallocation of labour between departments are examples). After all, each operational unit, just like each individual job, has its key result areas for which measurable objectives can be set within appropriate time limits. Once again, bar charts can be drawn up for use by top management in controlling these performance guides for whole production units.

THE FORMULA FOR DEVELOPMENT

Linking the theory of motivation* with the technique of management by objectives has led to yet a further step forward in efforts to improve the efficiency of an individual's work. People can be inspired to greater efforts by the challenge of their jobs: satisfaction accrues from being given responsibility, so that jobs should be designed to increase the demands made on the abilities of each employee to achieve some personal fulfilment of his own potential. In this context, each manager has the task of exerting pressure on his individual subordinates to acquire new skills or knowledge that can be used in their jobs. This may well, in turn, involve the provision of more advanced training to enable staff to gain a wider point of view and develop new attitudes.

This concept readily fits in with management by objectives, and with the task of top management of controlling the risks of their businesses. If senior managers will agree with all staff who report to them specific objectives which both meet important business needs and at the same time demand of individuals an enlarged body of knowledge or skill in order to achieve the objectives, then the key step in personal development will have been taken.

Growth of the business capacity of individuals is most rapid when they have to accomplish something entirely different from what they have been doing in their jobs in the past. But they must clearly know what is expected of them, appreciate its importance to the organization and to themselves in terms of career progress, and eventually be told whether or not they have accomplished these new tasks successfully.

* *See* Chapter 3.

The *formula for development*, then, may be summarized as in Figure 21.

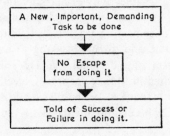

Figure 21. Formula for development

CONCLUSION

At the beginning of the previous Chapter, the first diagram (Figure 14) set out the role of the individual in an organization and the need for performance to be appraised from time to time. This can now be amended (Figure 22) to take into account the technique of management by objectives.

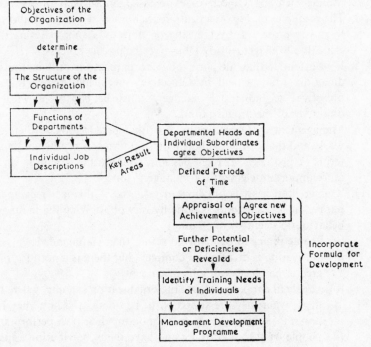

Figure 22. The role of the individual within an organization

Such a process clearly overcomes the 'insuperable' difficulties of conventional staff appraisals—subjectivity of marking and uniform standards—and ensures a positive approach to the whole problem of securing organizational growth, by concentrating on the deliberate expansion of the human resources available and directly seeking to improve the job performance and enthusiasm of individual managers working in it. This sort of analysis has resulted in Management by Objectives being eulogized as 'a new way of life for managers', or the first really comprehensive total system of management. The claims advanced to support these glowing statements include:

1. No organization should run except in terms of its aims and objectives. Its very existence presupposes aims. Action presupposes objectives. It is therefore essential that all organizations systematically set, define and review their aims and objectives. Management by Objectives provides the framework.
2. Effectiveness can be calculated only in terms of attaining aims and objectives.
3. Organization must have regard to objectives, not 'vice versa'. Management by Objectives exposes organizational obsolescence.
4. The resources of any organization are limited and must be allocated to satisfy priorities. By focusing on objectives and analysing them critically, Management by Objectives helps this process.
5. It is essential that all parts of an organization pull in the same direction. Management by Objectives specifically directs that the objectives of individual managers must be consistent with the objectives of the organization.
6. Management by Objectives ensures that people look at their own work, and that of their subordinates, in terms of results, and not in terms of processes. It identifies and concentrates attention on the more important elements of managers' jobs.
7. 'Our greatest asset is our human resources'—this is a meaningless phrase unless something is done by way of applying the findings of behavioural scientists, including:
   (*a*) People prefer to be involved rather than commanded;
   (*b*) motivation is diverse and complex, but there is a need for much greater emphasis on 'job enrichment';
   (*c*) people like to know where the organization is going, where they fit in, what they are supposed to be doing, and how they have done; if possible they want to monitor their own performance;
   (*d*) people want to contribute and have their contribution appreciated.

8. Any organization needs to make the best use of the talents and ideas of all its members. To achieve this, managers must create a climate of work in which constructive suggestions can flow naturally as part of the process. Management by Objectives performance improvement guides are so designed, and also pinpoint the responsibility for carrying forward the ideas that emerge.

9. Organizations need to develop their managers' abilities. The appraisal of performance will reveal and lead to the correction of factors which have impeded the attainment of objectives. Potential will be systematically uncovered also, so that training needs become exposed.

10. Motivation is increased by participation in target-setting, and by a connection between career progression and performance records.

11. Communications throughout the organization improve as managers become more clearly aware of their responsibilities.

12. Management by Objectives may reduce costs in a number of ways:
    (*a*) by leading to improvements in operational efficiency;
    (*b*) by drawing attention to work which need not be done at all;
    (*c*) by showing when new methods are demanded, rather than simply improving on the old.

13. The increasing use of specialists has the danger of their taking narrow professional views about management problems. Management by Objectives harnesses their specializations to the general objectives of the organization.

MBO—PRACTICE AND PROBLEMS

Numerous case studies have appeared in various publications over the years, the majority describing successful applications of MBO, but also pointing out the practical problems which must be overcome if failure is to be avoided. To illustrate the former, an analysis of 45 projects* carried out in different government departments during the period 1968–73 showed a wide variety of tangible and intangible benefits. These ranged from a staff saving of 13 per cent to 'more attention being focused on priorities', better delegation by managers to their subordinates, a 'flow of innovative ideas', improved communications, and the usefulness of having clearly defined job objectives when staff move between posts. The general impression gained by Civil Service Department advisers was that MBO is now commonly seen not so much as a means of gaining certain selected objectives, but rather as a comprehensive approach to better management in which an organization's activities are planned and controlled by reference to its

*'MBO in the Government Service', by C. J. Hancock, *Management Services Bulletin, 1974*, pages 16–26.

essential purposes and the atmosphere is one of participation and constructive change.

Experience over the years has shown how the threads, contained in the
sections of theoretical analysis above, come together. Of the basic problems
to have emerged, one* seems to arise from the fact that some organizations,
in their implementation processes, have lost sight of the philosophy which
underpins MBO techniques. Thus, in some cases, relative failure can be
attributed to management's attempt to use MBO as a method of propping
up existing authoritarian ideologies, at variance with the participative
approach necessary for success. The distinction between control from
above and self-control is of the essence, and when collaborative techniques
are used to bolster an authoritarian managerial structure, it is small
wonder that co-operation and commitment do not increase; indeed, the
level of organizational tension will often rise.

In such circumstances the superior-subordinate relationship may become the focus for win–lose struggles. It is open to the subordinate, for
example, to attempt personal targets at the expense of organizational
objectives. These targets may also be selected because they are simple
rather than complex; or are readily quantifiable; or where high risk programmes are avoided in favour of maintaining the system in its present
form. One case which clearly illustrated this danger was where a manager,†
faced with a choice of targets between allocating resources to developing
new products or further advertising an existing product, chose the latter.
In the short term this was highly profitable and he obtained a much better
position in another company on the strength of his success. But before long
his old company found itself foist with an out-of-date product and financial
crisis. This sort of situation is particularly prone to happen where some
objectives are easily quantifiable, while others are not.

It is widely recognized that senior managers increasingly find themselves
working as members of groups, yet it seems that target-setting and reviews
are rarely carried out on a group basis. Predictably, the common result is
increased tensions between and within management groups, when individuals strive independently to reach their own targets and standards.
Staff/line conflicts are frequent enough in any event; in trying to achieve
agreed targets, many staff managers, not least personnel specialists, must
have the co-operation of colleagues who function outside their control.
The behavioural sciences offer solutions to such problems. Motivational
theory clearly demonstrates that objectives which are settled within groups
will secure greater commitment from the individual manager than those

* *Cf.* 'Management by Objectives in Perspective', by C. F. Molander, *Journal of Management Studies*, February 1972.

† 'The Total Management Concept', by S. E. Bryan, *Business Topics*, Spring 1966.

given to him by an external authority. It may well be, therefore, that MBO would be most effective if target-setting was undertaken on a group basis. If relevant groups of subordinates set targets in conjunction with their superiors, who in turn accepted targets arrived at through their own group efforts, two main results would emerge: individuals would feel genuinely committed to those targets; and there would be less of the inter-group friction which so often arises when targets are set without reference to all the staff who may be affected, directly or indirectly.

Another problem which occurs in large organizations is that from time to time major changes in policy or procedures are imposed externally on managers who see such changes as damaging to their efforts to achieve objectives already agreed. Examples would be new projects, market developments which demand that resources be re-allocated, and new government legislation or policies.* Dealing with such situations in practice depends essentially on the time-span involved. Frustrating as changes may seem at first sight, if the change or new development is to be spread over a period of years, say, then one of the key result areas in the job descriptions of the managers concerned could be—'To plan for the introduction of... (what the change is).' Thus each manager would become committed to examining the required change, and the normal MBO methodology of control and feedback would come into play—even seeking improvements to that change concurrently with its application. Revised objectives of individual managers and the organization as a whole would thus be properly dove-tailed. Idealistic as this sounds, it would certainly be a great advance on what normally happens at the moment in trying to adapt to changes.

In terms of current management thinking, MBO must be seen in the context of Organization Development: that is, in a conceptual scheme of planned organizational growth which is itself clearly aimed at maintaining a participative managerial style. O.D. must be planned, managed from the top so as to be organization-wide, and designed to increase effectiveness through interventions in the organization's processes using behavioural science knowledge. Techniques for formulating the changes implied in such growth will include MBO, although a pre-requisite for its successful implementation may well be the provision of sensitivity training for effective team functioning.

MBO is a catalyst for change in the sense that, used as an incisive instrument for organizational analysis, it will expose weaknesses and thus point the way to more effective management. The identification and integration, vertically and horizontally, of the objectives of each manager and part of the organization will at the very least reduce enervating

---

* 'Management by Objectives—Quo Vadis?', by C. G. Pearce, *O. & M. Bulletin*, February 1971.

conflicts between line and staff, project teams and functional managers, and may even cool down the traditional battle between sales and pro- duction staffs. This must surely be the main practical value of manage- ment on a team basis, with each manager contributing to the objectives of the whole rather than a part, and accountable for meeting his agreed contribution to those objectives.

MBO, then can be justly claimed to offer the ultimate solution to the problem of participation, because right down through the management hierarchy it emphasizes the self-control elements of taking decisions, and subsequently evaluating results, directly aimed at optimizing efficiency. As a dynamic system of management, it can show each employee how he contributes individually to the total achievement of his organization. Thus a sense of participating in the whole develops, coincidentally with the satisfaction of personal needs in the work situation. It is not simply a matter of freedom from the traditional type of authoritarian control; each employee comes to see himself as an integral part of the total organizational system and not as a mere cypher chasing targets imposed from above. He is made responsible for creating the reality of the situation.

For the individual manager, MBO also offers a real chance of providing an environment for job enrichment; participation in controlling his task, the revealing of constraints or obstacles to progress (some of which may then be removed), the very process of discussing the job in detail with a superior—all add to enrichment. And achievement, recognition, and further responsibility are all inherent in the concept. But the attitudes of top management are crucial here: the installation of the ongoing processes of MBO must be positively encouraged, and decisions taken quickly about the constraints and weaknesses exposed; otherwise managers down the line will become disheartened and initial apprehensions about MBO as merely a gimmick may be confirmed.

FURTHER READING

The Human Side of Enterprise, by Douglas McGregor (McGraw-Hill, 1960).
Management by Objectives in Action, by John Humble (McGraw-Hill, 1970).
Management by Objectives in the Civil Service, by John Garrett and S. D. Walker. C.A.S. Occasional Papers, No. 10 (H.M.S.O., 1969).

There is also an excellent series of films produced by AB-Pathe Ltd., and featuring John Humble: (1) *Management by Objectives*; (2) *Defining the Manager's Job*; (3) *Performance and Potential Review*; (4) *Colt—a Case History*.

10 The Training Function

The purpose of training is to give employees at all levels sufficient instruction and guidance to enable them to perform their jobs effectively and prepare themselves for promotion. The personnel manager's task is to give advice and co-ordinate the training policy and programmes of the organization as a whole, but all line managers must directly control the development of the skills and potentials of their subordinates. The fact that the vast majority of all training takes place on the job makes this responsibility clear. Going off to outside courses or visits are infrequent experiences; the true training situation exists where there is a gap between the standard of performance demanded by a departmental head and that actually being achieved by the individual subordinate, and the main purpose of training is to close this gap.

Management of the training function itself is a four-fold process:

1. Assessing the need—determining training requirements for all types of staff, deciding priorities, and defining standards.
2. Programming—plans and procedures aimed at fulfilling the needs: policy on internal or external courses; individual development plans; deciding the best techniques appropriate to each type of training.
3. Organizing—how best to use the staff, finance, and facilities available for training purposes.
4. Evaluating—how well the results meet the original needs; budgetary control of resources.

LEGISLATION

The Industrial Training Act 1964 provided the framework within which most recent developments in training have taken place. It came about because the Government realized the need to strengthen and improve the partnership between industry and the various educational authorities for providing effective industrial training. The serious weakness in the situation before the Act was that far too much training was left to the uncoordinated actions of a large number of individual organizations. Many employers complained about the injustice of investing large sums in training activities only to find their young people, once fully trained, being lured away by other firms who could afford to offer higher salaries because they used none of their resources for training purposes. Thus, while the benefits of training were being shared by all, the costs were borne by only a few.

The main objectives of the Industrial Training Act were therefore:

1. To ensure an adequate supply of fully trained workers at all levels of industry.
2. To improve the overall quality of industrial training.
3. To bring about a fairer spread of the costs involved in training.

To achieve these objectives the Department of Employment (then Ministry of Labour) was given powers to set up Industrial Training Boards, which were to be responsible for seeing that the training needs of their respective industries were met. Twenty-four of these now exist, covering about three-quarters of the working population.

Then the Employment and Training Act 1973 was passed to reform all the arrangements for promoting the efficient working of the labour market in Britain. A Manpower Services Commission was set up to control the employment and training services previously provided by the Department of Employment, with two executive agencies, the Employment Service Agency and the Training Services Agency. The actual running of the services is carried out by the two agencies, while the commission concentrates on forward programmes of work and the annual budgets which have to be approved by the Secretary of State for Employment.

The Training Services Agency (T.S.A.) has three major responsibilities:

1. To co-ordinate the work of the twenty-four statutory industrial training boards, each different in size, complexity, and approach to meeting training needs.
2. To promote training in those sectors not covered by the I.T.B.'s.
3. To administer and develop the Training Opportunities Scheme (T.O.P.S.).

Overall, the T.S.A. has a role in the total national training effort, which, in its entirety, embraces not only the three aspects above, but also the efforts of employers in training their own staff and that considerable part of the further education system which is concerned with industrial training in one form or another. Weaknesses have existed in these provisions in the past, which it is intended that the T.S.A. should correct. Firstly, efforts were unevenly spread—geographically, industrially, and occupationally—and training coverage did not always reflect relative need. Secondly, there seemed an obvious need to develop a unified strategy to tackle common problems. Thirdly, there was evidence of under-use of some of the wealth of experience and valuable facilities available within the total training system. These weaknesses served to define the task of the T.S.A. in co-ordinating and supporting the national training effort.

Thus it must now approve the levy/exemption criteria submitted by each I.T.B., and backs this with key training grants allocated to support training throughout British industry, as well as directly paying the administrative and operating costs of I.T.B.s. The Agency has its own training centres, in addition to those which receive T.O.P.S. trainees, and also plans to expand its service of sponsored training for employers. Finally, it can undertake specialist advisory services and finance development work and research: for example, it supports the Industrial Training Research Unit at Cambridge.

Faced with the alternatives of spreading resources over a large number of possibilities and projects, or concentrating them in a few selected priority areas, the commission and T.S.A. have chosen the latter course. In strategic terms, this means that the Agency takes on the dual role of catalyst and co-ordinator. As the former, it aims to produce results which might not otherwise be obtained, or accelerate activities which otherwise would happen more slowly. As co-ordinator, it will support the entire training system, help to tackle common problems, and seek to obtain from the government of the day the resources required to meet the country's training needs.

INDUSTRIAL TRAINING BOARDS

I.T.B.s, dating from 1964, continue to have an important role to play. They are the bodies with whom responsibility and authority to improve training in their own industries rests, and their detailed duties include:

1. Establishing training policy within each industry, including such questions as admission to training (through apprenticeships or otherwise), length of training, registration of trainees, and provisions for appropriate attendance at colleges of further education.
2. Establishing standards of training and syllabuses for different occupations in the industry, taking into account the associated technical education required.
3. Providing advice and assistance about training to firms in the industry.

4. Devising tests to be taken by apprentices and other trainees during and on completion of their training.
5. Establishing qualifications and tests for instructors.
6. Running training courses in their own training centres.

All the Boards have deliberately been allowed considerable latitude in deciding their specific activities, so they have tended to plan their training efforts in different ways to fit their varying circumstances. Thus the Engineering Board, the largest and wealthiest, from the start set itself the mammoth task of meeting the whole range of training needs throughout the industry. The Wool, Jute, and Flax I.T.B. began by training factory-floor instructors; the Construction I.T.B. concentrated initially on the development of managers and supervisors; and the Iron and Steel I.T.B. started by establishing training standards for specific operations, beginning with apprentices and operatives. At the same time, this diversification led to problems of its own, for there are many jobs that are similar in different industries and there is an obvious need to safeguard against the danger of a massive duplication of training effort that might result. The predominant interest of particular Boards in certain trades and skills must be recognized, but each must then make allowances for the needs of other industries if the best use is to be made of the available educational resources. Substantial common interests may also exist in certain occupations (clerical, for example) where no Board has a predominant interest; again co-ordination becomes of paramount importance in this situation.

The Employment and Training Act set out new financial arrangements, replacing the original levy/grant system with a levy/grant/exemption system whereby each I.T.B. will exempt from levy any firm which in the Board's opinion trains its workers adequately. Criteria for 'adequacy' have been defined by each Board in consultation with its industry, and approved by the M.S.C. and Secretary of State for Employment. Boards thus set exemption standards which, together with the use of levy/grant for firms which are not exempt, aim to ensure that the existing standards of training are maintained and that there is a continuing stimulus to improvement.

This new system has, in fact, a combination of the factors of financial compulsion and of persuasion and advice*: the former, since the levy (maximum of 1 per cent of payroll) still applies to firms not meeting the basic level of training performance; the latter, since a training adviser is now in regular contact with each company, discussing their training problems and in a position to influence both thinking and action. The most

* 'The New Role of the Training Boards', by P. H. Saxon, *BACIE Journal*, September 1974, Page 107.

important strength of the new levy/grant/exemption system is that greater emphasis is laid on regular advisory contact with all firms, as opposed to the previous inspection and audit of only a sample of grant claims.

In this context, basic level of training means that firms have clear training policies and written plans based on an overall assessment of needs; that they do provide training to meet these needs, and that they use formal methods to evaluate its effectiveness. But another important strength of the training advisers is that they can help firms decide how they can most effectively go beyond this basic level, extending and improving training arrangements to their benefit. For example, the training adviser's review may reveal a problem of industrial relations training, which is beyond basic requirements, or how the smaller company may fit management training into its operations. The training adviser's role is thus at this stage largely diagnostic, and he can carry this out very effectively because of his close knowledge not only of his subject, but also of the industry and the individual company which he regularly visits.

The new framework of the 1973 Act also gives I.T.B.s new planning responsibilities. Five-year plans, updated annually on a rolling basis, must be submitted in order to obtain operating funds from the Exchequer. The great advantage that this process offers is the way in which it accentuates the need to work to objectives. Forward planning of this nature gives the opportunity to talk through ideas with all the firms in an industry, and thus enables each of them to relate their I.T.B.s policy to their own long-range plans. The fact that the whole range of manpower intelligence will be co-ordinated by the M.S.C. will also help.

One aim of all the I.T.B.s, specifically required by the 1964 Act, is to devise adequate methods of forecasting future needs, so that training can be organized efficiently, in co-operation with the D.E's Manpower Services Commission and with Industrial and Regional Development Councils. Such forecasts were advocated in Chapter 1. They need constant scrutiny, as technical changes and economic conditions alter the demand for different categories of labour. The Boards have legal powers to obtain all the necessary information from employers on their manpower, which enables them to devise questionnaires of a much more searching character than has ever been possible in the past.

The number of training officers required justifies the view that a training job should become a recognized step in every manager's career. Obviously the occupants of these posts must have sufficient ability to earn the confidence of the senior managers whose staff they are developing; equally, most will be expected to have a sound technical knowledge of the industry concerned. Such men will only be found among the ranks of present junior and middle management, and firms must be prepared to second those who have the right qualities to the Boards for a short time during their careers. They must, of course, be adequately trained to fill this specialized role.

Evaluation must take the initial objectives of the Act into account. The first major aim, that of ensuring an adequate supply of properly trained workers at all levels of industry, is very wide: it embraces accurate manpower forecasting for various grades of skill, questions of manpower utilization, and the retraining and redeployment of sections of the labour force where necessary. In the event, the numbers of apprenticeships and off-the-job facilities for craft and technical training have increased, and more emphasis has been placed on supervisory and management development. Several thousands of students have also completed introductory courses for training officers. The present major shortcoming is in retraining redundant workers, where the Boards' efforts are having to be heavily supplemented by the Government's own training centres.

The Act's second objective is to secure an improvement in the quality and efficiency of industrial training. Undoubtedly the Boards have made considerable progress in developing training standards. The module-training concept has gained wide acceptance, and a practical example, applied directly to personnel management, is given in the next chapter, p. 188. First-year off-the-job syllabuses have been developed by several Boards. The consultancy work of the Industrial Training Service has helped firms to develop skills in job analysis and thus evolve training programmes based on the tasks to be performed. The needs of small firms have been met by the promotion of group schemes, enabling them to co-operate in hiring skilled training officers and jointly provide suitable facilities.

THE GOVERNMENT'S DIRECT ROLE

Over the past decade the Government has greatly increased its assistance for industrial training and retraining. Apart from making grants and publishing advisory material, it also offers industry and workers, through the Department of Employment, a wide range of training facilities, including the following:

1. Vocational training courses at Skillcentres (formerly Government Training Centres), residential training centres for the disabled, technical colleges, or in employers' own establishments, encompassed by the Training Opportunities Scheme.
2. An instructor training service, and training development service for operator instructors.
3. Training Within Industry for supervisors.
4. Export office procedure courses.

At Skillcentres (G.T.C.s), workers without usable skills who are suitable for accelerated training are given it free in about fifty skilled trades; these embrace the traditional engineering and construction skills, but also aim to meet changing industrial needs and technological developments, for example, in hydraulics and electronics. Facilities are also offered for sponsored employee training, to enable workers nominated by their employers to acquire additional skills. This type of training consists of specially prepared courses, agreed after discussions with the employer and worker concerned, which enable the particular needs of the firm to be met. The scope of sponsored training is wide—conversion, additional skills, upgrading, or the provision of limited skills in all the trades taught at Skillcentres.

Other vocational training is imparted at four *residential training centres* for the disabled, run by voluntary organizations with financial support from the D.E. The *export office procedure courses*, which last five days, are also backed by the Board of Trade and a number of the I.T.B.s, and have two main objectives: to enable office workers to gain experience in export documentation and procedures; and to teach them how to pass on this knowledge to other staff in the most effective way.

The *instructor training service* has grown to the extent of turning out over 3,000 trained instructors annually. There are two specialized colleges, at Letchworth and Glasgow, for this purpose, and instructor training units attached to six of the Skillcentres in different parts of the country. An advanced instructor training course has also been introduced. Students receive intensive education in skills recognition, fault analysis and correction, training to high working speeds and effective training supervision; project work and the use of modern audio-visual aids are features of these courses. The training development service specifically provides training for selected operator instructors, who are taught how to instruct other operatives in a programme devised for 'in-plant' training. An information session for managers and a briefing session for supervisors precede a comprehensive five-day course for the selected operatives.

The T.S.A.s responsibility in all this is for the Training Opportunities Scheme (T.O.P.S.), which has effected a transformation of the direct training effort of central government. T.O.P.S. is based on two beliefs: that the needs of society and the economy during the rest of the twentieth century will mean a much greater demand for training and retraining, particularly of adults; and that it is the right of all adults to have the opportunity at any time to acquire a skill for the first time or to retrain for a new skill.

The numbers alone reveal the significance of the new scheme. In 1970 the Government's direct training effort produced about 15,000 trainees; by 1973 this had risen to 40,000; present aims are 70–75,000 by 1975–6, with an ultimate target of 100,000 trainees a year. (Impressive as such growth may appear, E.E.C. comparisons show that 290,000 workers are trained annually at government-supported centres in France, and 190,000 in Germany). Moreover, training is taking place not only in Skillcentres: 60 per cent of T.O.P.S. trainees are now being trained in colleges of further education, in employers' own establishments and in private training institutions. Nor is it only the unemployed who are undergoing training; in 1973, 45 per cent of those trained under the scheme left their previous jobs in order to train, and then moved straight into jobs using their new skills. Over a third of the intake of skilled craftsmen into the construction industry in recent years have been provided by the scheme, and it is also one of the largest trainers of clerical and commercial skills in the country.

The T.S.A. has the task of dove-tailing this increasingly important scheme with the training efforts made elsewhere, so as to derive maximum advantage from this big addition to the nation's training facilities and effort. It has already been resolved that these facilities should be given a much brighter image, through publicity similar to that designed for the new employment service. They will also pay special attention to the needs of workers in the declining industries, and generally aim at increasing the pool of trained labour in the assisted areas as well as elsewhere. A range of other training services, besides T.O.P.S., is also available free of charge to all firms in assisted areas. These services are: training of firms' own instructors; training of experienced workers in instructional techniques; provision of mobile instructors to train people on employers' own premises; training of supervisors; and special schemes to provide retraining where there are major redundancies.

INDUCTION TRAINING

Induction training is carried out in order to help recruits to an organization to overcome their sense of strangeness, secure their acceptance by existing employees, and develop in them a sense of belonging. A large proportion of labour turnover occurs during the early weeks of employment, mainly because no effort has been made to enable the newcomer to feel at home: he thus becomes unhappy and leaves to find another job in a more congenial atmosphere. This type of training is in effect an introduction to the organization's purpose, policies, and practices, seeking to establish the right links between each individual, his work, and his outside life in the community, by explaining:

1. His place in the organization.
2. The relationship between his work and the finished products.
3. The relationship between his firm, its industry, and the world outside.
4. How he can put his point of view to management.

In small firms this introduction has to be done informally, largely by the recruit's immediate supervisor. But in large organizations a planned induction programme is often given. A typical example is:

1. Welcome by a Director, whose talk would include a history of the firm.
2. Films showing firm's activities—flow of production, from raw-material sources through to the marketing of the finished article.
3. Talk on personalities of the firm, including an organization chart.
4. A conducted tour of the works.
5. Talk about social and welfare facilities available.

Such a programme would be carried out as frequently as the number of recruits warranted it, and would be organized by members of the personnel department. It is essential that directors and other senior executives are involved in the talks, however: this adds prestige to the occasion and gives the newcomer a sense of importance.

Clearly the content of this type of course would be of common interest to all newcomers no matter how junior or senior their positions may be. In particular, office as well as production workers should be included, and the relationships between different grades of staff made clear, so at least they start off by feeling members of one team. But this general information would then have to be supplemented by supervisors in each department, to provide the more domestic details. These include: a tour of the department, explaining how each job fits in to the main flow of production, and departmental rules about time-keeping, refreshment breaks, accident prevention, protective clothing, the actions to be taken in the case of emergency, procedure for reporting sickness, and observance of hygiene. In explaining how the new worker can put his views to management, arrangements for joint consultation and the structure of works committees should be outlined, together with the firm's policy about trade union membership. The purpose and procedures of any suggestion scheme might be included at this stage. On wider personnel issues, recruits must be told whom to approach among management if they want help with any private domestic matters. The training officer should explain the firm's promotion policies and any schemes to help employees improve their qualifications or broaden their education. Finally, it is important that all aspects of remuneration are clarified: methods of payment, incentive and bonus schemes, profit-sharing, superannuation and sickness benefits, and any other compulsory or voluntary deductions from pay.

All this information given verbally may be consolidated in the form of an employees' handbook, setting out the organization's policies, rules, and regulations in black and white. When the newcomers have settled in and had the opportunity of reading the handbook, the last stage of the induction process should be a formal follow-up session when questions would be answered and any points of misunderstanding removed. This may all appear to involve considerable effort, but unless special attention is given to the problems of integrating new employees with the organization, the risk of high labour turnover with its attendant costs is great.

Particular attention should be given to the induction of school leavers taking their first jobs; their reception will not only give them an impression of that particular firm, but may colour their attitude towards industry for the rest of their lives. Special emphasis should therefore be laid on the background to the job and its relation to the outside community; and on encouraging them to equip themselves for better jobs in the future.

JOB TRAINING

All jobs in industry and commerce call for the exercise of certain skills and the application of different forms of knowledge, and they will not be carried out very effectively unless these skills and knowledge are properly imparted in the first place. This means that the learner must be made aware of what he is doing, and why, and then be allowed actually to do the job for himself. Skills are thus taught through a mixture of demonstration, explanation, and practice. The majority of people seeking jobs, especially school leavers, are attracted by promises of proper training, the effectiveness of which is usually reflected in the rate of turnover among people during their first few weeks with a firm.

Job training methods generally fall into two types, depending mainly on the size of the organization and the resources it can devote to training. These are:

1. The understudy method, popularly known as 'sitting next to Nelly', when the learner is attached to someone proficient in the job and picks it up by copying that person.
2. The use of a separate training section, set aside especially to teach jobs to newcomers before they actually start work in the main production areas.

The success or failure of the first method undoubtedly lies in the hands of the experienced person giving the instruction. No matter how skilled he is at his job, unless he is good at teaching it too, his efforts and those of the learner will be of little avail. There is the possibility of his using bad working methods—short cuts that he may have evolved during years of experience which might not be suitable (sometimes positively dangerous) to teach to someone new to a job. If he is on piece-rates, and the demands of production are all important, he may have little time to devote to the trainee who will become bewildered by the speed of everything around him and the impatience of his instructor. In any event there is likely to be considerable wastage of materials by the learner and also the risk of damage to valuable production machinery.

With so many disadvantages to this method, the concept of having separate training facilities is obviously to be preferred. Full-time qualified instructors in properly equipped training workshops can exercise much better control and ensure that the correct methods are taught. The learners receive the full attention of these instructors whose thoughts are not absorbed by production demands, and emphasis can be placed on gradually building up skill at the job before transfer to the main production areas (in the process, induction is helped, too). Nevertheless, when the transition does take place, it still becomes a traumatic experience for many workers who find the change from the unreal and less urgent atmosphere of the training room to the pace of the factory itself more than they can cope with. This is a matter of great concern to management who naturally do not wish to see expensively trained recruits leaving soon after starting on actual production. Everything should be done during the training period, therefore to simulate real working conditions—inspection of the products made, with constantly increasing rates of output emphasized, for instance—in order to develop confidence.

Of course, in small organizations it may be physically impossible to have separate arrangements. The numbers of people to be trained and the frequency of demand for courses determine the methods used. Costs therefore need to be examined very closely in the light of these factors, with special regard to the savings in time taken to reach proficiency when newcomers are dealt with separately (as much as a half in many cases, compared with 'sitting next to Nelly'). Where traditional methods have to be used, supervisors must be careful in selecting the instructors: often someone who has himself recently learned the job is best, provided he can also be given some guidance on how to teach newcomers satisfactorily. On the other hand, if separate training is undertaken, supervisors must realize the importance of maintaining personal contact with trainees intended for their departments. This in itself can be a problem to those supervisors who are conscious of their own initial lack of background education. Nevertheless, they must be made to accept that training and development can never be completely delegated elsewhere, for by their very nature they are part of every supervisor's responsibilities.

PROGRAMMED INSTRUCTION

One modern training method that is increasingly coming into use is *programmed instruction*, which enables learners to work on their own from prepared texts or teaching machines, while still having the expert help of an instructor available when necessary. The former Central Training Council commended this method to Industrial Training Boards and asked each of them to establish small teams of training specialists well qualified in job analysis to consider the needs of their respective industries and prepare programmes for individual jobs. The merits of this method are:

1. Since the teaching material is prepared by an expert, his services may be made available to a wide audience through his programmes.
2. Individuals may be trained more economically and at the most convenient times, particularly when the rate of intake of trainees precludes the formation of a group.
3. The instructor in charge of the trainees can give closer attention to individual needs as they emerge.
4. Learning at one's own speed is less likely to be tinged with the anxiety which sometimes arises from an inability to keep up with the learning group.
5. The instructor in charge will have a quick and accurate measure of a trainee's rate of learning.
6. Training is more likely to be achieved in the time best suited to each trainee.
7. Instructor preparation time for training sessions can be reduced.

The main disadvantages are:

1. Self-teaching on an individual basis may militate against the good personal relations which the instructor builds up in a teaching group.
2. The abler trainee may become bored if the programme is too easy for him.
3. The less good instructor may tend to rely too much on the technique and not play his full personal part.

APPRENTICESHIPS

In large organizations there may well be several hundred apprentices of varying types, ranging from craft apprentices who usually serve five years training from their sixteenth birthday to the graduate apprentice who signs his articles with a firm only after obtaining his university degree. The variety is best illustrated by a chart Figure 23.

All these apprenticeships comprise a mixture of theoretical and practical training. Theory is usually given in one of three forms:

1. Day release at a local technical college.
2. 'Sandwich' type courses, with alternating periods of several months at a time at work and at college.

Type of apprenticeship	Age for signing indentures	Type of school or college	Educational qualifications for entry
1. Craft	16	Secondary Modern	None essential
2. Technical	16	Grammar or Technical School	G.C.E. 'O' level: 3 or 4 passes
3. Student (a)	16	Grammar or Technical School	G.C.E. 'O' level: 5 passes
(b)	18	Grammar or Technical School	G.C.E. 'A' level: 2 passes with 3 at 'O' level
4. Undergraduate	18	Grammar or Technical School	'A' level, 3 passes (necessary for University entry)
5. Graduate	21+	University or C.A.T.	Degree

Figure 23. Apprenticeships

3. Scholarships for full-time study at an advanced stage of the apprenticeship.

The latter two methods are generally preferred both by training officers and educationalists, for they provide much better opportunities to design well-balanced programmes for the students; the first method, on the other hand, is much more a form of cramming for an eventual qualification, with little chance to develop any potential or include much by way of vocational education to broaden the student's outlook. Apprentices receiving these types of training should ultimately acquire trade or professional qualifications, culminating for the best in membership of the appropriate professional institution.

Trade unions are, of course, very interested in the whole subject of apprenticeships, and many agreements on the subject have been negotiated between employers' federations and trade unions; for example, a comprehensive apprenticeship scheme is administered by the Joint Apprenticeship Board, which is a standing committee of the National Joint Council of the building industry. Certainly most craft unions in effect preserve their bargaining power and privileges by restricting the number of apprentices allowed to enter that craft each year.

Within the firm itself, if the number of apprentices warrants it, the best form of guidance and control they can receive is from a full-time apprentice supervisor. He is normally a member of the personnel department, probably directly responsible to the training officer; depending on size again, he may have a number of assistants or instructors under his control. Where training workshops are provided with machine tools and equipment set aside for apprentices, the time spent in these shops will have to be organized according to a curriculum. The progress of individuals must be recorded and discussed with their practical instructors and college tutors. There should also be provision for movement from one type of apprenticeship to another, according to progress or lack of it. The welfare demands of apprentices may also be considerable. Where they work at a distance from their homes, lodgings or hostel accommodation will be necessary, and must be properly supervised. Participation in any sports or social activities offered by the firm is probably best left to the apprentices themselves to organize, but there may be a need for some guidance here. The parents of apprentices may also be interviewed and given reassurance from time to time. The calls on the apprentice supervisor are thus numerous and varied, but it can be an enormously satisfactory job to play this vital role in influencing the development of these young men and watching their subsequent careers.

Providing practical facilities for apprentice training is simple in any large organization, but more and more small firms are being encouraged to help themselves, too. Many of these employ skilled men, but because of their size feel they cannot train apprentices. In fact, they do have a part to play, and a small general workshop undertaking a wide variety of operations could well offer as good training as a large organization. Where small firms only carry out specialized work, all-round experience can be arranged by their co-operating together in some form of group apprenticeship scheme. Firms continue to recruit apprentices individually, but their training programmes are arranged to include periods in the workshops of all the firms involved.

RETRAINING OLDER WORKERS

The employment problems of older workers have already been examined in Chapter 7. Retraining is likely to become a much greater problem in the future than it is at present, however, because occupational mobility will inevitably increase as technological advances occur more and more rapidly. This is what is implied by sensational press predictions that a man's working career in future will demand retraining for two or three different jobs in the forty to fifty years he spends at work.

Middle-aged and older workers tend to be conscientious, responsible in their attitudes, disciplined in attendance and time-keeping, and loyal—all qualities that employers should value when considering whether to take on and train older people. Certainly they are more expensive to train than school leavers, because their rates of pay are usually higher, and they start with inherent disadvantages compared with younger men and women: neither their basic education nor their existing skills may be as good, they take longer to learn new tasks, and they may never succeed in reaching the same standard of proficiency. But, on the other hand, widely held prejudices about the inability of 'an old dog to learn new tricks' ignore the findings of research surveys* about training methods.

Some of the difficulties encountered by the older person in learning a new skill have been studied at the London Postal School in training manual sorters. Perhaps the most important outcome of these studies has been the conclusion that the older trainee benefits most from learning by discovery —by free decision or discrimination in a fairly open situation. Learning by this method achieves more than when learning is governed totally by instruction, probably because the latter permits the trainee to become mentally passive. Every stage of a task must be adequately challenging to the older worker who resents being treated like a child at school; it may seem helpful to break a task down into its component parts and teach these one by one, but this technique is in fact rejected as 'kid's stuff'.

Such reactions must be taken into account when designing appropriate training methods. The G.P.O. studies suggested that although the man of 40-plus was unexpectedly good at acquiring information, he had relative difficulty in retaining what he learned. When he was asked, for example, to learn A, then B, then C, he learned each very well; but if he was then asked what he remembered of A, there was every chance that he had forgotten it. Because of this, long sessions of practical work were found advisable. These relatively long periods also provide the opportunity for him to tackle a sizeable job and to let him see the result of his studies. He favours knowing where he is going even if he prefers getting there under his own steam. Thus it was found expedient to offer a framework in which the 40-plus could structure his own learning rather than to break the task down for him. This self-structuring has the advantage too that it allows for the many different starting points of learning of a group of men drawn from different backgrounds and experiences. For this reason, the new technique of programmed instruction seems particularly relevant for older workers.

Practical analyses of this nature are essential in facing the situation that Britain has one of the oldest work-forces in the world, with forecasts suggesting that the proportion of older workers (especially female) will increase through the rest of the century. Thus the training of older workers must be high on the list of priorities of every personnel department in the foreseeable future, and will require a four-fold approach.†

'Green' labour from declining industries must be trained for employ-

* *Problems in Adult Retraining*, by Eunice and R. Meredith Belbin (London: Heinemann, 1972).

† 'Older Workers Retrained', by J. M. Smith, *New Society*, 4 July 1974.

ment in expanding industries (cotton industry workers moving into car manufacture, for example); this kind of retraining poses the greatest problems because the workers concerned have to learn the traditions and knowledge of an entirely new industry. Secondly, workers may have to be retrained in the same industry, because of a desire to upgrade skills, technological advances, or changes in fashion; for example, hosiery firms were forced to retrain large numbers of workers almost overnight when women's stockings were replaced by tights. Thirdly, there may be an increased need for versatility, again to meet changing needs or to avoid bottlenecks in production; this may go hand in hand with manning or productivity agreements which remove old demarcation lines between jobs. Finally, there is the 'booster' type training, aimed at raising production to more acceptable levels. Each of these four approaches makes a distinctive contribution towards industrial efficiency, and their differences need to be recognized to ensure that no area is overlooked.

FURTHER READING

Manpower Training and Development, by J. Kenny and E. Donnelly (I.P.M. and Harrap, 1972).
A Glossary of Training Terms, Department of Employment (H.M.S.O., 1971).
Induction, by Roy Van Gelder (Industrial Society, 1967).
Programmed Instruction for Industrial Training, by Bernard Dodd (Heinemann, 1967).

11 Training Supervisors and Managers

Both policy and practice for the training and development of supervisors and managers should be based on the technique of manpower planning within an organization.* The fundamental concept quite simply is that it is better to plan for job succession through internal promotion whenever possible, rather than wait to see if anyone is available when senior posts become vacant (and then perhaps have to search outside the firm for suitable candidates). In trying to put this concept into effect, and make training arrangements as a result, responsible managers will base their plans on the answers to these questions:

1. Are we providing adequately for our future requirements for senior staff?
2. Are we promoting the right people at the right time?
3. Are we getting the best results from existing foremen and managers?
4. Are we doing all we can to help our staff prepare themselves for promotion to supervisory and managerial positions?

SUPERVISORY TRAINING

The basic problem in training supervisors is to get them to accept new ideas and to build up confidence in their technical knowledge, organizational ability, and social skills. Concern for solving this problem has grown consistently since the war for a number of reasons. Full employment has brought about great changes in the general social climate, while the increased importance and influence of trade unions has had a direct impact on the industrial climate. The constant demand for higher productivity has led to increased specialization and radical changes to machinery, equipment, processes, and working methods. The trend towards larger units with more complex organizations in turn has caused relationships between employees to become impersonal, detracting from the significance of the individual and stifling his sense of responsibility. Almost everything that

* *See* Chapter 4, pages 53–58.

can be done to counteract these influences and enable individuals to feel that their contributions within a vast organization are important, depends ultimately on the calibre of first-line supervision—thus emphasizing the vital nature of this aspect of training. Conditions of full employment have made discipline based on pre-war 'carrot and stick' concepts of fear and insecurity ineffective. The alternative is discipline by consent, but this does not occur spontaneously in the absence of sanctions—it requires qualities of leadership based on understanding of subordinates' points of view. This at a time, too, when the status of the first-line supervisor is in question, particularly since his authority is constantly being eroded by the activities of specialists, such as production planners, quality inspectors, and work study engineers.

The main requirements of any supervisor are that he should regularly achieve production targets and increase productivity. To do so, he must be technically competent, be able to administer his department and organize its work, and establish proper relationships with his subordinates, colleagues, and superiors in both line management and service functions. His training should therefore be designed to:

1. Keep abreast of the current technical demands of his job.
2. Provide him with all the background information about the organization's policies and activities that he must know in order to act effectively and confidently.
3. Teach him the techniques and methods of management appropriate to his level and how they might best be applied under existing conditions.
4. Instruct him in the principles of personal leadership and develop his ability to exercise them effectively.
5. Teach him to cope successfully with changing conditions.

Of course, there is an enormous diversity in supervisors' jobs, depending largely on the size of firm and type of department, but certain forms of training are suitable for them all. One investigation* concentrated on the problems facing supervisors and the areas in which their performance was often inadequate. There are two ways of identifying the problems—individual interviews and a 'critical incident report' procedure. Critical incidents are recorded by asking supervisors at the end of their working day to describe briefly in writing the problem they found most difficult to cope with that day. These reports can then be analysed to detect what needs are common, and general training schemes developed. In addition, specific job training can be designed and given separately to individual supervisors.

*D.E.P. *Training Information Paper No. 2*, by P. Warr and M. Bird (H.M.S.O., 1968).

A wide variety of external courses are available for training supervisors, but these should always be introduced cautiously, at a pace which allows both the desire and ability to learn to be fostered. Otherwise, the results achieved are likely to be disappointing and any early hopes which may have been raised in the minds of senior management will founder. In any event, external training should always follow an internal course about the firm's history, activities, organization, policies, practices, and procedures, which will provide a general background against which subsequent training can be viewed in perspective. It makes no difference whether this programme is implemented on a group training basis or through a series of talks given by appropriate managers in the normal course of their work, as long as a properly planned syllabus is devised initially and then consistently adhered to. There must be a thorough preliminary appreciation of the supervisor's job and his place in the organization (by applying the technique of job analysis) before he attends any external training courses.

Many of these, for all levels of supervisors (both before and after appointment), are run by local Colleges of Technology in their business studies departments, and they have been greatly stimulated by the work of the National Examinations Board in Supervisory Studies set up in 1965. The Institute of Supervisory Management also offers a comprehensive programme. Probably the best known, however, is Training Within Industry (T.W.I.), a series of courses run by the Department of Employment, which have been officially described as follows:

The *job relations* programme aims to develop leadership qualities. It puts forward a pattern of behaviour for supervisors to follow in obtaining and maintaining good working relationships. In addition it trains them in a method of handling relationship problems.

The *job instruction* programme trains in the skill of imparting information to others whether by instructing a learner, briefing a more experienced worker, or in the normal process of communication. In many firms the instruction of newcomers is carried out by skilled workers rather than by supervisors and experience has shown the value of giving this programme of training to such instructors.

The *job methods* programme trains in the use of a technique for improving existing working methods. It helps supervisors to make better use of available resources. Additionally, it does much to ensure their cooperation, on a basis of understanding, with method study or planning departments.

The *job safety* programme emphasizes the need for and the supervisors' responsibility towards industrial accident prevention. It shows them how to spot dangers and how to take appropriate measures to deal with these dangers.

In an industrial setting, these four courses are normally given separately: the job methods programme requires 15 hours, but the other three take only 10 hours, and they are designed for learner groups of 6–12 supervisors. The Department of Employment also runs instructor courses, to qualify individuals to return to their own organizations and run the T.W.I. programme in turn.

In addition to training in basic supervisory skills, there should be specific courses to cover such subjects as quality control, departmental costing, plant maintenance procedures, materials handling, 'good housekeeping', and effective communications, with a broad approach linking these various aspects and so enabling the supervisor to appreciate all the techniques available for the achievement of efficiency. Particular attention must be paid to the supervisor's special problem of establishing and maintaining proper relationships with his colleagues and senior managers in the service departments, with whom most of his contacts take place. The aim here should be to make clear the ways in which senior staff responsibilities merge and overlap, especially between production and service departments, so that each person concerned will come to understand the other's problems and see the contributions they can make towards increasing each other's effectiveness. Clearly this could only be done internally, which emphasizes the fact that management cannot contract out of supervisory training; external courses can help enormously, but training on the job is the most vital part of the process and can only be carried out by the supervisor's own manager (who should take some trouble to acquire knowledge of modern supervisory training techniques).

Highly formal training is normally associated with large organizations which have all sorts of teaching aids and comprehensive facilities available. (An example of the detailed content of an internal supervisory training course is shown on the next page). The principles apply equally to small firms, however, where entirely individual training, carried out in the privacy of the offices of appropriate senior staff, can be given with considerable benefits. The small firm also has the advantage that training can be implemented at optimum speed; in big companies, the numbers involved in training programmes are often so large that time-lags inevitably occur between training courses, and their impact may consequently be diminished.

Interest and enthusiasm generated through special training efforts will wane, in any event, unless something positive is done to prevent this happening. Apathy or misunderstanding on the part of colleagues or superiors may well frustrate a supervisor when he tries to apply the knowledge he has acquired from training. Here again his own line manager is clearly responsible for proper follow-up and encouragement. The firm's training officer can also help by organizing:

1. *Departmental competitions:* for example, in 'good housekeeping' or safety.
2. *Discussion groups:* a forum for raising problems, keeping up with current technical developments, and also a useful means for communicating news about the company and any changes likely to occur.
3. *Exchange visits:* to see how other factories are run, or even to work in them for short periods of time.
4. *External refresher courses:* providing the opportunity to exchange experience with other supervisors from a wide variety of activities and backgrounds.

MANAGEMENT DEVELOPMENT

The job of a manager can be analysed into five types of activity, thus:

1. *Defining the organization's aims*, which will be achieved by the co-ordinated efforts of all staff.
2. *Planning* the best use of all available resources (labour, money, equipment, accommodation, time, and ideas), in order to achieve these aims.
3. *Taking action* to put plans into effect.
4. *Measuring* the results achieved by this action, and *comparing* them with specified performance standards.
5. *Taking corrective action* if there is any deviation from the recognized standards.

Apart from the necessary qualifications and grasp of administrative principles, this analysis of management shows that it differs from the work of other employees by demanding the use of judgment, the balancing of arguments, and the taking of decisions. The distinguishing feature of management training, therefore, is that it aims to cultivate these skills.

In as far as management is now regarded as a profession, training for it may be said to go through the same three phases as all professional education. Firstly, background studies orientate the student towards his chosen career (science for the engineer, for example): for management, this background is often considered irrelevant, although nowadays there may be some bias towards economic or sociological subjects. Secondly, there is the phase of on-the-job learning—a carefully controlled and supervised apprenticeship, with actual responsibilities slowly increasing as time passes. Parallel with this is the third aspect, a series of supplementary experiences—courses on special topics, attachments, secondments, reading lists—providing off-the-job training with the aim of achieving better performance on the job. External courses are thus seen as carefully timed supplements to development, which can be evaluated in terms of improved knowledge and skill when the trainee returns. This event itself demands that the climate of opinion in the working group concerned is such that criticism and suggestions will be encouraged or indeed expected of the returned member.

The emphasis in management training, then, must be placed on the development of individuals, and they should be allowed every opportunity of trying their hands at bigger jobs by deputizing for their superiors. Every person concerned must also be made aware of the importance of a planned career and of the self-development steps he must take, through personal study and reading, to equip himself for promotion. For their part, all senior managers must accept that the organization's dependence on the successful career development of their subordinates must take precedence over the convenience of their own local operations. They must therefore be prepared to give up subordinates for other jobs and take on in their place people from elsewhere in the organization who will be less knowledgeable but are themselves in need of instruction and broader experience.

This method of transferring staff to gain experience is a common means of training. As already mentioned, job rotation* is very useful in developing people early on in their careers, but may not be such good practice at senior levels. Where it is used for management trainees, great care must be taken in handling relationships between them and other staff within the departments through which they move. Trainees who are clearly destined for top jobs can arouse great jealousy, so their own behaviour needs to be circumspect and tactful at all times. If they are given projects to carry out, the limits of their authority as regards departmental supervisors must be precisely defined, and it is better for them not to be given a completely free hand.

More and more universities and colleges of technology are opening management departments, and the Diploma in Management Studies is now recognized as a qualification demanding a high calibre of student. Visits to other organizations can be of great value especially if the trainees are briefed beforehand on what they can expect to see: points of similarity and contrast with their own organization's structure and methods should

* Chapter 6, page 90.

be indicated and discussed on these occasions. It might even be possible to make mutual arrangements for trainees to spend longer periods of time with each other's firms, if potential advantages are obvious.

Many organizations send their managers on residential courses at a variety of staff colleges and management centres. The Administrative Staff College at Henley and the Business Schools at London and Manchester are perhaps the most famous of these in Britain; but several banks and many large private companies, for example, have their own staff colleges—all offering courses designed to stretch the intellectual ability of those attending and to provide close contact with other practising managers. External courses perhaps have the added advantage of getting members away from the possibly parochial atmosphere of their own industries. (Shown below are the content and methods of a management training course, designed to last eight weeks, which has been adapted from the programme of my own staff college.)

But the key factor in all these approaches and methods is the continuous inter-face between the manager concerned and his own immediate superior. One important question in any performance appraisal scheme is to ask the boss—what specific action do *you personally* intend to take to develop your subordinate or to remedy his shortcomings? Only after they have together considered what can be done to bring about development and improvement should they call in (if at all necessary) the management training specialist.

Even then, senior staff must be pressed further to secure an absolute commitment to action. A written policy, for example, will indicate sincerity about training: the 3M company policy on management development states, 'Every manager will plan, organize, and delegate to allow himself sufficient time to (*a*) participate in activities planned to further his own development and (*b*) assist in the development of his immediate subordinates.' As a further check on positive action, there is then a clear directive—'The achievement of effective results in the development of his immediate subordinates will be an important factor in the appraisal of a manager's results.'

AN EIGHT-WEEK SENIOR MANAGEMENT COURSE— OUTLINE OF CONTENT AND METHOD

1. *Membership*

The Course is multi-disciplinary in nature and is intended for twenty-four senior members of the health service professions, normally at the second in line officer level. In addition to the nursing and administrative

professions, officers from the specialist functions, e.g. work study, supplies
and engineering are also included.

2. *Duration*

The Course is of eight weeks' duration based on a five-day working week
with a mid-course long weekend break. All members return for a two-day
review conference a year after completion of the course.

3. *Timetable*

The programmed hours for the eight weeks amount to approximately
212. Normally four periods of $1-1\frac{1}{2}$ hours are scheduled per day, but on
average one of these periods each week is set aside for private study and
reading. In addition to this, members have to devote a considerable amount
of extra time to reading and work in connection with projects in their own
time in the evenings—probably a further ten hours per week on average.

4. *Objectives*

The purpose of the course is to improve the managerial effectiveness
of individuals in the health services.

Specifically, the expectations are that the experience of the course will
enable the individual member to:

(*a*) gain an increased comprehension of systems related to health—organizational, economic, social, political and environmental;

(*b*) comprehend a range of management techniques and their application;

(*c*) develop logical and analytical skills;

(*d*) evaluate individual and organizational performance;

(*e*) gain more insight into his own motivation and the effect of his behaviour on others in the work situation;

(*f*) develop the ability to innovate and achieve change.

5. *Content*

The following analysis indicates the broad content of the course together
with the approximate time allocated to each area of learning:

	Hrs
(*a*) The economic and social setting of the health service	22
(*b*) Structures of Organizations, including the principles of manage-ment organization analysis, and the application of social science to the study of the structure and management of the health service.	34
(*c*) Management and the individual—including the techniques of personnel management, development of personnel policies, com-munications, styles of management, sources of motivation and morale and group decision processes.	38

Hrs

(*d*) The skills of management including Management by Objectives, Management Audit and Management Survey. 19

(*e*) Management on a technical basis:

    (*a*) Finance 6

    (*b*) Statistical methods and Health Statistics 6

    (*c*) Cost benefit analysis. 6

    (*d*) Management's use of specialists and techniques such as Work Study, Computers and data processing, etc. 15

(*f*) Planning of Health Care including Health Services in the Community. 32

(*g*) Management and Change. 14

(*h*) Course administration, orientation, personal interviews and private study periods. 28

220

N.B. This total exceeds that referred to in paragraph 3 due to double counting where private study is an optional alternative.

6. *Training methods*

The syndicate method is used extensively on the course with four syndicates each of six members, each syndicate being representative of the mix of professions on the course itself. The syndicates change three times during the course, once at the end of each of the first three projects.

A variety of other methods are used as the following analysis of a typical timetable shows:

Syndicate Projects	33 *per cent*
Visits	8 *per cent*
Films	4 *per cent*
Exercises (including role playing)	15 *per cent*
Lectures and discussions	32 *per cent*
Private Study	8 *per cent*

THE CIRCUIT SCHEME

The *circuit scheme* of exchange visits is another useful training device for senior staff, whereby teams of managers visit each others' organizations, with collective meetings arranged between the teams and between individual specialist executives making up the teams. The purpose is for each person to report back on the differences in method, approach, and costs observed, and suggest points about his own organization which might be investigated. Where such exchanges can be made, teams might be made up of a representative of general management, an accountant, a production engineer, a work study officer, salesman, and personnel officer.

Obviously this can be done much more easily in the public services than in private industry where secrets have to be safeguarded against competitors. Where this method has been tried between administrators from different hospitals, for instance, quite dramatic results have been achieved. Examples of the conclusions from one such series of meetings include: re-siting of time-keeping clocks; supervision over certain grades of staff to be strengthened; the P.A.B.X. telephone system to be introduced; variations in costs for cleaning services to be investigated; further discussions to be held on the benefits of direct labour or contract labour for maintenance work; and the saving of appreciable sums of money by making certain medical equipment locally. The general feeling was that the exercise was a great stimulation to all those who took part in it. Every member of each of the teams gained some new idea that he was anxious to put into practice, and they all felt that their outlook had been considerably broadened.

TRAINING PERSONNEL MANAGERS

Reference has already been made (p. 164) to the development of modular training schemes. One important report* advocates their use in training specialists in personnel management through an initial course, cohesive and theoretically orientated but providing introductory practice in basic skills, and a second stage involving a selection of appropriate modules, each of which would deal in depth with specific areas of personnel management. The content of the initial course, for people entering personnel management, would be related to the kinds of work likely to be encountered early in their careers. No attempt would be made at this stage to provide a package of knowledge and expertise in techniques for use later in higher posts, for this would be educationally inefficient and, because of the rapid development of personnel work, would be out of date by the time of use. A fivefold structure is put forward as the best means of achieving this early understanding of personnel management:

1. Basic knowledge—for example, industrial and trade union law, how I.T.B.s operate, and the main sources of staffing information and statistics.
2. Behavioural sciences.
3. Industrial psychology.
4. The organizational role of personnel, especially manpower planning.

* 'A Modular Approach to Training', by the 'Edinburgh Group', *Personnel Management*, July 1969, page 28f.

5. Fundamental techniques—for example, job analysis and interviewing.

Subsequent training should consist of short, intensive courses on
particular techniques or aspects of personnel management in which there is
a desire to specialize. Teaching in this manner should be much more
effective than in general courses: it can incorporate the most recent developments, and is likely to stay fresh in the trainee's mind. The modules
themselves could change from time to time, reflecting the development of
training needs.

The whole concept can perhaps be best presented in the form of a
modular diagram (Figure 24), illustrating the subject-matter of the
specialized, intensive courses.

The D.E. report *Training for the Management of Human Resources** went
into greater detail in analysing the training needed by the professional
specialist to enable him to function as an integral part of an organization's
management team, making a cost-effective contribution towards achieving
its overall objectives. The report suggests that there are three levels of
intensity: common core knowledge and skills; general knowledge of
functional areas; and specific practitioner competencies.

The main functional areas are listed thus:

Organization Review and Analysis
The continuing review and analysis of an organization's operations in order
to determine appropriate work structures, roles, relationships, responsibilities and levels of authority.

Manpower Planning, Recruitment, and Selection
The forecasting and planning required to meet the present and future needs
of an organization for sufficient qualified people to man all its operations,
and the taking of the necessary steps to acquire them.

Manpower Training and Development
The provision of facilities and opportunities for people to acquire the skills
and knowledge needed to perform the jobs for which they are employed,
and to develop their own personal potential to meet the present and future
needs of the organization.

Industrial Relations
The promotion of effective communications between all parties in an
organization, and the establishment of procedures for the resolution of

*(H.M.S.O., 1972).

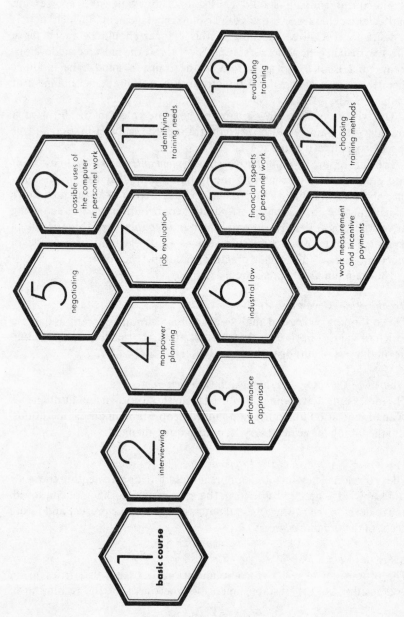

Figure 24. Modular diagram

personal and institutional differences, e.g. by means of collective bargaining and joint consultation.

Employee Remuneration

The development, implementation and administration of appropriate systems of remuneration (including, for instance, job evaluation, wage and salary structures, incentive payments, fringe benefits, and non-financial rewards).

Employee Services

The establishment of satisfactory services relating to the safety, health, and welfare of all employees.

Administration and Records

The design, implementation, and control of adequate records and administrative procedures to provide information for planning purposes and for the documentation of all employed personnel.

The ways in which these functions, and the degrees of competency required to work in them, interact, is illustrated by this diagram:

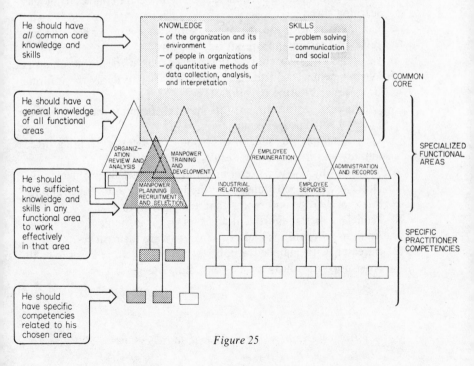

Figure 25

EVALUATION OF TRAINING

The purpose of evaluation is to determine whether or not the objectives and content of training courses are consistent with the aims and current needs of the organization; if these objectives are being reached in the most effective and economical manner; and, if not, what changes should be made. In the final analysis, of course, evaluation must be based on measuring the performance of employees before and after their training periods.

Comprehensive evaluation starts with assessing training plans in relation to defined needs based on job and task analysis. Decisions as to whether this training should be provided internally or through external courses must be kept under review. The quality of the methods, instructional materials and training aids must be assessed, as must be the ways of measuring students' progress during the training period. The results achieved on the completion of training can be examined, and subsequently the level and quality of employee performance can be appraised over a period of time.

The methods of evaluation have been listed* thus:

1. Comparison with the findings of educational research: for example, can programmed instruction be applied in specific courses to increase learning speed?
2. Comparison with job performance requirements, with continuous review to ensure appropriate adjustments.
3. Inspection of instructors, using a check-list of desirable qualities.
4. Written achievement tests, examining ability to apply the information received during training.
5. Questionnaires to trainees: this may be of limited value if trainees have no standards of comparison.
6. Questionnaires to supervisors—both to identify training needs initially and to specify the results of training.
7. Trainees' interviews—useful in highlighting specific problems.
8. Observation of performance on the job, before and after training.
9. Study of records and reports analysing achievements.
10. Proficiency tests: shorthand and typing, for example.
11. Analysis of problems and accidents, seeking their causes.
12. Research with matched groups, one having received training, the other not—obviously a time-consuming business.

* *Training and Development Journal*, May 1968, page 38f.

FURTHER READING

Approaches to Supervisory Development, by K. Thurley and H. Wirdenius (I.P.M., 1973).
Developing Effective Managers, by T. J. Roberts (I.P.M., 1967).
The Training of British Managers, by T. W. Leggatt, for the Institute of Manpower Studies (National Economic Development Office: H.M.S.O., 1972).

12 Wages and Salaries— the National Scene

COLLECTIVE BARGAINING

Until recent years, during which the Government has considered it necessary to exercise much more direct control over incomes, wage rates for the vast majority of workers were settled through the process of *collective bargaining*. This term relates to those arrangements under which wages and conditions of employment generally are decided by agreements negotiated between employers' and workers' organizations. Such agreements cover not only rates of pay, but may include working hours, special allowances for overtime, night duty, and shift work, piece-work rates, and other incentives, guaranteed minimum weekly payments, holidays, allocation of work, apprenticeships, and redundancy schemes.

An individual applying for a job may make his own private deal with a prospective employer, irrespective of the conditions of his new fellow-workers. An entirely different situation obtains when that employer is a member of an association which has signed an agreement with relevant trade unions about the conditions under which all workers in that industry will be engaged. The obvious advantages of this type of arrangement are that, on the one hand, all workers gain equality of conditions, and, on the other, every employer knows that his competitors who have signed the same agreement will not have lower wages costs than himself. Indeed, the significance is wider: for the terms of agreements are usually observed by employers throughout an industry, even if they are not actual signatories. Similarly, of course, the terms apply equally to all employees and not just to those who are members of the unions that successfully negotiated them (hence the main reason why union members object to working alongside non-union workers).

The development of collective bargaining practice has long rested on the principle that it is a voluntary system, depending on the mutual consent of both sides of industry and their loyal acceptance of decisions reached. This principle carries the implication that there will be no outside interference in the manner by which wages are settled; but economic circumstances in recent years have dictated otherwise, and there is now a large measure of policy control exercised by the Government.

As far as the *content* of collective agreements is concerned, basic wage rates are the prime consideration, of course; these are settled nationally in the first place, but usually leave scope for subsidiary or local agreements (as in the building industry). Trade unions always seek to maintain differentials between occupations, based on elements of skill, danger or variety in the work, and the actual scarcity of labour. More than one-third of the industrial workers in this country are at present operating on piece-rates or bonus systems. Rates for particular jobs are usually settled on the spot, although collective agreements often provide that incentives should enable an average worker to earn a specified amount, say 25 per cent, above the time rate. The extra effort of overtime working, night shifts, and weekend work are usually provided for, and minimum weekly pay may be guaranteed whether the full number of hours have been worked or not. Holiday payments are commonly settled, as in the past were sick pay benefits and compensation for redundancy, but these have increasingly come under statutory control.

FACTORS IN NEGOTIATING WAGES

The conclusion of most wage negotiations is a compromise, decided by the effective strength of each party's case. Their arguments have traditionally been based on the following factors:

1. INCREASES IN THE COST OF LIVING

Negotiations on this point revolve around movements in retail prices, since these directly influence the purchasing power of wage packets. But the volume of industrial production, labour costs, import prices, and wholesale prices all in turn affect the Index of Retail Prices, thus limiting the extent to which it can be used in wage negotiations. In any event, a narrower view of a particular industry usually needs to be taken, whereas the Index of Retail Prices is more a reflection of the state of the national economy as a whole. It may also be more important to consider earnings rather than basic wage rates; published sources (e.g. the *Department of Employment Gazette*) provide this information, so that average earnings for average hours worked can be compared with movements of retail prices to show whether *real wages* have risen or fallen.

2. PROSPERITY OF A FIRM OR INDUSTRY

Making sure that its members get 'a fair slice of the cake' is, of course, a main concern of every trade union, and frequent references will be made during negotiations to an industry's record of production and its financial position. The difficulty of applying this information, however, lies in apportioning the credit for improved performance, for example, between the shareholders' additional investment in new machinery and any increased effort on the part of the labour force. Higher dividends often lead to demands for higher wages: it is a complex subject when so many factors —such as managerial ability, financial turnover, size of funds for capital development, and delivery dates—all contribute to the higher dividend payments. But the fact remains that if the shareholders are consistently being made more prosperous, trade unions will press the claims of their members at the same time.

3. COMPARABILITY

Where the type of work carried out in different industries is similar, then wage rates in them will tend to keep close together. Although no two organizations are identical, the preparation of wage claims (done annually in many industries), involves careful consideration of increases awarded in other sectors, which may then be quoted in advocating the particular claim in hand.

The best-known example of comparability in practice is the Civil Service Pay Research Unit, which was created in 1956 to apply the techniques of fair comparison with outside organizations in determining salaries and working conditions for civil servants. But, however equitable this approach may appear in theory, many practical problems arise over the enormous amount of detail that accumulates during comparison studies; analysis takes longer, interpretation varies, and inevitably there are considerable delays in settling a claim.

4. TRADITION

The history and development of different industries and the unions associated with them vary greatly and have brought about differences in approach towards negotiations. Improvements in conditions do not always relate mainly to wage rates; factors of security of employment, higher status for manual workers, fringe benefits, shorter hours, and longer holidays—all these to some extent depend on traditional attitudes taken towards negotiations by both employers' federations and unions. The amount of progress already made generally as regards wages or various aspects of working conditions will also be a significant factor in determining the future policy of both bodies.

5. THE INCOMES NORM

Until the early nineteen-sixties, it would have been accurate to say that wage rates were influenced almost entirely by the four factors described above. But since 1960 successive governments have been much more insistent on measures to tackle inflation and balance of payments problems, and the concept of an *incomes norm* has been added to the relevant factors in wage negotiations. This norm, officially published or unofficially observed by the Government, depending on the party in power, specifies the average rate of annual increase of money incomes per head that is consistent with stable prices.

6. PAY RELATIVITIES

Relationships between the pay of different groups of employees lies at the heart of all pay determination. Relativities are inherently complex, being influenced by economic, social, and institutional factors which are often difficult to reconcile; but two factors are of major importance—the labour market and fairness.

In so far as pay relativities reflect differences in skill and responsibilities sought for particular kinds of employment, they help to distribute available manpower between jobs, occupations, and industries in accordance with the varying demands for workers' services. But, on the other hand, people's views of the fairness of their pay in relation to that of others frequently lead to pressures for changes in wage levels, and these may conflict with the operation of market forces. Fairness is subjective in the first place, and liable to change in meaning as circumstances change.

Collective bargaining usually facilitates the settlement of pay differences within single negotiating units (differentials), but there is no machinery for dealing with pay differences between different negotiating units (relativities). Although adjustments to relativities which occur all the time improve the position of some groups in relation to others, the effects are often offset wholly or in part as the result of later negotiations in which those others seek to restore their former relative positions.

Claims for changes in relativities are based largely on comparisons, which may be made between specific jobs with broadly similar skills and responsibilities, or they may be expressed as a generalized reference to movements in average pay for all jobs or for some large category like manual or non-manual occupations. Negotiators rarely confine themselves to one type of comparison, nor do they wish comparisons to be the sole determinant of pay; furthermore, each group has justifiable reasons for preferring one kind of comparison to another. There is no simple, universal set of pay comparisons which can be urged on all groups, and no single technique of general application for solving relativity problems.

Thus the task of devising procedures for considering claims by groups for a relative improvement of their position in the community is formidable—not least because of the absence of agreed criteria for deciding what relationships should be changed, and how this can be done in a manner that is fair to both beneficiaries and those whose relative position would become worse. Fairness, after all, is in the eye of the beholder, and the basic objectives of trade unions are to protect and improve the lot of their members—not to be fair to each other or to the community at large. The great practical difficulty is the need for consensus: 'on the assumption that the amount available for all wage increases in limited, other groups of employees must bear the cost of any special treatment. In other words, the relative position of some workers can only improve if others suffer. Will the unions representing the latter ever accept the reality of this situation?'*

GOVERNMENT INTERVENTION

There have always been exceptions to the principle of complete freedom of action on the part of employers and unions in wage negotiations. The need for some form of compulsory control during war-time was obvious, of course, but apart from this there has been the need to afford extra protection to less well organized groups of employees. The best known examples in practice are wages councils, the Terms and Conditions of Employment Act, 1959, and Fair Wages Resolutions. The Government's own role as an employer, directly or indirectly, of nearly a quarter of the total working population also has an obvious influence on policies concerning wages and conditions.

WAGES COUNCILS

Some 3½ million workers in Great Britain have their conditions determined by agreements which are enforceable at law, rather than being based on the voluntary acceptance of collective bargains. Examples of the types of workers covered are: baking, boot and shoe repairing, hairdressing, laundry workers, milk distribution, tailoring, the retail food trade, road haulage, and toy manufacture. Regulations affecting the wages and conditions of all these workers are decided by wages councils, the activities of which are provided for mainly by the Wages Council Act, 1959, which consolidates a large amount of previous legislation. The other significant statute is the Agricultural Wages Act, 1948, covering some 800,000 agricultural workers.

The constitution of a wages council allows for equal numbers of members representing employers and workers, together with not more than three independent members (often drawn from universities and the legal

* 'Problems of Pay Relativities': Pay Board Advisory Report 2 (Cmnd. 5535, H.M.S.O., 1974).

profession): the Minister usually appoints one of these three as chairman. In fact, he appoints all the members of wages councils, bearing in mind the main types of establishment and classes of workers affected and the principal centres in which they are employed. A council's actual work is concerned with fixing minimum wages, holidays and holiday pay, and with making proposals with regard to any other conditions of employment in the industry concerned.* Minimum remuneration may be laid down in respect of time rates or piece-work rates covering a large number of specified operations.

Wage regulation proposals must be published in the *London Gazette* and details must be sent to every employer affected. In turn, employers must exhibit the proposals so that workers can read them. Employers or workers may then make representations to their wages council within fourteen days and, after considering these, the council will submit its proposals with such amendments as it thinks fit to the Minister. The Minister will then either make a wages regulation order to give the proposals legal effect, or refer them back to the council for reconsideration as a whole; he cannot reject or amend the proposals submitted. Wages regulation orders made by the Minister to give effect to the proposals of wages councils are issued as statutory instruments, and wages paid to workers must not be less than the minimum fixed by these orders. Employers must keep records of payments of wages for three years and these must be made available to the Wages Inspectorate.

There has been mounting criticism in recent years from trade unions who allege that, although wages councils were created to protect workers, nowadays they protect employers instead. In particular, union leaders point out the facts that wage council awards are generally smaller than those obtained through collective bargaining,that trade unions have comparatively little influence on the awards, and that it is the employers who want to retain wages councils rather than replace them with any other system of wage negotiation. On the other hand, unions find it very difficult to organize workers in those industries affected by wages councils—thousands of small hairdressing shops, for example. They are industries which employ a large proportion of women who tend to show little interest in union membership; many workers reject unions simply because they can see no advantage in contributing to union funds when their wages are fixed by law in any case. Small wonder that union officers become disillusioned with recruitment drives aimed at such workers. On the whole, it seems a moot point whether employers would be more able and willing to cope with the new situation if legal protection were replaced by voluntary bargaining in many of

* The powers of wages councils are extended by the Employment Protection Act, 1975: they can now fix all terms and conditions of service.

these industries. In any event, current economic conditions indicate that changes designed to strengthen the position of low-paid workers would have to overcome another hurdle, for at present any new wage regulation orders can be easily controlled or delayed by the D.E. So Government policy inevitably means that it is going to be opposed to giving unions any greater freedom or autonomy when negotiating wages in the immediate future.

An alternative to both wages councils and voluntary bargaining would be a law setting a *national minimum wage,** enabling the earnings of the country's lowest paid workers to be kept under constant review. A model for this can be seen in the U.S.A., where the Fair Labor Standards Act, 1938, is now used to improve the purchasing power of underprivileged wage-earning groups. 'Imaginative legislation of this kind could conceivably play its part in the fulfilment of the seemingly disparate objectives of helping the underpaid, sustaining free collective bargaining, and bringing about an effective and socially just incomes policy.'

THE TERMS AND CONDITIONS OF EMPLOYMENT ACT, 1959, AND EMPLOYMENT PROTECTION ACT, 1975

Whether wages and conditions are settled by collective bargaining or by regulations issued by wages councils, the Government has given workers an extra measure of protection since the Terms and Conditions of Employment Act, 1959. This mainly concerned 'claims' which arose when a particular employer was alleged to have fallen short of the established terms and conditions which had been settled for that industry. The Act was repealed by the Employment Protection Act, 1975, and replaced by new provisions. These will enable a trade union or an employers' association to make a claim to A.C.A.S. that an employer is observing terms and conditions of employment which are less favourable than the recognized negotiated terms and conditions for the trade or industry. If there are no such terms and conditions, a union or an employers' association may claim that an employer is observing terms and conditions or employment less favourable than the general level in the same trade or industry in the district. A.C.A.S. may settle the claim by conciliation, but if this fails the claim can be referred to C.A.C. which may make an award.

---

* This argument is developed in a note on page 178 of *Personnel Management*. December 1966, by Dr. E. G. A. Armstrong: 'Public policy and the lower-paid worker—a national minimum.'

FAIR WAGES RESOLUTIONS

These express the will of Parliament about safeguarding the interests of workers employed by firms who are awarded Government contracts. Their basic purpose is to ensure that all such employers shall pay rates of wages and observe hours and conditions of employment not less favourable than those established generally by machinery for negotiations or by standard practice. The original aims were to prevent the 'sweated labour' of the nineteenth century and the abuses that arose from the sub-contracting of work.

To a large extent these aims were achieved by the Resolutions of 1891 and 1909, which were eventually superseded by the Resolution of 1946, with main provisions as follows:

1. Any employer undertaking work for the Government must pay wage rates and offer conditions not less favourable than those commonly accepted in the district.
2. If no such rates or conditions exist locally, then the contractor must offer conditions similar to those of other employers whose general circumstances in the same trade or industry are comparable.
3. The fair wage clause applies to all the employer's workpeople, not just those engaged on the government contract.
4. If sub-contractors are employed, the same obligations fall on them and the main contractor must ensure their observance.
5. All workers employed on the contract must be free to join trade unions if they wish.

To try to ensure that everyone is aware of these obligations, a copy of the Fair Wages Resolution must be displayed at every place of work of the contractor. Any disputes that arise may be referred by the Secretary of State to an independent tribunal.

THE GOVERNMENT AS AN EMPLOYER

The Government itself employs a very large labour force—some $5\frac{1}{4}$ million people working in the public sector as civil servants, local authority employees, or for nationalized industries. The basic problem is that most of these work in 'non-productive' services which have inflexible wage rates. Although incomes compare unfavourably with those in private industry, where incentive payments greatly increase take-home earnings, these workers are often unable or unwilling to take militant action or strike to further their interests. For its part, the Government's problem is to reconcile its role as an employer of large numbers of workers with its wider responsibilities not to allow wage increases which might harm the national economy. Indeed, in the past, the Government has rejected specific pay increases (for example, in 1961 to teachers and local government officers): such action naturally causes great resentment among public service staffs affected, who argue that the Government takes advantage of its position to single them out for special treatment, making its own employees bear the brunt of any sacrifices that have to be made.

It is in this area of public employment that the Government has been urging a wider view than the 'fair comparison' formula allows, and insisting that the country's economic difficulties will never be solved unless wage increases are restricted to what can be afforded. Wages must not be allowed to increase on average faster than the average increase in national productivity. The public sector has features that make it easier to apply a national wages policy: the Government clearly has the necessary authority, as far as its own employees are concerned, and the wage negotiating machinery itself is centralized and uniform. Not that the public sector should be treated in isolation, but, in terms of number of employees alone, it will inevitably play an important role in wages policy. An answer must therefore be found to the problems of ensuring that public servants do not suffer a pay disadvantage compared with workers in private industry, especially in those services, such as the railways, which are run at a loss.

ATTEMPTS AT A NATIONAL WAGES POLICY

THEORY

By and large, collective bargaining as a method of negotiating wages and conditions has a history of success throughout British industry, and most agreements have been reached without disputes involving stoppages of work. Even so, the system has been subject to mounting criticism over the years:

1. The 'pattern' which has emerged encourages inflation, since wage increases agreed in key industries tend to be followed by claims in less prosperous industries with arguments based on comparability and their need to maintain traditional pay differentials.
2. National negotiations about basic wage rates are unrealistic, because the minimum rate under review will invariably be earned by only a tiny minority of workers in that industry: 'local circumstances' are such that actual earnings usually far exceed the basic rates.

Despite these criticisms, employers and trade unions alike have consistently declared their opposition to any policy superimposed from outside taking the place of the free collective bargaining process. Yet, since the early nineteen-sixties, the view has strongly developed that the determination of wage rates cannot be left exclusively to a system that involves sectional claims by trade unions, piecemeal bargaining, and eventual compromises motivated by self-interest. More and more the Government has insisted on the concept of a national wages policy taking the place of such methods, as one means of trying to ensure a measure of stability in the national economy. The 'pay pause' and the 'guiding light' of the late nineteen-fifties were policies with this end in view, as was the creation of the National Economic Development Council ('Neddy') and the National Board for Prices and Incomes.

But the theory of a national wages policy is beset with many problems. In the first place, all-round increases obviously will not promote efficiency. What is needed is a system which allows wages to rise in expanding sectors relative to contracting industries; otherwise labour costs in the latter will be too high to enable them to recapture demand, while the former will have no inducements to attract the extra labour required. Secondly, criteria must be found on which to base changes in wages. To use solely 'increased productivity' is too simple an approach, for any improvements must be measured against general industrial stability: in an inflationary economy, therefore, this proposal would be doomed from the outset. Nor can 'cost of living' be used exclusively, because there would be no reward to workers for increased productivity nor any incentive towards greater efficiency. Thirdly, no policy involving the central control of wages, while leaving salaries, fees, dividends, and other forms of income uncontrolled, would be acceptable to trade unions or to workers at large. (Indeed, the converse view can be taken, that if only rational price and dividend policies could be devised, then many wages problems would disappear.)

Certain guarantees are therefore necessary before trade unions can be expected to give up any part of their traditional freedom to negotiate wages and conditions and accept a policy of wage restraint:

1. Real wages must be maintained in the face of rises in the cost of living.
2. Real incomes must improve as productivity increases throughout the economy.
3. There must be provisions for wage flexibility: for example, to reward special skills or to induce labour mobility.
4. The national system of planning and control must ensure that any extra effort or any concessions by workers would not be dissipated by wasteful Government expenditure in other directions.
5. Unions must be given assurances about their members' future, as far as an adequate rate of investment in industry can promise this.
6. The Government must check inflation and keep prices steady: this may demand rent controls and action against monopolies, *inter alia*.
7. A socially just budget must be enacted year by year, widening the tax base, attacking business 'perks' and expense accounts, closing avoidance loop-holes, and ensuring that a fair proportion of capital gains pass into the national exchequer.

It is part of the growth of economic realism that most of these measures, which only a few years ago would have been dismissed as political cant, are now widely accepted as part of the give-and-take that is essential in trying to create conditions of economic stability and growth that will benefit the nation as a whole.

PRACTICE

Nothing has spotlighted more clearly the difficulties of putting all this theory into practice than the concept of *wages drift*, which describes the success of some sections of the labour force in evading Government efforts to try to restrain the size of wage increases. It is largely attributable to the increased control over earnings by local shop stewards, who continuously aim at pushing the price of labour upwards. The personnel manager, for his part, must try to ensure that the wages paid by his firm are fair in the light of what it can afford. He may feel some concern for the national economy and the Government's policy, but he also has to face up to the practical reality of keeping his firm's production lines running smoothly.

Certain criteria* for judging whether or not increases in prices and money incomes were in the national interest existed during the period 1965–72:

1. Trends in national productivity.

2. Considerations of the national interest—

    (*a*) affecting prices: a sound price policy would depend on vigorous efforts by management to increase efficiency, to avoid cost increases, and wherever possible to stabilize or reduce prices;

    (*b*) affecting incomes policy: a 'norm' must be laid down indicating the average rate of annual increase of money incomes per head which is consistent with stability in the general level of prices.

3. Employment incomes: the new element in the Government's policy was its insistence on an incomes norm becoming the most prominent factor in wage negotiations.

Increases in wages and salaries above the norm had to be confined to cases in which exceptional treatment could be shown to be required in the national interest. Such exceptional increases would have to be balanced by lower-than-average increases to other groups if the overall increase in wages and salaries was to be kept within the norm.

* Prices and Incomes Policy: Cmnd. 2639 (H.M.S.O., 1965).

Exceptional pay increases were to be confined to the following circumstances:

1. Where employees accepted more exacting work or a major change in working practices, thus directly contributing to increased productivity in a firm or industry.

2. Where the national interest dictated a change in the distribution of manpower, and a pay increase would be both necessary and effective for this purpose.

3. Where it was generally recognized that existing wage and salary levels were too low to maintain a reasonable standard of living.

4. Where the pay of a certain group of workers had fallen seriously out of line with the level of remuneration for similar work and should be improved in the national interest.

5. General considerations to promote social justice, which included an appraisal of the way the distribution of the national income was being affected by the prices and incomes policy; for example, the Government pledged itself to correct any excessive growth in aggregate profits compared with the growth of wages and salaries.

Legislation in the form of the Prices and Incomes Acts of 1966 and 1968 gave the Government powers to impose a standstill on specified price rises and wage increases, and allowed it to impose heavy fines on offending firms, trade unions or individuals. No increases were permitted without Ministerial consent. Controversial as this legislation was, completely at odds with British traditions of free collective bargaining, the Government insisted on having these powers in reserve in order to deter the uncooperative selfish minority. Policy was aimed at trying to establish a sound basis for the resumption of sustained economic growth, and it was widely accepted that priority should continue to be given to encouraging settlements that promoted productivity and tried to increase the wages of low-paid workers.

Sound as this policy may have seemed, events conspired against it. Price stability became confused with other industrial relations problems, especially the control of strikes, after the Donovan Commission Report (*see* Chapters 14–15). Ultimately, in 1969, the Labour Government promised the T.U.C. to think again about its statutory incomes policy, in return for only the most general undertaking on the T.U.C.'s part about strike controls. The impression emerged that the Government was less concerned with price stability than with industrial peace, almost at any price, and the net result was an increase in both the size of wage claims and the incidence of strikes.

The Conservative Party was returned to power in 1970 and quickly abrogated the existing prices and incomes policy, disbanding the machinery created to administer it. To some extent this was replaced by the Office of Manpower Economics, set up to service three public sector pay review bodies: one for 'top' public servants, one for the Armed Forces, and the third for doctors and dentists in the National Health Service. This new Office also carries out *ad hoc* enquiries into pay structures, and conducts research into pay and manpower problems; for example, its early operations embraced studies of measured day work, equal pay, and the relationship between wage determination and earnings movements.

Whether there should be statutory control of wages, or whether collective bargaining should become a voluntary activity once again, was a major political issue during the two general elections of 1974. During the election campaigns the Labour Party, supporting a return to voluntary negotiation of wages, claimed to have a *social contract* with the T.U.C., whereby vigorous action on a Labour Government's part to control prices and to operate a fair and socially equitable policy on taxation, housing, pensions, and other social services would be reciprocated by the operation of voluntary restraint on incomes by the unions. T.U.C. officials and union leaders also stated that in return for programmes of economic advance and social equity, the trade union movement would respond by tempering wage demands in the light of the economic situation facing the country. But observance of the social contract during a period of runaway inflation became so hotly disputed that, in July 1975, the Government determined that pay increases during the ensuing year should be pegged to a maximum of £6 a week. For 1976–7, a maximum of £4 per week was fixed.*

One of the difficulties of persuading the unions to accept any form of restraint on their freedom of action is the uncertainty about exactly what they want. 'Complete freedom' does not in fact mean that 'everything is up for grabs', for most unions are deeply committed, for example, to policies which aim at greater social justice through some redistribution of real incomes. This is not simply a belief that employment incomes should rise at the expense of profits or unearned incomes; it also encompasses a concern for the conditions of low-paid workers, for the sick and unemployed, and for pensioners. A realistic attempt to tackle these broad issues was seen in the setting up of the *Royal Commission on Incomes Distribution* in 1974 to report on such matters concerning the current distribution of

---

* At the time of writing this footnote, the prospect of a third year of closely-defined restraint, as opposed to impatient union demands for a return to free collective bargaining, was very much in the balance.

personal incomes, both earned and unearned, as may be referred to it by the Government. It will conduct special enquiries, for example on top salaries and directors' remuneration, self-employment incomes, and the control of dividends. Organizations such as the T.U.C. and C.B.I. are consulted about the membership, duties, and enquiries of the Commission, which will work in close co-operation with other organizations involved in related areas: these include the Advisory, Conciliation and Arbitration Service, the Pay Review Bodies, the N.E.D.C., the Price Commission, and advisory bodies on employment and social security. Thus the many threads of linking the control of prices, incomes, and industrial relations are woven ever closer together in an attempt to project and foster the interests of the nation as a whole.

SUCCESS OR FAILURE? THE WAY AHEAD

It now seems generally accepted that, during the 1960s, the prices and incomes policy did enable the Government to keep inflation within tolerable limits with less unemployment than there would otherwise have been. Large pay and price increases were postponed at times when they would have embarrassed the economy, and the policy helped, by encouraging productivity bargaining and managerial efficiency, to accelerate economic growth. The general advocacy of more rational pay structures may also have resulted in some groups of workers (but certainly not all) coming to feel that there was more equity in the system than in a free-for-all.

Modest as they were, these were real achievements—so what went wrong? Basically, the refusal of trade unions, which exist to improve their members' terms of employment, and firms, which exist to maximize their shareholders' profits, to accept for any prolonged period severe restraints on their freedom to exploit such positions of strength as they may possess. Frustration at the failure of real incomes to rise, after tax, is another part of the same story, for it tends to increase trade union militancy. A growing realization that the policy was being applied more firmly to wages than prices did not help. Income norms were expressed in precise terms, but price norms were qualified by policy statements about rising costs or the financing of necessary new investment. Little attempt seemed to be made in practice to offset any price increases with reductions elsewhere, as had been promised.

Another objective of the prices and incomes policy was to raise the relative position of lower-paid workers, but it failed partly because no definition of 'low pay' was ever agreed. In many cases attempts to improve the lot of these groups of workers was inhibited because there was no way of preventing similar increases being passed up the scale to higher paid workers in the same industry, in order to maintain previous pay differentials. Wages drift went on, too, so that employees who shared in bonus and other incentive schemes benefited markedly; other workers, largely in the public sector, whose jobs could not be measured thus in production terms, fell further behind.

Productivity bargaining, intended to be a main exception to the restraint policy, often exacerbated the situation. It was justified at the outset because workers involved would be increasing the intensity of their efforts or the scope of their responsibilities, which also meant that the nation would benefit. In fact, although some productivity bargains were genuine, many others were struck just to prevent industrial conflict, and meant nothing— so much so that they became a loophole in the incomes policy. This is the only possible conclusion when reflecting on the distinctly marginal improvement to the rate of national economic growth achieved by some thousands of such agreements. Much of the productivity growth achieved might well have happened in any case, as technological advances inevitably brought about changes in working methods or as troublesome pay systems came up for revision. All that many so-called productivity bargains actually did, then, was to justify exceptional wage increases. With hindsight, it seems obvious, too, that productivity develops much more rapidly in some industries than others, due to such inherent factors as the nature of their technology or the rate of capital investment; so workers in such industries were lucky, and they gained more in wage increases than employees of the social services, for example, where it is difficult to measure productivity.

The rapid spread of workplace bargaining in recent years was largely encouraged by the prices and incomes policy and recognized by the Donovan Commission report. Yet, in practice, it conflicted with the declared objectives of the Government, for it proved comparatively easy for workplace negotiations to avoid close scrutiny under the incomes policy controls. That some workers were able to benefit doubly—from national agreements and from workplace bargains—was a situation that the policy mechanisms were never able to counter effectively. In fact, it must be recognized that all attempts by individual organizations to undertake local negotiation of wages and other conditions of employment serve to add an inflationary element to the industrial relations system. Any decentralization of such activity makes it less amenable to incomes policy restraints.

A third set of objectives was considered by many to be the most important—to improve payments systems and industrial relations generally and to make the labour market work more smoothly. But traditional factors cannot easily be set aside. For example, customary ideas of equitable wage relativities, usually relying on the principle of fair comparisons, were expressly forbidden by the policy; yet this remains probably the most important single factor in the minds of workers, for it is logical and just that people working with comparable skills, effort and conditions should be paid equally.

In trying to look ahead and assess if it is at all possible to make progress in this difficult area, it is clear that the basic economic problems remain the same: the achievement of price stability, together with full employment, an adequate balance of payments, and a positive growth rate in the national economy. At the same time 'fair comparison' as a factor in pay-determination will have to be observed, and the problem of the lower-paid tackled more resolutely.

There can be no avoiding the fact that compulsive comparisons are the mainspring of many claims: miners, railwaymen, postmen, and nurses alike have based recent claims on the positions they feel they should occupy in some sort of national hierarchy of wages and esteem. One way* of trying to resolve the dilemma of relating public to private sector wage levels is to compare the former with wages in the manufacturing economy by a combination of job evaluation and nationally-agreed wage regulators. But this in turn would depend on the freedom of private firms to negotiate wage settlements using the labour share of added value to the basic control index. This scheme is based on the principle that a certain ratio—for

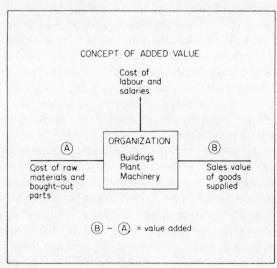

Figure 26

*'Relating Public To Private Sector Wages', by G. H. Webb, *Personnel Management*, February 1974.

example, labour cost/sales value – is allocated as an entitlement for wages. Any surplus arising from the difference between this entitlement and the actual wage costs creates a bonus fund which is apportioned between the firm and the participants in predetermined proportions. Such an approach would avoid periodic 'special cases' pleading by providing for a continuous process of pay settlements which reflects adjustments and adaptation to social and economic changes.

This formula recognizes that the prime source of the national revenue is that generated by the manufacturing industries: the earnings of their workers are what public services employees compare their own wages with. It is also a fair assumption that those industries which generate the highest added value per employee are those which reach settlements most satisfactory to the trade union movement. As the highest levels of added value correlate with the levels of investment, it follows that the economic performance of these companies best serves the national interest. So the manufacturing industry would reach wage settlements within a mathematically derived relationship between its total pay bill and its added value of production: the State would then carry out its own evaluation and pay grading programmes in order to regulate the wages and salaries of its own employees. As a starting point in this exercise, of course, there are many employees who do comparable jobs with those in industry, while others can be related to industrial practice by acceptable analogies. Indeed, important rudiments of such an approach already exist within the Civil Service Pay Research Unit and the Office of Manpower Economics, and the occupational links provided by jobs in the technician, maintenance, clerical, transport, and stores grades. The Government would thus acquire an effective method for managing the economy: a range of occupations and industries would be chosen as guiding lights of the wage economy, and a realistic effort made to ensure that the essential public services were staffed at competitive rates of pay by flexibly linking their wages and salaries to the producers of national wealth.

Another possible future development could be concentration on price stabilization – keeping the graph-line of *average* price increases horizontal.* This could be done by ensuring that rising prices are offset by falls elsewhere. Whatever Government agency might be devised to this end, it would have to be given strong power of enquiry and reserve powers of price control. Price targets would have an immediate effect on demands for wage increases, because employers would be prevented from passing on higher costs to the consumer. The strategy need not inhibit genuine productivity bargaining; at the same time it could check inequalities of pay

* Lerner Memorial Lecture, given by Professor H. A. Turner at Manchester University, February 1970.

developing as a result in areas where productivity naturally rises more quickly, by imposing tighter price targets in those sectors.

The whole question of Government control in this area remains topical, for the abandonment of a statutory prices and incomes policy was followed in Britain by a period of serious inflation. Achieving an objective of rising living standards without inflation requires steady economic expansion, careful price scrutiny, fiscal and social service measures designed to protect people with low or fixed incomes, measures to ensure the public accountability of private firms with significant market power, and broad agreement with the unions for the planned growth of incomes. A policy based on these factors carries conviction, because it clearly operates to the benefit of the majority of the population. At the same time, it seems that a workable incomes policy must be essentially voluntary: compulsion so antagonizes the parties that it is counter-productive.

LONG-TERM WAGE AGREEMENTS

Another variation on traditional practices can be seen in the way that many important industries and large groups of workers are now covered by long-term wage agreements which are increasingly taking the place of collective bargains which last only until the next claim is submitted (often within a year). Engineering and building workers, local authority staffs and manual workers, and those employed in electricity, gas, printing, and furniture manufacture are included in this new type of agreement: about 25 per cent of the working population (some seven million workers) are affected altogether.

When long-term agreements are negotiated only once every two or three years, the pressure on both employers and trade unions is clearly reduced. On one hand, employers, more confident of industrial stability, are better able to calculate the costs of future production, without having to face demands for higher wages; on the other, trade unions do not have to face the expense of frequent industrial action, especially strikes, in support of their wage claims. Overall, management can assume that the settlements reached under long-term agreements will not cost any more than those reached after annual wage negotiations. In any event, they are relieved of the practical periods of bargaining usually associated with recurrent wage demands and often accompanied by restrictions on output or strikes which further strain industrial relations. For their part, unions have usually been very satisfied with the size of the awards made under long-term agreements, especially when sliding scales have been included to protect their members against rises in the cost of living during the two or three year period negotiated. Union officers are thus left much freer to provide a fuller service to their members, when they no longer get caught up in annual wage negotiations. Finally, several unions seem to have regarded long-term agreements as providing the opportunity to try to achieve better fringe benefits and shorter hours on a phased basis for their members.

The advantages to both sides are such as to warrant the prediction that long-term agreements will play an increasingly prominent part in collective bargaining in Great Britain. In fact, improvements or refinements are already being suggested, along the lines of guaranteed annual wages, protection against temporary redundancy, better unemployment and sickness benefit schemes—all substituting long-term benefits for immediate wage increases, and together forming a much more complete plan for easing industrial tension. All this assumes that inflation can be kept in check, of course.

PROBLEMS OF LOW PAY

The intractability of the problem of low pay in industry continues to raise considerations of equity, the misuse and under-utilization of economic resources, and social policy regarding poverty. Before it was disbanded the National Board for Prices and Incomes completed a report* on the subject in which it concluded that there could be no single remedy for low pay since there was no single cause. An industry might be declining or might be faced with severe competition and falling profits; managements might be slack; the jobs themselves might be ill-suited to modern needs; workers might lack the skills necessary for better-paid jobs, or they might simply prefer convenient and undemanding work; trade union organization might be lacking or ineffective; wage-fixing arrangements might be inadequate; and wage-payment systems out of date.

The problems of low pay, however desirable it may be to alleviate it, is only one of our industrial problems, and it is primarily for the Government of the day to decide what priority should be attached to it. The role of trade unions is also crucial, as it is not at all easy to change differentials. The unions, however, have not been particularly energetic in trying to improve the relative position of low-paid workers, possibly because that would mean a relative worsening of the position of others.

In its report, the N.B.P.I. thought that the use of appropriate redistributive measures through the tax and social security system (rent rebates and family income supplements) was the most practical method of helping them. Can anything else be done, without running into the inflationary danger of pushing any increases gained further up the scale and without

* Cmnd. 4648 (H.M.S.O., 1971).

leaving particular groups of workers behind in the general upward movement of incomes? Perhaps a National Minimum Wage will some day be accepted. Although no such minimum has even been defined in Government policy, the arrangements made by wages councils, which cover nearly four million people, in effect amount to a statement of a national minimum wage. It is noticeable, for example, that all the wages councils' rates for unskilled men fall very near the median rate. Thus the Government could announce annually that it would approve an increase in the current average wages councils' rate for unskilled workers by a figure representing at least its estimate of the national average increase in all wage rates. Workers whose pay was lower than that average could also be brought up to that figure—thus achieving the desired effect of producing a bias in favour of the lowest-paid workers.

Two practical devices which have been applied to ease the lot of the lower-paid are lump-sum pay settlements and threshold agreements. The former are actual cash settlements, as opposed to percentage awards, so that everyone involved receives the same amount of extra cash in their pay-packets, and the lower-paid thus become somewhat better off in relative terms, compared with more highly paid workers. In 1972 a series of pay settlements took place on this basis, and in a few cases senior public servants gave up a proportion of their awards so that those receiving the lowest basic rates of pay could receive more. The Government's imposition of a £6 a week cash ceiling on 1975–6 pay increases is a more recent example.

While the statutory arrangements lasted, *The Price and Pay Code for Stage* III* included a 'threshold safeguard' which enabled pay to be increased as the cost of living rose: thus an extra 40p per week was paid when the Retail Price Index reached a mark seven per cent above that of October 1973, and further increases of 40p were paid for each subsequent one per cent rise. In the event, after five such payments had been made, it became open to question as to whether these payments were themselves further stoking the inflationary fires. But the fact is that in our kind of society it is impossible to have a system of total price control over all goods and services, so the application of threshold agreements must be viewed in this context. Import prices cannot be controlled, and comprehensive subsidies to prevent any increases in retail prices would be too expensive and distorting to resource allocation. Threshold agreements have their place in any form of broad agreements on the general rate of increase of money incomes which might, at least in part, replace a system of completely free, sectional, uncoordinated bargaining. They also impose a

*Cmnd. 5444 (H.M.S.O., 1973).

heavier responsibility on the Government to apply a more vigorous price policy, which is no bad thing in the battle against inflation.

THE EQUAL PAY ACT
AND SEX DISCRIMINATION ACT

The perennial controversy about equal pay and conditions for men and women doing the same jobs was statutorily resolved by the Equal Pay Act, 1970, through its three main provisions:

Section 1 (4) requires pay to be equal where it can be shown that a woman's work is the same or broadly similar to the work of a man in the same employment;

Section 1 (5) refers to job evaluation: jobs normally done by both men and women must be evaluated by the same criteria, and must not be given different ratings because of the sex of the workers concerned;

Section 3 refers to collective agreements; if these contain discriminatory clauses, they may be reported to the Industrial Court (now the Industrial Arbitration Board) which is given power to amend them.

Legislation of this nature is one thing, however, but does it get to the root of discrimination against women in employment? Feminists have always claimed that women's pay is low because the male and female labour markets are separate, the latter mainly confined to lower-paid jobs. If that analysis is correct, the position can only be improved fundamentally by allowing women to take jobs hitherto reserved for men. Employers' attitudes and prejudices thus remain the chief obstacles to real progress.

The problems of the training and maximum utilization of the married woman returning to work when her children are old enough needs to be dealt with (*see* Chapter 7). It is believed that such employees are often absent and that their wastage rate is high, but research shows that, as the level of women's employment rises, so their reliability and stability increases: in other words, the better the job, the greater are the efforts made to hang on to it.

The Act called for equality of pay by 1975. The D.E. calculated that the cost of this would amount to some $3\frac{1}{2}$ per cent of the national salaries and wages bill. Indirect costs could add an even greater proportion, depending on the strength of male opposition and insistence on maintaining traditional differentials. Carried to its ultimate extreme, of course, this would destroy the whole purpose of the Act. Employers, therefore, claim that they must be allowed greater flexibility in the employment of women, especially as regards hours of work and shift working. In other words, the present situation is one of 'wanting both the penny and the bun'.

In the long term, equal pay offers considerable potential economic gains. Faced with higher labour costs, employers will seek to make better use of women at work. The integration of the male and female labour markets should, in turn, have a double benefit: women will produce work of higher value than at present, and their influx into new occupations will ease any existing shortages of manpower, which is a root cause of wages drift.

It may be difficult to implement the Act. Appeals about the correct evaluation of women's jobs compared with men's may present particular problems. Traditionally, such matters are best resolved by negotiation between local experts, familiar with the detailed structure of an industry. The D.E.'s own conciliation officers can often lend a useful hand here. Such arrangements seem much more sensible than the proposal to refer appeals to industry tribunals, which normally deal with matters of fact or law: trying to resolve differences of opinion would impose a potentially overwhelming work-load.

Policy stated in the White Paper *Equality for Women* (H.M.S.O., 1974) tackles the whole question of discrimination against women, not only in employment and training, but in education, housing accommodation, the provision of goods, services and facilities and advertising. A Bill* is to be put before Parliament which makes it unlawful to discriminate on grounds of sex or marriage as regards recruitment or opportunities for training or promotion, or in actions which may be detrimental to employees such as short-time working or dismissals. The only exceptions intended are the clergy, armed forces, and cases where a person's sex can be shown to be a genuine occupational qualification for a particular job: also the special provisions relating to women in the Factories Act, 1961 remain in being.

Complaints are heard by industrial tribunals after initial consideration by officers of the independent Advisory, Conciliation and Arbitration Service, who try to help the parties reach a settlement. A tribunal, satisfied that unlawful discrimination has occurred, can award compensation or recommend a particular course of action. If the discrimination is in a general form, then the case may be forwarded to the Equal Opportunities Commission for consideration.

The main functions of the E.O.C. are: to investigate areas covered by the Act and to take action to eliminate unlawful practices; to assist and represent individual complainants in appropriate cases; to conduct enquiries into matters affecting the relative positions and opportunities of the sexes; and to conduct research and take action to educate and persuade

* Now the Sex Discrimination Act, 1975.

public opinion. When an unlawful practice is disclosed, the Commission has the power to issue 'non-discriminatory notices' which can, if breached, be enforced through the civil court. It can also seek a general injunction, in the public interest, dealing with unlawful discriminatory practices.

13 Wages and Salaries—the Individual and Productivity

Within the framework of Government policy and national wage agreements signed by employers' federations and trade unions, each individual organization has to work out its own salvation. Its personnel manager will be expected to advise on how best to build up a wages structure which must primarily be attractive enough to ensure the recruitment and retention of a labour force of the right size and quality to meet the circumstances in which production is carried on. It will need to offer financial incentives to stimulate improvements in performance. Its own brand of personnel policy and attitudes towards human relations will also have an effect on remuneration, and it will have to take into account local representations on such matters as differentials. There is no one 'best' pay system capable of universal applications for the benefit of all, and because of the difficulties involved, it is imperative that pay should always be regarded as a most important aspect of management policy. One thing is certain—that inefficiency will follow from a poor wages system, even though the opposite cannot be proved. Highly paid executives may regard the minor anomalies of a complex pay structure in a large organization as trivial in the extreme; but the workers affected will see them simply as examples of unfairness, and their irritation will inevitably strain industrial relations.

By definition, the manager should be an agent of innovation, constantly seeking improvements in the use of production facilities for his organization to survive in an era of constantly rising costs. In fact, most managers feel themselves to be prisoners of their wages structures—for every change presents the unions with negotiating opportunities and confirms the benefits of intransigence. There may be many other serious defects in any particular wages structure: informal limits on work-efforts may hinder productivity; methods changes may be negotiated and subsequently forgotten; 'wages drift' realizes earnings over and above productivity agreements; supervisors become frustrated at the lack of discipline and corruption of work standards; unnecessary overtime is 'engineered'; senior managers have illusions about incentive schemes which they believe encourage high effort, but which supervisors know have long since been out-manoeuvred. The personnel specialist's role, in such situations must, in effect, be to return to first principles and then consider all relevant details in advising on a wages and salaries system appropriate to his own organization.

DIFFERENTIALS

All large employers have established ranges of wages and salaries and use a variety of more or less scientific methods to calculate the relative worth of the complete list of jobs from shop-floor employees to senior executives. Unfortunately, in practice the usefulness of this evaluation of *differentials* is marred by a number of factors: the local scarcity of certain skills distorting wage scales; the inevitable tendency for full employment to bring about a labour auction; and the effects of present high progressive taxation, tending to remove rewards for additional skill and reduce real earnings compared with scheduled rates of pay.

Even when these problems have been tackled, the maintenance of differentials remains one of the most common sources of industrial strife, and emphasizes the need to consult the personnel manager, in his role as administrator of wage agreements, before any variations are made in rates of pay. The best intentioned actions by management, such as giving a slightly higher rate to reward the particularly good work of one small section of workers, can have the most far-reaching consequences. For as soon as the wages of that group are raised, the differential between their pay and every other group's pay is destroyed. There will inevitably be a clamour for these differentials to be restored, not by removing this recent rise, but by adding it on to all employees' wages. If this happens in a federated* company, then its rates of pay will become higher than those of other firms, and a chain reaction will exert pressure on the federation for a general increase in wage rates. Thus a rise of a couple of pence an hour for a handful of workers in an obscure factory could result in a nation-wide claim throughout that industry involving millions of pounds. For this reason it is essential that any alterations in rates of pay should be made only after due process of negotiation, and that any variations should be permitted only within the framework of existing agreements.

INCENTIVES

These agreements do not preclude the many forms of *incentives* which are commonly offered to stimulate production, nor the techniques of

* *See* Chapter 14 for an explanation of 'federations' of trade unions and employers.

job evaluation and *merit-rating* which are widely used to try to distinguish between individual effort.

In an industrial setting, incentives are anything which cause a person to work harder, urging him to some form of action and at the same time satisfying his subjective desires. The worker's main interest is earning more money, while management is concerned with reducing costs: it is therefore to both their advantages for the best conditions for work to be established, leading to more output, less effort, higher earnings, and lower costs. In this way incentives can achieve cumulative benefits, increasing efficiency which thus makes better incentives possible.

On the practical side, payments made under incentive schemes must stand up to certain tests. In the first place, workers must be satisfied that the output required is within their capacity, that they are being offered a just rate for the job, and that proper skill differentials are being maintained. Once time and output factors have been determined, management must not subsequently reduce the rate paid unreasonably. Payments must be easy to calculate so that workers can know how much they have earned up to a given moment. Any incentive scheme must offer an adequate income, taking into account abnormal conditions outside workers' control. In some cases minimum earnings are stipulated, or some form of 'attendance money' is provided for, as used to be the case with the dockers' labour reserve pool. Voluntary agreements sometimes legislate for piece-rate earnings, enabling these to be as much as $37\frac{1}{2}$ per cent higher than time rates in the boot and shoe manufacturing industry, for example.

The main types of financial incentives are:

1. Flat payments added to basic wage or salary, such as annual or cost-of-living bonuses and profit-sharing schemes.
2. Payments based on rate-fixing—the work is measured and a price per piece or time allowed for the work is settled by negotiation, usually between local management and shop stewards. Both workers and management may benefit directly from the cost saving which results from increased effort, as in the Halsey and Rowan schemes.
3. Geared incentive schemes—used where the volume of work fluctuates and earnings need to be related to average output. Bonus payments may start at a low level of output, but tail off at higher outputs, in order to stabilize workers' earnings.
4. Accurate work-measured schemes—the normal piece-work concept where payment is directly proportionate to additional effort and higher output; this means that the work content of jobs must be measured beforehand, and methods and conditions must be standardized. Gangs or groups of workers, as well as individuals, may be

rewarded in this way, earnings being determined by dividing total production bonuses between the members on an agreed basis. (Operators of steel melting furnaces may use this method, for example.) A variation of this type of payment is the commission earned by many salesmen, based on turnover or sales; this, too, may be paid to individuals or on a group basis, and in some cases represents a very high proportion of total income.

5. Lieu bonuses—these are sometimes paid in working situations where additional payments cannot be linked directly with production: they are, in effect, payments to compensate those workers whose jobs do not allow them to earn production bonuses, such as men employed on machine maintenance work.

6. Measured day work and high day rates—both depend on the initial calculation of the amount of work expected to be done in a normal eight-hour day and agreement on this through joint consultation. Under measured day work, an employee is paid time rates, plus a bonus awarded so long as he maintains the agreed level of output. The high-day-rate method simply means that he receives a high time rate so long as he keeps up the standard of output agreed.

Incentive schemes are intended to stimulate improved productivity, but their introduction is often only one feature of a series of complex organizational changes taking place at the same time, and it is quite impossible to isolate the effects of the changed pay structure in itself. Indeed this has led many progressive firms to suspect the effectiveness of piece-rates, and they are abandoning them in favour of high time rates or measured day work linked with sophisticated work study and job evaluation techniques.

The advantages of piece-rates are:

1. They may contribute in part towards solving the problems of raising productivity.
2. The pace of work is maintained with the minimum of supervision.
3. To a large extent workers can set their own pace, choosing when to speed up and when to ease off.
4. Workers on piece-rates can be relied on to keep the flow of raw materials moving steadily, so it need no longer worry management.

But there are drawbacks as well:

1. It does not automatically follow that people on piece-rates work as hard as they can, for group pressures often impose limits on output.
2. In practice, piece-rate systems are often not settled objectively, but are calculated on an assessment of what an acceptable weekly wage packet would be; some systems are so complex that they take up far

too much management time, spent in manipulating jobs so that all employees receive reasonable wages.

3. New rates are subject to such compromises, in the attempt to avoid friction, that exceptionally high earnings result once workers see how they can gain from the new system; inequalities of pay between departments often emerge in this way, too, making it difficult to transfer labour within the workplace.

4. Piece-rates encourage wages drift, because even when higher rates can be justified in terms of increased productivity, they often result in claims from time workers who want the previous differentials to be restored.

5. There is a fundamental concern that piece-rates undermine trust, reflecting management's lack of confidence in their employees' willingness to work, and, indeed, in their own inability to get them to work.

This last criticism is particularly telling since many large organizations have been experimenting with such methods as measured day work to try to find an alternative to the traditional piece-work. But, although management may undertake the most careful preparations of such schemes, the fact remains that they have to be put into effect by first-line supervisors. Throughout British industry, it seems that only a small proportion of these supervisors possess the background training and qualities to meet the additional leadership demands made by this new situation and which are now required in large measure to motivate the workers under their control. Piece-work rates must therefore be expected to play a major role in wage determination for many years to come.*

At the same time, experience suggests that measured day work may provide a greater incentive to effort than time rate payments and prove less of a stimulus to conflict than payment by results. At the end of 1972, nine per cent of all workers were being paid on a measured day work basis, whereby the pay of employees is fixed on the understanding that they will maintain a specified level of performance, but that pay will not fluctuate in the short term with actual performance.

The O.M.E. report *Measured Daywork*† concluded that this system of payment helps both employers and workers to meet their objectives. Employers can forecast both output and costs better, will find more flexibility in manning, fewer sectional disputes, and easier maintenance of quality. Workers can rely on stable incomes, especially when employers

* Cf. analysis by H. A. Clegg, 'The Lessons of N.I.C.', *New Society*, 11 March 1965.

† Office of Manpower Economics (H.M.S.O., 1973).

agree to maintain levels of pay during delays and breakdowns, and can look forward to greater opportunities for job enlargement and enrichment. Even the economy at large will benefit through a more structured wage system, less wage drift, increased performance, and fewer disputes.

These advantages will accrue, however, only if certain dangers are guarded against. Pay relativities tend to be highlighted by measured day work and can lead to pressure for comparability-based pay claims. There is also a risk that effort and performance may drift downwards unless the scheme is well maintained. So measured day work, like any other pay system, can degenerate. For it to be successful, managers must maintain and use control data, review work standards periodically, and be aware of the continual need to improve the ways they employ people.

Many group bonus schemes rely on the fixing of a ratio between total labour costs and the value of sales achieved, so that any subsequent reductions in this ratio (i.e. higher productivity) bring about savings which are distributed among the workers concerned as their bonus. The difficulty is that the ratio becomes progressively less realistic as time goes on: new capital investment or organizational changes may improve efficiency, but any attempt to readjust the ratio must then inevitably be unfavourable from the workers' point of view and will naturally be resisted. Workers also become very dissatisfied when their bonuses fluctuate: even if their own efforts become more efficient they may get smaller bonuses, or none at all, if sales fall off at the same time. These reasons explain why, for example, the 'Scanlon Plan' has not caught on in British industry, although it is a type of group incentive scheme that is widely used in the U.S.A. and has received much publicity here since the war.

JOB EVALUATION

Job evaluation is a technique of assessing the worth of each job in comparison with all others throughout an organization. Job contents are fully described, and a variety of methods may then be used to enable one to be compared with another. These include 'job ranking', 'job classification', 'points rating', and 'factor comparisons'—each resulting in a progressively more detailed analysis of jobs as such, without regard to the abilities of the persons doing them. The biggest problem in job evaluation is that of counter-balancing the personal judgments of the departmental heads who make the assessments; although jobs, not people, are being studied, friendliness towards or dislike of particular subordinates may well play a part. Again, trade unions are very interested in payment differentials between jobs, and may exert such pressure that the results of systematic assessments become distorted. Even so, it is sensible to allow full negotiations on job evaluation to take place, as a positive step towards ensuring confidence in the scheme among those employees affected.

An example of the procedures involved in job evaluation is that recommended for local government, following its reorganization in 1974, by the Local Authorities' Management Services Advisory Committee—thus:

1. The post holder completes a detailed job questionnaire concerning the constituent parts of his job and signs it.
2. This goes to the post holder's supervisor for him to agree and countersign.
3. The job questionnaire then becomes an 'aide memoire' for the job analyst who after assimilating its content will interview the post holder. This must be done adequately so that a fully rounded picture emerges in the analyst's mind of the total job, and also to satisfy the post holder that a fair estimate is made of the job content.
4. The job analyst on the basis of the job questionnaire and interview prepares a job description to a common format.
5. This job description which, incidentally, can have many valuable subsidiary uses, then goes to the post holder for signing if he accepts that this fairly reflects the content of his job. Where he does not do so, then he should identify those parts of the description with which he disagrees in order that a tripartite meeting between post holder, analyst, and supervisor can take place until an agreed formula is arrived at.
6. The agreed job description is considered by a panel of three or four senior evaluators who consider the job factor by factor using a manual of definitions to assist them in arriving at the appropriate level for each factor for the job concerned. They may also have present to assist them an officer from the post holder's department who is able to provide supplementary factual information about the job on request from members of the panel.
7. The effect of the panel's consideration is that a responsibility level under each factor is selected for the job concerned. These chosen levels are then related to a standard matrix which indicates the appropriate points (or numerical value) for each. The sum of these pointings provides a total numerical value which then provides in concrete form a clear relationship with the points totals accorded individually to the other jobs.
8. The points totals are then converted into grades within the national grading structure using salary administration techniques.

None of the available methods of job evaluation claims to offer a precise scientific formula for establishing the correct relationship of pay to responsibilities. However, the procedures are codified and, where judgment is required, helps through the adoption of the consensus principle. In particular, in the public services, an objective attempt at establishing the right grades for jobs has far-reaching implications not only for pay but also for promotion and career development.

MERIT-RATING

Merit-rating attempts to recognize and reward the personal abilities that an individual brings to his job, measured by the extent to which his output or the quality of his work exceeds the minimum that can reasonably be expected for his basic rate of pay. This definition may appear straightforward, but many problems have to be solved when trying to put a merit-rating system into practice. First, the desirable qualities relating to each job and their relative importance have to be decided, so that the right weight can be attached to each. The actual method of rating must be settled, and a formula devised for converting the ratings into cash payments. Policy about the duration of a merit award must also be determined beforehand—is it to be permanent, or reviewed from time to time? If the latter, what procedure of warnings or appeals must be created to cover the possible removal of merit awards?

Clearly any scheme will stand or fall on the fairness and consistency of the ratings. As with job evaluation, the personal attitudes of departmental heads need to be carefully guarded against. Many tend to be over-generous in their attempts to get as much money as possible for their subordinates; others are unperceptive enough to hope that top management will think that a department holding a large number of merit awards must necessarily be efficient, thus redounding to their own credit. The basic trouble, of course, is that the assessments asked for concern factors which have to be judged subjectively, so that there are likely to be considerable differences in the standards of assessment between departmental heads. These can only be prevented by a rigorous training programme to try to ensure that they all understand the scheme in the same way. Whether such training can also overcome the other criticisms levelled at merit-rating is another matter. These allege that any system of award based entirely on the personal opinion of the boss is bound to cause friction, since it is wide open to charges of favouritism; and that, in any event, length of service will be the factor uppermost in supervisors' minds when considering the awards. These points can only be refuted by recording that, on the other hand, many managers and personnel specialists clearly see merit-rating as an incentive and a means of rewarding sound all-round performance, both in terms of immediate cash payments and as an indicator for future promotion.

SUGGESTION SCHEMES

Another type of financial incentive directly linked with improved performance is the suggestion scheme, now operated in a very large number of organizations up and down the country. The concept of asking employees to put forward suggestions for the more efficient running of their firms emanates from the pre-war study of worker motivation carried out by industrial psychologists. In common with the principles of joint consultation and joint production committees, suggestion schemes operate on the theory that the boss cannot know everything about work processes, that workers are experts in their own fields, that their detailed knowledge of the jobs and operations performed in their departments is of great value, and that they have some desire to share actively in the success of their organization. A *suggestion scheme*, then, is a type of incentive designed to stimulate this particular motivation and desire on the part of the workers, by offering them payments or prizes to encourage their ideas on improving efficiency.

The sort of ideas required can generally be summed up as:

1. Improving the quality of any product.
2. Improving production, by economy in materials, avoidance of waste, better methods, or modified designs.
3. Improving processes or general workshop procedure.
4. Improving safety and welfare of employees.
5. Suggestions for new products.

The initial problem to be overcome when launching a suggestion scheme is the reluctance of people to put forward their ideas. This may be due to a variety of real or imagined reasons: fear of making fools of themselves in their mates' eyes; fear that the foreman may interpret any suggestions as implied criticisms of his own efforts and retaliate in some way; fear that ideas may be rejected, then filed away and introduced later without recognition or reward; fear that they will lose patent rights on inventions by disclosing them to the company.

The mechanics of the scheme must therefore be designed to overcome these fears. In the first place, arrangements can be made for all suggestions to remain anonymous (except to the administrator of the scheme) until after they have been fully considered, so that neither an employee's mates nor his supervisor need know about his idea. This can easily be done by providing suggestion forms with perforated sections, but numbered on each part.

An example* is given in Figure 27 where the suggestor writes his idea

* This form is reproduced by kind permission of C.A.V. Limited, Warple Way, Acton, London, W.3.

on the middle section and signs the bottom half; he posts the suggestion, after tearing off the top slip for his own record. The secretary of the scheme then tears off the bottom section, for his reference, which leaves the suggestion part to be considered by the panel of judges: only after they have reached a decision may they be told the identity of the person concerned, when the secretary brings the two parts of the form together again. Distrust of the scheme, shown by the fear that rejected ideas will be used later, can be dispelled by dealing quickly and scrupulously with all suggestions, and, above all, by giving the fullest reasons to suggestors whose ideas are turned down. Strictly speaking, inventions

---

COUNTERFOIL　　　　　　　　　　A　2141

Write your Suggestion on the Form below, sign the Acknowledgement Slip,
tear off this counterfoil and post the Suggestion Form in one of the Suggestion Boxes.

Keep this Counterfoil to prove your right to any reply or award.

| TEAR OFF HERE | FOR YOUR RECORD | Date Submitted............ | Details............ |

SUGGESTION FORM　　　A　2141

PLEASE WRITE CLEAR

Date............　　　　　　　　　　Comp't No............

This Suggestion concerns ....　　Tool No. ....

I Suggest :—　　　　　　　　　　Oper. No. ....

(USE OTHER SIDE IF NECESSARY)

(NOT TO BE DETACHED BY SUGGESTOR.)　　**ACKNOWLEDGEMENT SLIP**　　A　2141

Signed Mr. Mrs. Miss ....　Works No. ....　Dept. ....
　　　　　　*Staff　　　　*Staff Grade............

N.B.— Your name will be known only to the Secretary, except in the event of your Suggestion Being granted an award, when your name will be posted on the "Box Notice Boards" If you do not want your name to be published, please write "NO" in the following space ( )　　*Delete whichever does not apply.

FORM NO. 3321-8　　　　　　　　　　　　　　　　　P.T.(

Figure 27. Suggestion for

made on a company's premises, using its equipment and in its time, are that company's property; but enlightened employers nowadays take out joint patents with the employee concerned and thus safeguard his interests as well as their own.

Suggestions should be considered by a panel of people, possibly a section of the Joint Production Committee, with representatives of both management and workers. They should be able to call on whatever technical advice may be necessary to evaluate a suggestion. A decision should be reached as soon as possible, together with an assessment of how large an award should be given to the suggestor. The chairman of the panel there-

---

WHAT TO SUGGEST. Suggestions should contain ORIGINAL Ideas and will be welcomed on any of the following or similar subjects:

WORKS SUGGESTIONS.

Improvements in the Quality of any Product,

Improvements in production by:　(i)　Economy in Materials.
　　　　　　　　　　　　　　(ii)　Improved Methods.
　　　　　　　　　　　　　　(iii)　Modification to Design

Improvements to Processes or General Shop Procedure.

Development of New Products.

STAFF SUGGESTIONS.

Improvements in Accuracy and Quality of Work,

Speeding up the flow Work by:
　　(i)　Improvements in Office Procedure or Methods.
　　(ii)　Improvements in the design and Layout of Forms.
　　(iii)　Elimination of unnecessary or Duplicated Work,

Economy in Stationery or other Office Expenses,

Development of Office Equipment.

Improvement in Safety Appliances.

Details of Suggestion—(continued)

USE ADDITIONAL SHEETS OF PLAIN PAPER IF NECESSARY.

After the necessary investigation has been completed, you will be notified of the decision of the committee. We should like to explain that many suggestions are of such a nature as to require considerable time to investigate. In some instances it is necessary to conduct lengthy tests or contact various departments, all of which tend to delay our final decision. We want to assure you however, that there will be no unnecessary delay involved and that the investigation will proceed as rapidly as possible.

We will keep you informed as to the progress of your suggestion, and in the meantime if you have any other ideas, do not hesitate to send them in. We always welcome them and assure you they will receive impartial consideration.

and back)

fore needs to be an executive sufficiently senior to pledge the company's credit in this respect.

Wherever possible, the size of the payment should be related to the savings as a result of the suggestion, either as a lump sum or as a percentage of these savings. Promotion, wages increases, royalties on sales—these are other established methods of rewarding the man with ideas. Payments are often made, too, for the 'good try'—the idea which is rejected for valid reasons but where it is obvious that the suggestor has put considerable thought, effort, and time into formulating his ideas.

It is usual for a rule to be made about the eligibility of staff for awards. In some cases all are included, but many schemes allow only the lower-graded workers to take part, on the grounds that thinking up improvements is part of the supervisor's or manager's normal job. When the scheme is so restricted, to perhaps the less articulate part of labour force, it is important to offer help in writing up suggestions or drawing any diagrams needed to explain them.

Finally, if a suggestion scheme is to have permanent impact, it must be given continuous publicity, backed by obvious enthusiasm from top management. Methods used might include:

1. *Poster publicity*, bright and arresting, and frequently changed. (Over-humorous examples do not produce the most creative results.)
2. *Pay-packet enclosures*—making sure that every employee is reminded of the scheme at regular intervals, in a manner that gives him the chance to read at leisure what the scheme has to offer.
3. *A departmental suggestions league*—a prestige competition between departments, with additional awards or a trophy given to the department that scores the highest total of successful suggestions.
4. *Directors' special awards*—given annually to the best suggestions put forward, in addition to the normal award already made. These could be substantial amounts in outstanding cases and would have great publicity value as reminders of the benefits that might come to anyone from taking part in the suggestions scheme.

The main requirements for a successful suggestions scheme can thus be summarized as—good publicity, worthwhile awards, and, above all, swift and fair treatment. All suggestions should be acknowledged immediately, and the actual results announced within a few weeks. Sometimes delays are unavoidable if prolonged tests have to be carried out; the suggestor should be kept informed of these. Nothing will discredit a suggestions scheme as much as unnecessary delays or inadequate explanation of what is happening about the suggestions submitted.

PROFIT-SHARING

In 1954, some 520,000 employees of just over five hundred firms took part in profit-sharing schemes; these numbers are roughly the same today.* Such arrangements confer on labour a share of the success of a business and must therefore, in the first place, be regarded as incentives to greater output. But they are also obviously intended to have a psychological impact on employees in terms of loyalty, thrift, and a sense of security, which in turn can help build up the reputation of the organization as a good employer. There are other objectives, such as the preservation of the spirit of capitalism and the linking of earnings with the prosperity of the business cycle—but these seem too remote and academic to make much impression on the average employee.

The theoretical advantages of this type of incentive are: that it stimulates a greater collective interest on the part of all employees, from senior managers to shop-floor workers; that everyone becomes more conscious of the need for economy and prevention of materials wastage; that suggestion schemes become much more realistic as a means of improving efficiency; and that costs of labour turnover are greatly reduced, because people establish a much closer personal link with the organization. Unfortunately, these theoretical advantages are opposed by several practical disadvantages. The profit share-out is often so small or so long in coming that it loses its impact as an incentive, and, in any case, the efficient worker is no better off than the inefficient. Workers have considerable suspicions that their employer may be getting proportionately more than they are; accounts are difficult for them to understand, so that they become uneasy when profits are low; above all, they are conscious that profits are influenced by factors outside their control. Trade unions generally oppose profit-sharing schemes for two reasons: firstly, that dissension is caused between workers when, as is often the case, some are included in the arrangements and others left out; secondly, they fear that the underlying purpose is to win workers over to management's point of view. Not that this is necessarily so, for even shareholders sometimes complain about such schemes, particularly that workers share in the profits but suffer nothing when there are losses.

SALARIES

One of the distinguishing features of 'staff status' is the receipt of salaries rather than wages. A salary is normally expressed in terms of an

* *Attitudes to Efficiency*: Ministry of Labour report, page 25 (H.M.S.O., 1966).

annual figure, and is paid monthly by cheque or transfer into a bank account, whereas wages are paid weekly in cash. Earnings tend to remain steady, month by month, since salaried staff are seldom paid for overtime nor under any piece-rate system. In private industry, most salaries are a matter of private negotiation between the employer and the man or woman concerned, although there is evidence of a mounting interest in white-collar unionism, as executive and professional staff strive to restore differentials that existed in the past between their earnings and those of manual workers. The recent rapid growth of the Association of Scientific, Technical and Managerial Staffs under Clive Jenkins's leadership is a case in point; and draughtsmen, for example, are now urged not to accept jobs for salaries less than the recognized scales.

There are many differences in pay policy between staff and manual workers. Salary scales tend to be much more progressive, not stopping at the age of twenty-one as for craftsmen, so that salary increases act as incentives in place of production bonuses. Rate-for-age scales apply in many professions, sometimes rising until the age of thirty.

In most of the public services, salaries increase by fixed annual increments, which are often not as large as individuals may receive in private industry. It would be wrong, however, to infer from this that comparable jobs are better paid in the private than the public sector; there may be some temporary lagging behind from time to time, but periodic negotiations sometimes result in quite dramatic boosts for the scales themselves. Nevertheless, there are difficulties in the application of fixed scales and increments: when a man reaches the top of his scale he has no prospect of any further increase until that scale itself is reviewed; and, it is impossible to reward differences in the quality and ability of individual staff or in the amount of effort they put into their work and the success they achieve.

In private industry, salaries are usually periodically reviewed on an individual basis. Obviously this method does allow flexibility in recognizing standards of performance, types of responsibility, and the degree to which success depends on personal effort; age and length of service can also be taken into account. On the other hand, this method can so easily give rise to anomalies and the discontent that follows. Employers traditionally try to keep salary payments secret; if there are variations in the amounts paid to individuals, then the reasons for them are not published, in an attempt to avoid any embarrassment that might arise from personal grievances. The personnel manager's advice on salary administration will no doubt be based on the principle that there should be no anomalies, and that corrective action should be taken immediately if it is found, for example, that higher salaries than existing staff are paid have to be offered to attract newcomers. The least that should be done, where salary maxima have been settled for particular jobs, is for the staff concerned to be told how long it should take them to reach these levels, assuming satisfactory work on their part.

Salary reviews usually take account of the following factors:

1. The personnel manager administers a procedure which calls for periodic recommendations (usually once a year) from departmental heads: these are based on merit.
2. External features, such as changes in taxation and the cost of living, are also taken into account at this stage.
3. A continuous comparison is maintained with the salary levels of other organizations, by studying staff advertisements or exchanging information with other local firms who employ the same categories of staff.
4. There are special considerations relating to some types of staff:
   (*a*) The differential between supervisors' salaries and the total earnings of individual employees under their control is a perennial problem that is only partly covered by the better general conditions offered to the foreman.
   (*b*) In order to attract youngsters of the right calibre for future development, it may be necessary to offer them high initial salaries, which may lead to slower progress as they get older.
   (*c*) Similarly, research staff tend to be highly paid early on in their careers, so that if their interest in research wanes later on and they want to switch to general management, there is little scope left to recognize any managerial ability they may show.

One study* of the values and remuneration preferences of managers in one large British company revealed, *inter alia*, that although they varied considerably in their detailed views about pay, there was very strong support for remuneration based on individual performance, and there was also consistent support for remuneration to be sufficiently flexible to handle special individual cases. The administrative structure required to manage a salary system designed so as to provide motivational stimuli must have these characteristics: flexibility, to cope with individual differences; provision of the fullest information about the remuneration system to all managers involved; and the means of monitoring the effects of the system on performance.

SALARY STRUCTURE

The overall concern, of course, is to relate individual salaries to relative jobs and merit. In pursuing this aim, comparison with similar jobs else·

* *Motivating Managers Financially*, by Michael White (I.P.M., 1973).

where has only a very limited use because job titles and the responsibilities they carry vary enormously from company to company. Systematic evaluation of job content is the only real answer, which in turn demands the writing of precise job descriptions from the outset.

But even when it seems that individuals are being properly paid, the question of whether the salary structure of the organization as a whole is correct still remains. This question has been analysed by Harry Pearson,* Director of Personnel of Rolls Royce Ltd., to show what salary levels should be within an organization, taking its size into account. 'The structure of salaries is subject to a general law, known as Pareto's law, which says that in any large organized society there is a definite relation between income and the number of people having this income.' The graph in Figure 28 illustrates that if n is the number of people with an income greater than S, then if $\log S$ is plotted against $\log n$, an approximate linear relationship will result. This graph, plotting the income of the labour force in Great Britain, clearly shows a mathematical relationship between a salary and the number of people with that salary or greater. The salary

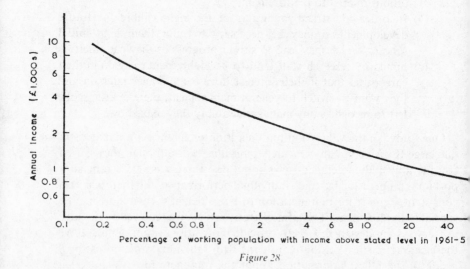

Figure 28

structure of any organization should in fact appear as a straight line when plotted in this way. Salary administrators should carry out this exercise for their own organizations, and if there are marked deviations from 'the straight line', they should look closely for the reasons.

* 'How to Pay Salaries', *Management Today*, December 1966, page 62.

PRODUCTIVITY BARGAINS

Productivity bargaining is the process through which management hope to obtain greater efficiency by offering improvements in wages, and perhaps better working conditions, in exchange for the elimination of restrictive practices. This simple definition, however, must not be allowed to obscure the vast amount of investigation, analysis, and hard negotiation that must be put into the satisfactory conclusion of such agreements. Work systems must be analysed to decide where change is needed, deep-rooted traditions of worker behaviour must be modified, and inter-group jealousies smoothed over by giving carefully considered reassurances about the future.

One of the best-known productivity bargains is that reached in 1960 at the Fawley refinery of the Esso Petroleum Co. In essence, the company offered its workers a 40 per cent wage increase, spread over two years, and a reduction of working hours from 42 to 40, in return for:

1. The redeployment of 300 craftsmen's mates, virtually abolishing this type of job.
2. A considerable easing of rules about job demarcation.
3. The reduction of overtime from 18 to 2 per cent.

Within two years, the productivity of process workers had risen by 45 per cent and of maintenance workers by over 50 per cent, and additional plant worth £12 million was being operated and maintained by a labour force that had fallen from 2,461 to 2,266.

Productivity bargains are in essence, then, attacks on under-employment. For far too long British industry has been bedevilled by the contrivance of 'policy overtime' by managers simply to produce higher wage packets for those employees whose jobs do not lend themselves to payment by results or to any type of production bonus. In other words, the system of wage payment actually encourages workers to waste time. The feeling that high overtime is inevitable in the competition to get workers is typical of management's casual approach to the use of labour resources. Yet how can employees be persuaded to clamp down on materials wastage, or to try to get more out of their machines, or to accept work study investigations to improve working methods, when they are aware daily that their own time is being wasted in so many ways?

Naturally, too, long-term overtime working creates income expectations that makes its elimination virtually impossible when management faces up to its responsibilities for increasing productivity. But there can be no dodging: management created the situation of excessive overtime in the first place, as a means of attracting scarce labour, and must now take action to get rid of it and all the other restrictive practices that reveal collective control by workers over the pace of work. Unions themselves oppose overtime in principle but, because of their members' income expectations, they argue for higher basic rates as the best method for reducing its working: they certainly will not propose cuts in overtime as such, with subsequent loss of pay. The only answer, therefore, is for management to take the initiative and be prepared to finance increases in basic rates out of the gains from higher labour productivity.

Management must take the lead in this because it is basically concerned with the efficient use of resources to produce the best results. The search for improvement, and the introduction of the changes that this often entails, are management tasks—but workers and their unions will resist if the achievement of these tasks bring insecurity of employment in its wake. Nevertheless, unions recognize that in the event they can do more for their members in an efficient firm than in one that is inefficient. Hence an understanding of management's problems develops, to form the basis for negotiation and co-operation aimed at removing both inefficiencies in production on one hand and workers' grievances on the other.

In no circumstances is productivity bargaining to be thought of as a means by which management can buy itself out of trouble. There is no question of bribing workers to abandon restrictive practices, and passing on to the customer additional labour costs thus incurred. The concept is essentially a method by which wage improvements are financed, not through higher prices but from the cost savings made as the result of agreed changes in working arrangements. There is already abundant evidence that this is a much more successful way of achieving greater productivity than all the after-dinner invocations by Government ministers and industrial leaders since the war.

These bargains are, of course, local agreements, and they have already been criticized as being inflationary since they inspire wage claims elsewhere (to maintain previous differentials) which by no stretch of the imagination are supported by any evidence of greater efficiency. Another difficulty arises in trying to extend productivity bargaining more widely, say on an industrial basis. It lies in the essential thorough preliminary analysis of the working system which can only be done locally and under the control of managements who will accept a direct responsibility for administering any changes which they may subsequently negotiate. On the other hand, the concept must not be allowed to provide an excuse which enables control over rising wages and inflation to be subverted. Such bargains can only be allowed when it can be proved that productivity actually has increased.

There are many other subsidiary problems involved in the process of negotiating these agreements. The rewarding of improved productivity by increasing basic wages immediately exposes the salaries of supervisory and managerial staff. A reappraisal of the management structure must therefore be carried out, preferably before the stage of negotiating with trade unions begins, with an intensive investigation of the responsibilities and relative earnings levels of all salaried staff. Not that this is a straightforward matter of salary administration. The N.B.P.I. rejected one claim for an increase from clerical staff in the electricity industry because it had grave doubts about the inflation of salaries as a side effect of productivity agreements with manual trade unions; again the acid test of asking for evidence of improved productivity was applied. Restrictive practices and job demarcation are virtually non-existent among salaried staff, so there is little to bargain for by offering more pay for increased productivity in this respect. On top of this, when manual workers were previously earning more than them, salaried staff became reconciled to the fact, knowing they were working ten to twenty hours overtime a week in order to earn large wage packets. The productivity agreement that completely changes this situation makes it essential to reappraise the position of salaried workers. In reality, of course, other factors are at play besides labour cost and effort put into the job; salary administration demands that account is taken of the availability of managerial and supervisory skills, the added responsibilities that follow technical changes (including the working arrangements of the productivity agreement), and the constant revaluation of job gradings. This degree of thoroughness is essential to remove the risk of salaries inflation, which is inevitable if the problem is tackled simply by giving a flat general increase. In association with productivity bargains, the answer might be to increase basic salaries and reduce the progression scales.

But although productivity bargaining has made a real contribution to improved labour relations in recent years, it cannot be regarded as the panacea for all industrial troubles. The concept can only be applied successfully where management is imaginative, takes the initiative in identifying the practices that it wishes to modify, and carefully calculates what it is prepared to pay, in terms of cash and security of employment, to obtain the required concessions from its workers. Secondly, experience has shown that wage increases can most easily be absorbed in those industries, like oil refining, where the capital–labour rate is high. Thirdly, it is difficult to negotiate productivity bargains on a national scale: it seems that local flexibility and adaptability are key factors in agreements. Fourthly, productivity bargaining may only be successful as a once-and-for-all experience; this is shown by the second attempt at Fawley to obtain further concessions from the unions, when the price proved too high for management to pay.

In a statement published in 1969,* the N.B.P.I. suggested that the more embracing term 'efficiency agreements' should be used, 'productivity agreements' in the generally accepted sense being included. The guide lines are:

1. It should be shown that the workers are contributing towards the achievement of constantly rising levels of efficiency. Where appropriate, major changes in working practice or working methods should be specified in the agreement.
2. Measurements of efficiency should be based on the application of relevant indices of performances or work standards.
3. A realistic calculation of all the relevant costs of the agreement and of the gains attributable to the workers' contribution should normally show that the effect is to reduce the total cost of output or the cost of providing a given service.
4. There should be effective controls to ensure that projected increases in efficiency are achieved and that higher pay or other improvements are made only when such increases are assured.
5. There should be clear benefits to the consumer by way of a contribution to stable or lower prices.
6. An agreement to one group of workers only should bear the cost of consequential increases to other groups, if any have to be granted.
7. Negotiators should avoid setting levels of pay or conditions which might have undesirable repercussions elsewhere.

FURTHER READING

Salary Administration, by G. McBeath and D. N. Rands (Business Publications, 1964).
Motivating Managers Financially, by Michael White (I.P.M., 1973).
The Realities of Productivity Bargaining, an Industrial Relations Committee report (I.P.M., 1968).

---

* Cmd. 4136, (H.M.S.O., 1969).

14 The Framework of Industrial Relations

The study of *industrial relations* may generally be defined as being concerned with the ways in which working groups, both formal and informal, behave and interact. More specifically, it describes the efforts aimed at securing co-operation between managements and trade unions at the workplace so that the most efficient methods of production may be achieved. All too often, however, these efforts must be viewed negatively— as means of overcoming conflict between 'authority' and worker groups. Mistrust, rooted in the industrial history of Great Britain, particularly the inter-war years of economic depression, is still very much at the back of workers' minds, associating the words 'progress and change' with 'insecurity of employment'. Tradition plays a prominent part both in the principles and structure of industrial relations, neither of which have developed much during the twentieth century (indeed, to say that they have stood the test of time is a common defence against any attacks). The trouble is that today we are beset with fundamental economic problems, such as the fight against inflation and the need to increase productivity, finding solutions to which is hampered by the institutional rigidity of the system.

TRADITIONAL STRUCTURE

Industrial relations are governed by a multitude of collective agreements, statutory orders about wages and working conditions, arbitration awards, management decisions, trade union regulations, court rulings which have established precedents, social conventions, and custom and usage—all referring to the employment of labour. Trade unions, employers' federations, individual private firms, and public authorities take part in making these arrangements, which often vary within the same industry from one part of the country to another. Such is the basic complexity of the subject.

The Trade Union Amendment Act, 1867, contains one definition of trade unions which is still accepted today:

'A trade union is any combination, whether temporary or permanent, for regulating the relations between workmen and masters, or between workmen and workmen, or between masters and masters, or for imposing restrictive conditions on the conduct of any trade or business.'

This was amended by the Trade Union Act, 1913, which provided that the above objects, together with the provision of benefits to members, must be the principal objects of a combination.

The Trade Union and Labour Relations Act, 1974 defines a trade union as an organization which consists of workers whose principal purposes include the regulation of relations between those workers and employers or employers' associations.

Although the sample is small, some insight into what workers expect of their unions can be seen from the analysis below of the views of 66 Transport and General Workers Union members in Sheffield* about what their union should do:

WHAT THE UNION SHOULD DO:

	strong agree	agree	indif- ferent	dis- agree	strong dis- agree	no answer
make sure workplace is healthy and safe to work in	52	12	0	0	0	2
get best possible working conditions for the men	50	13	1	0	0	2
get best possible wages for the men	46	17	1	0	0	2
set up adequate procedures for handling disputes	45	18	0	1	1	1
seek co-operation with other unions to better the working man's life as a whole	42	20	1	1	0	2
fight against redundancies	42	14	3	5	0	2
fight for longer holidays	32	22	8	1	1	2
fight for shorter hours	31	19	10	2	2	2
get workers a say in management	31	19	7	7	0	2
run courses to instruct members in unions affairs	30	28	6	0	0	2
have a detailed knowledge of the firm's profits	25	20	9	4	1	7
have a say when new machines are brought in	21	24	8	6	3	4

*'What are Unions For?', by Michael Poole, *New Society*, 9 May 1974.

	strong agree	agree	indif- ferent	dis- agree	strong dis- agree	no answer
ensure seniority in promotion for shop floor jobs	18	13	10	15	7	3
ensure seniority in promotion for supervisory jobs	17	10	11	18	7	3
have control over apprenticeships	15	22	12	10	4	3
fight on a political basis for nationalization	15	11	13	12	13	2
sell unionism through advertising	14	9	12	21	8	2
develop social arrangements such as parties, clubs, etc	12	21	16	11	3	3

The overall purpose of a trade union is to bring together workers' aspirations into an effective force, and any appreciation of trade union attitudes must accept that these aspirations are different from management's. They may be summarized into four aims:

1. Efficiency in production must be realized with the minimum human cost; in particular, essential changes should result in the least possible threat to security of employment.
2. Constant improvement in working conditions—the *raison d'être* of the trade union movement. This covers claims for higher wages, shorter hours, guaranteed earnings, holiday arrangements and pay, improved environment, regard for seniority in promotion and at times of redundancy, and an overall policy of full employment. Adequate grievance procedures and provisions for arbitration over disputes are further safeguards.
3. The development of internal strength, better to achieve all the other objectives. Unions constantly strive to increase their membership, and hence their power, provide leadership to unorganized groups, point the way to further improvements in conditions and worker benefits, and are ever critical of the actions of Government authorities and employers which affect the labour force of the country.
4. In doing so, unions seek full recognition as the exclusive agents of employees who come within their respective purview. Thus they encourage workers to regard themselves collectively, rather than as individuals: rules of conduct and conditions of employment are established for all, with no special terms for individuals.

At the end of 1975 there were 488 trade unions in Great Britain, of which 258 had less than 1,000 members each, accounting for only 0·6 per cent of all trade union membership; on the other hand, the twenty-five unions with over 100,000 members each accounted for 77·6 per cent of total membership. The tendency for the number of unions to fall, through amalgamation, continues: 596 unions in 1964, 555 in 1967, and 488 in 1975. The total membership of trade unions, however, has increased in recent years: 1967—9,970,000; 1972—11,315,000; 1975—11,950,000.*

There are basically three main types of trade union, although very few fit exactly into one or other of the categories (it would almost be true to say that there are as many categories as there are unions):

1. The *craft union* which seeks to unite all workers of a particular craft, trade, occupation or grade of skill, irrespective of the industry in which they happen to be working.
2. The *industrial union*, which seeks to unite all workers engaged in a particular industry, irrespective of their craft, trade, occupation or grade of skill.
3. The *general union* which seeks to unite workers of every industry and occupation who are not catered for by either of the other two categories. Normally associated with general unions are unskilled or semi-skilled workers in industries where long-established craft unions recruit the skilled men, for example, engineering and building; workers of all grades of skill in new or recently organized industries with no tradition of craft or industrial unions; groups of workers in isolated pockets of their industry who are not catered for in either craft or industrial unions.

Such then is the pattern into which unions have grown over the years, spreading out along the lines of development which seemed appropriate and convenient at the time and in whatever direction was necessary to protect the interests of their members.

Craft unions are the oldest type of worker organizations (having developed from the medieval guilds). In addition to their concern with wages and conditions of employment, they are very conscious of the status of their craft and take a close interest in apprenticeship and other training schemes. They often have a strong element of the benevolent society about them, and their high rates of contributions enable them to pay generous benefits. Craft unions have tended to grow in two ways: the days of the small unions are passing and development has often involved the amalgamation of unions of related crafts; or, in industries where their members comprise a large proportion of those employed, they have enrolled workers of lower grades of skill. Within the category of craft

* A full analysis appears in the *Department of Employment Gazette*, November 1976, page 1250.

unions there are three sub-divisions: the 'pure' craft union, for example the former London Society of Compositors; the multi-craft union, for example the Amalgamated Society of Woodworkers; and those bordering on industrial unions, for example the Amalgamated Union of Engineering Workers, which admits machine operatives and labourers.

There are no *industrial unions* in the full sense of being without opposition in their own industry and organizing every grade of worker, including salaried staff, in that industry. Generally accepted as two good examples, however, are the National Union of Mineworkers and the National Union of Railwaymen. The former evolved as local coalfield unions came together, but there are some groups of maintenance workers who remain outside the N.U.M. The N.U.R. started out deliberately intending to become an industrial union by the amalgamation of several small unions of manual workers in the railway industry, but its efforts so far have always been frustrated by two occupational unions, the Associated Society of Locomotive Engineers and Firemen, and the Transport Salaried Staffs' Association; also, in railway workshops skilled men are often organized by the appropriate engineering unions. Unions in new industries, for example the Chemical Workers Union* and the Tobacco Workers Union, are striving to set up industrial unions against the competition of the general workers' organizations. On the other hand, some industrial unions have expanded in such diverse directions that there is little to differentiate between them and general unions. The Union of Shop, Distributive, and Allied Workers, for instance, was originally concerned with the business of distribution, but now includes van men, clerks, and workers in a variety of manufacturing industries and consumer services like laundries and catering.

No clear line of distinction can be drawn between industrial and *general unions*. Best known among the latter are the Transport and General Workers' Union and the National Union of General and Municipal Workers. Both are among the giants of the trade union movement and were formed by amalgamations in 1921. They organize unskilled and semi-skilled workers in a wide range of industries and occupations, and in some cases they have absorbed craft unions. Without having precise spheres of influence, in general the T.G.W.U. covers roads, transport, and docks, while the N.U.G.M.W. organizes manual workers in municipal concerns, gas, water, and electricity. Conflict between them and with other industrial and craft unions sometimes arises over allegations of 'poaching' members.

The attempt to classify British trade unions is further complicated by the presence of large numbers of local unions which exist quite independently. Examples are the Sheffield cutlery unions, where the industry

*A case of failure—eventually absorbed into the T.G.W.U.

itself is localized, and the former London Society of Compositors which enjoyed territorial monopoly in a defined area although national organizations operated over the rest of the country. In the Lancashire cotton industry there are approximately 150 local unions but most of them belong to one of six federations. In addition, there are a large number of staff and professional associations, some with a horizontal structure, covering many different industries, such as the Clerical and Administrative Workers' Union, where a variety of non-manual workers within a wide range of industry are members, and others with a closed membership like the National Union of Teachers. The picture is further complicated by such bodies as the Civil Service and insurance unions, the structures of which are so complex that they are impossible to classify. The growth of these 'white-collar' unions and staff associations has been a phenomenon of the nineteen-sixties, and can, therefore, be traced to more modern aspirations —particularly as regards the employee's need to combat the increasing impersonality of his environment and remoteness of senior management. Staff want greater influence over the decisions that affect their working lives, and, to this end, they want their representatives involved in decision-taking and answerable to them.

The basic unit of most trade unions is the *local branch* or lodge which elects its own officers and discusses matters affecting its members' interests (*see* Figure 29). Purely domestic matters are normally decided on the spot; issues of wider importance are sent forward to the union's district or national centres. Branches vary in size from a handful to thousands of members, although the average in craft union branches is about 100. Each branch usually has a secretary and a small number of other officials; they are voluntary and undertake their duties in addition to their normal employment, receiving very little if anything by way of payment.

In many industries union membership is also organized on the job,

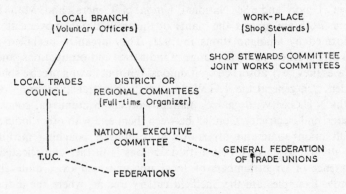

Figure 29. Trade union structure

where the lead is taken by *shop stewards*. Their range of duties varies in practice: they may do nothing more than collect weekly dues; at the other extreme, they may try to obtain higher rates of pay or to settle grievances by negotiating directly with management. They may be responsible for union recruitment, contacting newcomers to the factory, and also for detecting any encroachment upon recognized working conditions. Shop stewards of different unions within the same organization may be linked by a *steward's committee*, and may also sit on joint committees representing management and workers.

On a district or regional basis, trade union branches may appoint representatives to local *trades councils* to consider questions of common interest to trade unionism in that area. Most of these councils are based geographically on a county or group of counties. One of their important functions is to act as channels of communication between local unions and the Trades Union Congress, which lacks any local organization of its own; with national executives of trade unions they are the only bodies which can contact the T.U.C. direct. Although membership of local trades councils is voluntary, the advantages to union branches are obvious: apart from offering a voice in high places, trades councils play a prominent part in the education and training of local union officials, and are usually represented on local employment committees and other joint bodies in which the interests of the working community are involved.

The members of a union's local branches elect delegates to represent them on district and national committees of the union, and particularly at the union's *national conference* when policy and any alterations to rules are decided. Most unions have some kind of *regional organization* with full-time paid organizers, either elected by members or appointed by the national executive committee, and the bigger unions also have networks of regional committees or councils which often have great influence on behalf of their members in their area.

The central organizations of the larger unions follow the same general structural pattern. Each controls its own funds and has a head office with full-time staff. A permanent body of officials, including a *general secretary*, is responsible to a *national executive committee* of the union, which may be part-time or full-time, and is usually elected at the national conference of branch delegates. The executive committee plays a major part in the running of the union, carrying out the policy decisions of the delegates between conferences and preparing reports which, together with resolutions submitted by the branches, form the basis of conference agenda. The general secretary is normally a full-time paid official, in most cases elected by a vote of all members, but sometimes by the delegate conference. He normally takes part in all important union meetings, in negotiations with employers, and is usually one of the union's delegates to the annual Trades Union Congress. Most unions also have a *president* (again full-time or part-time) who is usually of comparable importance to the general secretary.

While trade unions are often accused of conservatism towards change, they do reorganize themselves from time to time in attempts to increase effectiveness. For example, the E.T.U. took note of some of the comments in the Donovan Commission Report and abolished its old area committees, setting up four industrial conferences in their place. Now all the E.T.U. shop stewards in the shipbuilding, electrical supply, engineering, and contracting industries meet separately for annual area conferences; every other year each group has a national industrial conference. There are also industrial branches at local level. The E.T.U.* then, has moved towards a trade group structure based less on regional and more on work groupings. Perhaps the greatest significance of this is that all the stewards who attend area and national conferences speak the same language and have practical experience of the problems brought up for discussion.

The distinction between craft and industrial unions is further complicated by the fact that in a number of industries *federations of trade unions* have been formed to enable collective bargaining to take place on an industry-wide basis. The number of trade unions affiliated to such federations is large, and several trade unions are members of more than one federation. Some of these decide policy and take action on behalf of their particular unions: for example, the Confederation of Shipbuilding and Engineering Unions and the National Federation of Building Trade Operatives; others act purely in a consultative or co-ordinating manner. In national negotiations workers may therefore be represented by more than one body, but although the authority of federations over constituent unions varies, ultimate power as regards action about disputes always rests with the individual union.

Yet another part of the total structure is the *General Federation of Trade Unions*, established in 1899 by the T.U.C. as a central body which today, in practice, mainly takes responsibility for financing trade union mutual-aid services. Any of the fifty-six member unions of this federation can draw upon a central fund to supplement its resources in the event of a strike or lock-out. This federation also provides research, statistical, and educational services of the type which large unions can afford from their own resources.

Most of the large and important trade unions are affiliated to the *Trades*

---

* Further merger talks are taking place, at the time of writing, between what is now the Electricians and Plumbers Trade Union and the General and Municipal Workers Union.

Union Congress, which caters for a total membership of over eleven million workers. The official functions of the T.U.C. are:

1. To do anything to promote the interests of all or any of its affiliated organizations.
2. Generally to improve the economic and social conditions of workers in all parts of the world and to render them assistance whenever necessary.
3. To affiliate to or subscribe to or assist in other organizations having objectives similar to those of the Congress.
4. To assist in the complete organization of all workers eligible for membership to its affiliated organizations, and (subject to its rules) to settle disputes between the members of such organizations and their employers or between such organizations and their members or between the organizations themselves.

In furthering these objectives the T.U.C. operates in the context of a comprehensive political and social programme, including nationalization, the extension of social services, adequate participation of workers in the management of public services, a maximum working week and minimum wage for workers in all industries, cash benefits and training for the unemployed, industrial health and welfare services, full educational facilities, adequate housing, and adequate pensions.

Annually in September, delegates from affiliated unions meet to settle future policy and elect a *General Council* to implement decisions taken at the Congress. The duties of the General Council are to co-ordinate industrial action of trade unions, to promote legislation affecting labour, to foster common action on general conditions of employment including wages, to settle differences between affiliated unions, and generally to seek in every practical manner to strengthen the trade union movement. The Government usually consults the General Council before deciding policies or taking action on any matter affecting the nation's labour force.

But although the scope of these duties is very wide, the T.U.C.'s executive powers over the individual unions affiliated to it are limited. Its resolutions cannot bind any trade union, which remains completely autonomous. The General Council will never intervene in any dispute, unless requested by the affiliated unions involved, so long as there is any prospect of a settlement being achieved through the traditional methods of negotiation. If a deadlock is reached, and particularly if this affects workers in other industries, then the Council may take the initiative in trying to effect a settlement.

Another important function of the General Council is to apply the *Bridlington Agreement* which states the general principles necessary to ensure smooth working relations between unions. Under this agreement the Council may investigate disputes between unions, usually relating to demarcation of work or competition in the same industry to attract members. In the last resort, any union which does not accept the decision of the General Council in such a dispute may be excluded from membership of the T.U.C.

The General Council consists of thirty-seven members elected by the whole Congress, representing nineteen trade categories on a proportionate basis. The T.U.C. has a permanent headquarters and its staff come under the supervision of the general secretary. It maintains a liaison with government departments, employers' organizations, and many other bodies. It has five group committees, each covering a number of related industries, and also a number of standing committees dealing with problems of organization, economic affairs, education, and international issues.

More and more important economic decisions are being taken internationally by worldwide corporations. It has been estimated that as much as 25 per cent of British industry will be owned by American firms by 1980, and entry into the European Economic Community is another recent event. Trade unions are clearly becoming conscious of the implications in this development, such as employers wielding new economic weapons—switching investment between countries, for example, or even placing orders elsewhere if one area is faced with industrial strife.

International trade unionism thus sees the need to develop beyond its past 'fraternal' phase. Typical of the action already taken are attempts by unions to regulate relationships with the Bowater and Michelin groups. Representatives of the unions concerned hold periodic meetings in Geneva, where they exchange information about the companies' profitability and how much members should hold out for in their respective countries when they negotiate with these firms. Thus they work out common objectives and seek to get better terms than if each were to negotiate separately.

EMPLOYERS' ORGANIZATIONS; THE N.J.A.C.

Employers' organizations, like trade unions, have grown in an entirely haphazard manner; possibly more so, since there are some 1,600 of them. They fall into three main groups:

1. Those which deal with questions of labour relations and negotiate with trade unions to settle conditions of employment and avoid disputes.
2. Those which deal with these purposes and also deal with trading and professional questions.
3. Those which deal only with trading matters.

Just as their functions vary so do their structures, although for purposes of settling working conditions most employers are organized upon an industry basis, both locally and nationally. Most of the major industries in the country have local or regional organizations, combined into national federations. But, like their counterparts in the trade union movement, these federations have very limited executive authority over their individual members, especially as regards wages and working conditions. The activities of many employers' federations are very comprehensive in safeguarding the interests of their members, providing them with advice and assistance on a wide range of problems, and undertaking the organization of training courses for management.

A survey of members of employers' associations was carried out by the Donovan Commission, which listed many benefits accruing: collective action and uniform decisions; technical information; advice on trade union matters; representation and liaison with government bodies and trade unions; advice on wage rates; advice on pricing policies; information and advice on government and local authority regulations; advice on training schemes and on holiday arrangements. Some associations also provide management consultancy services and assistance with work study and productivity bargaining.

Representing employers of some 70 per cent of the working population engaged in private industry throughout the country, the *Confederation of British Industry* is the employers' equivalent of the T.U.C. Its aim is to secure the co-operation of employers' national federations in dealing with all industrial relations questions affecting employers and their workers. A General Purposes Committee takes executive action and there are many other standing committees corresponding to those of the T.U.C. There are regional associations in several parts of the country, either where most activities are centred (for example, shipbuilding on the Clyde and in Belfast) or sectional bodies dealing with the manufacture of particular products within an industry.

The final piece in the elaborate structure of industrial relations is the *National Joint Advisory Council*; originally established early in the Second World War, this Council constitutes permanent formal machinery whereby matters of common interest to employers, workers, and the Government can be discussed. Its membership has fluctuated over the years, but now comprises equal numbers representing management and labour in both private and nationalized industries. Typical of its deliberations are problems of automation as related to employment, restrictive practices, the training of young workers in industry, and the development of joint consultation.

DISPUTES MACHINERY

The machinery for the settlement of disputes (Figure 30) involves negotiation in the first place, and in some industries there is a chain of reference upwards from local disputes to national level.

This procedure for settling disputes may lead to State intervention: the parties involved may ask for this voluntarily, or it may take place compulsorily. The Secretary of State for Employment himself is obliged under certain circumstances to offer his assistance, particularly when he feels the national interest is at stake, to prevent and settle disputes. In the

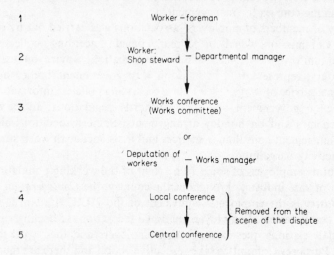

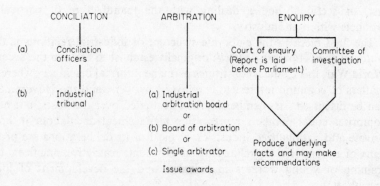

Figure 30. Settlement of disputes

first place, conciliation officers may try to effect a settlement at any stage of a dispute by bringing the parties together and informing public opinion of the facts behind it. The Minister may also order an enquiry in one of two forms. Where the public interest is seriously involved, he may set up a Court of Enquiry which has formidable powers and can compel witnesses to attend and give evidence under oath; it lays a report before Parliament and may make recommendations from which a reasonable settlement of the dispute can be expected. This form of impartial public examination has often been successful in the past. Under the Conciliation Act, 1896, the Minister may also appoint a Committee of Investigation which is normally employed where the national interest is not so closely involved. Its procedure is less flexible and its report is not laid before Parliament. Finally, arbitration may be tried, with the consent of both parties, when all other means of settling a dispute have failed. Both parties must agree to such action, for there is no means under the Conciliation Act, 1896, or the Industrial Courts Act, 1919, of compelling an unwilling party to go to arbitration. Arbitration awards under both these Acts are not legally binding on the parties concerned but, since they arise from a joint desire to settle a dispute by arbitration, the question of enforcement rarely occurs in practice. Once awards have been acted upon, they form part of a normal contract of employment.

The Secretary of State may refer cases for arbitration to the Central Arbitration Committee or to one or more persons appointed by himself. Most cases are dealt with by the former, which is a permanent and independent tribunal free of any form of governmental control. The members of the C.A.C. comprise independent persons and representatives of employers and unions. Most of the cases that it has dealt with since its establishment in 1919 (as the Industrial Court) have related to wage increases, hours of work, and holidays with pay. It may also be asked by the Secretary of State to give advice to him on questions which, in his opinion, ought to be referred to the C.A.C. Its awards are normally expressed in the form of decisions with full statements of the opposing arguments, but without discussion of the merits of those arguments or of the factors on which the awards are based. Many industries have voluntary agreements providing for the reference of unsettled disputes to the C.A.C. and, most important, for the acceptance by both parties of its findings. The Advisory, Conciliation and Arbitration Service may refer disputes to the C.A.C. for arbitration if the parties concerned agree.

There is, nevertheless, scope for improvement in arbitration through the Central Arbitration Committee, for at present the process has two weaknesses. The fact that no reasons for awards are given is certainly no help to either trade unions or employers' federations in trying to settle their future policy. Secondly, the C.A.C. has no resources to pursue any enquiries they might like to make into the background of claims presented to them. In this respect the thoroughness of their investigations falls short of what the staff of the N.B.P.I. were able to achieve by way of research during the early stages of claims; they were also able to receive informal representations (meetings between officers, telephone calls) as well as formal submissions.

No-one would regard arbitration as a panacea for all industrial relations problems. In no way is it a substitute for collective bargaining; but it is a logical extension of existing processes, and there is much to be said in favour of arbitration being written in to all organizational policy statements on industrial relations as the final step in negotiations. Arbitration is especially suited to the settlement of disputes of right, demanding the interpretation of existing written agreements or contracts. These must be distinguished from disputes of interest, for example where a company's ability to pay or comparability with similar workers elsewhere is in question. Most managers, supervisors, and shop stewards alike probably require further training in this area to ensure that they fully understand the aims and processes of arbitration. Finally, a practical issue: it is vital to ensure that the act of arbitration works speedily and without external pressures of any kind.

Actually, the procedure described above for the engineering industry is one of only a few cases where anything more than the most general rules are laid down for settling disputes. Most managers and shop stewards rely on informal custom and usage rather than written rules; and even where procedures are most closely defined, they are often applied in a very flexible manner. Both sides normally realize the need to allow for settlements that reflect variations in local circumstances, and accept that any dispute may take a course which does not strictly follow procedure. After all, precise procedures cannot of themselves be expected to solve industrial problems; in view of the rapidity of technological development, conflict is almost inevitable and indeed may help to clarify the situation and speed the way for any necessary changes.

THE PROBLEMS FACED BY THE DONOVAN COMMISSION

Trade unions, which were granted a privileged legal position early in the twentieth century when they were very weak compared with employers, have now become extremely powerful. In turn, society has come to question this position, believing that unions should suit their policies and actions to the national interest, and that the welfare of the majority of the community should not be sacrificed to the sectional interests of a few. It was in this context that the Royal Commission on Trade Unions and Employers' Associations was appointed in 1965, to examine these specific problems:

1. The role of trade unions and employers' associations in accelerating the social and economic advance of the nation.
2. Relations between management and employees.
3. The role of trade unions in promoting the interests of members, and the comparable role of employers' associations.
4. The law affecting the activities of trade unions and employers' associations.

These problems had manifested themselves over the years in the following ways:

Demarcation disputes, between workmen and workmen, rather than with their employers.

Unofficial strikes, which accounted for the large majority of working days lost (7,197,000 in 1973).

Union power over individual members, including the withdrawal of a union card, thus depriving a man of his livelihood. The intimidation of individual workers, especially during unofficial strikes, was another common abuse of power.

The closed shop, where union power was exercised over workers who were not members of the union at all.

The question facing the Royal Commission was whether practical solutions to all these problems lay in new legislation or in internal union reform. Those favouring the latter approach saw the T.U.C. playing a key role: members should be prepared to endow it with greater powers, enabling it to take a positive lead in raising union rules to an agreed standard; arbitration in all cases of inter-union disputes could be made compulsory; and expulsion from the T.U.C. should become a much more significant penalty than it was. The obvious lack of co-ordination between the policies of individual unions also called for an initiative from the T.U.C.: this could take the form of consultation between the General Council and union executives before their respective national conferences so that common tactics on wages, hours and other working conditions could be agreed.

Some structural reorganization of trade unionism would also help to resolve past difficulties. What is lacking is any form of local organization with responsibility for looking after the interests of trade unions as a whole in their area and seeing that inter-union disputes are referred to the appropriate machinery. This role could be undertaken by regional councils of the T.U.C. if they were given full-time staff to tackle demarcation problems, carry out local employment research work, and conduct recruitment drives to increase union membership.

THE TWO SYSTEMS

In its *Report*, the Donovan Commission distinguished between two systems:* the formal system employed in the official institutions, and the informal system created by the actual behaviour of trade unions and employers. Industry-wide collective agreements, which are supposed to settle pay, hours of work, and other conditions, form the keystone of the formal system; but the informal system, or what really happens in practice, is often at odds with the formal. Over the past thirty years there has been a decline in the extent to which industry-wide agreements determine actual pay, and today local plant bargaining is usually much more important.

National negotiators have also concluded procedural agreements in the past, providing means for conciliation or determining disputes that arise between organized workers and their managers (*see* Figure 25), but many of these procedures have been subjected to strain by the transfer of authority in industrial relations to the local workplace—in particular, much impatience has been shown at the length of time it takes to work through the formal channels.

The decline of the formal system provides an explanation for the pattern of strikes in this country. Official strikes represent only 5 per cent of the total, and there has been little tendency for these to rise in recent years. The other 95 per cent are unofficial strikes, lacking the support of the appropriate trade union authority; they are also usually unconstitutional, taking place before the various stages of the procedure for dealing with disputes have all been used. Very few of these strikes are concerned with industry-wide issues, but normally develop from disputes on the workshop floor and are settled locally.

The decentralization of collective bargaining took place under the pressure of full employment during postwar years, which greatly encouraged bargaining about pay at local levels. Employers often bid up pay rates, without much prompting, in order to retain labour, and thus became responsible more than anyone else for the phenomenon of 'wages drift'. But this intensely local activity has led to a decline in the authority of

* *Royal Commission on Trade Unions and Employers' Associations, 1965–8* (Cmnd. 3623, H.M.S.O.), Chapter 3.

employers' associations with which the practice of industry-wide bargaining is closely bound.

On the other hand, there has been a comparable shift of authority within trade unions. Certain features of their structure and government have helped to inflate the power of work groups and shop stewards within individual organizations. Among these is multi-unionism in most British industries and factories: four out of five trade unionists work in multi-union establishments, and about one in six belongs to a grade of worker in which two or more unions compete for members. The disproportionate numbers of giant and very small unions (*see* page 235) also serves to strengthen the position of work groups and to increase their independence. Since many trade union branches consist of small groups of members from a number of different factories, the branch is somewhat divorced from the real business of the union at the place of work, and full-time union officers cannot easily keep in touch.

In summary, the Commission found that the existing system of industrial relations had many shortcomings: the tendency for extreme decentralization and self-government to degenerate into indecision and anarchy; the propensity to breed inefficiency; and the reluctance to accept change—all these are characteristics that become more damaging as they develop, as the rate of technical progress increases, and as the need for economic growth becomes more urgent.

Hence the Conservative Government returned in 1970 decided that a legislative programme was necessary to improve industrial relations in Britain as opposed to the alternative of encouraging rapid internal reform by the unions themselves. Thus the Industrial Relations Act, 1971, was introduced. It produced a storm of bitter controversy, culminating in vows of non-cooperation from the trade unions.

In the event, contrary to the objectives of the Act, the number of official strikes rose as a proportion of all stoppages, and so did the number of days lost through them. In two major cases, the railwaymen's ballot held under the Act simply served to show their enthusiasm for the strike; and in the docks there would have been no strike at all if events connected with their union's defiance of the Act had not led to five dockers being committed to Pentonville prison. The Act was intended to boost union recognition and recruitment, but all that happened was a complicated union scramble for members, especially among the growing white-collar unions. The closed shop, which the Act was supposed to make void, continued as before; the 'agency shop', which was supposed to replace it, made little or no headway. No firm invited investigations of its disputes machinery, as had been hoped, to improve efficiency. The Government wanted union–employer deals to become legally binding, but very few such agreements were ever concluded. Thus the Act's true potential was never tested, for the simple reason that the T.U.C. forbade its member unions to have anything to do with it. Legislation that fails to attract a minimum of support from the people it is directed towards is bound to be a flop. A Labour government was returned in February 1974 and promptly repealed the 1971 Act.

THE TRADE UNION AND LABOUR RELATIONS ACTS 1974 AND 1976*

In order to avoid the uncertainties and, in some respects the loss of rights which a straightforward repeal of the Industrial Relations Act would have caused, other legislation was required. Hence this 1974 Act was passed to make provision for the law relating to trade unions, employers' associations, workers and employers, including the law relating to unfair dismissals, and the jurisdiction and procedures of industrial tribunals. Some provisions of the Industrial Relations Act were re-enacted; at the same time, some institutions which it set up were abolished, and the status and legal immunities of unions and employers' associations redefined.

The National Industrial Relations Court and Commission on Industrial Relations (C.I.R.) were abolished, and with them went the concepts of 'unfair industrial practices' and 'agency shop agreements' which they dealt with. The Secretary of State for Employment lost his powers to apply to the Industrial Court for orders for the discontinuance or postponement of industrial action, for 'cooling off' periods of up to sixty days, and for orders for ballots relating to industrial action. Registration of trade unions and employers' associations was taken over by a Certification Officer (E.P.A. 1975): each of these bodies registered must conform to the 'business rules' set out in the Trade Union and Labour Relations Act.

The Act continues a Code of Industrial Relations Practice. The law returns to the position it has occupied for most of the twentieth century, that an action by a person in furtherance of a trade dispute is not actionable. Legal recognition is given once again to 'closed shops', now called 'union membership agreements': these are defined as arrangements which have the effect of requiring the terms and conditions of employment of every employee to include a condition that he must be or become a member of one of the unions which is party to the agreement.

The position of collective agreements also reverts to the pre-1971 situation—they are not legally enforceable, unless they are in writing and con-

---

* The 1976 amendment mainly concerned the law dealing with dismissals for non-membership of a closed shop union. A clause providing for a charter on press freedom was included.

tain a provision stating that the parties intend that they should be legally enforceable contracts.

The Industrial Relations Act introduced the right to complain to an industrial tribunal about unfair dismissal, the onus of proving that a dismissal was not unfair being on the employer. The 1974 Act effectively continues these provisions, so that the case law built up since 1972 will continue to hold good. There are also two significant amendments. An employee is entitled to prove that he has been 'constructively dismissed', a phrase which covers termination by an employee of his contract of employment in circumstances such that he is entitled to terminate it without notice by reason of the employer's conduct. The employer is also given the right to dismiss an employee fairly if the employee refuses, other than on religious or other reasonable grounds, to belong to a trade union with whom the employer has a union membership (closed shop) agreement.

Where an employee considers he has been unfairly dismissed, he may make a complaint to an industrial tribunal. A conciliation officer of the Advisory, Conciliation and Arbitration Service will receive a copy of the complaint, and will normally intervene to try to obtain a voluntary settlement, thus avoiding the need for the case to be brought before a tribunal. The first priority is seen as the reinstatement of the dismissed person; if this is not practicable, an attempt must be made to get the parties to agree on the amount of compensation to be paid.

CODE OF INDUSTRIAL RELATIONS PRACTICE

The Trade Union and Labour Relations Act continues the responsibility of the Secretary of State for Employment to maintain a Code of Industrial Relations Practice. Thus the former Code, which supplemented the 1971 Act, and which was originally conceived as the most significant long-term basis for reform of industrial relations policies, is to continue. The Code has never been legally enforceable as such, but any proceedings before industrial tribunals are examined in light of practices recommended in the Code. The onus for good leadership is placed on the shoulders of management in implementing the advice offered in its seven main sections:

1. The responsibilities of managements, unions, and individual employees.
2. Employment policies, which should be drawn up and maintained by employers.
3. Communications and consultation.
4. Collective bargaining—structure and agreements.
5. Employee representation at the place of work: i.e. the work of shop stewards.

6. Grievance and disputes procedures.
7. Disciplinary procedures.

INSTITUTIONS

One way of further comprehending the scope of current legislation and its application is to look at the roles of the institutions which now exist to assist in the smooth running of industrial relations in this country.

(a) ADVISORY, CONCILIATION AND ARBITRATION SERVICE (A.C.A.S.)

This is headed by a ten-man council appointed by the Secretary of State for Employment, and consists of a chairman and nine other members, three appointed after consultation with the C.B.I. and three after consultation with the T.U.C. The service has the duty of offering advice, conciliation and mediation in both private and public sectors, where this is considered likely to be of assistance. Having regard to the procedural agreements already existing in an industry or area of employment, the service does not normally seek to intervene, unless and until there had been a failure to obtain a settlement within those procedures.

Conciliation is undertaken by the full-time professional staff of the service, although outside people may be called in as mediators if it is thought fit. At the joint request of the parties in dispute, single arbitrators or boards of arbitration may be appointed to determine differences on agreed terms of reference. A panel of people experienced in industrial relations has been set up for this purpose.

As a complement to conciliation, the service has also taken over the advisory functions of the D.E.'s former Conciliation and Advisory Service. Aimed at promoting better industrial relations, advice is available on such matters as procedural agreements, communications and consultation, labour turnover, job evaluation, payments systems, and progress towards equal pay. The advisory function of promoting the improvement and extension of collective bargaining machinery, the purview of the defunct Commission on Industrial Relations, has also been taken over.

The government's intention is eventually to establish the A.C.A.S. by statute, when it is envisaged that it will also take over the functions of the Registrar of Friendly Societies and the Industrial Arbitration Board and have other statutory functions.

(b) INDUSTRIAL TRIBUNALS

Originally set up in 1964, these tribunals already exist to adjudicate on matters arising from the Contracts of Employment Act, 1963, the Industrial

Training Act, 1964, the Redundancy Payments Act, 1965, and the Equal Pay Act, 1970. They sit in regional centres, and now also deal with individual cases and complaints under the Trade Union and Labour Relations Act;* they have powers to award compensation and make orders determining the rights of individuals or organizations. Their procedures are informal, and they are required to offer opportunities for conciliation between the parties before hearing a case.

(c) CENTRAL ARBITRATION COMMITTEE

This is the old Industrial Court, given a new name, and as such will continue to deal with claims under equal pay legislation, for example. In addition, the A.C.A.S. will refer to it for arbitration claims by registered trade unions that an employer has failed to disclose information to them, or has not complied with a requirement to negotiate with them. Disputes may also be referred for arbitration, if the parties concerned agree.

(d) CERTIFICATION OFFICER

The registration of trade unions is intended to ensure that, in order to benefit from the rights and privileges originally established by the Industrial Relations Act, trade union rules comply with statutory minimum standards. These standards, which also apply to employers' associations, refer to the constitutions, management, links with members, property, and the financial arrangements of all registered organizations. The Registrar's tasks are to check on these rules, ensure that they are observed in practice, and to vet the administration of unions and employers' associations so as to safeguard the public interest, and protect the rights of members and those seeking membership. He can investigate complaints against registered organizations, and may take unresolved cases to the A.C.A.S. for adjudication. He is responsible for certifying the independence of trade unions under the Employment Protection Act, 1975.

(e) EMPLOYMENT APPEAL TRIBUNAL

This body hears appeals from the decisions of industrial tribunals on points of law (previously went to the High Court). It also hears appeals from the decisions of the Certification Officer.

FURTHER READING

The System of Industrial Relations in Great. Britain, by H. A. Clegg (Blackwell, 1970). *Report of the Royal Commission on Trade Unions and Employers' Associations 1965–68* (Cmnd. 3623, H.M.S.O.).

* Also the Race Relations Act, 1976.

15 Labour Relations at the Workplace

No general framework of industrial relations can of itself create the harmony and trust between management and workers in individual organizations necessary to develop the spirit of co-operation so essential for achieving success in business. Responsibility for establishing good relations rests with both management and workers, but there can be no doubt that the initiative must be taken by the former. Confidence must be earned over years of consistent dealing with day-to-day personnel problems, in a manner which reflects management's attitudes towards the basic need of individual employees for a satisfactory working environment in its fullest sense.

Maintaining contact and spreading understanding between management and workers is the purpose of communications in industry. Slowly it has come to be realized that improvements in efficiency, leading to increased productivity, depend in large measure on the co-operation of workers, and that this can only be obtained if they are told of and comprehend management's aims and plans. The achievement of effective communications is the subject of the next chapter: the point to be made clear here is that experience shows that the most important factor in communications is the quality of relationships within the organization between management, supervisors, and worker groups.

SHOP STEWARDS

Key figures in labour relations at any workplace are shop stewards. Their emergence can be traced to the remoteness of union branch and district officers whose concern for all workers in their areas means that they can devote comparatively little time or effort to any single establishment. The strength of the shop steward movement has always been based on the argument that rank-and-file union members must act for themselves in their own local interests, even if this means taking unofficial action with unofficial leaders.

Typical of the constitutional powers that have been granted to shop stewards are the conditions set out in the 1922 agreement between the Engineering and Allied Employers' Federation and the engineering trade unions, which established a procedure for the ventilation of grievances and for dealing with questions raised at the workplace by shop stewards. The agreement permitted workers who were members of trade unions employed in federated establishments to appoint shop stewards to act on their behalf. The names of these stewards were to be intimated officially to management on election by the trade union concerned. Shop stewards were to be subject to the control of the trade unions they represented and could act only in accordance with agreements signed by the employers and unions. The employers, for their part, agreed that shop stewards should be accorded facilities for dealing with questions raised in their departments, including time to carry out their duties in connection with works committees and power to visit other departments of the establishment while doing so. Both employers and shop stewards were forbidden to enter into arrangements contrary to any agreement between the employers' federation or local association and the trade unions.

A shop steward is the main link between the members of a trade union working in a particular department and the full-time local officials of that union. Although his election normally must be confirmed by the branch or district officers of the union, he is not himself an official of the union. But he is accepted by his employer as the union's accredited representative and spokesman, providing a recognized point of contact, especially in large firms where employee representation on works committees may be confined to shop stewards. He will assist in settling complaints and disputes between workers and management at workshop level, and may also take part in such technical matters as rate-fixing on piece-work operations where it is desirable to take workers' points of view into account. In big organizations it is usual for shop stewards to have their own committee under the chairmanship of the most senior steward, called the *convenor*.

As regards his union, the shop steward's chief functions are to recruit new members, to maintain membership, and in some cases to collect dues. Through union branch meetings he may assist in formulating policy, and is then responsible for reporting back and explaining that policy to the members he represents. Conversely, he reports to the union about wages and conditions of employment in his firm. He may also play an important part in the initial stages of claims in respect of industrial injuries incurred by any of his members.

It is an important prerogative of shop stewards in most establishments that they have direct access to management. Although it is unusual for them to take part in any national machinery of negotiations for their industry, there is an increasing movement towards local negotiations for the adjustment of central agreements, and stewards play an obvious part in these; in fact they often take the initiative in presenting claims to management for local increases on negotiated rates. But the role of shop stewards in the settlement of disputes, including those relating to demarcation of work, manning of machines, and redundancy, is generally limited to the stage at which those disputes, having failed to reach settlement at workshop level, pass into the hands of full-time union officials at branch or district level. In recent years, judging by the incidence of unofficial strikes, there has in fact been a marked increase in the number of disputes dealt with entirely by shop stewards. These usually relate to demands about working arrangements, rules, or discipline; the amount of work considered reasonable for a given wage; changes in working methods and the use of labour; and the treatment of individuals by supervisors and departmental managers.

Discussing all these subjects with management places shop stewards in the van of the movement towards industrial democracy, aimed at integrating managerial authority with the rights of individual employees. The onset of a higher level of unemployment, such as occurred in the latter part of 1966, for example, also increases shop steward activity. The threat of unemployment no longer puts unions on the defensive, as it did during the nineteen-thirties; instead, they fight to preserve the security of employment and stability of earnings that are part of the ever-rising level of expectations among workers about their just entitlements from industry. They also demand the right to participate with management in reaching decisions that affect their well-being.

Authority to call a strike on their own initiative is rarely given to shop stewards by their unions. Nevertheless, by reason of the influence which their activities give them at the place of work, they sometimes do call workers out on strike without the permission of their union officials and sometimes in breach of agreements. But since the unions concerned have not sanctioned this 'unofficial' action, the workers involved do not receive any strike pay.

This analysis of the place of the shop steward in the local structure is echoed in the advice on good policy given in the Code of Industrial Relations Practice, which in turn was supplemented by a C.I.R. report on the facilities that should be afforded to shop stewards.

In the first place, it is suggested that trade unions need to clarify the steward's functions and responsibilities—election arrangements, the issue of union credentials, the observation of agreements, how to handle grievances, communication with members—all matters that could be dealt with in a more standardized way, and hence more efficiently. Employers should also review their present attitudes towards shop stewards. Although the latter are now generally recognized as making a valuable contribution in the field of industrial relations, it should be management which takes the initiative, and which sets the tone of the relationship by actively seeking their help.

The functions of shop stewards that are of joint concern should be jointly reviewed, especially as regards the facilities necessary to carry them out. In trying to apply industry-wide agreements, it must be recognized that the key areas are usually at company or unit level. Management and unions, therefore, need to decide on constituencies, the number of stewards to be appointed, the range of their duties, and the facilities needed for them to perform effectively.

The growing significance of plant bargaining is relevant here, of course, for it is likely to develop further as processes become ever more specialized and capital-intensive industries strive to retain their skilled labour. A major consequence is the shift of power and authority on the shop floor from union executives to the shop stewards. Productivity bargaining, which cuts through the complexity of wage agreements, job redefinition, shift-work and overtime payments, has added to this local power. Shop stewards, whose original tasks were largely limited to recruiting members and collecting subscriptions, now find themselves negotiating local agreements, explaining their nature to the workers they represent, and even supervising the way they operate.

Many trade unions undertake their own educational activities, and as long ago as 1948 the General Council of the T.U.C. urged unions to consider the training of shop stewards in such subjects as the elements of production and costing as well as industrial relations. The growth of the use of work study in industry also stimulated this type of training, which has since been taken up by technical colleges and universities. Some progressive employers, when introducing work study practices into their organizations, arrange for shop stewards to train in the technique so that union members might have greater confidence in it. Since 1951 the T.U.C. has run full-time courses in production and management for shop stewards and members of joint production committees; their main purpose is to assist workshop representatives who act on behalf of unions in negotiations and joint consultation to increase their competence by acquiring knowledge of the terminology, principles, and elementary techniques of management. The subjects studied include industrial efficiency, works management, work study, wage systems, costing, company finance and accounts, and problems of productivity. The more progressive trade union leaders thus seem convinced of the need for wider training of their future officials, but many unions still do little or nothing in this direction. A further interesting development is the decision of several Industrial

Training Boards (initially shipbuilding, construction, and water supply) to make grants to employers who release their shop stewards for approved training courses. So employers who do not believe in training trade union representatives in the firm's time in future will be indirectly subsidizing those who do. Again, the Code of Industrial Relations Practice urges management and trade unions to review the type of training most appropriate for the steward's needs, and to take all reasonable steps to ensure that stewards receive this training.

Each union should also take care to see that its own shop stewards are adequately informed about its policies, organization, and the agreements to which it is a party. Management, too, should ensure that stewards are well informed about its objectives and employment policies.

WORKSHOP RULE

Some industries appear to be much more prone to friction between workers and management than others, and there often seems to be a hard core of firms within each industry which have continuous trouble over workshop regulations. Since other comparable organizations have much less trouble, the only conclusion must be that it is not only collective agreements and union rules which lead to workshop friction, but also worker–management relations in each individual establishment. These relations are intimately connected with the operation of workshop rules which are usually out of reach both of union control and national agreement, but are very much the concern of the shop steward. It is most important to appreciate this 'separation', because it is not a fact that is advertised by either unions or employers' associations. Officials who are ultimately responsible for maintaining union authority and agreements no doubt feel that their position would be weakened if they were to acknowledge that a considerable part of shop steward activity was beyond their control. It is, nevertheless, one way of describing the 'unofficial system' identified by the Donovan Commission.

In addition to union rules and legislation (such as the Factories Act) a wide variety of domestic rules apply in each workplace. There are agreed rules about procedure and conditions of work which supplement those made in district and national agreements between unions and management; these may be written or simply based on custom and practice. Then there are works' rules laid down by management as part of workers' contracts of employment; these must be written, but often overlap into works' custom. Finally, there are work-group rules established by workers on the job, usually dealing with such matters as the pace and sharing of work.

Many of these rules are made unilaterally by workers or management until challenged by the other; they normally then form the basis of negotiation and, once settled, both sides are obliged to see that they are kept. Some managers feel that the existence of shop stewards makes rule-making and enforcement easier, others believe the opposite. It is obvious, however, that a system which includes worker representatives is more democratic than one which relies exclusively on management decisions.

In addition, an element of self-government is reflected in decisions on two broad groups of topics: those matters in national agreements which are left to be settled locally, and matters that are essentially domestic to the establishment itself, such as complaints about the canteen or the settlement of holidays. In either case the calling of meetings to discuss problems, together with informal discussion between stewards and workers, constitutes a type of self-government in the workplace. The implications of this for trade unions are of the utmost importance. If low attendance at branch meetings makes the self-government of trade unions difficult, and if workshop groups, in themselves largely self-governing, become the active focus of membership participation, the possibility of strain between workshop, branch, and outside officials increases. At the moment this apparent gap is bridged successfully because shop stewards often form the core of branch membership attending meetings in any case, and union officials themselves usually take great trouble to maintain close contact with the shop stewards in their areas.

A large proportion of shop stewards accept the need to play a responsible part in maintaining works discipline, one reason being that discipline is in the general interest. It can be argued therefore that management should never try to weaken the hold of the steward over his members but rather provide him with opportunities for strengthening their confidence. The existence of agreed rules between workers and management on the factory floor give responsibilities to both sides, but trade union members are often unable to see the practical limits to a steward's militancy. They feel that if he acts in a 'constitutional' manner he may become a part of the management team, and this is one of the main reasons why some unions are opposed to giving formal powers to shop stewards. In practice, however, 'constitutional' stewards often achieve better results than their more militant colleagues, as there is a great deal to be said for not pressing opposition to its ultimate limits. Stewards are obviously unable to change their management and they are wise to recognize that successful negotiation includes the ability to save the other side's face, so that a working relationship profitable to both sides can be continued.

Thus an accurate analysis of the roles of shop stewards seems very difficult, closely involved as they are with their unions, the policies and behaviour of local managers, and the collective agreements, traditions, and organizational problems of the industry in which they work. It is an over-simplification to regard them merely as subordinate trade union officers carrying out instructions or applying national agreements within their local spheres. Indeed, operating in such a variety of different situations, shop stewards need considerable latitude if they are to represent workers effectively, and it therefore seems almost impossible to subject them to detailed control by their unions. Union leaders themselves are faced with a dilemma, knowing that stewards' activities at the workplace are essential, yet ever aware of the threat they pose to the cohesiveness of union policy and standards of discipline. Since stewards cannot be rigidly controlled, can they not at least be more strongly influenced to accept the objectives and priorities laid down by their union's leadership? To a large extent each union must find its own solution to this problem, mainly by improving communications with its ordinary members and their workplace representatives. The T.U.C. could also help by trying to give a much clearer sense of direction to the shop steward movement as a whole.

Even so, the ultimate responsibility of management for controlling industrial relations in the workplace cannot be avoided, despite the fact that all too little thought has been given to the development of harmonious relations with worker representatives. Appeals are frequently made to unions to discipline their stewards when they cause trouble, overlooking the fact that the events to which stewards react in the workplace are shaped by management's own decisions or lack of them. Management rarely takes the initiative in putting forward proposals to improve wages and working conditions; more commonly it merely responds to union pressures. When the lesson is made so clear that coercion achieves the best results, obviously unions cannot be asked to prevent their members from acting on it, nor can they be expected to relieve management of the responsibility for avoiding stoppages by providing alternative and more attractive methods of settling conflicts at the workplace.

The fragmentation which inevitably results from the existence of 1,600 employers' associations clearly contributes to management's piecemeal and largely defensive role throughout the whole field of industrial relations: a role which usually means waiting for demands to be made and then trying to contain them within practical limits. The net result can only be to leave employers open to a progressive series of demands. Forward plans are made for finance, sales, and production—why not for industrial relations? The future pattern of demands for shorter hours, longer holidays, improved fringe benefits, and wage increases linked to the state of the economy is normally fairly clear to those who take the trouble to look —so that most organizations should be able to forecast where they will stand for at least a few years ahead. They should therefore be in a position to take the initiative in influencing the order and timing of claims for improvements, thus avoiding the present practice of dealing with demands in a piecemeal fashion without considering their cumulative long-term consequences.

JOINT CONSULTATION

WORKS COMMITTEES

Works committees date from a recommendation of the Whitley Committee set up in 1916 to investigate means of securing a permanent improvement in relations between employers and workers. In addition to proposals affecting industrial relations at national level, it was suggested that works committees representing both managers and workers should be set up in individual establishments, in the hope of giving employees a wider interest in, and greater responsibility for, the conditions in which their work was performed. As long ago as 1919 a Ministry of Labour industrial report listed the following as suitable functions for works committees:

1. The issue and revision of works rules.
2. Questions of discipline and conduct as between management and workpeople (for example, sickness, malingering, and bad time-keeping).
3. Terms of engagement of workpeople.
4. Arranging lectures on the technical and social aspects of the industry.
5. Training of apprentices and young people.
6. Suggestions for improvements in methods and organization of work.

Other matters which commonly form the subject of joint discussion nowadays include the settlement of grievances, holiday arrangements, the distribution of work and other production problems, and social functions.

Some subjects clearly must be dealt with at national level, but there are many others which can only be settled locally within individual establishments. These fall into four main groups:

1. Terms of employment which are normally decided as matters of company policy: for example, pension schemes, sickness benefits, long-service awards, and redundancy agreements. All are subjects for consultation and discussion rather than negotiation.
2. Those terms of employment that are normally settled within the individual establishment: for example, incentive bonus schemes,

merit-rating, and payments for abnormal conditions. These are typical plant bargaining matters of great importance to individual employees, for such payments often account for a substantial proportion of their wage packets.

3. National agreements which cannot be applied at local level without some interpretation of their terms to the particular needs of individual firms; for example, agreements to reduce the length of the working week without loss of earnings often result in a great deal of bargaining at company and factory level.

4. The application of industrial agreements which fix minimum rates and conditions only. This form of agreement is often deliberately concluded in order to give much greater flexibility between companies whose profits may vary considerably, whose factories are located in different parts of the country, and who therefore face very different problems in trying to secure adequate supplies of labour.

The idea of extending joint consultation to production matters dates from the Second World War, originating with pit production committees in coal-mines at the end of 1940 and quickly extending to ordnance factories, shipbuilding yards, and other establishments under Governmental influence. The Minister of Labour issued a general call for regular discussions between management and worker representatives aimed at increasing production, and as the idea spread, employers quickly found that workers often had worthwhile suggestions to put forward and that consultation had great value as a means of improving morale. Since the war, the Government, the T.U.C., and the C.B.I. have all actively supported joint consultation, and in April 1947 the National Joint Advisory Council urged that *joint production committees* should be established where they did not already exist. Such machinery should be voluntary and advisory: it should not deal with questions relating to terms and conditions of employment, and each industry should decide the best form for this workplace machinery to take.

SPECIMEN CONSTITUTION FOR A JOINT PRODUCTION COMMITTEE

Objects

The Committee will operate in an advisory and consultative capacity and will provide for the following functions:

1. A direct means of communication between management and all employees.
2. A basis for constructive co-operation in obtaining—
   (a) The best possible shop efficiency.

(*b*) The best possible shop conditions.

(*c*) The well-being of all employed in the works.

3. A channel for discussion and consideration of any other matters concerning employees except those covered in the agreements between the company and the trade unions, such as wage rates and hours of work.

Membership

1. Management will be represented on the Committee by the Chairman, Secretary, and up to four other members.

2. Employees will be represented on the Committee by ten representatives, covering all departments.

3. Election of employees' representatives will take place in January of each year and will be by ballot. Management representatives will be appointed by the management.

Duties

The Committee will consider and make recommendations on any matter referred to it, provided such matters come within the scope of the objects.

Sub-committees

The Committee may set up temporary or permanent Sub-committees to which it may co-opt additional members to enable them to operate effectively. The Committee will elect the employees' representatives on the following Sub-committees and on any other Committees that are from time to time set up:

Economy of Materials Sub-committee
Quality Sub-committee
Safety Sub-committee
Fuel Economy Sub-committee
Welfare Advisory Sub-committee
Suggestions Scheme Sub-committee
Competitions Sub-committee
Works Collections and Charities Sub-committee.

It is Government policy to encourage rather than to compel private industry to discuss its problems with labour. This policy has been generally followed in the case of the *nationalized industries* with the exception of the coal industry which has a statutory obligation to set up joint consultative machinery. Section 46 of the Coal Industry Nationalization Act, 1946, reads:

It shall be the duty of the [National Coal] Board to enter into consultation with organisations appearing to them to represent substantial proportions of the persons in the employment of the Board, or of any class of such persons, as to the Board's concluding with those organisations agreements providing for the establishment of joint machinery for

(*a*) the settlement by negotiation of terms and conditions of employment, with provision for reference to arbitration in default of such settlement in such cases as may be determined by or under the agreements; and

(*b*) consultation on
   (i) questions relating to the safety, health or welfare of such persons;
   (ii) the organisation and conduct of the operations in which such persons are employed and other matters of mutual interest to the Board and such persons arising out of the exercise and performance of the Board of their functions.

As opposed to this statutory compulsion, Section 53 of the Electricity Act, 1947, provides:

Except in so far as they are satisfied that adequate machinery exists for achieving the purposes of this section, it shall be the duty of the Central Authority to seek consultation with any organisation appearing to them to be appropriate with a view to the conclusion between the Authority and that organisation of such agreements as appear to the parties to be desirable with respect to the establishment and maintenance of machinery for

(*a*) the settlement by negotiation of terms and conditions of employment, with provision for reference to arbitration in default of such settlement in such cases as may be determined by or under the agreements, and

(*b*) . . . the discussion of other matters of mutual interest to the Board and such persons, including efficiency in the operation of the Boards.

The fact that these forms of joint consultation take place in public rather than private industry does not in itself seem to have removed traditional management–labour difficulties. It appears that workers, accustomed to regard negotiations as trials of strength between two opposing parties, cannot readily appreciate the full significance of this new situation. Not that consultation should ever be regarded by trade unions as a handicap to their basic function of protecting the interests of their members. Indeed, these can be furthered by discussing such subjects as productivity, methods of working, and training; safeguarded, too, when issues arise which threaten their conditions of employment (for example, the introduction of new machinery, the closing down of departments, or transfer of workers within an organization). Trade union representatives will seek guarantees from management that their proposals in any of these areas will not adversely affect their members.

There are many basic difficulties to be overcome in making joint consultation work effectively. Trade unionists tend to object to joint machinery when non-unionists become members of the committees concerned. (In practice, methods of selecting representatives vary considerably; in most cases there is secret ballot of all workers, but in many firms representatives are elected or appointed by the local union branches.) Then there is the historical mistrust of management by so many trade unionists who feel they have nothing to gain from discussing improved methods: that it is not their concern to make suggestions which may result in higher profits for shareholders, and that ideas for new processes might mean working themselves out of their jobs. For their part, employers in the past have objected to joint consultation on the grounds that trade unionists are not primarily loyal to their firms and therefore may not be trusted with much of the information that is necessary for joint committees to function efficiently. Worker representatives have been charged with using joint committees to debate political matters and to re-open questions that have already been settled at a higher level of district or national negotiation. Many managers see in joint consultation a surrender of their prerogatives to direct and control. They are often unable to perceive that, by consulting the workpeople in the same way as they would consult their supervisory staff, they are not in the least lessening their own responsibility for the final action decided upon. Managers who take employees into their confidence, far from losing their prerogatives, may secure intelligent support for decisions because there is a better understanding of the motives and considerations underlying them. When managers use consultative methods enthusiastically and without reservation, they are as a rule met with a corresponding attitude. Suspicion breeds suspicion, however, and apathy indifference.

While the manager brings to joint consultative meetings facts and figures and a broad view of the plan to be followed, the worker can also bring something of value to the table. He is familiar with processes and materials, and by reason of long practical experience he knows the limitations of each. No one is more aware than he of the causes of waste, both of time and materials, or why work is rejected on inspection. While the manager is versed on the effects of these deficiencies, the worker is often best qualified to speak as to their causes.

Complaints that joint consultation is a waste of time seem to arise mainly in organizations where relations are bad. ('Management gets the shop stewards and union representatives it deserves.') Once again much depends on top management initiative and on the attitude of the chief executive, in particular. Many organizations are still paternalistic in outlook, very willing to consider employee welfare services, but they refuse to allow any important policy or production matters to be discussed at works committee meetings, so that many of the charges of abuse of joint consultation made against workers can often be traced back to earlier management attitudes. A policy of ensuring discussion at every level of the organization is the best way in which confidence and mutual respect between management and employees can be built. This requires management to take the initiative in fulfilling the need of each individual employee for satisfactory working conditions in every respect.

Despite its rather chequered history, and doubts expressed about the benefits for the effort involved, the principle of joint consultation continues to be actively encouraged in the Code of Industrial Relations Practice: 'Consultation means jointly examining and discussing problems of concern to both management and employees. It involves seeking mutually acceptable solutions through a genuine exchange of views and information ... Consultation about operational and other day-to-day matters is necessary in all establishments whatever their size. Establishments with more than 250 employees should have systematic arrangements for management and employee representatives to meet regularly.'

The right approach to joint consultation is where management clearly shows its belief that workers can contribute to an organization's efficiency. Consultation does not mean telling worker representatives about management decisions after they have been reached, so that they can then be communicated to the factory floor; rather, it is a process of obtaining workers' views *before* the decisions are taken. (Failure to grasp this distinction is undoubtedly the reason why so many joint consultative schemes have floundered from the outset.) Management must realize that time taken up in joint consultation is very well spent; those who feel it is wasted must be made to appreciate that it takes far less time to clarify policy in advance in the right atmosphere than to dispel the misunderstandings that often arise through failure to hold preliminary discussions. The main value of works committees thus lies in the good management–employee relationship engendered: on the one hand, workers feel satisfied because they can clearly identify themselves with the projects on which they are engaged; on the other, management will better be able to eliminate misunderstandings, to apprise themselves of the views of employees before decisions and policies are finalized, to know about matters on which strong feeling exists, and to become aware of employee attitudes on countless domestic situations.

BEHAVIOUR AT THE WORKPLACE

Works rule-books are now used in a large number of business organizations as the basis for the behaviour of everyone working in them. The compilation of these rule-books is an obvious opportunity for joint consultation, as this will ensure understanding of the purposes of the rules and will also offer a guarantee of support for their enforcement. Many attempts have been made in the past to administer rules through joint machinery: absentee committees, theft committees, safety committees—all are examples of efforts to deal with disciplinary matters that have met with some degree of success. Where punishment of offenders may be involved, principles of natural justice demand that there should also be appeals committees, but these have been slow to develop in any significant numbers within British industry.

The main reason for this limited application can be traced again to management attitudes, based on doubts whether worker representatives possess either the ability or impartiality to pass judgment on their fellows. The procedure is complex: obtaining and weighing evidence which may often be conflicting or incomplete, reaching a verdict, and imposing punishment where appropriate. All too often it appears that management and worker interests are so different as to inhibit a satisfactory decision. For example, individual employees in a large department generally seem to lack social conscience and see little wrong in taking the odd day off work to go racing or decorate a room at home; but to management such absence may mean reorganizing the work of a section and overtime working to meet delivery dates. In situations like this, can worker representatives on joint disciplinary committees be relied on to reach impartial decisions, irrespective of the views of their fellow-workers? As far as theft and safety are concerned, everyone has a common interest—but many doubts remain about the partisan attitude of workers over problems relating to time-keeping, absenteeism, and appeals against disciplinary action.

Trade unionists themselves are very sensitive about their shortcomings in this respect, and include guidance on joint consultation for worker representatives attending their own training courses. Their aim is to provide those taking part in joint committees with knowledge of the techniques of the job. It is wrong to expect workers from the factory floor to pick up these points as they go along, so unions often ask employers to help train worker representatives to understand committee papers and agenda, to acquire reasonable facility in self-expression, to develop skill in finding facts from cross-examination and passing judgment upon them, and to report back to the workers they represent in the most effective manner.

One good example of a company allowing employee representatives to participate in disciplinary matters is the Misconduct Committee of the Firestone Tyre and Rubber Co., Brentford. Its function is to hear all charges of misconduct brought by management against process workers and to decide what disciplinary action, if any, has to be taken. There are four permanent members of the Committee: the Chairman is appointed by the management from the staff of the personnel department and three shop stewards are elected from the Works Committee; either the manager of the department in which the offender works or the Chief Security Officer also attends. The company genuinely acknowledges that the shop stewards have shown a willingness to judge each case on its merits. The Committee deals with all breaches of company rules, which have previously been discussed with trade unions and well publicized among employees. Examples are: an employee clocking out someone else's time card; insubordination; an employee missing from his workplace; failure to report an accident; driving a car in the wrong direction from the company's premises; and serious or continued bad workmanship. The sanctions which management have available to them are: reprimand, suspension, downgrading (which could mean £200 a year reduction in earnings), and dismissal. After each case has been considered, the decision is posted on notice boards throughout the company. It is important to appreciate that, far from taking authority away from management, the number of sanctions available has been increased; the threat of being brought before the Misconduct Committee and its subsequent publicity has had a very salutary effect.

Experience over the years has led some industrial relations experts to doubt the value of joint consultative committees. Even the Ministry of Labour, in its evidence to the Royal Commission on Trade Unions and Employers' Associations, commented that joint consultation has had comparatively little impact in Great Britain.

The reasons for this may be partly due to traditional mistrust between management and workers, but there have also been basic misconceptions about the technique which have led to an increasing number of complaints about the triviality of the subjects that joint committees are asked to discuss—'tea, towels, and toilets'. Managements jealously guard their 'right to manage', and in any case often doubt the sincerity of workers' contributions in joint discussions about ways to improve production; consequently they have tended to avoid putting really important matters on the committees' agenda. (A cartoon comment appears in Figure 31.)

A survey* carried out by the Office of Population Censuses and Surveys in 1974 was a wide-ranging study of the shop floor, the most thorough since the Donovan Commission's report. It analyses a growing trend towards informality where there is a written procedure or agreement between management and workers, which in turn is helping to make workplace

* *Workshop Industrial Relations*, by Stanley Parker (H.M.S.O., 1974).

Figure 31

relations easier on the level of personal contact between employees, stewards, foremen, and managers. There is a good deal more flexibility where face-to-face contact is possible, so that grievances can often be settled amicably and more speedily than written procedures allow.

By and large, workplace relations are self-contained and self-regulating, with full-time union local officers playing only a marginal role. Shop stewards play a full part in affairs as representatives of employees, and managers generally regard them as moderating influences. For their part, employees surveyed (some 2,000 of them) rated management as being strict rather than indulgent in the way they applied procedures.

The most frequently mentioned suggestion for improving industrial relations was better communication, especially through consultative procedures. The report reveals that although most workers agree that they have a voice in deciding how their shop stewards deal with specific issues, they themselves play little or no part in making changes in their overall working circumstances. Workplace relations are based on fairly well-developed systems of representation in most unionized establishments. Networks of informal practices and short-cuts are common, whether or not written procedures exist. Little evidence was found in the survey that stewards are more militant than their members—indeed they are usually viewed as exerting reasonable and sometimes moderating influences. Where the parties have adapted to the idea that there may be occasional clashes of interest, then they can usually achieve a high level of mutual tolerance and acceptance. Certainly a large majority of employees and stewards said that they preferred going through agreed procedures to strikes or any other form of pressure.

REMOVING RESTRICTIVE PRACTICES

The fact remains that some of the changes which are necessary to remove restrictive practices and thus increase productivity can only be effected by joint action between management and employee representatives. The term *restrictive practices* covers a wide range of activities, including strikes, go-slow action, late starting, lengthy tea-breaks, persistent absenteeism, informal group restrictions on the amount of work produced by members of that group, demarcation of work rules, and opposition to new methods, work study, and incentive schemes: in fact, any arrangement whereby labour is used inefficiently and which cannot be justified on social grounds. They may be caused by many factors—tradition, custom and usage, the desire for security, as a means of strengthening bargaining power, or the weakness of management—and obviously are intended to protect the interests of whichever party operates them. A distinction can be drawn between three main types of restrictive practice:*

1. Those which both parties see as justified, but outside observers do not (for example, excessive overtime working, questioning acceptance of the use of mates on traditional lines).
2. Those which one of the parties sees as justified but which the other considers should be discontinued (for example, many practices found in printing and shipbuilding).
3. Those which simply amount to managerial inefficiency (for example, bad time-keeping, excessive tea-breaks, and out-of-date incentive pay systems).

Only management itself can deal with the latter; but it should also take the lead in removing all other opposition to production plans. Senior staff must be prepared to undertake hard negotiations on the subject, however, for the co-operation of trade unions and worker groups is unlikely unless their members benefit as a result. In some cases this may amount to productivity bargaining as already discussed in Chapter 13, for the removal of most restrictive practices would undoubtedly have a direct impact on national output and improve standards of living. But although union leaders show in their public speeches that they fully appreciate the truth in this logic, they seem to have great difficulty in persuading their rank-and-file members that it has personal validity for each one of them. It is up to employers to take more initiative in publicizing the idea that higher

* *See Ministry of Labour Gazette*, February 1964, page 128.

productivity benefits everyone, rather than to go on maintaining the concept of 'two sides' of industry. No matter how good management is, it can be made better by establishing even closer relations with workers in this way.

'THE REFORM OF COLLECTIVE BARGAINING AT PLANT AND COMPANY LEVEL'

This report*seeks to analyse the action necessary at local level to rectify many of the defects in the existing system of industrial relations identified by the Donovan Commission. There are, in fact, many pressures, external and internal, which are constantly forcing both sides of industry to look anew at their relationships. The opportunities to effect improvements usually present themselves at times of change—mergers, productivity bargains, and organizational changes in management are good examples. Success in dealing with such events seems to be much more certain if the organization concerned has developed a series of long-term objectives to act as guidelines in preparing proposals. For their part, trade unions tend to press for the extension of agreements into areas hitherto regarded as management prerogatives.

To the degree that employer-union relationships have taken on permanent features over the years, it can be said that a *bargaining structure* has been created comprising four elements—levels, units, scope, and forms. Negotiations may be conducted at the national, company, plant or sub-plant *bargaining level*, and the *bargaining unit* may comprise all employees at that level or there may be separate units for different groups. The subject coverage, or *bargaining scope*, of negotiations may be wide or narrow; and the *bargaining form*, in which agreements are expressed, may be written or unwritten, signed by the parties or only confirmed verbally.

The realization of long-term industrial relations objectives, or *bargaining principles*, may require the adoption of particular types of bargaining structure. To secure successful improvements, first a careful analysis of present arrangements must be made to identify any structural weaknesses; secondly, a consistent set of bargaining principles must be developed; and thirdly, these must be harmonized with all other aspects of the bargaining structure. Thus, in the interests of bargaining consistency, it may be necessary to centralize negotiations at company or plant level, to seek wider bargaining units and more formal bargaining forms. (This is an interesting reflection on the Donovan Commission's remarks about the present dominance of informal systems.)

Experience shows that the role of the personnel specialist is paramount

* Department of Employment, 1971.

in the taxing and time-consuming task of analysing complex information and preparing management proposals on industrial relations problems. The most effective arrangement seems to be that whereby personnel managers take the lead in negotiations, with essential support from appropriate senior line managers at the bargaining table. In this way the advantages of bargaining expertise, specialist knowledge, and line management commitment can all be attained. It is vital in the process, however, for management negotiators to be vested with authority to reach decisions, since general frustration and undermining of credibility can result from constant reference to higher authority.

On the union side, pressure has grown over the years for the inclusion of shop stewards in negotiating teams. Their detailed knowledge of conditions on the shop floor complement the bargaining skills of the full-time union officers, and facilitate communications with the membership during the course of negotiations; this can be very important, of course, if provisional agreements require speedy ratification by the union membership.

Perhaps the most important factor in the successful operation of agreements is the determination shown by managers and unions alike in monitoring their progress and seeking to ensure that they function according to plan. Here again central co-ordination is best undertaken on the management side by the personnel specialist, and on the union side by the senior steward.

A degree of flexibility undoubtedly plays a large part in the successful operation of disputes procedures. Informal consultation between official meetings is commonplace, and usually contributes significantly to resolving disputes within a plant, without having to go outside. Having separate procedures for handling disciplinary, work study, and job evaluation issues also tends to be advantageous. They help to achieve consistency of practice, bring specialists more quickly to bear on any problems, and relieve the main disputes machinery of the bulk of such issues.

The aim can thus be seen as the achievement of a greater consistency in handling industrial relations problems, through the introduction of more formality into the bargaining system and the development of a central co-ordinating and monitoring capability. More attention must also be given to ensuring that line managers and the work-force fully understand new agreements. No single model for bargaining reform can be regarded as universally applicable; indeed the process of adaptation and improvement probably has no end. What is required is a readiness to make a careful appraisal of the existing system and a willingness to discuss proposals for sensible and beneficial change.

One of the most famous examples of recently concluded procedural agreements is that of the British Leyland Motor Company, and an outline of its provisions serves as a practical summary of many of the points discussed in this chapter:

1. Scope and purpose.
2. Formal confirmation of union recognition and encouragement of trade union membership.
3. Provisions relating to shop stewards.
4. Provisions relating to joint negotiating bodies, e.g. the establishment of a joint works council in each plant.
5. Principles on the basis of which the plant procedures will be established.
6. Provision for a single external stage.
7. Provision governing the management of change including certain *quid pro quo* arrangements.
8. A 'peace' clause.
9. A Corporation undertaking that the whole procedure can be operated, if necessary, within 20 working days.

TRADE UNIONISM AMONG WHITE-COLLAR WORKERS

Already, in 1974, 45 per cent of all workers are 'white-collar' rather than 'blue-collar', and within a few years white-collar workers will be in the majority. By the same token, the growth of white-collar unions (which in recent years has averaged 6% p.a.) and the decline of blue-collar unions (membership falling by 5% p.a.) means that by 1980 the T.U.C. affiliation of white-collar unions will account for 50 per cent of its total membership.

There are several reasons for this growth. Economic expectations have undoubtedly provided the main impetus, for many white-collar workers have felt themselves to be losing ground in relation to other groups of workers and believe that they could achieve immediate financial benefits if they obtain professional assistance with collective bargaining. Secondly, the increased size of organizations means that staff relationships in the working environment become more and more impersonal; staff therefore seek ways of obtaining greater influence over the processes whereby decisions are taken which affect their lives at work—they want their own representatives involved in such decision-taking. Size and remoteness have also meant a growing awareness of loss of status among white-collar workers: gone is the separate identity and sense of privilege of years past, to be replaced by a need for protection, through joint action, against **arbitrary decisions taken by top management.**

On the other hand, the current industrial relations climate embraces the view that management also derives tangible benefits from procedural agreements between employers and unions; for these provide constructive avenues for resolving differences and problems. It has been suggested* that employers would find it to their advantage, therefore, to draw up policy statements, recognizing white-collar unions, and including such detail as:

1. Criteria to decide which unions should be recognized.
2. Union representation of clerical, technical, supervisory, professional, and managerial staffs.
3. Negotiating rights and negotiable subjects, with the appropriate units, agents and levels for bargaining.
4. Training and communication requirements.
5. Facilities to be granted to union representatives.
6. Consultative and negotiating machinery, and domestic procedures for dealing with disputes.

The initial criteria for recognition highlights the developing controversy between staff associations and trade unions. Membership of the former is always confined to employees of one organization, which enables them to claim the advantages of being led by officers with intimate knowledge of that employer; officers whom the members know well, and whom they can readily remove if necessary. All members have a vested interest in their organization's prosperity, and so they behave in a reliable, responsible manner which, they claim, produces results of benefit to their members without having to resort to extreme action.

Trade unions, on the other hand, tend to look down on staff associations, questioning whether negotiations over differences of interest can truly be conducted by a body which is patronized by the employers and must therefore be subservient to some degree. The essential element of independence is missing, and this is necessary to convince members that their interests are being pursued as firmly as possible.

Collective bargaining nowadays is so wide in scope that trade unions can certainly claim advantages in their comprehensive information and research facilities which staff associations could never possess. Professional expertise has its own attractions, of course, as well as the horizontal approach throughout industry and commerce. Most importantly, in this context, unions have the ability to monitor salary movements for white-collar workers across the board, so that increases in one sector can be swiftly converted into claims in others.

CONCLUSION

Industrial relations troubles occur most frequently in three types of industries: those which deal in perishable goods—docks, markets, trans-

* C.I.R. report 'Recognition of White-Collar Unions in Engineering and Chemicals' (H.M.S.O., 1973).

port; those where processes are long and complicated—engineering; and those where trading conditions fluctuate widely—building, car manufacturing. In the first, management fear stoppages much more than in most industries, and this plays into the hands of militant worker representatives. In engineering and other complex industries, there is a greater than usual need for co-ordination and expert negotiation by management with worker representatives who know where and when best to exert their strength. As for the last, much of the trouble could be removed if management succeeded in forecasting labour requirements more accurately, thus avoiding periods of labour shortage followed by redundancies.

Solving industrial relations problems at the workplace therefore demands a variety of approaches:

INCREASING JOINT CONSULTATION

This means more worker participation in management. Such an increase would inevitably mean greater delegation of authority over worker discipline, and many managers would probably be willing to concede this if worker representatives agreed to co-operate more in raising productivity. Not that the idea is without opposition, for both supervisors and union branch officials see such a move whittling away some of their own methods of control. Nevertheless, consultation helps to ensure that management will lead as well as command.

BETTER TRAINING

The better training of everyone involved in labour relations will in the long term help to remove the opposition of supervisors and union officials just mentioned. There can be no doubt that managers, supervisors, union officials, and shop stewards alike would benefit from fuller training in the techniques of industrial relations, negotiating skills, and joint consultation.

PUBLICITY FOR GOOD PRACTICE

One method for improving standards throughout the country is to devise a means of examining and publicizing instances of good or bad industrial relations. Best done by neutral investigators, the position of the A.C.A.S. seems apposite here, since the preparation of its annual report would provide an excellent opportunity to publish the results.

MANAGEMENT LEADERSHIP

This emerges as the most important factor in improving industrial relations at the workplace, for the initiative must come from management in any drive for co-operation. It is management's responsibility to keep production flowing, to deal with any threats to efficiency, and, above all, not to allow awkward problems to degenerate into crises and disorders. It is vital that managers and supervisors understand that in fulfilling this responsibility they must do everything possible to harness the abilities of their labour force with their own to create an effective team. Leadership of the quality demanded can itself cause resentment among workers and fellow-employers. It needs strength of character, courage, and integrity to maintain, and only rarely at present can there be found industrial leaders who work in anticipation of claims, who spot potential grievances, and are prepared to take constructive action to prevent them actually materializing.

Not that too naïve a view should be taken of methods to secure industrial peace. In reality a constant conflict takes place between labour and management (regulated to an increasing extent by the State) over sharing power and dividing income. This conflict centres around eternal issues of individual freedom, the desire for economic progress and improved standards of living, resistance to change by vested interests—problems that man has always struggled with all over the world. Clearly there are no permanent solutions to these eternal issues, so that the practice of industrial relations becomes a matter of effecting minor adjustments from time to time in order to secure a balance between the contenders for power.

THE EMPLOYMENT PROTECTION ACT, 1975

Introduced following the Labour Government's re-election in October 1974, this Act covers a number of disparate subjects: the rights of individual workers; the Advisory, Conciliation and Arbitration Service; rights of trade unions; reform of wages councils; handling redundancies; and issues arising from the Trade Union and Labour Relations Act.

A main section of the Act protects workers by creating a system of guaranteed weekly payments. Workers who are not covered by better voluntary schemes should be paid a guaranteed rate for hours within the normal working week when employers can give them no work (for example during short-time or lay-offs). A method of calculation is suggested, with the guarantee initially limited to £30 per week: this will eventually be raised to a full week's wage as the economy permits. Two examples illustrate that a £24 a week worker on a three-day week would get £14.40 pay and £9.60 guarantee—full earnings, in fact, because he is below the £25 limit; a man normally earning £48 a week would get £28.80 plus £10 in guarantee.

Another major section deals with maternity. Any woman completing two years' continuous service is on pregnancy entitled to national insurance maternity allowance made up to her normal week's pay for a minimum of six weeks; and to reinstatement in her old or a similar job for up to 29 weeks after her baby is born.

Legislative proposals are made in the Act to codify time off allowed with pay: for officials of recognized independent unions for carrying out union activities; and for employees with more than two years' service who are faced with redundancy to enable them to seek new jobs or re-training. Time off should also be allowed for duties as members of public authorities, although not necessarily with pay.

Trade union membership and activities are covered by proposals that employers must not prevent or deter employees from belonging to and joining in activities of independent unions or the unions party to a closed shop arrangement; nor must they require an employee to join a union except in a closed shop situation (with exemption provided for objectors on religious grounds).

The law on dismissal was also changed when the Act reached the statute book. A new scale of minimum notice entitlements was introduced, ranging from one week after four weeks' service to twelve weeks after twelve years. When dismissal is found to be unfair, it is suggested that priorities should be: reinstatement; re-engagement to a comparable job; where the employee is partly to blame, re-engagement on less favourable terms; only then—compensation. In order to help an industrial tribunal judge on re-instatement, employers will be required to provide information about vacancies in their own or associated organizations. For compensation, an employee judged to have been dismissed unfairly should get a minimum of two weeks' pay or the equivalent of his redundancy entitlement which-ever is the greater. Employers will also have to provide written reasons for dismissal when employees ask (this will help the dismissed employee make any complaint).

Better protection is also offered to employees when their employer goes into liquidation. Instead of having to take their chances with other creditors, the Department of Employment will meet in full all claims by employees for arrears of wages, holiday pay, unpaid pension contribu-tions, and pay in lieu of notice.

Part I of the Act makes the new Advisory, Conciliation and Arbitration Service (A.C.A.S.) into a statutory body, taking on, *inter alia*, the task of the former Registrar of Friendly Societies. In addition to its existing func-tions (*see* page 252) A.C.A.S. will prepare a new guide on policy which will replace the Code on Industrial Relations Practice. A Central Arbitra-tion Committee has been established, which can make awards enforceable on employers concerning wages and other conditions of employment in establishments where no independent union is recognized, or where the employer is not conforming to an agreement reached for the industry.

Complaints that employers have not provided unions with information needed for effective bargaining will also be dealt with: A.C.A.S. guidelines are expected to cover financial, manpower, and earnings information in this respect, and further information requirements may well be included in a future Industrial Democracy Bill.

Wages Councils feature in the Employment Protection Act, in so far as it is intended to speed up both the procedures of statutory wage-fixing and the transition to collective bargaining. Councils will make their own wages regulation orders, and no longer have to submit them to the Secretary of State for approval. At the suggestion of the unions the Secretary of State may withdraw the chairman and independent members so that a council, while keeping its power to make orders, will become composed of two parties only; it would thus become a statutory Joint Industrial Council, and may replace the public service secretariat with its own and also dispense with the use of inspectors to enforce its minimum standards. (This move recognizes that wages councils seem to be declining in effectiveness: originally intended as a prop to help weak bargaining organizations to grow, they may have served only to prolong this weakness by making it less necessary for the workers concerned to join a union.)

New rules about notification of redundancies seek to protect workers further. An employer planning redundancies is required to consult the appropriate trade unions about their implementation, and to take note of and reply to any representations made by them. Length of notice of redundancy will also be controlled, depending on the number of workers affected.

FURTHER READING

Trade Unions, by W. E. J. McCarthy (Penguin, 1972).
Industrial Relations and the Personnel Specialists, by Peter Anthony and Anne Crichton (Batsford, 1969).
Industrial Relations Procedures, by Norman Singleton: Manpower Paper No. 14, Department of Employment (H.M.S.O., 1975).

16 Communications

THE PROCESS OF COMMUNICATING

In management terms, the word *communications* describes the process of conveying messages (facts, ideas, attitudes, opinions) from one person to another so that they are understood. The key word in this definition is 'understood', and many organizations would profit by giving more attention to this simple fact rather than trying to develop increasingly sophisticated systems of communications that add confusion to complexity. Most people in senior managerial posts spend the majority of their time communicating with other staff, and for this reason alone the need for efficiency in this aspect of their work is clear. Management activity has previously been analysed in Chapter 11, and the relevance of effective communications to this analysis can be explained in parallel terms:

Management Activity	*Importance of Communications*
1. Setting objectives	(*a*) Information required from clients, potential customers, suppliers, competitors, local and national government. (*b*) Internal information required, e.g. labour turnover and scrap rates.
2. Planning use of resources	Information required about these resources (labour, money, equipment, accommodation, time, and ideas), their availability, quality, and advice on how best to use them.
3. Taking action	Giving instructions; devising procedures.
4. Measuring results	Understanding of the standards set—quantity, quality, costs, time taken.
5. Corrective action	Giving revised instructions where necessary.

The passing of a message from the mind of its sender to the mind of the receiver may seem a straightforward affair. The fact that it is not so in practice is the reason why communications pose perennial problems in all business organizations. A model of the process will serve to illustrate the nature of the barriers which must be overcome if communications are to be successful (Figure 32).

Apart from human frailty, such as forgetfulness, there are five barriers:

ABILITY TO EXPRESS MEANING

This is obviously essential to the understanding of any communication. It is a difficulty keenly felt by many first-line supervisors, promoted to such positions because of their outstanding technical skills, but who sometimes lack a sound background education and hence the ability to express themselves clearly either verbally or in writing.

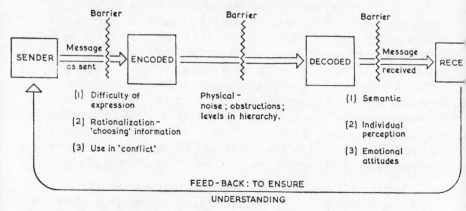

Figure 32. Model of the process of communication

RATIONALIZATION

Rationalization is the selection of information passed on, so as to enhance the position of its originator. Thus he feels important, as being the only person in a group who knows everything about a situation. Or if an atmosphere of conflict exists where relationships are bad between certain sections of an organization, information can be used virtually as a weapon, being conveyed or withheld as the advantage of either party dictates (cf. Stephen Potter's concept of 'one-up-manship').

PHYSICAL BARRIERS

Any obstruction, noise, or discomfort on the part of the receiver (workroom too hot or too cold, for example) will increase the likelihood of a message being conveyed inaccurately. The number of levels through which a message has to pass from top management down to the shop floor also forms a series of physical barriers, as each level has an unfortunate tendency to cut off a piece of the message or embellish it in some way before passing it on.

SEMANTIC BARRIERS

These refer to the difficulty the receiver has in understanding a message. This is the obverse of the supervisor's difficulty in expressing himself, and is obviously a great problem in those industries and public services which employ large numbers of immigrant workers. Just as any lecturer must try to pitch his talk at what he believes to be the level of comprehension of his audience, so the supervisor must give instructions or make requests in simple words which his subordinates, whose educational background may leave much to be desired, can understand.

THE PERCEPTION OR EMOTIONAL STATE OF THE RECEIVER

The receiver's likely reaction should always be taken into account by the sender. For example, a departmental head may want a subordinate to deal with an emergency which crops up late in the day: he may ask him to do so in a manner intended to convey his confidence that this particular man is the best person to deal efficiently with the crisis. But, at that moment, the subordinate may have a variety of reasons for wanting to get home early, so that his reaction may be bitter, silently accusing his boss of dodging difficult problems and passing the 'dirty work' on to him.

All these barriers complicate the seemingly simple task of passing messages between people. The important point to grasp is that, if a communication system is to be efficient, it must include a feed-back mechanism whereby the sender can check that he has succeeded in overcoming the barriers. In small businesses this is comparatively easy, because most communications take place face to face between individuals and understanding can be checked immediately. The problem is much greater in large firms where individuals may not have such close contacts: communications become more and more impersonal, and verbal exchanges are replaced by circular letters or papers pinned on notice boards. Some organizations have appointed executives charged with the special responsibility of ensuring that communications flow smoothly by 'auditing' the system continuously, removing bottle-necks (caused, for example, by a departmental head's absence), and generally effecting improvements.

WHAT TO COMMUNICATE

Shared information is one of the key factors in the morale of an organization and hence in its efficiency. Obviously everything cannot be communicated to everybody all the time—no other work would get done. What should be communicated will largely be determined in practice by the direction of the communication. This may be downwards in the form of policy or instructions from senior staff to subordinates; or upwards, as reaction to communications received or as control information supplied to senior staff; or horizontal, as part of the normal business procedure of keeping staff 'in the picture'.

Management's aim in practice should be to communicate downwards all relevant information that will enable employees to give their best to their jobs. This will include:

1. Information about the job itself—its importance, its duties and responsibilities, its relation to other jobs, and the relation of the person doing it to other staff and the general public; the aim of the job and how it fits in with the work of the organization, accepted standards of performance, cost consciousness and the need for economy; accident prevention; and reasons for changes being made in the job.
2. Information about conditions of employment—calculation of wages or salary, sick pay, superannuation, length of notice, holiday arrangements, welfare and social amenities; promotion opportunities, provision for further training; the employer's attitude towards membership of trade unions and professional organizations, staff complaints procedure; and suggestion schemes.
3. Information necessary for staff to carry out their work—management plans and policy, objectives and targets to be reached, day-to-day instructions, and the quantity and quality of production expected.

On this subject, the Code of Industrial Relations Practice advises management regularly to provide employees with information about:

1. the performance and plans of their organizations;
2. organizational and management changes that affect employees.

All managers, including supervisors, should regard it as one of their principal duties to explain organizational policies and intentions to their subordinates; they must, of course, themselves be supplied with the right information to be able to do so.

Basically, the upward flow of communications from staff to their superiors supplies information for management control purposes. As already mentioned, there must be feed-back of reaction to instructions or plans, so that top management can be sure that these have been understood; indeed, depending on the nature of this reaction, original ideas and concepts may need to be modified before finally being put into effect. Other communications received by management will include a constant flow of data, statistics, and reports, all giving information necessary for decision-making; and subordinates will submit requests from time to time as well as putting forward suggestions to improve efficiency.

Horizontal communications take place between units and departments within a business, with the basic aim of keeping all staff informed generally of what is going on. No industrial organization is likely to expand unless its staff are fully aware of each other's efforts, achievements, and problems; for example, unless horizontal communications are good, there is the risk that two research sections in different parts of an organization may be duplicating each other's work. Apart from such tangible factors, the development of a good corporate spirit upon which morale and productivity greatly depend can be attributed to the effectiveness of this type of communication.

HOW TO COMMUNICATE

The principles of good communications are simplicity itself—so much so that they are commonly taken for granted, which inevitably means that they are neglected in practice. Communications will be effective when the barriers in Figure 27 are overcome—by trying to see things from the receivers' point of view and taking account of their feelings and levels of perception. Conciseness, clarity, and concentration on reactions are other precepts that appear easier to preach than perform. It is essential to provide for two-way flow, or feed-back, so that questions can be answered and difficulties resolved. The system of communications itself must be well understood throughout the organization and consistently applied so that all staff have confidence in it.

In most business organizations, three main methods of communication are used:

1. Managers talk to supervisors and employees.
2. Written material is used—circular letters, papers put on notice boards, news-sheets, and house journals.
3. Information is given to, and news exchanged with, employee representatives at formal meetings of joint consultative bodies.

The first method of face-to-face contact is widely practised, of course. Speech has all the advantages of direct two-way communications. It enables the mood, attitude, and responses of the receivers, whether individuals or groups, to be taken into account, and gives some guarantee of understanding by allowing questions to be asked and alternative courses of action to be discussed—all of which provides managers with clear-cut opportunities to exercise effective leadership.

There are disadvantages, however. No matter how much care is taken, some risk of varying interpretation of the communication by different people still remains. Spoken communications can also be very time-consuming; apart from the problem of securing full attendance at meetings, it takes much longer to communicate in this way or by seeing people individually than sending out a written memorandum. Then there are many organizational problems, too, which inhibit the effectiveness of verbal communication. In large complex units there may be several levels of supervision and many specialist departments away from the main flow of information; shift working adds to the difficulty since some senior staff and supervisors may not see each other for days at a stretch. All these complications contribute to the dangers of inaccuracy and misunderstanding: details tend to get lost as information is passed orally from one grade or section to another. The position of the foreman is often tricky in complex organizations. He seems to be best placed to convey information between management and workers; but to his embarrassment, fuller and more prompt information is often given to workers by their union representatives. It is difficult to decide the right course of action in such situations. If information reaches the shop floor direct from the supervisor, workers may feel that management is acting in an arbitrary manner; if it comes from the union, it shows that there has been full consultation, but supervisors may feel aggrieved. One solution lies in having staff and foremen representatives as part of the arrangements for joint consultation.

A communication in writing, on the other hand, usually means that the tone and choice of words can be carefully considered and checked with colleagues or supervisors before being sent out, thus providing less scope for ambiguity or misinterpretation. Obviously, too, a permanent record exists of what has been communicated. The disadvantages are that since contact is impersonal, there is no opportunity for questions or discussions; indeed, there can be no guarantee that the communication has even been read, let alone understood. The effectiveness of written material therefore depends largely on whether it can command attention; a well known illustration of this precept is the practice of some firms chalking urgent messages on a wall facing, or on the floor immediately inside, the factory entrance where it must be seen.

In reality both verbal and written methods of communication are used. Verbal are usually considered more suitable for complex or controversial subjects, which may be discussed first and then confirmed in writing, and written for transmitting routine information which staff need and expect. Visual communications must also be mentioned: films and slides are used extensively for training purposes, of course, and they can also be applied as aids to solving such management problems as the introduction of work study or new production processes.

Reference has already been made in Chapter 10 to the use of a *works handbook* in induction training, providing newcomers with essential information. The contents may well start with a brief history of the organization, notes about its links with the neighbourhood, and a description of its products. It should include full information on terms and conditions of employment, with notes for the guidance of any employee in specified circumstances, such as sickness, accident, and change of address; what to do when he wishes to purchase some of the company's products; what to do if he is late or absent or desires leave of absence; where he may and may not smoke (and why); what to do if he comes in contact with an infectious disease; and all the other information essential to the smooth running of a business organization. If the company has working agreements with particular trade unions, the terms of these agreements could be included in the handbook, and the new employee be given information about how to join the appropriate union.

It is essential that there should be strict control over a company's *notice boards*. They must be positioned so as to be readily accessible, but not so as to cause traffic congestion by crowds of employees trying to read the notices at the same time. Using a standard pattern, size, and colour for all notice boards will help to make them familiar; those placed out of doors probably need to be locked and protected by a glass cover. All notices should be posted and taken down by the central department controlling the boards (usually the personnel department); the notices should be dated and handed in to this department, with a copy for filing. No notice should be allowed to outlive its usefulness, being taken down immediately after it has served its purpose.

Many organizations publish a regular *news-sheet* giving information about their activities, past, present, and future, of a technical, financial, and social nature. This kind of internal publicity is invaluable for passing on authentic information which employees should know, and greatly helps to prevent the circulation of wild rumours, thus removing the necessity of the traditional 'grapevine'. As far as the costs of news-sheets are concerned, some firms make a nominal charge for them, mainly on grounds that anything free is little appreciated, while other firms prefer to give them away; this is possibly a subject on which the opinion of worker representatives might be sought at the outset. The method of distribution varies: in this country they are usually handed around within the organization, but in the U.S.A. some firms go to the expense of posting their news-sheets to employees' homes, seeking in this way to gain the moral support of their families.

The publication of *house journals* or *magazines* is an extension of the use of news-sheets, the difference usually being in the length of time between publications. News-sheets are issued frequently, full of news and urgent in their appeal; magazines are more leisurely in tempo and are more concerned with long-term policy. A house journal is often printed with an eye to outside publicity for the company, in which case it is likely to be edited by the company's publicity department and be a charge upon advertising costs. Nevertheless, it may still be of social significance in fostering a deeper understanding of the working of the organization as a whole and of the problems of staff in other departments. Reactions among employees are generally favourable, but it is evident that a modicum of entertainment and humour is essential for a successful publication. Most editors experience difficulty in obtaining articles from staff, and the organization of a group of unofficial and keen news reporters throughout the firm is very desirable. Although house journals vary considerably in both content and presentation, several definite principles emerge: clarity, brevity, and honesty in presentation of official information must be keynotes, and regularity of publication is also of prime importance. Staff appreciate information regarding future plans and, above all, explanations of actions or delays which, at times, with insufficient details available, are very hard for them to understand or accept: a great impact on morale can be made in this way.

Of course, some workers will always tend to dismiss all this written material as propaganda, and there can be little doubt that news-sheets and house journals alike are of limited value unless supported by as much personal contact between top management and the shop floor as possible. In the same way as an organization's advertising costs are sometimes challenged, so it is virtually impossible to measure the return obtained from the considerable sums of money often spent on these publications. The effectiveness of their role in any communications system can only be demonstrated negatively—by ceasing publication, and assessing their value in this way.

It is unfortunately true that some house journals are started for the wrong reasons, often merely as a status symbol to impress the shareholders or satisfy the vanity of the board of directors. It is also true that some senior executives look on the value of these journals purely as means of reporting social events, and not for any serious or important company purpose. But explaining costs, a new pension scheme, a department's closure —these are ideal and vital subjects for house journal treatment, and journals clearly do have a value in providing background information on complex subjects (for example, circulating new agreements among managers, supervisors, and worker representatives prior to discussing their implementation). The question for those who doubt the house journal's role as a serious medium for communications is—how else can top management effectively keep in touch with several thousand employees?

The success of the N.C.B.'s *Coal News* has resulted from a deliberate attempt being made to explain problems and policies. It was set up as the industry's newspaper with freedom of editorial comment on all aspects of the Board's activities, and its use in this way undoubtedly helped to smooth away many staffing problems associated with the closure of mines and the reduction and transfer of staff. Here is an excellent example of a journal being used as a bridge for the two-way traffic of ideas and information, and the establishment of confidence and understanding between management and men.

For some years the Industrial Society has advocated the system of *briefing groups* as a simple but effective means of communication. These are groups who meet their immediate superiors regularly to hear and discuss proposals and decisions that affect their jobs or conditions of work. The organization of the groups depends on the number of levels involved and the working arrangements, but their membership should not exceed twenty. Thus, with two levels in a management hierarchy, information can be quickly disseminated among 400 employees; with three levels, this rises to 8,000. That is to say, directors and senior managers brief heads of departments, who in turn brief groups of supervisors, who then brief their subordinate staff.

The formula for successful *joint consultation* has already been described in the previous chapter. To work effectively as channels of communication, joint committee meetings must be held regularly, with formal agenda and arrangements for the fullest possible distribution of minutes. There are always very real problems associated with worker representatives reporting back to their constituencies—problems arising from the numbers of employees represented, shift working, and lack of ability on the part of representatives. Where decisions taken after consultation are felt to be unpalatable, worker representatives find themselves placed in a position of stress, in that they are being asked to do management's job in conveying information to shop-floor workers. Some of these problems are being overcome by giving worker representatives proper training in their duties. In any event, it can be argued that only a minority of employees take any active sustained interest in joint consultative discussions of policies and plans; nevertheless, the knowledge that information is available for the asking, and will be discussed with worker representatives, greatly helps to establish an atmosphere of confidence throughout an organization.

Sweden provides an excellent example of the way good communications help to achieve harmony between management and workers (albeit in their favourable circumstances of having a much smaller working population and industrial trade unionism). Works councils were established by an agreement signed in 1946 which stated two purposes:

1. Setting up a scheme for regular contact between management and workers, as one means of improving productivity.
2. Meeting workers' demands for better insight into the management of the organization for which they worked.

These purposes are founded on a general recognition of the desirability of workers understanding the importance of their own jobs against the background of the organization as a whole.

It should be clearly understood that these main methods of communication—through management, by means of written material, and through joint consultation—are not alternatives to each other: rather they are complementary. In fact, there can be no standard pattern or one correct system of communications. The methods used must be those which match up to the peculiar circumstances of each organization, the way work is carried out within it, and the quality of relationships between all its staff. An organization is structured in its own particular way to enable it to carry out its business in the most efficient manner, having regard to the morale of its employees. If the emphasis is placed on vertical communications, work may be done quickly, but comparatively few staff will know what is going on around them; they will derive much more personal satisfaction from a situation where horizontal communications are stressed so that staff throughout the organization are informed and consulted about plans and policies. Good communications will bring about good relations between staff, but these will not then bring about efficiency defined exclusively in terms of achieving speedy results. In most organizations a balance has to be struck between such efficiency and employees' morale.

Even the generalization that communications should always be two-way must be questioned, despite the fact that it is democratic and makes for greater staff satisfaction. There are significant qualifications. Two-way communication is best when accuracy is essential and when a situation is changing, but it is time-consuming; when routines are well understood and speed of response is all important, then one-way communication may be more effective. The personnel specialist asked to advise top management about communications should therefore not waste his time looking for the ideal answer; rather, he must try to predict the outcome of the various methods available, and decide which offers the greatest advantages in balancing efficiency against staff morale.

The communications system of every organization is linked closely with many other aspects of its management. For example, good communications must be backed by sound personnel policies and the mutual confidence between management and employees that only the application of these policies can build over the years. Efficient communications also will increase the satisfaction people get from their jobs. This is particularly important in the case of supervisors, whose jobs tend to become diluted by the incursions of experts; a conscious effort needs to be made to enlarge jobs by building variety, responsibility, and opportunities for individual judgment and initiative into them. Where this has been successfully achieved, a high degree of co-operation and enthusiasm on the part of employees has resulted.

THE ART OF PERSUASION

Staff problems often pose difficult situations where a full appreciation of communications techniques can decide a course of events. How does one explain to a man who has been passed over for promotion why a job has been given to someone with far fewer years' service? How can a sophisticated training scheme be introduced into an organization whose senior executives have all 'come up the hard way'? How can one's boss be persuaded to take a different course of action from that which he has set his heart on?

These things can be done by communicating effectively: by presenting a case that is irrefutable. The construction of such a case demands careful thought along these lines:

1. First convince yourself and clarify your objectives. Make sure you are aware of all the facts. You may not necessarily use all these facts but remember why you discard any of them.
2. Learn the views of others in controversial matters and what is desired and what is not. Try and anticipate any awkward questions.
3. Your preparation must be thorough and your ideas realistic. Present your case in terms of what the other person wants and can understand. Practice your approach, adapting it to the type of person you are dealing with. If possible, 'lobby' or convince key people of your goals.
4. Always present your ideas in a way that enables any one of your audience to change his mind without loss of prestige. Establish common ground at the outset so that you start with agreement. Avoid as much argument as possible and direct criticism to existing weaknesses showing how improvements can be achieved.
5. Do not force your ideas on to the other person nor make him feel he is being obliged to accept a proposal against his better judgment. Let him be satisfied completely.
6. Finally, you should be ready to follow up with supplementary facts and figures once initial agreement has been established and policy is being planned in detail.

MEASURING SUCCESS IN COMMUNICATING

A successful communications system will only be achieved if top management are determined that it shall be so. They must set good examples themselves, clearly expect others to follow them, and check from time to time that there are no bottle-necks. The personnel department can provide the necessary help here. One simple method is by questioning— for example, why someone is doing a particular job or why a change has been made: if explanations are inaccurate, or if the person does not know, the personnel officer should take the matter up with the employee's supervisor. When major changes have been introduced, it is good practice for the works committee to discuss how the communication aspect has been handled and if it could be improved. Projects can be devised for management trainees to examine the communication network: a senior executive could provide examples of recent decisions and the trainee would then follow these through. Whom did managers talk to? When? How? How did the next level of staff hear? When? How? Such investigations will show not only if a decision becomes lost, but when and why. Finally, written surveys can be used. Staff may be asked to complete a questionnaire about a recent decision showing if they were informed through their supervisor, by the company news-sheet, whether they read it on a notice board, were told by a representative, or heard a rumour. Another method is the attitude survey where employees are asked (anonymously) what they know of their firm's policies and what their attitudes are to conditions, supervisors, managers, and their own jobs.

General attitudes towards communications in industry have been well summed up in *People at Work* (page 5):

'The management of nearly all the firms visited believed that good communications would give employees a better understanding of their work and of factors, such as the state of order books, which might affect it. They also believed that good communications would help employees to work intelligently and efficiently and to accept the need for change when it arose. Most managements also held that there was value in letting employees know what was going on in the firm generally and that in the absence of facts, rumours, often unfounded, would take their place. Most managements also were anxious to know what employees thought about the firm and the way it was run, so that they could take this into account in shaping their plans and policies. For their part, employees felt that they should have clear and definite information on matters necessary for carrying out their jobs; also that they should be given full information about their terms and conditions of employment. Employees also attached importance to arrangements for raising and discussing with the management matters affecting their jobs and working conditions, and also the general running of the firm.'

If there is such a thing as an 'art of communicating', it surely lies not so much in giving information as persuading people to listen. What matters is not what is said or its tone, but how it is *heard*; and what is heard is judged against the accumulated experience, favourable and fearful, of each individual and working group throughout the organization. Thus the key factor in communications emerges as *confidence in management*, built up over years of fair dealing, so that what is heard is believed.

FURTHER READING

People at Work—A Report on Communications in Industry (H.M.S.O., 1963).
The Manager's Responsibility for Communications, Notes for Managers No. 2 (Industrial Society, 1964).

17 Problems of Morale

DEFINITION OF MORALE

The state of *morale* in any business organization can be judged by the degree of willingness its employees show towards their work. Basically, as with so many other aspects of industrial efficiency, much depends on the quality of the initial selection of staff, particularly for senior posts. But satisfaction at work is the principal factor in high morale, which means that pay must represent a fair reward, the duties of the job must hold the employee's interest, and above all, he must enjoy the social contacts established at his workplace. No matter how well-paid and interesting jobs are, if the people performing them do not get on well together and respect each other's abilities, then morale will be adversely affected. In the last resort every organization is a sum of individuals whose morale depends on their mutual adjustment. If this is satisfactory, then an integrated work community develops into which newcomers will be readily accepted and will quickly acquire the prevailing good corporate spirit.

One of the main functions of every manager and supervisor controlling other staff is to create and maintain a level of morale which evokes their full co-operation in obtaining maximum operational efficiency throughout the organization. There may well be certain influences which are outside the individual manager's control; company policy, the industry's history of labour relations, and economic conditions in the firm's locality may all have a bearing. Nevertheless, each manager can have more effect in determining morale in his department than any other factor, and should be expected to show a measure of social skill in creating an effective team spirit among his subordinates.

The links between morale and other aspects of personnel management are strong. Most departmental heads ensure for themselves that staff selected are suited to the jobs available. Some have the opportunity to influence the wage and salary structure of their organizations or departments in ways calculated to keep morale high. Communications are also important, for employees' interest cannot be roused unless they know what is going on; knowledge can therefore be used as an incentive to stimulate effort and as a means of inculcating pride in achievements. Every employee should fully understand both his own part in the life of his firm and the firm's purpose in the community as a whole, and should be made to feel that he is playing an essential role in achieving that purpose. A good manager will take pains to ensure that his subordinates have these attitudes. To do so, he must develop the ability to deal effectively with social relations between his staff, as well as showing technical and administrative skills. In short, he must be a leader of men, and if he is a good leader he may even be able to obtain a response from his team which prevails over external factors beyond his personal control which may tend to lower morale.

DISCIPLINE

Optimum performance in any organization depends on the willingness with which workers carry out the instructions of their supervisors and managers and the way they conform to the rules of conduct established to aid the successful attainment of the organization's objectives. If unreasonable rules are imposed, great damage may be done to morale. No matter how much value any man places on his independence, in the work situation he looks to his supervisor to lead him, and as long as he gets what he considers to be a proper lead he accepts the concept of discipline. This is, in effect, *self-discipline*, resulting from positive and intelligent leadership and the willing co-operation of subordinates within a framework of policies, procedures, and rules which controls the organization as a whole. Thus it is wrong to conceive of discipline as something restrictive which is imposed by force or threats of punishment: it can only be maintained by self-respecting workers who follow a leader in whom they have confidence.

Where this is so, there need be only the minimum of rules about conduct, safety, and efficiency, making clear to all employees and new recruits the responsibilities they have towards each other. Once a work group is fully aware of the standard of discipline required by its supervisor, it quickly becomes a matter of tradition, and the members of the group will themselves insist on its acceptance by newcomers: 'We don't do things like that here' is the common cautionary phrase. Any breach of discipline or disobedience of rules is usually attributed to thoughtlessness or deliberate intent, but are these the right reasons? For, in reality, few workers would ever be so undisciplined as to refuse to carry out a superior's orders, provided the actions demanded are reasonable. Once again the importance of communications emerges here, for the words with which instructions are issued must make sense to workers, having regard to their training and experience.

It is sound policy to have as few rules as possible, for their proliferation breeds contempt for the very concept of discipline; in such a situation, often very little effort is made to enforce the more unpopular rules, thus undermining management's authority. In any case, breaches of disciplinary rules may be tolerated to some extent in practice, as illustrated by this simple diagram of the *Line of DisciplinE*:

D represents the absolute enforcement of a rule, where no breaches are tolerated (matches forbidden in a coal-mine). E represents the situation where there is complete non-enforcement (for example, an office rule against receiving phone-calls). The line DE is thus the maximum possible range of toleration, although in practice it is rarely as great as this. A point T lies somewhere between D and E, and the degree of toleration is DT for most rules. Thus if a couple of men were loitering at an exit waiting to clock off, their supervisor might think they had special reasons for wanting to leave promptly, and do nothing about it; if three or four men were there, he might wonder if he should do something, but decide not to; if five or more men were concerned, however, he definitely would take disciplinary action. In this case, T represents five, where the point of toleration is crossed.

Tension arises between management and workers when they disagree about where point T appears on the Line of DisciplinE. This is frequently the case, for instance, with no-smoking rules. There is one story of a worker who was using an oxy-acetylene burner near some flammable gas tanks and was suspended because he was smoking. The farcical nature of the rigid imposition of a no-smoking rule in this case caused his fellow-workers to strike for his reinstatement. Finding, for each disciplinary rule, a point T on which management, supervisors, and workers agree is a matter of compromise which follows recognition of the causes of conflict and the discussion of remedies. This is often done with a no-smoking rule by specifying certain areas within the workplace where smoking is permitted.

One cause of tension which can have an impact on staff morale is the disagreement that sometimes arises about the range of toleration of indiscipline between senior managers who do not directly control labour and first-line supervisors who do. Top management may be prepared to put up with some degree of disorder, as long as production targets are reached; similarly they may decide to turn a blind eye to such things as bad time-keeping or absenteeism during periods of acute labour shortage. Disciplinary policy in these circumstances tends to be one of expediency, with supervisors being placed in the difficult position of having to vary point T from time to time to meet the demands of production.

The supervisor, for his part, wants to see order maintained and no large-scale breaking of rules allowed, especially in big departments where the situation could rapidly get out of hand. Of course, there must be some allowance made for people's needs as human beings: this means the strict enforcement of medical and safety rules on one hand, but a much more permissive view taken of such things as chatting, provided it does not go too far, on the other. Finally, toleration cannot be permitted to exceed the point where the status and prestige of managers and supervisors is jeopardized.

Most supervisors do not seem to consider it necessary to have direct disciplinary authority over workers, as long as they can rely on the powers of their managerial superiors: that is, they must have confidence in the consistency of management policy, know that management will back them up in their relations with subordinates, and be assured that workers fully realize that their supervisors have effective powers in the last resort. The supervisor normally has all the authority he needs to deal with minor infringements, but when considering sanctions for more serious offences, prior consultation with senior management has two advantages: it avoids the risk of decisions being reversed at a later stage and helps to develop the supervisor's resources of personality and leadership. These benefits will only be gained, however, if there is a consistent management policy about discipline throughout the organization.

DEMOCRACY IN INDUSTRY

One of the most important factors influencing workers' attitudes towards their employers appears to be how much opportunity is given to participate in the managements of their organizations and the policy decisions which govern staff relationships within them.* 'Government of the people, by the people, for the people' is the classic definition of democracy, and there are many advocates of the personnel manager's responsibility for trying to apply its principles within industry by achieving a fuller co-ordination between management and workers and making them realize the mutual benefits that will come from pursuing the common aim of increasing productivity.

But can the principles of democracy be applied in business situations in practice? Obviously industrial leaders cannot be elected, but at least it should be appreciated that 'leadership by consent' is only possible if the managers and supervisors appointed within an organization possess personalities and job-skills which command the respect of their subordinates,

* A major conclusion of Dr. Elliott Jaques's investigations at the Glacier Metal Co., for example.

and that they should be properly trained to deal with human relations problems and grievances. Regard for individuals and the right of appeal are other principles which should continuously be observed, and a great deal of industrial strife has been caused in the past by their omission; there have been many cases, for example, of unions calling strikes to secure the reinstatement of individual workers who have been arbitrarily dismissed from their jobs and allowed no appeal.

The most important principle of democracy, of course, is that everyone should share in deciding Government action. Its application to industry has seen the development of joint consultation, particularly as a means of agreeing rules of behaviour within the workplace and discussing changes that are likely to affect employees. Practice has shown that joint consultation is a cumulative process, success in one area leading to its progressive adoption in others: nowhere is the personnel specialist given better opportunities of directing the energies of management and workers alike along constructive lines.

The extent to which *participation* is practised within an organization is closely related to morale and productivity, and once the true significance of this concept is recognized, enlightened managers will go on finding new ways to utilize it in building up effective teamwork within their organizations. Applications include policy development, with joint discussions leading to better understanding and administration; sharing the solution of job problems between managers, supervisors, and workers—such matters as safe working, the running of superannuation and sickness benefit schemes, and methods improvement to reduce costs; and open discussion sessions aimed at breaking down barriers to effective communications. These are all examples of how the morale of employees can be raised in the working situation.

The report *On the Quality of Working Life** presents the conclusions of a government-sponsored enquiry into this area of staff management. The themes of efficiency and satisfaction at work, and the links between them, are explored to see how it might be possible to plan for the better use of human resources with improved productivity and work satisfaction. The report also examines the influence of the environment and technology on the quality of life at work and how people's expectations from work have developed in recent years. In fact, this approach reveals that a number of modern methods of working cause stress, including: forced, uniform pacing, especially when the pace is high; repetitiveness and short-term cycles leading to monotony; triviality and meaninglessness at work; large, impersonal structures of organization, working arrangements and relations; and

* Report for the Department of Employment by N. A. B. Wilson: Manpower Papers No. 7 (H.M.S.O., 1973).

objectives which seem distant and unreal to the worker. Small wonder that, in reaction to such stresses, problems of absence, labour wastage, and under-utilization emerge.

In trying to counter these problems, the report takes the view that the largest single factor in job motivation is that people will work hard when they feel that in some sense they are working for themselves. The aim must be to increase job satisfaction by providing scope for development and autonomy, while maintaining productivity at the same time. This can be achieved, firstly, by giving people the opportunity and encouragement to be less passive, more versatile and more self-directed towards defined objectives; and secondly, by making all desirable work behaviour obviously rewarding by a combination of inherent and extrinsic incentives.

Looking back over their years of experience, many people now in senior management posts suspect that the recent years of super-specialization in business activities have gone too far in de-skilling jobs and diluting supervisory responsibilities, with subsequent adverse effects on employee satisfaction. Some organizations have consciously tried to reverse this trend through the processes of job rotation, job enlargement, and job enrichment. Behavioural scientists affirm that most employees are capable of more than routine repetitive tasks, the tedium and predictability of which, however, can be countered by building greater variety into them and allowing discretion as regards the time or order of their completion.

Job rotation, which has already been mentioned under training, relieves monotony, enables employees to acquire new skills, and increases flexibility in the staffing of departments. *Job enlargement* seeks to increase satisfaction by adding new tasks to existing work in order to make it more interesting or challenging. *Job enrichment* concentrates on responsibilities, allowing more discretion over such matters as quality control and the choice of working methods; in this way the fragmentation of tasks comprising individual jobs is reduced and there is much more scope for employees to identify themselves with what is going on around them. A much greater feeling of unification of purpose is thus achieved. Results of all three approaches have been very encouraging and higher degrees of co-operation and enthusiasm have been acknowledged, particularly when employees have been allowed to participate in planning their work, and have shared in setting personal objectives.

Morale can also be boosted by adopting a deliberate practice of introducing gradual changes in the workplace so that employees are constantly reminded of management's interest in their welfare. One factory in Essex programmed such changes thus: one month the main building was decorated; next month 'canned music' installed; then automatic vending machines put in for refreshments; next, a suggestion scheme introduced; then the vending areas upgraded . . .

One fascinating case study of employee participation in recent years has been the appointment of part-time directors, drawn from the labour force, to serve on Group Boards of the British Steel Corporation.* This came about largely as a result of the Corporation's own analysis of participation in practice: it includes being asked to advise before decisions are taken (consultation); being party to decisions taken jointly by management and trade unions (negotiation); and sharing responsibility for management decisions.

In the event, twelve employee director posts were created in 1967 (with four more subsequently added), the men appointed coming from a wide range of occupational grades: operators, maintenance men, clerical staff, supervisors, technicians and one assistant departmental manager. They were representative of the major trade unions in the steel industry and were also chosen in part on a geographical basis from the major works in the B.S.C.

Their need for preparatory training was recognized and a five-week joint T.U.C.–B.S.C. course was designed, with the object of making these very experienced people aware of the Corporation's problems and policies. They were also given an appreciation of general economic considerations, the role of the T.U.C., and the management techniques and procedures they would come into contact with. It was decided that a job description for these new posts was necessary, making it clear that the employee directors should be involved in working parties, advisory committees, formal and informal meetings of functional and line managers, as well as attending their divisional Board meetings.

Difficult as it obviously is to evaluate an experiment of this nature, an independent attempt is currently being made by a team drawn from four British universities: their report, analysing the success or failure of this extreme venture in participation, should make interesting reading.

The borderlines between such concepts as 'job enrichment', 'participation', 'involvement', and 'consultation' can never be exactly defined, for they all centre on attitudes of mind and managerial style, rather than formal techniques. They all share the same basic belief that people will give of their best when they understand the purpose of their work activity and the factors influencing it, and when they feel they are making a useful contribution towards organizing it. Two case studies must suffice as evidence of the results of applying this theory in practice.

The I.C.I. fibres factory at Gloucester is now a participative management classic. The work load on each different type of machine varied

---

* See Appendix B, page 375, for a summary of the Bullock Committee Report, which includes recommendations about worker directors on boards.

widely according to the type of yarn being manufactured; it was therefore thought that a computer would be the best means of arranging the necessarily very complex work plan for the machines. But the constants on which the computer programme was based were the performances of a standard man and a standard machine; it could not make allowances for such things as unplanned maintenance problems, nor could it appreciate that, by making voluntary alterations in their working patterns, the operatives had considerable scope to improve the efficient running of their machines. In fact they proved to management that they could make better decisions on how to adjust the work plan to meet day-by-day events than the computer could. The simple procedure now is for the work flow to be scheduled in pencil on a long roll of paper, with much rubbing out and dove-tailing by the time that everyone involved has made a contribution to the best solution. The main virtue of the case lies surely not in the triumphant reaction to the impersonal computer, but because the development took place without any directives from I.C.I. 'top brass'—enlightened local managers saw the opportunity to encourage their operatives to use their own knowledge and ideas. This untapped reservoir of experience and common sense must surely exist in all organizations where the planning function is carried on remote from the men and machines actually producing the goods.

Fred Olsen Ltd., which operates a cargo-handling terminal in London dockland, claims benefits of high productivity and efficiency directly resulting from its participative management style. The lynchpin of this is a works committee comprising five management members and five representatives of the work force, which meets once a month and sets down the working methods for the terminal. It decides manning arrangements, allocation and rotation of working groups, holiday rotas, canteen subsidies, and everything else which affects employees' working lives. The general manager also meets a group of thirty men for an hour a week for informal discussions of the terminal's activities. Other committees include—equipment, the members of which present the general manager with lists of their requirements, having first asked manufacturers to bring their products to the terminal for inspection and testing; safety, and here committee members, having received safety training themselves, work on a rota system to provide safety cover for all shifts; social, which runs one restaurant for all staff; and a protective clothing committee. The high degree of involvement of the men in their working conditions, and the freedom of speech they have in their own committee meetings, are generally considered themselves to be highly motivating factors. Direct benefits claimed since this participative style was introduced in 1966 include the absence of unofficial strikes and an infinitesimal labour turnover.

DEALING WITH INDIVIDUAL STAFF PROBLEMS

From time to time every supervisor and manager has to tackle problems posed by individual subordinates, usually of a personal, domestic, or disciplinary nature. Help may be sought from the personnel department, but it is important to observe correct procedure: a problem should always be dealt with by an employee's immediate superior initially. With personal matters, which the employee wishes to discuss only with a senior manager or someone in the personnel department, he should nevertheless speak to his foreman first, to make the necessary arrangements.

Having to deal with individual problems in human relations is a part of the job which seems to cause great concern, being raised time and time again on training and development courses by supervisory and managerial staff of all levels. They are most conscious that the delicacy of many of these situations inevitably produces an atmosphere of embarrassment, which in turn often results in a problem being handled clumsily, leaving both superior and subordinate dissatisfied at the outcome. The basic difficulty, of course, is that at this point in time the relationship between them is entirely different from their normal day-by-day working contact which is rarely founded on close personal feeling.

Experienced personnel managers find that the best way of dealing with these situations is for a manager deliberately to detach himself and 'cold-bloodedly' apply a set procedure for solving them. One such procedure that has successfully stood the test of time is taught on T.W.I. courses for supervisors. It consists of the following steps:

GETTING FACTS

Obtain all possible facts about the individual. Note the rules and customs affected by the problem. Note the possible effect of the problem upon other people. Talk with appropriate people and get their opinions and feelings.

WEIGHING FACTS

Fit them together and consider how they may relate one to another. Consider gaps and contradictions. Seek further facts if necessary.

DETERMINING AN OBJECTIVE

Decide what you wish to accomplish by considering the effect you want on the individual, the staff, and the work of the section. What would be a really satisfactory situation?

DECIDING UPON THE ACTION TO BE TAKEN

Determine possible alternative actions. Consider which of these will best conform to the practices and policies of the organization. Which will have the best effect on the individual, the staff, and on the work of the section. Which is most likely to achieve the objective?

TAKING ACTION

Consider who is the best person to take the action and who should help in the matter. Decide if seniors should be consulted. Determine the best timing for the action.

CHECKING RESULTS

Decide the timing and frequency of the follow-up. Watch for changes in attitudes, relations, and the output of work. This problem may lead to others.

The most important part of this procedure is *determining an objective*. Supervisors and managers appreciate the need to collect all the relevant facts, but so often then go straight on to consider what action to take, without pausing to decide exactly what they are trying to achieve: thus the advantages of various courses of action become muddled together and a confused solution emerges. If, instead, a clear objective is first defined, each alternative course of action can be considered in the light of its likelihood of realizing this objective.

To take a simple example, if a good workman is frequently late because of inconvenient buses, two objectives are open: either to do everything possible to retain his services, because he is good at his job; or to dismiss him, because he persistently breaks a disciplinary rule. But only if his superior clearly decides on one of these objectives (once he has gathered all the facts about where the worker lives, bus times, alternative transport, his duties on arrival) is he likely to take direct action to solve the problem, without dithering or postponing the outcome.

ABSENTEEISM

There are various signs of low morale in an organization—poor production methods, numerous complaints about quality, lax discipline, bad time-keeping, and high rates of absenteeism and labour turnover. From the point of view of the personnel manager, perhaps the latter two are the most significant.

Working time lost through strikes and restrictive practices makes sensational headlines for the press, while absenteeism rarely rates a mention. Yet it is a hundred times the problem of strikes: in recent years an average of some 3 million working days per annum have been lost through strikes; yet nearly 300 million working days are being lost each year through absenteeism. This amounts to about 12 days a year for each employee—an obvious figure to concentrate on in trying to increase productivity.

Absenteeism falls into three main categories, based on the reasons which cause it: illness, when medical certificates are usually demanded after three days, and frequent absences of up to three days are regarded with suspicion; permitted leave, which the firm knows about beforehand; and voluntary absenteeism, usually for personal reasons which may not be revealed in detail, or sickness may be feigned. Identifying and dealing successfully with this last category is fundamentally a management problem. Progress in solving it will not be achieved by public pronouncements at national level about malingering, but only by detailed effort by local managers. Their problems are not helped by the seeming inability or unwillingness of anyone to define the degree of illness that justifies staying away from work. Every General Practitioner is placed in the peculiar quandary of never being able to prove that a patient is not sick or in pain if he insists that he is; and no doctor will take the legal risk of sending someone back to work even when he strongly suspects him of malingering. Doctors, in effect, refuse to do what they regard as really the manager's job.

There can be no doubt of the significance of absenteeism to management. It means idle machines, the reorganization of production, reduced output, increased costs, and extra strain upon those employees who do turn up for work. In fact, where production depends basically on a spirit of co-operation and teamwork, workers should always be impressed with the problems caused by absenteeism, in the hope that this may have some impact on their social conscience when contemplating staying away.

The personnel manager is concerned, too, about the way absenteeism reflects morale, especially the extent to which high absence rates in particular departments may indicate bad management there. It means work for the personnel department in other ways as well: records must be kept, enquiries and interviews held, and there may be subsequent labour turnover if men are dismissed for persistent absence from work. Periodic reports must be prepared, including statistics showing time lost through absence as a percentage of total working hours, so that top management can consider whether any general action or changes in personnel policy are needed.

Three major factors are consistently associated with the level of absenteeism:

1. personal, which are controllable to a certain extent through the organization's selection policy: thus age, sex, the length of journeys to and from work, length of service, and family responsibilities are all relevant;
2. organizational, which are very much under the direct control of local management: for example, the heaviness or unpleasantness of jobs, the stress involved, shift-working and the amount of overtime, income levels, and employee morale generally;
3. external: factors such as local levels of unemployment, which are largely outside the control of individual organizations.

Responsibility for the control of absenteeism should rest squarely on the shoulders of supervisors: they are most closely involved in the problems arising, know the individuals concerned best, and can assess the truth or otherwise of reasons given for absence. But this immediate authority must be supported from above by a clear personnel policy on absenteeism, which can be strengthened if initially agreed with the unions. Such a policy must be made known throughout the organization; it should obviously lay down that good attendance is required, and should clearly set out the procedure to be followed in the event of absence. Above all, it must be applied consistently.

The well-established fact that absence rates are highest in large units gives another clue to help in tackling the problem. The crucial point is that in small organizations the boss can keep in personal touch with all employees and can see them when they come back to work from sick leave; he can also arrange for them to be visited if they are away for long. Achieving such close personal contact in large organizations involves willingness by top management to delegate authority. An experiment in the electricity industry, at Blackburn Generating Station, has produced noteworthy results in this respect. Heads of sections were made responsible for interviewing workers on all possible occasions—lateness, working well or badly, and on return after illness. Within a month the sickness absence rate fell by 30 per cent. As a result, complete authority was delegated to section heads to give time off for domestic reasons, and it was arranged that a nurse should visit workers off sick. The sickness absence rate promptly dropped still further, and for the past two years it has remained 40 per cent lower than previously. The secret seems to be that workers now know that not only will notice be taken of their absence, but action will follow—a visit from a qualified person and a polite but firm interview when they return.

Since absenteeism is a disciplinary matter, affecting both efficiency of production and the well-being of employees remaining at work, a strong case can be made for the creation of joint absentee committees to investigate all cases of seemingly unjustified absence, with the main objective of directing moral censure against absenteeism. Many firms practice methods of rewarding workers with good attendance records, bestowing upon them a certain status and prestige. Others set themselves the specific target of reducing absenteeism throughout the working week to its level on pay-day (invariably the day of lowest absence).

Every employer must carry out his own research to identify the precise nature of his absenteeism problems. Statistical analyses should lead on to an assessment of people's predisposition to stay away: working conditions may then be investigated as well as the quality of supervision in the departments affected. Finally, positive efforts must be directed at developing human satisfaction at work. Genuine team spirit must be inculcated among groups, largely by training supervisors to deal with human relations problems properly; if this could only be achieved, the pressure from members of the team exerted on those who tend to 'dodge the column' would be far greater than management would ever dare to impose.

LABOUR TURNOVER

Labour turnover is the term used to describe the movement of workers into and out of the employment of an organization. To enable the problems involved and their causes to be seen in proper perspective, an index of labour movement has been devised, expressing the total number of workers replaced as a percentage of the average number of employees during a year:

$$\text{net labour turnover} = \frac{\text{total replacements}}{\text{average working force}} \times 100$$

$$\text{or } T = \frac{100R}{W}$$

Since some separations are unavoidable (married women leaving to have babies), or in some cases desirable (men may be encouraged to leave to get advancement their present firm cannot offer), the formula may be adjusted to take these factors into account, in which case:

$$T = \frac{100(R - U)}{W} \quad \text{where } U = \text{unavoidable separations}$$

An annual calculation is considered the best, since shorter periods may contain particular unusual influences; sometimes, however, quarterly indices are produced when it is felt that they may indicate seasonal trends.

There is, however, one great weakness about this method of calculation, since it obscures the extent of the stable element of the labour force. For example, a labour turnover index of $33\frac{1}{3}$ per cent could mean either of two things: if a different third of employees left each year, none of the original employees would be left after three years; but if labour turnover affected a particular third of jobs, the holders of which constantly left after only one year's service, then two-thirds of the original employees would still remain after three years. These two situations differ markedly in the degree to which the labour force consists of experienced workers; so an index of labour stability also needs to be calculated at the same time as that of turnover. Two such indices are:

$$\text{skill dilution index} = \frac{\text{No. with over 1 year's service now}}{\text{total employed now}} \times 100$$

and

$$\text{skill wastage index} = \frac{\text{No. with over 1 year's service now}}{\text{total employed 1 year ago}}$$

(These assume a worker to be experienced after one year, but the actual period may be adjusted as necessary.)

Returning to the traditional method of calculating labour turnover and the criticism that it takes no account of the length of service of those leaving, an alternative measure of an employer's ability to retain labour is to calculate the *half-life period*—the time taken for a group of new recruits to be reduced, by separations, to one-half of its original size. This concept is easy to understand and compute, yet readily provides a means of comparing different firms and different batches of entrants.

Labour stability and turnover are relative terms: no employer wants to lose too many of his staff, but equally a low turnover can adversely affect promotion prospects for able younger employees and reduce opportunities of injecting new ideas from outside. Turnover statistics should therefore be compared with figures of other employers, available from such sources as the *Department of Employment Gazette*, Employers' Federations, the Institute of Personnel Management, and the Industrial Society.

There can be no doubt about the unfavourable effects that employees leaving have on the minds of those remaining, undermining morale and interest, and lowering efficiency. Considerable costs have to be faced in replacing the leavers and training their successors, and there are also the hidden costs of lessened effectiveness throughout the organization. Excessive turnover is a bad thing socially, too, low morale being reflected by the unsatisfactory relations that exist between management and workers: it shows that management has not established the links that bind individuals to their working groups. Workers who leave soon after starting jobs because they do not feel at home demonstrate how management has failed to carry out one of its main functions, that of influencing workers' behaviour towards co-operation. Just as it has been said of the Army, 'There are no bad soldiers, only bad officers,' so industry can be accused—'There are no bad workers, only bad managers.' Every disgruntled employee is a source of ill-will towards the firm he leaves and is likely to damage its reputation.

The costs of replacing staff vary, of course, with the seniority of appointments and the amount of advertising involved. But with even the lowest-graded jobs, costs probably exceed £50 per replacement. Firstly, there are administrative recruitment costs associated with advertising, interviewing, medical examinations, and processing the necessary paperwork. Further expense is incurred while the newcomer is relatively inefficient during the early weeks of a job, which is also a time when accidents, damage to equipment, and wastage of materials are most likely to happen. Training costs must be added—induction, and the time of supervisors and other staff devoted to job instruction. During the time that vacancies exist, capital equipment is probably standing idle. And, finally, there are the intangible costs of lower staff morale and frustration for supervisors when there is a continuous movement of employees in and out of jobs.

Any study of the causes of this turnover that leads to constructive action will therefore be an attack on threatened instability among workers still remaining and a means of pin-pointing where management is lacking. The measurement of labour turnover must first be supplemented by knowledge of the reasons why employees leave. *Exit interviews* are the most commonly used technique, aimed at determining the real cause of leaving as opposed to the stated reason. This is a procedure that requires the most tactful application, for human motives are complicated and it is very difficult to achieve the desired standard of accuracy. Sympathetic and sensitive interviewers can obtain a great deal of useful information, however, which will have a direct bearing on their firm's personnel policies and practices, and hence their employment situations, as well as retaining leavers' goodwill. The occasion should not be used to try to persuade an individual to withdraw his resignation. The interview must be held in private and the person interviewed assured that it will be treated confidentially. If it proves impossible to interview an employee who has resigned, a questionnaire may be sent to him after he has left.

Separations fall into three main categories: voluntary, which are potentially avoidable; those due to management action; and involuntary separations which are unavoidable. Employees who leave of their own accord do so usually because they dislike the job, its pay and conditions, or the people they work with; personal welfare matters, such as poor transport or accommodation difficulties, may also be involved. Whichever of these reasons is appropriate, the leavers think they will be able to do better elsewhere. Employees dismissed by management leave for reasons of unsuitability (inefficiency, incompatability); breaches of disciplinary rules (insubordination, persistent lateness, or absenteeism, for example); or redundancy due to trade recession or reorganization. All these reasons are capable of a certain amount of management control. Within limits, jobs can be made more attractive and pay and conditions improved; better selection methods will reduce the number of unsuitable employees and proper induction will help recruits settle into existing work groups; and there are techniques designed to improve such matters as time-keeping, staff health and welfare, and the quality of supervision. Only trade recessions are beyond management control, but even then there are many ways by which the effects of redundancy can be minimized. Above all, management must treat employees as individuals, keep them informed of matters likely to affect their working lives, and try continuously to imbue them with the idea of co-operation for a common purpose. All this effort on the part of management is necessary if employees are to identify themselves with the organization and if morale is to be maintained at a high level.

Viewed positively, all this amounts to the management of retention (rather than turnover) by reinforcing the 'right' reasons for staying—a combination of job satisfaction and environmental reasons which themselves relate to the organization's goals. In contrast, the 'wrong' reasons for staying are those which are beneficial to neither employee nor the organization. Ultimately, rightness and wrongness, whatever their specific meanings to individuals, will require the provision of a work environment that is broadly compatible with employees' personal goals and their values in working and living. Managers must realize that 'the average worker' does not exist, and develop personnel policies and practices which are responsive to the disparate values of employees. Only then will it be possible to develop strategies aimed at retaining employees; if an organization reinforces the right reasons for staying and abstains from reinforcing the wrong reasons, its turnover—as distinct from turnover rate—might be more satisfactory.

MERGERS AND TAKE-OVERS

Obviously there are many similarities between labour turnover and redundancy situations and what happens to the morale of staff when they become involved in mergers and take-overs. In fact, there may be no personnel problems at all if the amalgamation of two organizations is purely a financial arrangement and both carry on trading as before. On the other hand, staff fears are likely to be great where take-over efforts become a struggle, which is eventually lost, against the advice of the board of the firm taken over. Many mergers take place when trading conditions are at a low ebb and it is hoped to revive matters by creating a more efficient operating unit: but inevitably this means streamlining the two organizations, centralizing administration and services, closing departments, and making considerable numbers of employees redundant. The application of a carefully prepared redundancy policy, as discussed in Chapter 6, is therefore one essential in such a situation.

In the first place, the maintenance of morale is a public relations exercise: policies (humane) and procedures for the period of amalgamation should be fully explained to everyone concerned in both organizations, trade union representatives consulted, and relevant local bodies (employment exchange, press, and local authorities) informed. It is often the case that the firm taken over is smaller and less efficient than its new parent organization. Its employees will be very conscious of their inferiority, and if their morale is allowed to deteriorate so that good men leave, some of the anticipated benefits of the merger will be lost to the new organization. The only way of forestalling this problem is for top management deliberately to demonstrate the same attitude towards all staff and to bring conditions of service throughout the new organization into parity. Unified rates of pay and fringe benefits, and common facilities for trade union representation are among the essential requirements if charges of prejudice against the taken-over staff are to be avoided. Where individuals are likely to suffer financial hardship as a result of the amalgamation, personal arrangements should be devised to cushion the blow over a period of time.

Again, a comprehensive programme must be worked out, if possible, for the mixing of staff of the previously separate firms: visits perhaps to start with, then job rotation for short periods throughout the new organization, and sharing in training courses and discussion groups—all building up to full integration. Above all, the employees of the taken-over firm must not be allowed to feel that they have lost promotion opportunities.

Traumatic as the initial impact may be, the economic facts may very well be that a firm caught up in a merger or take-over is in reality being presented with the prospect of a more prosperous future than it had before. This in itself can present hope or a challenge that can be stimulating to morale. It is unfortunate that, financial speculators being as they are, merger negotiations often have to be cloaked in secrecy. For the evil reputation which mergers and take-overs have developed is due entirely to their impact on individual employees in the organizations affected; most of their fears could be readily dispelled if they were given the maximum amount of information early on, and they would then be able to view the immediate future with much more confidence.

One survey* of a number of mergers reached the conclusion that while people were naturally anxious about their jobs, initially they felt excited rather than despondent about the future. But feelings of anxiety then came to be projected into every situation, and all new events, large and small, tended to be considered a direct result of the reorganization: for example, strangers visiting a particular location are likely to be thought of as new officers spying out the lie of the land; by contrast, lack of visitors may lead to fears that the unit is considered not worth visiting.

The amount and nature of the information given out during a change in control forms the most important single factor in reducing anxiety. Statements that people have nothing to fear, or that jobs will remain secure, and that there will be no major changes in work patterns, are *not*, by themselves, reassuring or convincing. Employees will be reassured more by precise knowledge of the direction that affairs are taking than by general expressions of benevolence. Equally important, notice of the changes to be expected should be given as soon as possible, for nothing causes more unrest than continuing uncertainty.

FURTHER READING

Labour Turnover? Towards a Solution, by P. J. Samuel (I.P.M., 1969).

Absenteeism, Manpower Papers No. 4, Department of Employment (H.M.S.O., 1971).

Experiments in Participation, by George F. Thomason, (I.P.M., 1971).

The Right to Manage?, by W. W. Daniel and Neil McIntosh (A P.E.P. report: MacDonald, 1972).

The Human Implications of Mergers and Takeovers, by P. F. Barrett (I.P.M., 1973).

---

* *After the Take-over*, by Raphael and Zimmerman (N.I.I.P., 1963).

18 Working Conditions, Welfare, and Status

PHYSICAL ENVIRONMENT

The physical surroundings in which people are employed have an obvious effect on the amount of work that can be produced. They also have a psychological impact on workers, considerably influencing their attitudes towards their jobs. Thus it has been alleged that as much as 30 per cent of all absence from work is caused by illness stemming from anxiety neuroses which develop as reactions to the type and conditions of work. This is the essence of the practice of occupational medicine—how far a patient's condition can be attributed to his or her work. (This is discussed in more detail in the next chapter.)

GOOD HOUSEKEEPING

The concept of *good housekeeping*, in the sense of insisting on cleanliness and tidiness of working areas, is as important in industry as anywhere else. The environment in even the dirtiest and most unpleasant industries should be made as amenable as possible by providing good lighting, using bright colours to cheer the appearance of depressing buildings, and by covering wet surfaces with impervious materials. Considerations of comfort should also take into account the temperature, ventilation, humidity, and spaciousness of workshops. In offices, too, much can be done to ensure high physical standards by proper maintenance: floors polished and windows washed regularly are examples. Providing the best furniture and equipment the organization can afford will benefit morale: first-class executive and clerical staff deserve good desks and chairs and equipment to use. Order and system in a firm's activities are generally appreciated by employees of all grades, and management should never permit any departure from the highest standards of good housekeeping.

FATIGUE

One of the first investigations carried out by research workers* in industrial psychology was concerned with the question of *fatigue*, which can

* There was an Industrial Fatigue Research Board during the First World War.

always be identified by reference to a firm's production curve throughout the day. Where it presents a problem, obvious remedial measures include the reduction of working hours and the use of refreshment breaks during the day. Time and motion studies can help to evolve easier methods of work, particularly by devising mechanical aids to alleviate the drudgery of heavy jobs. Much depends, too, on the quality of managers and supervisors: on their ability to adjust the speed of production lines so as to obtain optimum performance from their subordinates, and on their handling of human relationships so as to avoid the emotional strains that cause nervous fatigue.

NOISE

Most normal people find that certain types of *noise* 'get on their nerves' and are a great source of annoyance when they are trying to focus their attention firmly on some task. Continuous, meaningless, loud noise is usually accepted by workers as part of the working situation, but noise which has meaning, especially if it is elusive, like partly heard conversation, can be very distracting. Sharp, intermittent noises (those which make people jump) cause strain, as does human speech which is only just distinguishable above the background noise level. The learning of new jobs, specially if they involve mental effort, can easily be upset by unfamiliar sounds. Thus noise imposes upon the senses of workers, competing with what is relevant to their jobs; it may be meaningless, but it is insistent, and the workers affected have to turn their attention to it from time to time to make sure that it is meaningless. This constant shifting of attention has been called 'mental blinking', during which significant events may go unnoticed or be misinterpreted. Since distractions of this nature inevitably have adverse effects on production, noise is an aspect of the physical environment that management cannot afford to neglect. Positive measures may include isolating the offending machines or processes, installing silent mechanical parts, and lining walls and ceilings with sound-absorbing materials.

MONOTONY AND BOREDOM

The *monotony and boredom* that arise from repetitive work also have physical effects, although different individuals will not have the same feelings about their jobs. Monotony and boredom are products of people's minds, but it is generally accepted that the more intelligent a person is, the more bored he will become with repetitive tasks. So the fact that a process is repetitive does not necessarily mean that the operator concerned will find it boring; there are monotonous aspects in almost all jobs, especially those associated with mass production in many factory industries, but many operatives get considerable satisfaction from 'long runs' with no interruptions to their work, particularly when their piece-rates are good. The problem must therefore be viewed in the right perspective, and its basic solution lies in the initial selection of workers whose employment history shows a record of adjustment to routine work or who possess 'knitting-minds'.

There are a variety of palliatives for jobs that are entirely repetitive. Operatives can be trained to perform several different tasks and then alternate between them. They can change their positions from time to time, for instance by fetching their own materials for processing. Even their outlook can be changed occasionally by rearranging the workroom if possible. Rest pauses provide obvious breaks in routine, but these must be properly planned to avoid production losses likely when workers make up their own reasons for pausing. Music-while-you-work and chatting are usually permitted within reason. Work study specialists are interested in this problem, of course, and it is noticeable that several of the remedies suggested serve as reminders to them that the task of obtaining the greatest output in the quickest time must take the human factor fully into account. Other positive measures to relieve boredom include attempts to stimulate workers' interest through proper induction, so that they understand how their jobs fit into the overall scheme, and by invoking a feeling of competition through the regular display of production records.

ERGONOMICS

The study of all aspects of the working environment and its effects on workers' productive capacities, and the application of anatomical, physiological, and psychological knowledge to the problems arising therefrom, is known as *ergonomics*. Its emphasis is on fitting the job to the man, and it has been the subject of a great deal of research work during and since the war. Studies have included taking measurements of averages and ranges of the population at large, and determining the maximum force that can be applied by arms and legs in different positions—both of which have influenced the design of vehicles, many types of mechanical apparatus, and the optimum heights for seats and work-benches. Maximum working periods under arduous or very hot conditions have been calculated and better results obtained through various experiments with rest, refreshment, and shielding from heat sources.

As modern machinery and equipment improves, however, so the psychologist comes more into this field. No longer is the concern so much with relieving workers of heavy work as with their problems as receivers of communications—taking in data, ordering it, perceiving its importance, and doing something about it. Men can only absorb a certain amount of information or carry out a given amount of activity in a set period of time: it is important to try to measure these perceptual limitations if performance is to be improved, otherwise instructions may be presented to operatives in a manner which makes unreasonable demands on their powers of understanding. Control indicators on highly mechanized equipment have been investigated too, leading, for example, to the development of methods (for equipment that seldom fails) whereby sound signals first attract an operative's attention to dials which display more detailed information about something that has gone wrong.

These are examples of how applying the principles of ergonomics can overcome problems where exacting or confusing equipment is in use, making work easier, safer, and less likely to be disrupted by sudden crises. All this can help the personnel manager in advising on working situations which cause strain and dissatisfaction among workers, as well as guiding design engineers in their work on machines and equipment that take into account the limitations of the human beings who have to operate them.

HOURS OF WORK

Most civilized concepts of the length of the *hours of work* accept that the demands made on workers should make allowance for their needs as human beings taking part in other spheres of personal and community life. During the past century the number of hours in the standard working week has been progressively reduced from 60 to 40. Actual hours worked have also fallen, but not by as much.

The report *Hours of Work, Overtime and Shiftworking** showed that since the Second World War the British workman does not work less than he used to: in all that time the average number of hours actually worked has fluctuated slightly around the 47 hours a week mark. In other words, he has preferred to take the benefits of rising prosperity in increased earnings rather than greater leisure.

In fact, overtime has become an established feature in the lives of a substantial proportion of all workers, especially men in their thirties with growing families. Contrary to popular myth, high overtime workers have relatively low sickness and absenteeism records, for clearly pay is their major motive. Low basic rates provide the main stimulus, but highly skilled workers will also do overtime in order to preserve their differentials. Another constraint can be found in the fact that, quite apart from compulsory overtime worked in some public services, in many firms, particularly construction and engineering, production schedules and man-

* National Board for Prices and Incomes (H.M.S.O., 1970).

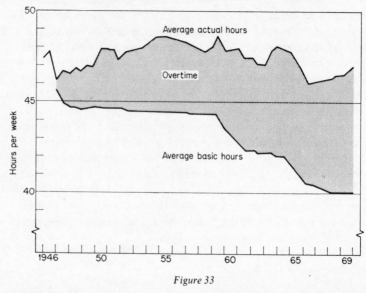

AVERAGE ACTUAL HOURS AND NORMAL BASIC HOURS
PER WEEK, 1946–1969: ADULT MALE MANUAL WORKERS

Figure 33

power levels are planned, and contracts accepted, on the assumption that regular overtime will be worked. Yet most managements still maintain that they regard overtime as voluntary, while accepting many reasons why they might wish it to be worked. These include the need to maintain plant; the demands of the type of service provided, for example, transport; to meet emergencies or occasional peaks in demand; and because it is cheaper than recruiting extra labour. Less impressive reasons are those of increasing workers' pay and meeting normal demand for products or services—both readily admitted in the P.I.B. survey. In very few cases was a coherent management policy towards overtime found, and in less than 20 per cent of cases had any comparative measurements of productivity as between normal and overtime hours been made.

A wide variety of factors—legal, social, domestic, male or female, young or old—influence the number of hours worked. To take two examples: the married woman's desire to augment her family's income may well be satisfied by a part-time job only; while the need to study or the desire for leisure may curtail the hours worked by a young man, although marriage and a family may then change his preference to one for immediate cash return from overtime. Levels of income determine that labourers generally work longer hours than craftsmen and technicians, and manual workers longer than clerical and administrative staff: one result of this, of course, is the effect it has on wage structures of narrowing the gap between skilled and unskilled workers. Methods of payment have a bearing too: time-workers have little opportunity to make extra money apart from overtime, whereas piece-workers can always earn more from an extra effort during normal hours. Men with family responsibilities tend to work longest; the trouble is that for some of them overtime becomes virtually an addiction, a self-sustaining activity usually devoted to acquiring more and more luxury goods. The value to production of the very long hours worked by this minority is very doubtful, since they almost certainly involve a lower average effort over the total hours worked, so that the input–output ratio in fact moves adversely in terms of labour costs.

Employers seem traditionally opposed to any reduction in the length of working hours. Premium payments for overtime were originally developed, in part, to induce workers to continue beyond the limits of the ever-contracting standard week, while trade unions saw the premiums as penalties which would persuade employers to take on more men rather than work existing employees for longer hours. The facts are inescapable, however, that when overtime is worked, or if hours are reduced while weekly pay packets stay the same, unit production costs must rise unless there is an equivalent rise in output.

A reduction in the actual as well as standard working week may not mean that everyone will work fewer hours than at present—they may well find supplementary part-time jobs elsewhere. A Gallup survey in April 1964 showed that 16 per cent of workers in Britain already had a second job: 5 million more employees said they would like to have a second job and would be prepared to work an average of 12½ additional hours. Even those workers who do not take an additional job are available to do more household chores, thus giving more married women the opportunity to work. A shorter working week is not the only way in which greater leisure could be secured: longer weekends and more holidays are both possible developments. There is a growing demand for four weeks' annual holiday and it seems fairly certain that this will be conceded generally within the next few years. British workers lag behind their Continental counterparts both as regards annual leave (Swedish workers were recently awarded four weeks) and the number of paid public holidays.

Most factors with a contracting influence on working hours are growing; in particular, the proportion of the total labour force which tends to work shorter hours—skilled workers, married women, professional staff—is continually increasing. Economic factors including income, productivity, the balance of payments situation, and the net effect of all these influences on the supply of manpower, are difficult to assess. There may very well be a fall in the total man-hours worked in the years ahead, so that the aim must be to use the hours which are worked more efficiently. Much will depend on the rapidity of the changes and how well management can adjust its activities to cope with them.

Making the best of working hours is always a matter for each individual organization to investigate for itself, of course. Dramatic results can be achieved when this is done, as in this case of the Industrial Solvents Division of the Distillers Company. Specifically designed kiosks, vending machines, and the introduction of safe smoking areas have enabled fixed canteen breaks for 650 workers to be replaced by natural breaks, with the result of an estimated 25,000 extra productive man-hours a year. Taking tea-breaks 'off the clock' in a factory where smoking was almost entirely forbidden, and where no ignition source is allowed within fifty feet of any production unit, was first considered during National Productivity Year. A joint consultative body was set up, which stimulated thought on the elimination of the fixed break, improved working conditions, and increased productivity. Employees are trusted to use the facilities sensibly whenever there is a natural break in their work, and results show that they maintain their rate of working more easily.

SHIFTS

The numbers of workers employed on *shifts* continues to rise and there may be a very rapid increase in the near future. Overhead costs are spread over a longer production day in this way; but overtime is not necessarily eliminated, and double-shift and Sunday premiums are commonly found in practice. Capital equipment and labour can be used more efficiently in shifts, although their introduction will not be readily achieved if workers' net wages are reduced through loss of overtime. The appeal of shift working then, like most other changes in conditions, will largely depend on how attractive it is made to workers financially.

When shifts are first contemplated in a discontinuous process where employment has previously been day work, the double-day system (say, 6 a.m.–2 p.m.; 2 p.m.–10 p.m.) probably offers the greatest advantages to all concerned—for management because the second shift is the one which alleviates fixed charges most; for employees because the physical and social difficulties are much less than when night work is involved. Of course, there should be the fullest consultation and discussions before any system is actually implemented.

The main problem about working a three-shift system is the 'unnatural' aspect of night work. Some difficulties are physiological (body-temperature rhythms, digestive disturbances, inability to sleep during the day), but the real unpopularity of continuous shift-working is due to the social disturbances caused. In particular, complaints are directed at the 'dead fortnight', when afternoon and night shifts virtually preclude any normal evening social life. In order to overcome these problems, the Continental, or 3–2–2, system is coming more and more into use, and is already firmly established in the chemical and iron and steel industries. It entails more frequent changes than the traditional pattern, with the result that employees concerned can take part in normal social activities at least two or three times *every* week. The rotation of shifts over a four-week cycle is three mornings, two afternoons, two nights, three rest days, two mornings, two afternoons, three nights, and two rest days, thus:

| | *Weeks* | | | |
	1	2	3	4
Monday	6–2	—	10–6	2–10
Tuesday	6–2	—	10–6	2–10
Wednesday	2–10	6–2	—	10–6
Thursday	2–10	6–2	—	10–6
Friday	10–6	2–10	6–2	—
Saturday	10–6	12–10	6–12	—
Sunday	—	10–6	2–10	6–2

Average weekly hours 42

The two notable features of this arrangement of hours are that it gets away entirely from the 'dead fortnight' and that there is a 24-hour break between each section of the 3–2–2 shifts. On the debit side, there are the possible difficulties a family may have initially in following the system, and the fact that there are no entirely free weekends (although the different Saturday hours partly help to overcome this).

Good reports have come from industrial organizations using the system: I.C.I. operate it in two of their factories, and a survey of 5,000 employees showed an 86 per cent response in its favour. Shorter and more frequent spells on each shift were found to be less tiring and the variety was more enjoyable. Employees said that they seemed to have more time off, and obviously opportunities were much better for social and family life. Senior staff, for their part, found it much easier to keep in touch with shift workers and supervisors.

Enlightened management might well take the view, in any case, that because shift working is inherently unpopular, the system of operation should be decided by those involved, as long as productive efficiency is not adversely affected. This should leave scope for administrative ingenuity to meet the personal convenience of employees whenever possible as regards the frequency of shift changes, starting and finishing times, and when rest days occur.

In summary, management's aim must be to make the physical environment at work as congenial as possible, having regard for the 'inner man' as well as creature comforts. It is important to take action when employees are dissatisfied with their conditions generally, and to help individuals by means of unguided interviews when they appear to be brooding over some anxiety or worry. Such interviews may very well give the clue which reveals underlying grievances about working conditions.

FLEXITIME

Flexible working hours represent an approach to attendance at work which, within limits set by management, enables individual employees to vary their hours day by day and, to that extent, come and go as they please. Several advantages are claimed for such systems, many of which have now been put into practice, largely in commercial and government offices employing clerical workers. Flexible working hours operate best when individual workers are responsible for activities which do not require the presence of others. In most industrial jobs, certainly on production lines, this is rarely possible.

Morale is improved by allowing staff to arrange their days to fit their particular needs and leisure pursuits and to make the best use of available transport; the stresses and strains on individuals can thus be reduced with consequent benefits to their health and efficiency. The pioneering schemes have demonstrated that absenteeism is reduced because there are no longer fears associated with being late for work, and the temptation to take the odd day off is also reduced. Very important is the encouragement to married women to work by being able to adjust their hours to the demands of running a home.

The major management constraint quite obviously is so to control the scheme that neither general efficiency nor service to customers suffer in any way. This means that most offices have a 'core time', commonly 10.00 to 16.00 hours when all staff are expected to be present—the flexibility lying in actual starting and finishing times. Flexible hours permit employees to work more or less hours in a working day than is normal, but over a period of say three weeks or a month, the full contracted hours must be worked. A rule must therefore be agreed about how many 'credits' or 'debits' of hours any employee may carry forward and for how long. Hours may be worked so that the occasional day or half-day off may be taken, although management has to control this so as to prevent inefficiency due to periods of under-staffing. It is also necessary that time off should not lead to regular 4 or $4\frac{1}{2}$ day working weeks.

The practical consideration involved in operating a flexitime scheme were well illustrated by an experiment conducted in nine different offices

of the Department of Inland Revenue*, with almost unanimously favourable reaction being reported from each place. There was certainly very
little desire to return to the previously closely defined hours, and it was
generally felt that this single innovation had done more to improve staff
morale than all other recent changes put together. Fears of a revolt against
recording times in and out had proved groundless and there was very little
evidence of any abuse of the new freedom. Many people worked much the
same hours as before; very few wanted to work eccentric hours; everyone
was glad to have the opportunity to change hours, without fuss, when they
needed to. The experiment proved a boon to those with temporary personal
problems (like having to visit relatives in hospital); and, as anticipated,
married women made more use of the flexibility concept than any other
group of staff.

One inherent practical problem is the system for recording time. Small
units can usually manage quite happily without formality. In large units,
however, a greater need seems to be expressed for formal records and closer
supervision. Manual records maintained by the staff concerned and their
managers are possible, of course, but tend to be time-consuming, prone to
error in compilation, and productive of suspicion between fellow-workers.
There are also mechanical time-recording units available, but these are
expensive to install, and no mechanical system is ever entirely foolproof.
Challenging questions about the quality of supervisors and their relationships with subordinates must therefore be resolved before deciding on the
particular 'brand' of flexitime to be introduced.

WELFARE

The important thing about employee benefits and welfare services is
that they should spring from the right motives, otherwise management and
worker attitudes towards them might clash. If management regard them
as paternalistic acts of benevolence, preening themselves as good employers with their workers' interests at heart, they may very well be sur-
prised by a reaction alleging fraud. For employees often feel that the costs
of welfare provisions are used as a cheap excuse for refusing claims for
better working conditions, and that amenities provided unilaterally could
be withdrawn at any time without breach of agreement. The view is often
expressed—'Cut out the welfare, and give us the cash in our wages'.

Welfare policy must therefore be based on sound principles:

1. Management should never obtrude into the private lives of employees
   through welfare schemes (thus avoiding accusations of paternalism).

---

* 'Flexible Hours Experiment', by G. Galey, *Management Services Review*, 1973,
pages 182–7.

2. Amenities should be provided only when desired by employees. The sincerity of this desire may be judged by their willingness to administer the activities, clubs, and benefits themselves.

3. The amenities provided should be beneficial in the long run to both management and employees (thus avoiding charges of bribery or extravagance).

Figure 34

Practice in the provision and administration of welfare facilities varies enormously between different organizations, as does the extent to which their personnel departments become directly involved. Broadly speaking, however, the following seven services and amenities are normally considered to fall within the welfare sphere:

CANTEENS

These may be controlled directly by the firm or organized through outside caterers. In most cases the prices of meals are subsidized, apprentices getting very cheap meals, while senior executives pay near the economic price. Food can be a constant source of complaints, of course, and joint consultative committees are usually formed to deal with them and help the canteen manager with constructive suggestions. Outside working hours canteen buildings are often used for other social purposes and may be licensed as clubs.

ACCOMMODATION

Any large organization which recruits professional and technical staff from a distance will find it necessary to assist them in finding accommodation for their families. Help may take many forms, ranging from maintaining lists of approved lodgings or running hostels for single men, to advancing loans for house purchase. Many firms own houses and flats which they rent to employees and some have special arrangements with local authorities concerning council housing for key workers. Obviously the whole question of providing such assistance needs the most careful control, especially as regards the legal position of employees who leave a firm while still receiving its help with accommodation.

TRANSPORT

Linked with the housing problem is that of travelling to work. Here again practice varies widely: firms may own or hire fleets of coaches or lorries, provide senior staff with cars or car allowances, and will certainly make representations to local bus companies to arrange services convenient for their employees. In any given area there is a committee which advises the transport authority on local problems: the personnel manager must ensure that his organization's views are heard in that committee.

PERSONAL PROBLEMS

An employee should first notify his immediate superior if he wants help with a personal or domestic problem, but may ask to see or be referred to someone in the personnel department. All its staff should be prepared to help directly with problems if employees approach them as individuals: this is preferable to passing a person with worries on to a colleague unless absolutely necessary.

SICKNESS BENEFITS

The importance of firms' private benefit arrangements has been progressively reduced by State provision, culminating in the National Insurance Act, 1966, which introduced a scheme of earnings-related supplements to unemployment and sickness benefits. These are payable to men aged 18–65 and women aged 18–60 as long as they are entitled to flat-rate benefits and are earning at least £500 per annum. The supplement is approximately one-third of the amount of that portion of a person's average weekly earnings which lies between £9 and £30: for example, a man earning £15 would receive a supplement of £2. It is payable for six months, in addition to all other benefits, subject to a maximum of 85 per cent of average earnings. As far as firms' own sickness arrangements are concerned, a notable recent development is the tendency for the distinction made between payments during absence to 'staff' and 'workers' to disappear.

PENSION SCHEMES

Most large organizations now operate their own superannuation arrangements for professional and technical staff and many have schemes that include all their workers. These may have some value in attracting and retaining the steadier type of employee, although there is the contrary argument that a man's reluctance to lose pension rights is the wrong motive for staying with an otherwise unsatisfactory employer. An organization's own pension scheme may be contributory or non-contributory, and may be administered by its own trust or through an insurance company.

Here again State provision has caught up with some private arrangements, as a result of the Graduated Pension Scheme which was introduced under the National Insurance Act, 1959, to supplement retirement pensions. The scheme applies to all workers whose employers are not contracted-out on grounds that they already guarantee comparable benefits under their own occupational pension schemes (at present, private schemes cover more than one-third of the working population, including half of the men). The level of employees' earnings now affects both the rate of their pension contributions while working and their retirement pensions; graduated contributions must be paid by both employer and employee whose pay, before deductions, exceeds £9 per week. No contributions are paid by employers who contract-out, normally done when they have their own 'generous' contributory schemes.

LONG-SERVICE AWARDS

These are most commonly given at the conventional 'coming-of-age', twenty-one years' work with the organization, although further awards are often given for greater service. They can be of considerable motivational importance to those eligible, and the administration involved needs to be carried out carefully. When firms have traded only for twenty to thirty years, for example, or when they have expanded rapidly during that period, early staff records may be scanty or non-existent, and the Welfare Officer may have to undertake a considerable amount of 'detective work' among older employees to verify claims to awards. Obviously certain rules will have to apply to any long-service scheme: those relating to broken periods of service over the years are always crucial to the equitable treatment of employees when deciding on awards.

SOCIAL ACTIVITIES

These may range from an informal Christmas party or summer outing to the provision of a sports and social club with a large full-time staff to run it. Facilities on this scale are often the subject of controversy; certainly, extravagant provisions can never be justified while employees' more fundamental needs for improved working conditions or security of employment may be neglected. Nevertheless it is very useful to have social facilities where employees and their families can meet, especially in remote locations or small towns where little other entertainment is available in any case. Even when full-time administrative staff are provided, each section or activity should be allowed reasonable autonomy, within the social club's rules and subject to the firm's overall financial control, of course.

STAFF–WORKER STATUS

For many years efforts have been made to narrow the differences between 'staff' and 'workers'. The Institute of Personnel Management's Golden Jubilee statement of personnel policies declared support for the progressive removal of distinctions in security of employment and conditions of work, including fringe benefits, for different categories of employee, and more recently the Code of Industrial Relations Practice made the same point.

Fundamentally the distinctions are akin to those drawn between social classes. One group of employees work comparatively short hours and are trusted to carry out a reasonable amount of work during that time; and there is a larger group who normally work longer hours and are generally not trusted by their employers, their work being much more closely supervised and paid for in ratio to the hours spent in the workplace or the effort expended. There is no escaping the fact that this mistrust in turn causes a lack of confidence in management by employees—a general situation which is wholly unhelpful to labour relations.

Practical distinctions are commonly seen between security of employment, the amount of notice due, promotion opportunities, length of holidays, and generosity of sickness pay. It is commonplace to hear that a skilled craftsman with twenty years' experience in a firm works forty-two hours a week, has pay deducted if he is a few minutes late for work, draws only his National Insurance benefit when sick, and has two weeks' holiday a year. His teenage daughter, employed in the same firm's typing pool for twenty days, works thirty-five hours a week, loses no pay if late nor if she is away ill, and is entitled to three weeks' holiday. The historical distinction is that between 'office' and 'works', but several factors have served to blur this: the rapid increase in numbers of professional, techni-cal, and clerical staffs compared with production workers; the fact that so many women are employed in these groups (whose better conditions are envied by men); above all, the growing together of the interests of pro-fessional and technical staff and skilled operatives on the one hand, as opposed to office staff on the other. All these factors help 'workers' over the barriers that previously existed.

Recent reported attempts to make progress with this problem seem to be inspired by different motives on the part of management. In some cases, equality of conditions is aimed at in order to retain labour by building up loyalty towards the employer; in others, concessions have been made virtually as part of the process of productivity bargaining. Thus in 1965 an agreement was concluded between I.C.I. and the trade unions concerned by which higher status was given to manual workers. For their part, unions agreed that workers should be allowed to undertake a much wider range of tasks as the need arose, with considerable interchange between skilled and unskilled jobs. In return, workers received stable remuneration in the form of annual salaries paid weekly. Within each of eight different job grades minimum and maximum salaries were fixed, with overtime to be paid on a fixed hourly scale related to salaries. In addition, employees are now subject to four weeks' notice, and those with three years' service are entitled to up to six months' full pay during sickness. The approach of most organizations seems to be aimed at tackling equality of status step by step, either dealing with one aspect at a time or progressively granting improved status to certain types of staff according to their length of service, degree of responsibility, or general reliability.

One symbol of staff–worker distinction that regularly comes under attack is the clocking-in system. There is no clearer indication of mistrust of workpeople than this insistence on a record of the times they arrive and depart (irrespective of how much work they do while there). More faith must be placed in the responsibility of individuals by management, and indeed in the ability of supervisors to control the time-keeping and attendance of their subordinates. Apart from these emotional aspects of management and worker views on the subject, clocking-in is also ad-ministratively expensive. The experience of firms who have abandoned it is that their confidence has been fully justified by results; there has been no deterioration in employees' time-keeping, and new documentation for wages purposes was speedily evolved.

Many practical difficulties have to be overcome. Fixing annual salaries for workers accustomed to overtime pay, piece-rates, and production bonuses requires the most careful negotiations. Workers will reject offers which amount to less than their previous total earnings inclusive of overtime and other premium payments. If the offers are too high, on the other hand, management will be faced with greater costs unless increases in productivity are obtained at the same time. Professional and clerical workers inevitably react defensively to some extent, seeking to preserve their past privileges. This may lead to greater interest being taken in white-collar unions, the bargaining strength of which will grow, possibly straining staff relationships with management. On the financial side, wage agreements may have to be renegotiated to take into account the staff concept of pay increases based on length of service: although this may cut down on labour turnover, it means substituting incremental rises for the present practice of frequent (often annual) wage claims.

It is not easy to change employment conditions which have their origins in the dim past of industrial history, are largely based on the privilege of superior social class, and are resented for that very reason by the majority of workers. Traditional trappings of status are irrelevant in our contemporary economic circumstances, but getting rid of them calls for the closest co-operation between managers and trade union representatives, encouraged by the strength of public opinion, and stimulated by advice on good practice which is available from Government departments. There can be no doubt that success in this sphere would materially contribute to improving workers' attitudes to the whole social structure of industry.

FURTHER READING

Status and Benefits in Industry (Industrial Society, 1966).
Welfare at Work, by A. O. Martin (Batsford, 1967).
Physical Working Conditions, by Winifred McCullogh (Industrial Society, Gower Press, 1969).

19 Health and Safety

To a large extent the health and safety of workers are controlled by legislation, notably the Factories Act, 1961; the Offices, Shops, and Railway Premises Act, 1963; the Employment Medical Advisory Service Act, 1972; and the Health and Safety at Work Act, 1974. The important thing is that most employers accept these as enforcing only minimum conditions and are concerned to improve on them wherever possible.

THE FACTORIES ACT, 1961

The main sections of the Act refer to the health, safety, and welfare of workers, as follows.

HEALTH

Daily removal of dirt and refuse and a weekly cleaning of floors is required, as is the periodical cleansing, painting, or lime-washing of walls, ceilings, and partitions. The amount of space allowed for every person employed is a minimum of 400 cubic feet. The temperature of workshops where a substantial amount of work is done sitting must not be less than 60°F and standards may be laid down for efficient ventilation and lighting. All floors liable to be wet must be efficiently drained. The provision of suitable and sufficient sanitary accommodation is obligatory. Persons employed in rooms where poisonous substances or fumes are in use must have facilities to take their meals elsewhere in the factory. Other regulations relate to work in underground rooms, lifting excessive weights, employment involving lead processes, and the notification of industrial poisoning or disease.

SAFETY

Accidents causing loss of life or disablement of a worker for more than three days must be reported to the district factory inspector; certain dangerous occurrences must also be reported, even though no injury results. Several sections of the Act relate to the safeguarding of engines, prime movers, transmission machinery, and dangerous parts of other machinery. These requirements are most stringent: not only is the occupier of a factory required to fence such machinery securely but the person who sells or hires out any machinery not complying with the Act is liable to penalties. Hoists and lifts must be of adequate strength and construction, must be properly maintained, and examined every six months; similar regulations apply to all forms of lifting tackle—chains, ropes, and cranes. Every factory must have a certificate from the local fire authority to the effect that its buildings have reasonable means of escape: workrooms must be arranged so that there is a free passageway to the escape doors. Exits must never be locked when employees are in a workroom, and in all factories employing more than twenty people effective steps must be taken to ensure that they know the means of escape and the routine to be followed in case of fire.

WELFARE

Provision of drinking water and washing and cloakroom facilities are compulsory. All employees, male and female, must be provided with seats if their jobs allow opportunities for sitting without detriment to their work. Every factory must have a first-aid box or cupboard of the prescribed standard, with increased provision for every 150 persons employed.

The above are the main requirements of the Act. There are many other provisions relating to the protection of employees' eyes, limitations on hours of work of women and young persons, and provisions for 'outworkers' and piece-work. The factory occupier must keep a General Register, in which data is recorded showing that the prescribed requirements of the Act are being observed (for example, particulars of young persons employed, accidents, and industrial diseases). H.M. Inspectors have power to inspect every part of the factory by day and night; they may ask for registers and certificates, question any person in the factory, and may take samples for analysis. The officers of local authorities and fire services have similar powers in carrying out their duties under the Act. It is a sensible measure for the personnel manager to arrange that these visiting officials should always be received and conducted about the premises by the same member of his staff, thus ensuring that any action which may be necessary as a result of these visits will be consistent.

An interesting experiment started in 1974 was the reorganization of two areas of H.M. Factory Inspectorate, so that teams of inspectors became responsible for specific industries. Previously, most of the inspectorate was organized on a district basis, with individual inspectors covering the whole range of industries in their districts. Under the new scheme, principal inspectors with teams of inspectors will have responsibilities for particular industries throughout the whole of the new areas. It is hoped that by building up greater experience in the problems and hazards of particular industries, the inspectorate will be able to give a better service to managers and workers.

THE OFFICES, SHOPS, AND RAILWAY PREMISES ACT, 1963

The purpose of this Act was virtually to extend the requirements of the Factories Act to offices and shops, where some $7\frac{1}{2}$ million people are employed. Its main provisions are:

1. Suitable and sufficient sanitary conveniences and washing facilities must be provided and properly maintained, with effective lighting and ventilation.
2. Stairs and gangways must be of sound construction, provided with handrails, and be kept free from obstruction.
3. Drinking water must be provided and means for drinking it.
4. Arrangements must be made to hang up outdoor and working clothes and also to dry them.
5. Seats must be provided for employees who normally can sit at their work. In shops at least one seat must be provided for every three employees.
6. If employees in shops eat meals on the premises, suitable facilities must be provided.
7. No one under 18 may clean any machinery if this exposes him or her to risk of injury from moving parts. No untrained person may work at certain machines except under supervision.
8. No one may be required to lift a heavy load likely to injure him.
9. A first-aid box or cupboard must be provided. Where more than 150 people are employed, a trained first-aider must be available.
10. A room in which people work must not be so overcrowded as to cause risk of injury to health; account must be taken not only of the number of people in the room but also the space occupied by furniture, fittings, and machinery.
11. Workrooms must be of such a size that there is 40 square feet of floor space or 400 cubic feet of capacity for each person.
12. A reasonable temperature must be maintained in rooms where people are employed other than for short periods. Where work does not involve severe physical effort, a 'reasonable' temperature is specified as not less than 16°C after the first hour. Thermometers must be provided to enable employees to check temperatures.
13. The Act also covers fire precautions and means of escape, and the notification of accidents at work.

An investigation of fifty offices carried out in Hull* shows how much needs to be done in this field. The majority of them were classified as 'really

* 'Are Offices fit to work in?' by F. E. Heathcote, *New Society*, 8 September 1966.

poor', when the age of their premises, the quality of furnishings and decor, and the amount of space available were considered. All the firms employed less than fifty people, and it was the smallest of these which had the best office conditions: quality of conditions generally seemed to vary inversely with the size of the firms. There is every reason for believing that the high proportion of poor offices found in this local study is repeated in other commercial centres, but only further surveys will show how prevalent substandard conditions are. Office staff are rarely organized by unions, and they may be ignorant of the legal requirements or not know to whom they can complain, despite the fact that an abstract of the Act must be displayed.

Compulsory inspection of premises registered under the Act has already shown that few occupiers are reluctant to conform with the law once they are made aware of their obligations. The many defects found* show how necessary this protection for staff is. Low standards of cleanliness were noticeable in those parts of shops and offices not seen by the public. Temperature and ventilation were generally satisfactory, except in some partitioned premises: 'However, where adequate ventilation was provided, many office employees complained of draughts and sealed up the source of ventilation.' It was apparent that the planning of lighting had been neglected in the past and warranted particular attention. There were reports of insufficient or unsuitable lavatories and of the lack of running hot water. Few premises provided accommodation for drying outdoor clothing. Scope for ergonomic specialists was evidenced by complaints about the functional design of chairs and equipment. Enforcement of the regulations about floors, passages, and stairs is likely to cause most trouble, however. Inspection has shown innumerable cases of worn and loose floorboards and coverings, defective stairs with handrails not provided or ineffectual, and obstructions in a high proportion of passages and stairs.

OCCUPATIONAL HEALTH SERVICES

The principles of occupation health emanate from the answers to three questions:

Has a patient's illness been caused by his job?
Will his work retard his recovery?
Does his disability affect his capacity to do his job (for example, can a bronchitic be sent back to a dusty job, or should a manager who has been mentally ill return to a job where he controls other people)?

---

* Report on the Act for the year 1965, H.C. No. 144 (H.M.S.O., 1966).

The tasks that can be carried out by the staff of an occupational health service include:

1. Assisting in placing applicants in suitable jobs: this involves initial research to find out the health requirements of different types of work.
2. Intelligent medical surveillance; following up suspicions of hazards; looking at special problems (for example, older workers); examining employees, who are well at the time, to try to detect any early symptoms of illness.
3. Treatment services, which in themselves can provide a great deal of information about hazards to health: sophisticated statistical analysis should reveal where and why hazards are occurring.
4. Regular inspection of the working environment.
5. Involvement in the planning stages of new buildings, to prevent known hazards being built in to them.

The successful fulfilment of these tasks should in itself justify the expenses of the staff salaries, accommodation, and equipment of such a service. There will be tangible gains in terms of time saved as a result of quick treatment and through diagnosing of illnesses and industrial diseases at their early stages. But there will be other intangible benefits as well, in the effect on staff morale through knowing that medical treatment is immediately available, the preventive work carried out, the preliminary screening of potential employees, the planned rehabilitation of those returning to work after injuries or long illness, and the control exercised over the environment. The latter covers the elimination both of physical hazards and those which cause mental stress provoking psychosomatic illness and neurotic symptoms. The extent of services provided in practice varies with the size of the organization, and ranges from the minimum first-aid boxes prescribed by legislation to superbly equipped medical centres with full-time doctors and nurses in attendance. A specialist medical officer is rare in firms with less than 5,000 employees, however: small firms tend to employ part-time medical officers, often with a group of firms sharing the same doctor. Where a firm has a surgery of its own, a State Registered Nurse with specialist training in industrial nursing is usually in charge, and at least one nurse will be present during all shift hours.

Clearly advice on the detailed application of legislative requirements falls within the province of the medical officer, and much of his work will be closely linked with that of the personnel department. He will be concerned with the employment of disabled people, which is obligatory for firms working on Government contracts. He will make periodic inspections of canteen facilities. He may consider eating habits; for example, trying to find the number of workers who arrive without having breakfast, and so advise on canteen opening hours. He will review accident figures, consider their causes, and make recommendations accordingly; and his prestige should play an important part in safety education. His opinion will be sought on such difficult personnel problems as terminating the employment of people with prolonged illnesses, and on policy matters such as whether employees with colds should be encouraged to stay home to avoid infecting their fellows.

With so many close ties, it is vital that the correct relationship should be established between the personnel officer and the medical officer. In functional matters the medical officer plays his own part in securing the efficiency of his firm by maintaining the 'happiness' of workers, and in this he is a member of the management team (rather than having the solitary role of the G.P. in the community). He should consult with the personnel officer so that the co-ordination of personnel policy is made effective, but in professional matters he must have direct access to the highest level of authority, the board of directors. It is probably best in these circumstances that copies of all his proposals affecting employees should also be sent to the personnel department. It is essential to remember, however, that all dealings between doctor and patient, whatever the situation, are confidential, and this principle must always be respected. Over a period of time the works medical officer is generally able to establish a comprehensive medical history of every employee. This record is also confidential and may not be mentioned in other than general terms to the employer, unless the state of the employee's health demands some specific action (for instance, an employer may not place persons known to be suffering from certain communicable diseases next to other employees, or it may be necessary to transfer an employee from one job to another owing to some disability). Besides individual medical histories, the medical officer may also keep group records for statistical purposes.

A great deal of research work is being done both by individual doctors and by industrial health services, such as the famous pioneering venture at Slough. The emphasis is usually on preventive medicine: for example, trying to find links between anxiety neuroses, pressure of work and noise, the effect of hours of work on illness, or the ways epidemics spread in a workplace.

Such a wide range of activities smacks of the larger organization, but there are cases of quite small employers obtaining excellent results from combining resources to provide health facilities. There are, for example, four firms in Huddersfield* who provide such a service; located within a

---

* This scheme is explained in *The Nursing Mirror*, 14 October 1966, in an article 'A Health Service for the Smaller Industries'.

three-quarter mile radius, their total pay roll is only 730. A qualified nursing sister visits each mill at least once daily. Both the capital costs and the running expenses are borne on a *per capita* basis, fluctuating according to the average number of employees a particular firm has during any one year. A board of directors controls the whole scheme, composed of one representative from each firm. The objects are:

1. To deal promptly and efficiently with personal injuries whether occurring in the mill, at home, or elsewhere.
2. To give regular care to all skin abrasions, splinters, and boils in order to obtain rapid healing.
3. To give treatment for minor ills, such as headache, colds, sore throats, and stomach upsets.
4. In the case of more serious injury or illness to direct the patient promptly to hospital or a G.P.
5. To give advice on health and welfare matters or indeed on any subject causing a worried state of mind.
6. Above all, the service exists to try to prevent injury and illness and actively to try to promote good health as well as to deal with illness when it occurs. Suggestions for reducing the risks of accidents and for improving conditions generally are studied jointly by the nursing sister and management.

The nursing sister is trained in general nursing and also in occupational health. From time to time arrangements are made with the national scheme of mass radiography for checks for tuberculosis, and other simple testing is done, such as for diabetes, in an effort to discover the development of certain illnesses at an early stage. The effects of the scheme so far have been most satisfactory, and in decreased absenteeism alone its costs are saved. But the firms concerned regard the improvement in employees' well-being as more important in any case.

The benefits of occupational health facilities seem obvious, yet it is not a subject that is without controversy. Criticisms are sometimes heard about the lack of uniformity in the activities of industrial doctors and the fact that some of them have little or no specialist training. The value of routine medical examinations, upon which the practice of occupational medicine is largely based, has been questioned, too. But typical of the nature of the controversy was this statement* made at the 1966 annual conference of the Institute of Personnel Management: 'I am convinced that if a personnel manager attempts to solve a placement problem without

* Dr. W. Marshall, Group Medical Officer, Baker Perkins Holdings Ltd., in his talk on 'Physical and Mental Health Problems at Work'.

a medical report on his file, he is working with his eyes bandaged and his ears plugged'.

As a result of an Act of Parliament in 1972 there has been set up an Employment Medical Advisory Service, designed to become the focus for the development of occupational medicine in Britain. Part of the Department of Employment, it will be staffed by over 100 doctors, some part-time, based in the country's main industrial centres.

The new service will study and advise on the effects of a particular job on health; the medical precautions to be taken in working with poisonous or hazardous substances; and the medical requirements for different types of work, especially in relation to the disabled. Other duties will include advising employers, trade unions and employees on medical matters, helping H.M. Factory Inspectors to deal with health hazards, and carrying out medical investigations and examinations of workers. Liaison will be maintained with colleagues in hospitals and general practice, and with the D.E. service concerned with the resettlement training of disabled workers. Finally, the E.M.A.S. staff will be responsible for the medical supervision, guidance and examination of all those attending government training centres and industrial rehabilitation units.

The good intentions behind the creation of this service are backed with official powers. Thus employment medical advisers will have a right of entry to factory premises in the course of their duties, and also the power to require a factory occupier to permit them to carry out a medical examination on any employee whose health they believe to be in danger because of his work.

SAFETY OF WORKERS

Reported accidents in 1968 reached the record figure in peacetime of 312,430. These included 625 people killed—an average of nearly two for every working day. The 1975 figures were 427 killed; 243,140 accidents.

The personnel manager's function in the prevention of accidents is basically to reinforce and co-ordinate the efforts of the safety and medical officers. These should reflect concern for both the individuals who suffer accidents and their effect on the reputation, efficiency, and morale of the organization as a whole (indeed, it is not unknown for strikes to be called to obtain better safety precautions). Detailed activities include:

1. Ensuring that dangerous machinery is properly guarded, that there are adequate fire exits, and that all the other legal requirements are observed.
2. Atmospheric conditions, temperature, and humidity: the important factor here is that anything which makes the worker feel uncomfort-

able attracts his attention to himself and away from his work, thus making accidents more likely.

3. Lighting: more accidents occur in artificial light than in daylight; uniform lighting is also important, since accidents often occur when people leave well-illuminated workplaces and pass into dimly lighted surrounding areas.

4. Speed of production: the speed of machinery running throughout the day should be closely controlled in relation to the increasing fatigue of the machine-minders; on the other hand, too frequent changes in speed may affect workers' co-ordination and expose them more often to danger points.

5. Personal conditions arising, for example, from the immaturity and dash of young people or the inexperience of workers taking on new tasks; these considerations underline the importance of adequate training, no matter how simple the process is.

Particular attention needs to be paid to the fencing of dangerous machinery. Why is it that, despite all the educational effort and the publicity given to the huge annual toll of deaths and injuries, some employers still in effect get away with non-observance of the Factories Act? The simple truth seems to be that so few employers or machinery manufacturers fully appreciate what the law demands. The two most relevant judgments are: 'A machine is dangerous if . . . in the ordinary course of human affairs danger may reasonably be anticipated from its use unfenced, not only to the prudent, alert and skilled operative intent upon his task, but also to the careless, inattentive worker whose inadvertent or indolent conduct may expose him to risk of injury or death from the unguarded part.'* 'The duty to fence securely is an absolute one. The duty is not to be qualified by such words as "so far as practicable" or "so long as it can be fenced consistently with its being used for the purpose for which it was intended", and if the result of a machine being securely fenced is that it does not remain commercially practicable or mechanically possible, that does not affect the obligation.'† In the eyes of the law, then, the plea that a machine cannot be effectively guarded is unacceptable, as is the excuse that productivity or profits would be reduced if guards were to cover it properly.

The personnel manager must investigate all aspects of any accident: its nature; its cause, which is usually attributable to some fault in equipment, working arrangements, or negligence on the part of a worker; and its effect. Statistics of accidents are usually recorded for this last purpose, showing their frequency rate measured in terms of the number of accidents

---

* Mitchell v. North British Rubber Co. Ltd.
† John Summers and Sons Ltd. v. Frost.

causing loss of time per 100,000 working hours, and the severity rate, the actual number of working hours lost per 100,000 hours.

Carrying out these duties demands the closest liaison with specialist staff throughout the organization; with maintenance engineers to ensure the guarding of machinery and testing for safety of all new equipment; with designers, method engineers, and work study staff, to insist on safe working methods and if necessary the sacrifice of speed for the sake of safety. As the company may be sued at common law for damages resulting from negligence which causes accidents, the personnel manager must also keep in close touch with its legal advisers, to instruct them on any technical matters arising out of such actions, and to produce for their information all relevant records and reports. He must also see that the employer's obligations under the National Insurance (Industrial Injuries) Act, 1946, are fulfilled, and that those who are injured at work know how to make the necessary claims, confirmed by his departmental records.

Prevention is better than cure, and the basic necessity is to try to develop a responsible frame of mind on the part of all employees. The largest organizations usually appoint a full-time safety officer, and even small firms make one executive responsible for safety as part of his duties. The safety officer is usually backed up by the appointment of a safety committee, and there is no doubt that this represents one of the best examples of joint consultation in practice. Under the chairmanship of the safety officer, representatives of management, supervisors, and workers meet together to discuss ideas aimed at improving safety, studying reports of accidents that have occurred, and making surveys of their place of work to ensure that safety precautions are being carried out. Co-operation between employers and employees is a key factor, and H.M. Chief Inspector of Factories would like to see many more joint safety committees tackling the need to make industry safe.*

Some interesting psychological research is going on in industry at the present time on the question of *accident proneness*—a phrase which applies to that small minority of people who seem to be more susceptible to accidents than their fellows. It is possible to discover who some of these accident-prone people are: for example, there are tests for skilled workers which call for rapid and accurate co-ordination of hand and eye, intelligence, and mechanical aptitude. The results indicate that those who fail the tests have a higher accident rate than those who pass them. On the other hand, there is a body of opinion which believes that the concept of

---

* A survey carried out by the Factory Inspectorate in May 1967 revealed that nearly 8,000 firms in which more than fifty people were employed had joint committees concerned with safety: 73 per cent of these were considered to be effective.

accident proneness may be accepted too readily, since no one has yet succeeded in pin-pointing an accident-prone group and, by excluding that group, modifying the accident rate. Furthermore the intricacies of tasks, the experience of workers, and the conditions under which they work, can make it virtually impossible to establish valid comparisons. Another explanation, then, is that individuals may have 'accident spells' related to impaired health or domestic stress.

Considerable help in accident prevention is available from outside the organization, particularly from the Royal Society for the Prevention of Accidents (RoSPA) which plays a leading role in tackling the problem, by gathering statistics, through publicity, and safety education. The Society continually strives to improve its activities; during 1965, for instance, it appointed seven Regional Industrial Safety Organizers to stimulate the growth of safety consciousness and the development of company policies within their areas. The C.B.I. and T.U.C. have also shown their willingness to help by collaborating in arranging a series of joint conferences on industrial safety. To give greater cohesion and effectiveness to the efforts of all concerned with accident prevention, early in 1967 the Minister of Labour set up a new national body, the Industrial Safety Advisory Council. He himself is its chairman, and there are representatives of the C.B.I., T.U.C., RoSPA, the nationalized industries, and the British Insurance Association. Its first tasks were to give consideration to research and joint consultation on safety.

The form of safety organization adopted by a firm must be the one best suited to its particular circumstances. It must be properly conceived, with clear objectives, and must have the backing of the power of the boardroom. But the fact that accident figures continue to rise, despite technical and scientific advances, clearly emphasizes the human factor which is fundamental to the problem. Future research therefore might well concentrate on ways in which employee behaviour patterns in the workplace contribute to accidents. 'It must be driven home repeatedly that factories and building sites are not play-grounds for the irresponsible, but working places which require the exercise of discipline—especially self-discipline and self-restraint—in the potentially dangerous environment which they create.'*
A continuous process of education must go on, sponsored by the board of directors, the personnel manager, the medical officer, and the safety officer and his committee; all organs of joint consultation must be encouraged to make worthwhile suggestions and offer constructive criticism on the subject. The combination of all these efforts, applied in a sustained manner, will greatly help, but the ultimate solution to the whole tragic

* From the survey mentioned at the foot of the previous page.

problem of accidents will only be achieved when every employee conscientiously accepts personal responsibility for working safely.

THE HEALTH AND SAFETY AT WORK ACT, 1974

The most comprehensive ever system of law covering the health and safety of people at work, and the general public who may be affected by the activities of people at work, is provided by this Act. It arises from the recommendations of the Robens Committee and subsequent consultation with interested parties. A Health and Safety Commission and Executive have been set up to administer the legislation.

Besides the general purposes already stated, the Act also aims at controlling the storage and use of dangerous substances, and the control of pollution emitted into the air from certain premises. Basic obligations are backed by granting powers for Ministers to make regulations dealing with particular hazards to health and safety, and for the Commission to issue approved codes of practice for improving standards of protection of work people and the public in specific situations.

The Commission, with a chairman and up to nine members appointed after consultation with employer organizations, trade unions, and local authorities, has major research, educational, and advisory responsibilities. It also undertakes the continuing job of preparing proposals for revising, up-dating and extending the statutory provisions on health and safety at work and for issuing approved codes of practice.

The Executive was formed initially by transferring the existing government inspectorates covering factories, mines and quarries, explosives, nuclear installations, and alkali works. It has the power to enforce statutory requirements on safety and health. Local authorities have also been given certain enforcement powers. In particular, inspectors now have powers to issue improvement and prohibition notices, which would enable them to require practical improvements to be made within 'a specified time or require preventitive measures immediately without first having to obtain a court order.

The Employment Medical Advisory Service continues, and the Secretary of State has delegated running it to the Commission. Part III of the Act extends the power to make building regulations, so that as far as possible all requirements relating to the structure of new buildings can be made under building regulations. At the same time, the opportunity was also taken to extend the scope of the Building Regulations generally and to rationalize procedures.

The Robens Committee report emphasized the importance of 'self-regulation' by industry in safety and health: that precautions would best be left in the hands of those who worked with the risks. But the Government has not taken this to mean any reduction in statutory provision or enforcement in favour of a more voluntary system: indeed, the 1974 Act in no way weakened the existing system of statutory protection. Nevertheless, its aim quite clearly is to ensure that employees themselves should feel involved in the maintenance of safe and healthy working conditions.

In summary, the situation following the 1974 Act is different in many important ways from that which obtained under the previous legislation. It embraces *all* people at work, which means that over five million workers received protection for the first time. It contains very little detail, concentrating more on the statement of broad principles which call for positive action on the part of both employers and employees; regulations and codes of practice were to follow. Statutory backing was offered to requirements for a safe environment, with a demand for commitment at the highest level in every organization: written safety policies must be published, together with methods for implementing them; full information about risks must be given to employee representatives, and they must be consulted about the solution to problems.

The inspectorate must also try to give more information about hazards and their prevention, and must therefore have more direct contact with employees. Additional powers have been given to inspectors to issue improvement and prohibition notices, backed by the sanctions of much stiffer financial penalties than those which had existed hitherto.

FURTHER READING

Health and Safety at Work (Robens Committee), Cmd. 5034 (H.M.S.O., 1972).

20 Administering the Personnel Function

STRUCTURE

The structure of personnel departments varies greatly from industry to industry and among different organizations within the same industry. In saying that a 'typical' structure is represented by Figure 35, it is nevertheless a hypothetical model, and probably no single department exists anywhere exactly along these lines.

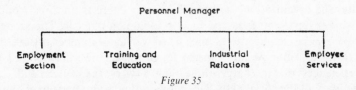

Figure 35

In charge of the function will be a *personnel manager*, supervising and co-ordinating the work of the department, probably dealing himself with senior staff problems, and controlling the personnel policies and manpower planning of the organization as a whole. There is considerable divergence of opinion as to whether the head of a personnel department should be a member of the Board of Directors; the overall importance of his role must be balanced against the fact that it is advisory in nature, whereas the position of a director is near the ultimate in executive authority.

The *employment section* is normally the largest: it involves the 'bread-and-butter' work of recruitment, transfers, promotion, and dismissal of employees, control over working conditions, and personnel records. The executive in charge would probably deputize for the personnel manager, and in a large organization might supervise a sub-department of the type shown in Figure 36. The staff of this section might well form a hierarchy, which would then represent a channel of promotion. Newcomers entering personnel management could profitably start as assistants in the records department or job review section; as they acquire experience, they could be given some interviewing to do until ready for promotion. The employment officer would therefore be a senior executive, in charge of personnel officers responsible for executive and male operatives recruitment, a lady recruitment officer for female operatives, and assistants in charge of records and job reviews.

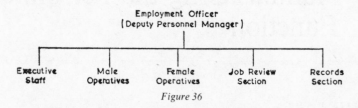

Figure 36

Another senior executive would control the *training and education section*, responsible for everything in this field from apprenticeships to the development of managers. In fact, where the range is so wide, and especially when an organization runs its own internal courses, a number of training officers will be required; these may well be men seconded from line management for a year or two. An experienced 'diplomat' would be the executive looking after the organization's *industrial relations* interests, in direct contact with worker representatives and local trade union officials. The scope of *employee services* might also be such as to warrant a number of staff subordinate to a senior welfare officer: for example, the safety officer, the domestic supervisor in charge of cleaning services, the canteen staff, and the secretary of the social club. The number of assistant personnel officers employed in each of these main sections would depend on the size of the organization, the amount of work to be done, and on the firm's attitude towards executive succession. There would also be an establishment of clerical staff (for records), secretaries, and typists.

The structure and range of activities of the personnel function in an actual major enterprise is well illustrated by the organization chart given as Figure 37.

THE DEPARTMENTAL BUDGET

It is a far from straightforward task to try to itemize the costs of running a personnel department. There are obvious direct costs like staff salaries and stationery supplies, but many of the services provided (training, for example) are so closely involved with the rest of the organization that it is virtually impossible to distinguish between charges which should be allocated directly to the personnel department and those that belong elsewhere. Nevertheless, when financial estimates are being prepared, some measure of definition must be agreed between senior executives so that a

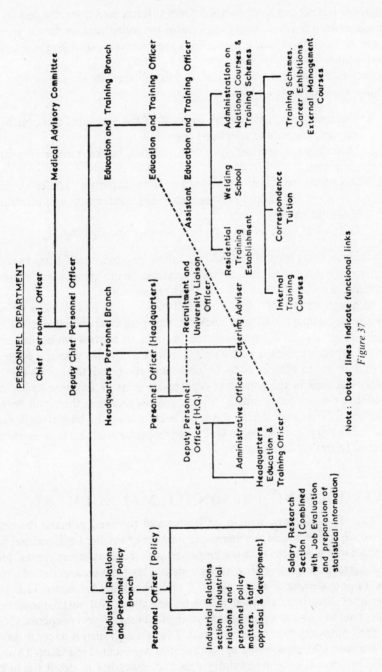

Note: Dotted lines indicate functional links

Figure 37

clear-cut budget can be established. Once this has been done, the personnel manager then becomes solely responsible for seeing that its provisions are kept. If, as time passes, modifications are necessary, then he should give instructions about how they should be effected.

Estimates and subsequent budget allocations can be sub-divided in many ways. One method is:

1. Expenses to be incurred by the staff of the personnel department—salaries, travel, and telephone costs.
2. Materials and services—printing, supplies, books, membership subscriptions.
3. Resources to carry out company-wide activities—students' fees, education and training courses, meetings, conferences and literature.
4. Consultancy fees.
5. Overheads, such as office rentals, heating, and lighting.

The actual categories of expenditure might be—basic staff costs (wages, stationery); education and training services; health provisions; canteen services; social activities; and other welfare amenities.

Although details of expenditure will be prepared and checked by accounts department staff and auditors, the personnel manager must be given copies of the figures produced in order to control deviations, and actual expenditure must be compared month by month with the original budget to guard against over- or under-spending and the possibility of fraud. All staff in the personnel department must be impressed with the fact that the budget is exactly what it means, and that there will be no additional funds allocated to the department during the budgetary period nor further expenses entertained. Proper recognition of this is an essential part of sound management.

INTRODUCING PERSONNEL MANAGEMENT

With the continuing scarcity of labour and the need to make the best use of what is available, an increasing number of smaller firms and public services which hitherto have not employed personnel managers are making such appointments. In doing so, they are having to overcome the difficulties of introducing a new specialist and obtaining his acceptance by managers already established in the organization. Not surprisingly, the latter tend to view with misgiving anything that they suspect of encroaching on their authority over their own staff. The first task then is to try to gain agreement in principle to the appointment of a personnel specialist. This is done by emphasizing his advisory role and indicating in detail the help line managers can expect in solving staff problems which they are often ill-trained to cope with themselves, as well as lacking the time to deal with matters which fall outside their immediate technical or departmental concern. They must be assured of retaining ultimate authority, but at the same time be made to appreciate the potential benefits of having expert advice available about likely staff reactions to management decisions.

The problem of status must also be resolved, for it is difficult to grade an unprecedented appointment in a way that will not cause resentment from some established executives who may feel that their own jobs are more important or more productive. Professional qualifications, training, and experience will be significant factors in solving this problem.

In making a new appointment, the applicant's knowledge of the relevant industry must also be taken into account. An experienced personnel specialist could be appointed from outside, and then be given the opportunity of acquiring knowledge of the technology of that industry or service after he has established himself. On the other hand, a person with some experience in the industry could be selected and then trained in personnel management. Each organization will need to decide such questions for itself, although staff representatives will usually press for the latter attitude because of the potential promotion involved.

Once in post, the new personnel manager must consolidate his position by working conscientiously to gain the confidence of his senior colleagues and overcome any resentment or personality difficulties. In practice, this may mean a deliberate programme of targets, tackling specific problems for different departmental heads until the time when they eventually come to seek out his help and advice on staff matters. Only the success of this positive approach can guarantee the co-operation of all senior managers throughout the organization.

HELP FROM OUTSIDE ORGANIZATIONS

To be fully effective, a personnel manager must not only know his job, but he must also use every available method of persuading people throughout the organization to act on his advice; influence brought to bear from outside often may tip the scales in his favour. In any event, many firms are too small to employ personnel specialists and therefore must look outside for guidance with their labour problems. Such help may come from a variety of bodies, including several Government departments, and may range from management consultants, who offer advisory services on every aspect of personnel work from recruitment to welfare, to professional associations and voluntary bodies.

DEPARTMENT OF EMPLOYMENT SERVICES

The most comprehensive aid is offered by the *Department of Employment* and includes the following, through the Employment Services Agency:

EMPLOYMENT SERVICES

1. Employment offices and job-centres which provide a free service for employers requiring workers and for workers seeking jobs whether employed at the time or not. Vacancies which cannot be filled locally may be circulated throughout the country.
2. Services are provided to meet the special requirements of ex-regular members of the Armed Forces, nurses and midwives, and disabled people.
3. Resettlement Transfer Scheme: by paying fares, lodging allowances, and household removal costs, this scheme encourages unemployed workers to transfer from one area to another and obtain permanent employment there.
4. Professional and Executive Recruitment Service: provided at thirty-nine of the larger employment offices, this is a service for professional people and those seeking managerial and trainee executive posts. Information is also given about careers opportunities in the professions and in industry and commerce.

The work of 364 *Local Employment Committees* must also be mentioned here. They are the main advisory bodies attached to employment offices, securing for the Minister the full benefit of local knowledge on industrial problems, and bringing the offices into close contact with local employers and with workers. The members of the committees are appointed for five years and are equally representative of employer and worker interests.

YOUTH EMPLOYMENT SERVICE

The Youth Employment Service is administered throughout the country by local education authorities. This service gives advice and vocational guidance to young people on their choice of work and the training necessary for it, helps them to find suitable jobs, and keeps in touch during their early years of employment. Employers are also helped to fill their vacancies for young workers.

TRAINING*

The Department of Employment, through the Training Services Agency, is at present responsible for overall supervision of the Industrial Training

---

* Dealt with more fully in Chapter 10.

Act, 1964 and the Employment and Training Act, 1973. It offers several services:

1. Vocational training—available free in about forty skilled jobs at Government Skillcentres throughout the country. Other arrangements can be made for individuals at technical or commercial colleges, or with an employer, and for severely disabled people.
2. Supervisory training—the T.W.I. scheme,* run by the Department's own training officers, or by instructing firms' trainers on how to run courses back at their local premises. Special versions are available for supervisors in shops and offices.
3. Instructor training—courses in teaching techniques for trade instructors, designed for staff who spend a considerable part of their working time giving job instruction.

REHABILITATION

Free courses are offered at twenty-five Employment Rehabilitation Centres to help people gradually readjust themselves to working conditions, with expert vocational guidance about suitable jobs.

SAFETY, HEALTH, AND WELFARE

The Department is responsible for the administration and enforcement of appropriate legislation by Inspectors of the Health and Safety Executive in factories, offices, and shops. The Industrial Health and Safety Centre in Horseferry Road, London, displays safety, health, and welfare methods and appliances used in factories.

PUBLICATIONS

These include the monthly *Department of Employment Gazette*, quarterly *Statistics on Incomes, Prices, Employment, and Production*, and a variety of pamphlets on current labour legislation, accident prevention, and careers.

MODERNIZATION

In 1972 a start was made on improving the employment service, and ridding it of its negative image, of back-street offices paying out 'dole' money. Indeed, one of the initial steps was to separate the providing of employment from the payment of unemployment benefits, both administratively and physically. A new framework has been established, so that the Employment Service Agency is now a self-managing unit within the D.E., controlled by its own Chief Executive, and directing its efforts towards four objectives:

* *See* Chapter 11, page 175.

1. doubling the number of vacancies notified by employers (some 2 million annually beforehand);
2. persuading everyone looking for a job, whether already in employment or not, to visit their local employment office (job centre);
3. providing an effective placing service for all grades of employee, from unskilled manual workers to senior managerial and professional staff;
4. improving its capacity to advise workers on alternative jobs, training facilities, and removal assistance; and advising employers about probable changes in their labour markets.

Thus the overall aim of the E.S.A. can be seen as one of providing better services to more people: varied and flexible responses will be offered to meet varied and flexible demands.* Relating directly to both employers and job seekers, employment services comprise information, advice, and guidance within the limits of the opportunities afforded by the labour market and the resources available: helping employers to fill jobs with the right people, and helping job seekers to select, prepare for, and obtain the right jobs. Access is also available to the Training Opportunities Scheme (*see* page 165), for there must not be any lack of cohesion between the public employment and training services.

Initial achievements of targets promise much for the future. In the first year of operation, there was a 25 per cent increase in the number of vacancies notified by employers, and the subsequent 1,650,000 placings were 6 per cent above the initial objective. By the end of 1974, about 140 job centres had been opened—attractive, modern, prominently sited, comfortably furnished and well decorated: they are an up-to-date advertisement for a new kind of employment service. The number of job placings in the areas affected has gone up by 40 per cent, and it is claimed that the numbers of job changers who are still employed but make use of the job centre services have gone up by about 300 per cent.

The first point of contact in every job centre is a self-service job information section. This is supported by an advisory service manned by a new professional corps of employment advisers—people for whom the D.E. has devised special training programmes to develop staff with the right blend of skill and sensitivity, of maturity and knowledge of the market, and of discretion and judgment to be able to offer the maximum possible help to the ever-varying multitude of job seekers and employers. By 1977 the intention is to have given this specialist training to some 3,500 employment advisers, in a deliberate attempt to improve the quality of the basic advisory services provided.

---

* 'The Employment Service Agency', by K. R. Cooper, Chief Executive, E.S.A., in *BACIE Journal*, September 1974, page 104.

The occupational guidance service is also being developed, with additional specialist training for the staff concerned. It is intended for the benefit of adults who may either be compelled to take up new types of employment or who may wish to change not simply to a new job but to work of a different kind. The service tries to help about 50,000 people a year, most of whom are under 25: many are students seeking their first jobs; about 20 per cent are people who are being compelled to change their occupation; about 30 per cent of all clients are women, a number of whom are returning to employment after some years away. The potential for extending this service was shown by an experiment in South Wales, when a special publicity campaign led to an increase of more than one-third in the number of applications for interviews.

As far as young people are concerned, one essential feature is the development of coordinated activity between local education authorities and employment services. For although the former continue to operate careers advisory services in schools, the 1973 Act abolished the age limit of 18: so the E.S.A. is now able to provide services to young job seekers who are looking for jobs and for advice and guidance with a view to work.

The gathering of labour market intelligence by the E.S.A. should be of particular value to personnel managers (who would otherwise have to do this for themselves). Systematic collation, interpretation and dissemination of the information is necessary, of course, but early experiments gave clear indications that the E.S.A. will be able to make a material contribution to the reading of labour market trends and needs, and to the development of programmes to meet them.

Improved methods of communications within the widespread network of the E.S.A. is at the heart of all its efforts, particularly the use of computer facilities. A facsimile transmission system exists to link offices in the major conurbations, thus enabling the rapid exchange of information about job vacancies and the faster matching of job seekers to jobs. In London, a computer-based job bank carries details of 15,000 jobs at a time, with plans for employment advisers to have terminals which will give them immediate access to the computer. If this works successfully, then the idea will be extended nationally, and by 1980 on-line job matching could be as radical a breakthrough as the initial job centre programme in helping to provide better services for more people.

In fact, the new Professional and Executive Recruitment Service has been computer-based from the outset. It is unique in its commercial approach, fees being charged to employers for placements on a scale which means that the service will eventually become self-sufficient financially. Special advertising services are also offered to clients, whereby they may select candidates for interview from a shortlist prepared by PER on the basis of a computer sift of its register of about 70,000 job seekers as well as those candidates who reply specifically to the advertisement. The initiative has also been taken, in conjunction with the Training Services Agency, to sponsor a variety of new training schemes for redundant executives, including self-presentation and in-company conversion courses.

MANAGEMENT CONSULTANTS

The obvious occasions to use *management* consultants are when specific major problems need to be examined but the organization concerned does not possess the skill or resources to do so for itself, or when its own experts are divided on the best course of action. Assignments need to be clearly defined and time limits set, so that the consultants are kept fully occupied and the best value is obtained for their fees. The terms of reference should require a specific estimate of the likely effects of any recommendations being implemented. It usually eases the consultant's investigations and his relationships with the organization's staff if worker representatives or local union officials are consulted beforehand about the reasons for bringing him in, and if one person is nominated as his main point of contact, introducing him to people and making sure he is properly briefed.

Which consultant to choose? The B.I.M.'s Management Consulting Services Information Bureau and the Management Consultants' Association supply appropriate lists. Having sought their advice, an organization must then approach perhaps two or three different consultants and try to assess which is likely to offer the best service in tackling its particular problems.

PROFESSIONAL ASSOCIATIONS AND VOLUNTARY ORGANIZATIONS

There are several professional associations and voluntary organizations* concerned with various aspects of personnel and welfare work.

THE INSTITUTE OF PERSONNEL MANAGEMENT

The *Institute of Personnel Management* is the professional body of men and women who are actually employed in personnel management jobs. Its general aims are to encourage and assist the development of personnel management by spreading knowledge and information about its practices, promoting investigations and research, and by establishing and maintaining through training and other services high standards of qualification and performance. There are five regional committees and two specialist groups,

* The addresses of those mentioned here are given in the Appendix.

the *Staff Management Association* and *Public Services Group*; and some thirty branches up and down the country, bringing the Institute's total membership to nearly 17,000.

The range of activities covered is:

1. Conferences, national and regional.
2. Courses in techniques and practices for people already engaged in personnel work; some last a week, others only a day, together with a series of seminars and 'workshops'.
3. An information service, which both answers members' queries and issues its own surveys of personnel practices.
4. Publications: a monthly journal entitled *Personnel Management* and the *I.P.M. Digest* of news and current affairs. Several new booklets are published every year, too, on matters of topical interest to personnel managers.
5. An appointments service of help to both potential employers and those looking for jobs. Appointments are now advertised in *Personnel Management* and *I.P.M. Digest* which are sent to all members: many of the jobs notified are not advertised elsewhere in the national press.
6. The general expression of views on current labour problems and submission of evidence to government commissions and enquiries.

Looking at appointments advertisements as a whole reveals a growing emphasis on the demand for personnel officers to be properly trained and qualified. The I.P.M. is itself an examining body: students may prepare themselves for its qualifications at some forty colleges throughout the country or by correspondence courses. In addition, fourteen universities and colleges run their own full-time diploma courses in personnel management, most of which last a year.

A *European Association for Personnel Management* was founded in 1963, of which the I.P.M. and twelve other West European associations of personnel management are members. The E.A.P.M. holds an international conference every two years, selecting different venues in Europe.

THE INDUSTRIAL SOCIETY

The Articles of Association of the *Industrial Society* state that it consists of persons interested in 'promoting the industry and commerce of the United Kingdom, in particular by improving management and industrial relations'. In fact its membership comprises over 3,000 organizations which include companies, nationalized industries, government departments, local authorities, employers' associations, and trade unions. The practical problems that the Society is concerned with are mainly the development of good leadership by managers and supervisors in works and offices, better management-trade union relations, the evolution of conditions of employment appropriate to the requirements of modern jobs, adequate communications, and the development of young employees to play a full role in today's changing industries. Some of its activities are very similar to those of the I.P.M., although in some cases on a rather larger scale. The Society provides a comprehensive advisory service for its members, including special surveys and reviews of conditions of employment; this is supported by an information service which deals with legal and general enquiries. A wide variety of short conferences and training courses are held in different parts of the country, and in-company training facilities for supervisors are offered to members who lack the resources or experience necessary to set up their own programmes. It, too, issues a journal and publishes booklets on current management problems, and gives specialist advice to firms who publish their own house journals. The more technical aspects of its work cover a catering advisory service and the production of sound-filmstrips mainly intended for training purposes. Finally, a special department exists to meet the needs of developing countries overseas: this includes a tutorial system for experienced men and women in personnel management and industrial relations, and running courses on management and supervision for overseas technical trainees completing their studies in Britain.

THE MANPOWER SOCIETY

Originating in 1967 as a study group of the Operational Research Society, the *Manpower Society* is basically concerned with a systematic approach to all manpower questions. It thus pays attention to manpower planning and to the development of techniques designed to ensure the maximum use of the human resources within an organization.

Jointly sponsored by the O.R. Society and the I.P.M., the Manpower Society aims to provide a forum where the personnel professional and the O.R. specialist can pool their experience of the management of manpower problems. Monthly meetings are held in London, with other meetings in Scotland, the North, and the Midlands. Annual conferences are held, with a biennial meeting with the French manpower planning group. A basic manpower planning course is run, and many other seminars; joint meetings are frequently held with the I.P.M., B.I.M., the Society for Long-Range Planning, and the Institute of Manpower Studies.

The reports of special studies are published, and have so far included papers on manpower costs, views on the Manpower Services Commission, and the improvement of manpower information.

THE BRITISH INSTITUTE OF MANAGEMENT

The *British Institute of Management*, as its name implies, has wider interests in the field of management than just the personnel function, but this nevertheless plays a significant part in its activities. Its claim is to be a national clearing house for information on management policies, practices, and techniques, and on management development, including education and training. Over 13,000 member organizations support its activities, and there are some 45,000 individual members organized into seven regions and about fifty branches throughout the country. As with the three previous organizations, the B.I.M. offers conferences and training courses, a library and information service, seminar and study group arrangements, and its own publications—books, pamphlets, the journal *Management Today*, and a quarterly series of management abstracts. Unique features of its work are the Management Consulting Services Information Bureau and the exchange of facilities with management organizations overseas.

OTHER BODIES

The Tavistock Institute of Human Relations investigates and advises on problems of relations and morale within industry. It runs specialized training courses and publishes books largely concerned with pioneer work and research within its sphere of interest.

The British Association for Commercial and Industrial Education arranges meetings, courses, and conferences, and publishes a monthly journal and a wide range of booklets, with the aim of encouraging educational and training work in industrial and commercial undertakings.

The Royal Society for the Prevention of Accidents deals with industrial accidents, supplies posters, films, and leaflets, runs training courses for safety officers, and gives advice to firms and other enquirers.

RECEPTION AND SECURITY

Reception and *security* are two aspects of administration which are often allied and come within the purview of the personnel department.

First impressions strike deep, and efficient and courteous reception arrangements do nothing but good, enhancing an organization's reputation and ensuring goodwill. It is wrong therefore to assume that anyone can do this work, that a reception desk can be manned by somebody who is not busy elsewhere at the moment or by an unsupervised business trainee as part of his learning to deal with the public. Reception work requires special skills which can only be exercised by a pleasant-mannered person, mature, experienced, of some seniority, and who has been properly trained. In a large organization it is a task which demands undivided attention, and no other work should be undertaken during periods on duty; any incidental pressures, or indeed fatigue towards the end of the day, results in enquiries or the arrival of visitors being treated as interruptions, and the consequent resentment is painfully obvious to the visitor.

The mechanics of good reception lie in giving prior notice to the reception staff of the names, expected times of arrival, and intended destinations of all visitors and new arrivals. This does not apply only to those expected by the personnel department but should be a standing rule for all departments. Where security is important, visitors should not only be checked in by receptionists, but also checked out again when they leave.

As far as security of property is concerned, joint disciplinary action against stealing has already been mentioned in Chapter 15. No one, manager and worker alike, feels comfortable knowing that a thief is on the prowl, and a works committee may very well be able to take effective action. On the other hand, some workers feel that an employer is 'fair game', and things left lying about are taken. Quite clearly this is illegal. An employee is entitled only to what his employer has agreed to give him; if he has been told to help himself to stationery or samples, then he is free to accept this offer. But such goods are the employer's property, and the employee has a right to them only as a servant, entirely confined to the arrangement made with him.

Does an employer have the right to search a worker suspected of stealing? Search an individual unjustly and he becomes an enemy. It is better to invite all staff, or the section affected, to turn out their pockets and handbags. If they agree, all is well; if they refuse, there is nothing that can be done. The best advice is not to try to detain or search anyone unless there is no alternative: call in the police to do this.

Many organizations employ security staff. The numbers, type, and duties of these vary considerably—commissionaires, gatemen, night patrolmen, with duties ranging from controlling traffic to the prevention of pilfering; often they have a direct link with the local police. It is a mistake to employ any but able-bodied gate police or watchmen in an organization where the pilferage risk is high and where security is important; the old-fashioned pensioner type of night-watchman is a bad risk. Security measures are often publicized on notice boards and by giving special instruction to employees. Losses due to carelessness or negligence should result in punishment. Few firms have any systematic approach to this or impose a fixed scale of fines. Demotions may be used for some offenders, with suspension for more serious cases, and dismissal as the ultimate sanction.

The Official Secrets Acts, 1911 and 1920, provide heavy penalties for unauthorized use of uniforms, falsification of reports, forgery or alteration of official documents, impersonation of official persons, or for passing secret documents or information to unauthorized persons. All visitors to Government offices, departments, and factories may be asked to sign a declaration which sets out the main provisions of this legislation.

THE RECORDS SECTION

An efficient records system is fundamental to producing the control information essential for effective personnel management. The boast of some senior staff that they know all about their subordinates is no substitute for this (and they should have better things to occupy their minds anyhow). In large organizations, the sheer volume of work involved in maintaining staff records and keeping them up to date is staggering, and demands that three sound principles must be applied in deciding what records of individuals and statistics for management should be kept:

1. The utmost simplicity in methods of recording information and in the design of any forms used.
2. The preservation of only absolutely necessary information: records are pointless unless they serve a useful purpose.
3. The avoidance of duplication, especially when considering needs for cross-reference.

The basic personal record is founded upon the application form, which is filed as the first document in each individual's folder. It is followed by his interview notes; as well as copies of correspondence between the company and the employee, the folder will come to hold such documents as his follow-up reports, time-keeping record, and notes of promotions or transfers. On its cover will be listed quick-reference personal data and brief information about his movements and progress within the organization.

There are many records systems marketed by firms specializing in this activity, designed to meet the general requirements of the average industrial and commercial organization; in addition, numerous records sections devise procedures and print forms to suit their own peculiarities. There is thus a great divergence of practice—some use a simple card-index system, some keep personal documents in index envelopes, and some keep them in folders. Probably the best and most convenient method is to keep all documents relating to an individual clipped into a manila folder which has its cover printed to receive the minimum essential details for quick reference, the whole kept in a suspended filing system with an easily visible name-title index. Folders are best kept in alphabetical order by name of person. For cross-checking, simple card-indexes can be used for such things as seniority by age or date of engagement, departmental order, membership of trade unions, rates of pay, occupations, or other ranges of information which may be useful from time to time. In very large organizations there will probably be punched-card or computer installations which can be used for tabulations for the personnel department. No matter which system is used, it needs to be reviewed from time to time (at least once every five years) and the personnel manager himself must keep abreast of new developments and systems, for example by attending the annual Business Efficiency Exhibition.

From these personal records statistical information can be collated which will be useful both to the personnel department and to line management as records of control. Thus the personnel manager should be able to submit periodic statements to the chief executive about manning and labour turnover, time-keeping, absenteeism, education and training, health, and accidents. The following minimum information about employees is essential for statistical analysis:

1. Basic data—age, sex, address, domestic responsibilities (tax code number provides this), date of joining, occupation, rate of pay; a record of previous jobs may also be an advantage.
2. Absence data—length of absence, date of last absence, shift work or overtime, if changes of job are frequent, job at time of last absence.
3. Sickness and injury data—diagnosis, whether self-inflicted, whether contagious, whether treatment continuing, whether change of occupation desirable.
4. Labour turnover data—date of leaving, reason, whether job performance had been satisfactory or not.

The personnel department is usually called on to provide weekly or monthly returns showing the numbers employed in each department and departmental costs of wages and salaries. It should also be possible to produce at short notice statements about the composition of the labour force, by age groups, by sex, and by length of service. Statistics must be prepared to show the relation between the actual and estimated labour strength in the various departments; line managers will want to know the proportions of skilled and unskilled labour employed, and how much of the labour force is termed directly or indirectly productive, for the calculation of prime and overhead costs.

Every departmental head is personally responsible for controlling the time-keeping and absence of the people working in his section. The personnel department, however, will keep a record of individual performance in this respect and will also collate this into departmental and factory summaries, giving an overall picture of time lost and an analysis of the known reasons for lateness or absence, from which management action can be recommended about supervisory training, or representations made to the local bus company, for example. The training officer will keep records of employees' educational progress, and these too can be collated as factual evidence available when manpower and staff development programmes are being prepared. The medical section is responsible for statistics on general health matters affecting the organization, including analyses of industrial diseases and accidents. Health records of individuals may be maintained separately, but since records department staff are always impressed with the confidentiality of the documents they handle, there is no real excuse for duplication. Medical statistics can be very revealing to the industrial doctor, who can associate problems with the working environment in ways that would never occur to scattered G.P.s each examining one or two patients from the same workplace.

Outside organizations, such as the British Institute of Management, the Royal Society for the Prevention of Accidents, the Department of Employment, and Government departments which place contracts with private firms frequently call for statistical information relating to labour strength. Since many of these returns are demanded regularly, the personnel department should familiarize itself with the forms in which they are required and design its tabulation methods accordingly.

The deficiencies of present records systems are largely due to non-observance of the three principles which should govern procedures. Sizeable sums of money are spent on systems that are not fully effective and, in particular, lack the simplicity which enables management control information to be produced quickly. It is very rare for any organization to prepare a single record which contains all the details likely to be needed, so that any new demand which calls for a thorough survey of personnel records may entail the vast task of gathering information from several different sources. In such cases, the natural tendency is to say that the information is not available, so that the problem which led to the request may then be tackled purely by guess-work. The actual systems used are often heavy and clumsy to handle, discouraging the continuous attention necessary if they are to be kept up to date. In the author's experience, one method originally comprised a reference for each employee spring-locked into three large metal-bound volumes each weighing nearly 10 lb; these were kept in a cupboard on the opposite side of the room from where the records clerks sat. It was eventually replaced by a system using much smaller forms which recorded only essential information, fitted into a number of light cardboard covers which could be kept in the clerks' desk drawers.

The difficulties posed by some systems are such that the accuracy of the more intricate calculations must be very suspect, especially when the work is done by junior clerks aiming for 'a quiet life'. This also applies to requests for statistical information from outside bodies and Government departments—if this is not readily available in the form specified, a records department is very likely to guess rather than impose hours of work on its clerical staff calculating accurate answers. Part of the trouble is that different definitions are used for standard terms, which makes comparisons between different organizations very difficult: for example, has labour turnover been adjusted to account for unavoidable separations, or do figures of lost time include employees with prolonged sickness absence?

In the light of these potential deficiencies, any efforts that may be made to improve personnel records will largely depend on the importance which management attaches to the information that records can provide. For example, because vacancies so often exceed applicants, selection procedures may become nominal; but an analysis of training costs for newcomers who soon leave sometimes shows that it is more economic to work short-handed with a stable and experienced labour force and to select more carefully to this end. Adequate and accessible records enable many complex problems of management to be investigated without delay.

USE OF COMPUTERS

The relevance of the computer to personnel records work is obvious, for its initial use in most organizations is the mechanical handling of vast quantities of simple paper work, such as wage and salary calculation and keeping employee records up-to-date. But it can also process data, selecting, storing, analysing, and presenting the information required by management. In this last respect, the most efficient method of functioning is to programme the computer on the 'exception' principle, so that information is only brought to management's attention when it deviates from what is normal or expected. This in turn, of course, depends on managements' ability to define its needs (at present, the greatest cause of the inefficient use of computers). The computer can also be used to check and control processes, and this has possible applications to the manpower planning activities of the personnel department. A logical extension of this use is in simulating future conditions so that decisions can be taken about changes to be effected deliberately by management (reducing working hours, new types of wage structure, for example). As these applications come more and more into common practice, the staff of personnel departments will be relieved of the tedium of sifting information and record-keeping, and the personnel manager himself will have a wider range of more accurate facts available to enable him to advise his line-manager colleagues on the human problems of their organization.

At the same time, the reasons for introducing computers must be right, and related to business needs and the efficiency of existing systems. They are *not* status symbols. There are manual systems in existence that can deal more cheaply than computers with up to 10,000 staff, so the obvious first step is to carry out a cost-benefit analysis and *prove* that savings can be made. Reported annual costs are in fact as high as £3·50–£4 per person indexed on computer programmes, and one analysis* quoting American experience shows that 60 per cent of all computer installations fail to achieve savings in operating costs.

Obviously, computers produce the most profitable returns when they operate on a variety of tasks, every day of the week round the clock. But such maximum use poses its own problems, for personnel records are usually accorded a low priority in data-processing, and *ad hoc* non-routine enquiries suffer particularly.

If a decision to computerize personnel records is taken, then the greatest benefits are likely to accrue in organizations that have these characteristics: an initial belief by top management that a computer is a 'good thing' to have; the minimum resistance from other levels of management; a personnel department having a high status, with its head regarded as an innovator; good staff relations, with favourable attitudes towards change; high labour costs; and technical expertise.

FURTHER READING

Personnel Records, Forms and Procedures, by W. Durham (Industrial Society 1965).
Statistics and Personnel Management, by M. G. Kendall (I.P.M., 1963).
The Computer in Personnel Work, by Edgar Wille (I.P.M., 1966).

* *Personnel Records and the Computer,* by Joan Springall (I.P.M., 1971)

21 Human Asset Accounting

Starting from the premise that if the personnel manager is to be really effective, he must have a means for measuring the resource for which he is primarily responsible, techniques of human asset accounting have been developed recently to record and present information about the value of an organization's employee resources which should prove of great value for managerial control and decision-making purposes.

The people employed by an organization are among its most valuable assets, and yet their value does not appear in statements of its financial position. The death of an outstanding company leader may cause an immediate fall in that Company's quotation on the Stock Exchange; key staff caught up in a take-over may decide to leave an organization, having a potentially profound effect on its performance: such are examples of the real value of people—yet there is no way of telling from the usual type of accounting information whether the human assets of an organization are increasing or decreasing in value, whether they are being used effectively, or whether a satisfactory return is being obtained on them.

Conventional accounting procedures treat expenditure on building up human assets as revenue expenditure, writing off costs of recruiting, training, and developing staff against the income of the period in which it is incurred. But are such costs revenue expenditure or are they really capital expenditure? If the latter, a proportion should be charged against the income of all periods receiving benefit from this expenditure, and this could have a significant impact on an organization's income statement and balance sheet. Furthermore, management's attitudes to such expenditures might well alter if such costs were not borne out of current income, but were looked at as contributing to the building of assets which will produce benefits for some time to come. This means accounting for staff in the same way as machines—as assets on the balance sheet, the costs of which are written off against profits year by year; if any machine becomes obsolete before the end of its anticipated useful life, its remaining book value is written off as a loss thus reducing the Company's profits. Viewing investments in obtaining and developing staff in the same way requires that the amount of cost not yet written off should be carried forward in accounting statements as an asset. A change of this nature in the treatment of expenditure on staff would have a marked effect on an organization's measurement of costs and income in any period and on its declared financial position at any particular point in time.

But the concept of human asset accounting is one thing—gaining its acceptance by existing managers is another. The difficulties of isolating and measuring the costs of human resources are formidable: so much accountancy is influenced by conventions which have stood from time immemorial; the need to capitalize human costs has not been as great in the past as in present conditions; and it is difficult to forecast the time period over which benefits will be received from expenditure on human assets. It is also true to say that managements of most firms do not think of their staff as assets in the same way as other property of the firm. 'Human assets' are not owned in a legal sense, and many people regard it as degrading to subject human beings to a monetary value in the same way as a piece of machinery. Yet it is the human resources which use the other assets of an organization to produce goods or render services: the other assets take on value because of their potential when combined with human assets. Thus a human asset accounting system would create information to show the investment made in staff and the financial effects of changes taking place in the human assets during defined periods of time.

TECHNIQUES

Although there are two major approaches, at least two other variations must be included in describing the methods so far proposed for human asset accounting. The Institute for Social Research at Michigan and its Human Resource Accounting Association have developed a technique which attempts to identify those costs which an organization expends in improving the performance of its labour forces in the long term: these include recruitment, training, and development costs. A variation can be seen in the case of Texas Instruments, who examine replacement costs for groups of people which take account of learning time on a job and the individual's salary during that time. The Institutes of Cost and Management Accountants and of Personnel Management have put forward a joint concept in Britain—of calculating the asset value of people by first computing a multiplier based on the price:earnings ratio and applying it to the total remuneration of the company. Finally, the concept of added value is sometimes used, an approach where the training cost attributable to an individual over his expected working life is examined and related to his improvements in performance.

Rensis Likert and William Pyle are the names most closely linked with the Michigan initiative in seeking a method to include a figure for people in company accounts, which represents the investments made to acquire and train people to expected levels of effectiveness in their respective occupations, less the amortization of this investment based upon expected tenure.* This is not the same as the idea, repugnant to so many people, of trying to put a cash value on individual employees: rather, the concept is one of developing methods for measuring an organization's investment in its staff and the rate at which those particular inputs are more productive than others. This approach relies on the historical cost of acquisition and development to give a present cost of replacement. It is thus primarily a method of monitoring how managers are utilizing their human resources over time; linking human asset accounting with conventionally measured business results will enable better insights on preferred management strategies of allocating, maintaining, and utilizing human resources. As a negative example of such strategy (but which serves to highlight the importance of including human assets in an accountancy system) Likert† makes the point that certain managerial styles have the effect of liquidating human assets while producing short term increases in profit. Conventional accounting reports an increase in profit, but the deterioration in the attitudes and motivation of employees and the increases in labour turnover, followed by costs of hiring and training replacements, result in reduced profits in the long run.

This American system requires a series of accounts to be opened for each manager, covering: recruitment outlay and acquisition costs; familiarization; formal and informal training; and development costs. Included in these accounts as investments in human assets should be all outlays which have an expected value extending beyond the current accounting period (usually one year). Thus the costs involved in recruiting and inducting a new manager are amortized over the whole working life of that person with the organization; outlays on his training and development are amortized over shorter periods of time. In this way what may be called the 'opening value' of a new employee is increased by further enhancing expenditure and decreased by amortization and wastage, for example, which diminish his asset value.

This approach has recently been further developed by the use of replacement cost methods. Historical costs, as already set out, are converted to

---

* Annual Report of the R. G. Barry Corporation, 1970.

† *The Human Organisation, Its Management and Value*, by R. Likert (McGraw-Hill, 1967).

current values in the same way that some companies provide for amortization on plant by estimating the cost of replacing each item with something similar at the end of its useful life.

The method developed jointly by the I.P.M. and I.C.M.A.* has the primary objective of placing some value on the human resource so that it can be included in normal credit/debit transactions. It would thus be useful in describing the total asset situation, for share evaluation and take-over purposes. It is concerned with total remuneration, together with a multiplier derived from the price:earnings ratio of that company.

This multiplier method is based on the assumption that there is no direct relationship between costs incurred on an individual and his value to an organization at a particular point in time. It is argued that there are many factors of motivation, attitude, and working environment which affect the person's value to the organization and which can only be expressed in subjective terms. Hence the valuation method must itself be capable of representing these subjective factors in a financially quantifiable form. This is achieved by the use of a multiplier which, when related to pay, can be used to weigh the value of different grades of staff within a total value for the organization. There are four grades: senior management, middle management, supervisors, and clerical and operative. Thus, for example, a movement summary may be produced for senior management as follows:

OPENING VALUES

Grade	Remuneration	Multiplier	Value
	£		£
Senior management	12,000	3·0	36,000
Middle management	7,000	2·0	14,000
Supervisors	25,000	1·5	37,500
Clerical and operative	80,000	1·0	80,000
			£167,500

MOVEMENT SUMMARY—SENIOR MANAGEMENT

Opening value			36,000
Inputs (training and development costs, etc.)	£1,000	3·0	3,000
			39,000
Outputs (turnover and terminal costs, etc.)	£1,200	3·0	3,600
			35,400
Amortization 15%			5,310
Closing value			£30,090

* *Human Asset Accounting*, by W. J. Giles and D. F. Robinson (I.P.M. and I.C.M.A., 1972).

PRACTICAL APPLICATIONS

The main benefit which must be claimed from this sort of analysis lies in the need to calculate the return on all investments. Unless it is made clear that expenditure on training and development offers long-run benefits and increases the profit-earning capacity of a company, it may be regarded as an expenditure the firm can only afford when profits are at a high level and may be dispensed with as soon as profits turn downwards.

As an example of the wider implications of human asset accounting, the problem of redundancies* may be considered. Present calculations concern the amount of compensation which will be incurred as a charge against the revenue of the company. In addition, personnel managers and trade unions are greatly concerned about the social and personal impact of redundancy decisions. In terms of human asset accounting, redundancies represent the scrapping by one user of a valuable resource and its transfer into a community pool from which it can be withdrawn and put to work by another. The unqualified factors in this process are: the real efficiency of the existing use of the resource; the cost to the community of retraining the redundant person; and the comparative cost of retention and retraining within the present user organization.

The efficiency of the use of human assets could be demonstrated by recalculating returns on capital to include this element in addition to conventionally measured assets. Clearly, if a company is relatively unprofitable and overstaffed this will only highlight a known deficiency. Nonetheless the existence of a valuation and the need for an acquiring company to show how it intends to utilize the assets would represent a considerable advance. Equally, an awareness of the value and return on human assets should create a real incentive for management to be more efficient. It could well forestall situations in which human assets are scrapped as part of a programme of stripping more tangible assets. It should also help management to decide on what is fair compensation in individual cases. Also, if the current and potential asset values of employees threatened with redundancy could be related to the retraining and unemployment costs which will fall on the community, more rational decisions could be taken within government on supportive policy.

ACCOUNTANCY AND PERSONNEL MANAGEMENT

Predictably, the novelty of this whole concept has led to criticisms, both from personnel managers and accountants. The concept itself has been

* 'Progression Human Asset Accounting', by D. Robinson: *Personnel Management*, March 1973.

challenged, and pointed questions asked about practical applications and the suggested measurements of asset values.* It follows that the specific uses of the concept for management is not yet clear. Nevertheless, although the techniques may call for refinement, the underlying philosophy is undoubtedly coming to be more widely accepted. In summary this may be restated thus: the employees of an organization are a valuable resource and it is important to know how valuable. They have great potentialities if properly trained, organized, and motivated: the effects of the programmes designed to realize these potentialities must therefore be properly evaluated. Yet, at present, managers seem to lay but little emphasis on the financial consequences of decisions about people. Cannon suggests that rather than attempt to account for human resources by a global asset figure, it might be better to develop a more comprehensive set of criteria in the form of a list of data for a human resource audit.

Cost breakdown
Cost of acquisition
Cost of yearly maintenance
Cost of performance improvement
Replacement cost

Manpower breakdown
Numbers joining, employed and leaving. (Reasons for termination)
Skill breakdown and changes in structure
Level of satisfaction (Areas of dissatisfaction)
Level of absenteeism (Reasons)

Productivity
Ratio analysis—profit/employee
    Controllable cost/employee
    Value added/pound of employee cost
    'Output'/employee
Organizational effectiveness

The closer and growing contacts between accountants and personnel specialists has been an interesting phenomenon in recent years. Besides the work described above, another example is an attempt to develop a cost-effectiveness approach† to industrial safety and health at work. Expenditure on reducing industrial risks could be distributed more

* 'Human Resource Accounting—a critical comment', by J. A. Cannon: *Personnel Review*, Summer 1974, pages 14–20.

† Research paper for the Robens Committee, written by T. Craig Sinclair, Science Policy Research Unit, University of Sussex, (H.M.S.O. 1972).

efficiently, and measures to improve safety and health standards at work should be related to their efficiency in reducing human and material costs: this is the concept underlying the approach.

In the past, prevention costs have been generally ignored in discussions on the costs of accidents. Setting up a safety programme imposes a financial cost on an enterprise and contributes nothing directly to output. At whatever level the prevention cost is fixed, it is likely that some accident risk will remain. If the prevention programme is increased at additional cost, the risk level should fall, and with it the cost of accidents. Therefore an economic optimum can be determined, and a relationship worked out between cost and risk for a particular industry or firm to provide a quantitative means of assessing priorities. Areas can be selected which will give the greatest return in terms of accident cost reduction for a given outlay, and in this way management can be provided with guidelines for framing policy.

As a practical example, Sinclair's analysis shows that while the risk of death in agriculture is ten times that in pharmaceuticals and equal to the risk in steel-handling, the expenditure on accident prevention in agriculture is less than 2 per cent of that in pharmaceuticals and less than 10 per cent of that in steel-handling.

Methods must be evolved to produce this sort of information about human assets readily, otherwise the administrative inconvenience involved will detract from acceptance. Once this has been done, the whole concept will become more attractive: the very idea that employees are a resource which is valuable and must therefore be utilized as such, rather than being an unmeasurable factor of production, is potentially a major step forward in the efficient management of organizations.

22 Auditing the Personnel Management Function

In the ultimate, the success of any business organization, private or public, comes as the result of the efforts of its employees effectively aimed at attaining the desired objectives. The nature of its achievements is a direct reflection of the abilities of everyone involved, from the board of directors to the lowest-graded worker. In assessing its own efficiency, management must consider this factor of the *quality* of employees above all, as well as the organizational structure within which they will work. No business can rise above the capacities of its staff; unless ratings of individual abilities are positive for the majority of employees, then it is unlikely to be successful or to develop in the future. The organization itself must function smoothly, too; even the best staff cannot work efficiently unless their responsibilities are clearly defined and there is an effective structure for the various levels of its hierarchy. The necessary information is clearly available within every business, and it should be used to carry out regular, objective assessments of individual abilities and organizational efficiency, which in turn should lead to action to correct defects and improve performance.

The purpose of this final chapter is, in effect, to summarize the main points made throughout the book by presenting a check-list which will enable any personnel manager to *audit* the activities of his particular department, methodically reviewing their whole range by reference to acknowledged good practices. The continuing theme to be kept in mind during this process is that every aspect of personnel management has an impact in two ways: one on business efficiency and the other on the individual employees involved. Both must be taken into account in assessing the success of the personnel management function.

TECHNIQUES FOR MANAGING TOTAL LABOUR RESOURCES

	Yes/No	Action

1. Has the organization a *manpower plan*? In detail, is the following information readily available:

(*a*) An organization chart?

(*b*) Precise job descriptions for all posts shown on the organization chart?

(*c*) An estimate of future labour requirements for five years ahead?

(*d*) A training and development programme, designed to meet the estimated labour requirements?

(*e*) A recruitment programme, designed to fill anticipated gaps?

(*f*) A genuine assessment of the impact on these detailed plans of such imponderables as technological advance, sociological changes, and other local, national, or industry-wide factors?

(*g*) A procedure for keeping the manpower plan under constant review, so that it is flexible above all else?

2. Has the organization *personnel policies* which are written, published, and fully understood by all employees?

3. Do the staff of the personnel department adhere to a *recruitment procedure* based on:

(*a*) Receipt of a full job requisition from the departmental head?

(*b*) A full analysis of the job, if this is not already available?

(*c*) Familiarity with all local sources of labour supply: above all, friendly, personal contact with the employment office manager, youth employment officer, and the careers masters in schools and colleges?

(*d*) Continuous check on the response, cost, and effectiveness of staff advertising?

(*e*) Adequate training of all recruitment officers in the techniques of dealing with applications, taking up references, and interviewing candidates?

(*f*) The use of selection tests and group selection methods where appropriate?

	Yes/No	Action

(*g*) The fullest preparation of members beforehand, when panel interviews are arranged?

(*h*) Follow-up of successful candidates to validate
the selection techniques used?

4. Are the problems associated with *transferring*
employees dealt with realistically throughout the
organization?

(*a*) Are supervisors impressed with the need to
spot signs of trouble which may eventually lead
to transfer requests?

(*b*) Do managers have a positive attitude towards
transfers, recognizing that some changes are
inevitable if an organization is to grow?

5. Does a clearly defined policy and procedure for
promotion exist within the organization?

Have these matters been resolved:

(*a*) Seniority or merit as the basis for promotion?

(*b*) The extent to which senior appointments shall
be filled internally or by recruitment from outside?

(*c*) Providing members of promotion boards with
full job descriptions, and their training in selection and assessment techniques?

6. Is there a *dismissal procedure* which is fully
understood by management and employees?

Does this allow individuals the right to state their
case personally?

And does it allow the right to appeal against dismissal decisions?

Has a redundancy policy been prepared, in consultation with worker representatives, so that it is
available should the need ever arise? In the event,
does the policy provide for everything possible to
be done to minimize the number of redundancies
and to help those affected to find other jobs?

7. In striving to obtain optimum use of available
labour, is special attention given to the problems
of employing:

(*a*) Married women?

(*b*) Older people?

(*c*) Disabled workers?

(*d*) Immigrant workers?

Have senior management agreed a code of
'affirmative action' in applying the Race Relations
Act?

	Yes/No	Action

8. Is *training* viewed positively throughout the organization as the best means of increasing the productivity of all grades of staff?

(*a*) Are training needs assessed effectively in the first place, priorities settled, and standards defined?

(*b*) Is a development programme then established for each individual likely to benefit from further training?

(*c*) Does the organization provide its own training officers by withdrawing executives from line management for short periods?

(*d*) Are those responsible for training and job instruction properly qualified in the relevant techniques?

(*e*) Have the advantages of using separate job instruction areas been fully evaluated, as opposed to the 'understudy' method?

(*f*) Do line managers fully accept the fundamental importance of training-on-the-job, as opposed to sending subordinates on infrequent external courses?

(*g*) Nevertheless, is the best use made of all the training facilities provided outside the organization?

(*h*) Are employees who return from outside courses positively encouraged to apply the techniques learned and to develop new ideas?

(*i*) Are relationships with neighbouring organizations such that a 'training circuit' can be arranged?

(*j*) Are results of all training efforts followed up and evaluated?

(*k*) Is full advantage taken of T.O.P.S.?

9. Do *rates of pay* allow for any flexibility within the limits imposed by collective agreements, legislation, and Government policy?

10. Is management prepared to face up to the realities of getting rid of *restrictive practices* through *productivity bargains*?

	Yes/No	Action

11. Does management take the *initiative* in improving working conditions and in developing better methods of wage negotiation?
Is it feasible to boost morale by a programme of regular changes in the working environment?

12. Has the organization a clearly defined attitude towards *trade union membership* of its employees?

13. Is management practice such as to encourage *shop stewards* to act in a constitutional manner?
Does management help in ensuring that shop stewards are adequately trained for their tasks as worker representatives?

14. Is *joint consultation* practised positively, as a method of obtaining employees' views on problems and proposed changes before final decisions are taken?
(a) Do senior staff take the lead in encouraging joint consultation?
(b) Are important items included on joint committee agenda?

15. Are the barriers to effective *communications* fully understood throughout the organization?
Do the job descriptions for managers and supervisors make clear their responsibilities for communications?
Is the concept of a feed-back mechanism emphasized as a means of ensuring that communications are understood?
(a) Are notice boards efficiently controlled?
(b) Does the organization publish a house journal or news-sheet?
(c) Are employees issued with a handbook containing information about the organization's structure, policies, working conditions, and the rules of conduct?
Is any one executive charged with ensuring that the communications system throughout the organization functions efficiently?

16. Are checks made to ensure that a *consistent disciplinary policy* is applied by all managers and supervisors?

	Yes/No	*Action*

17. Is *labour turnover* accurately recorded, and constructive use made of the information thus provided?
  Are exit interviews arranged with leavers, and followed up by management action on any deficiencies revealed?

18. Are *welfare services* provided for the right motives?
  Are social activities largely administered by the employees taking part in them?

19. Are there differences in the way '*staff*' *and* '*workers*' are treated in the organization? Is anything being done to remove these differences?

20. Does the organization's provision for the *health* of employees exceed the minima laid down by statute?
  Are occupational medical services provided?

21. Are continuous efforts made to impress on all employees that *accidents* will only be prevented when they accept responsibility as individuals for working safely?

22. Is optimum use made of *outside organizations* and the various types of help they can offer in solving personnel problems?

23. Is the personnel records system able to produce whatever management control information is required quickly and accurately?

GETTING THE BEST FROM INDIVIDUALS

24. Are individuals provided with precise *job descriptions*?

25. Are they properly *inducted* into the organization when they start?
  Especially school-leavers?

26. Are *standards* of job performance clearly laid down?

27. Is there a regular formal *assessment* of how well these performance standards are being realized?

	Yes/No	Action

28. Are managers kept aware of research findings about the behaviour of individuals at work and the ways they function in groups?

(*a*) Is the organization willing to participate directly in research work in this field?

(*b*) Do managers know how to promote *job satisfaction* and remove the *frustrations* which inviduals experience at work?

(*c*) Are managers and supervisors readily accessible to their subordinates?

29. Are the principles of *participative management* encouraged within the organization?
In particular:

(*a*) Do staff agree *targets* with their superiors for improved performance?

(*b*) Is special attention given to *enlarging the jobs* of individuals, and is the application of this concept discussed with them by superiors?

(*c*) During performance reviews, do staff help to identify *organizational shortcomings* which hinder progress?

(*d*) Does the organization run a *suggestions scheme* to encourage individuals' ideas on increasing productivity?

30. Is *joint consultation* practised in ways which allow problems to be dealt with by those employees whose working lives are directly affected?

(*a*) Initially to share in deciding the rules and regulations governing the behaviour of individuals in the workplace?

(*b*) To sit in judgment on any breaches of these rules?

(*c*) To try to exercise some measure of control over absenteeism?

(*d*) To share in the continuous campaign for safe working throughout the organization?

31. Are the techniques of *job evaluation* and *merit-rating* used to reward the efforts and talents of individuals?

	Yes/No	Action
32. Are employees interviewed by their departmental heads when they return to work after *absence*? Are they visited by someone from the organization during periods of absence which last longer than three days?		
32. Is special attention given to the *conditions* in which individuals work (e.g. environment, types of work, hours)?		
33. Could the social problems of *shift working* be overcome by adopting a Continental system of shifts?		
34. Have supervisors and managers been trained in an effective procedure for dealing with *individual staff problems*?		

Much of what has been advocated in this book as being good personnel management practice has now been incorporated in the provisions of the Trade Union and Labour Relations Act, 1974, and in the Code of Industrial Relations Practice.* The official view of a check-list of good personnel management may therefore be summarized in this way:

TRADE UNION AND LABOUR RELATIONS ACT 1974

	Yes/No	Action
1. Is it clear which managers are responsible for *recruitment*? Are they aware of each individual's rights under the Act? Do they ensure that each job applicant is informed of his rights to belong to a trade union? Do they keep a written record of the reasons for rejecting unsuccessful applicants?		

* A new version of the Code may appear in 1975 or 1976.

	Yes/No	Action

2. Do *contracts of employment* provide written notice to all employees of periods of notice?

Do they provide full details of holiday entitlements?

Do they give each employee in writing the name (or job title) of the person with whom grievances can be raised, and also outline subsequent steps in the formal grievance procedure?

3. Are specific managers designated with authority to *dismiss* employees? Are they aware of what constitutes fair dismissal?

Does dismissal procedure encompass the following stages:

(*a*) oral warning;

(*b*) written warning;

(*c*) opportunity for an employee to state his case, and to be accompanied by his trade union representative;

(*d*) right of appeal to a higher level of management?

Are written records of all dismissals kept for at least a year?

4. Do all your organization's procedural and substantive *agreements* comply with the terms of the Act? Do they match up to the recommendations of the Code?

5. Are your organization's policies as regards union *recognition* and the *representation* of manual, white-collar, and managerial staffs settled and clear?

6. Do all voluntary recognition agreements specify precisely the categories of employees they cover? (Great help in the future in forming bargaining units and in avoiding inter-union competition for members.)

7. Are all employees issued with an *annual statement* of the organization's activities? Does the information provided conform with Stock Exchange rules?

Do you ensure that your own managers receive this information beforehand?

	Yes/No	Action
8 Have you reviewed all existing procedures for the settlement of disputes in the light of the Code (adherence to which will be important evidence in unfair practices hearings)?		
9. Have you established which union representatives with whom you deal have the *authority to call strikes*?		
10 Are your *works' rules* of conduct up-to-date, and do they comply with the requirements of the Act?		
11. Are you aware of the facilities available to help settle disputes?		

The tasks of the personnel manager have already been described as basically those of advising on the planning necessary to make optimum use of total available labour resources and how to derive most benefit from each individual's abilities. If all the criteria listed above are accepted as good practice, then the job of the personnel manager is obviously a difficult one. It will involve hard work, some tedium (preparing precise job descriptions, for example), and a measure of embarrassment and discomfort when dealing with individual personal problems or tough negotiations with worker representatives. The fact remains that these difficulties cannot be shirked for the sake of 'a quiet life'—they must be tackled and successfully at that, if personnel management is to become increasingly respected as an honourable profession.

Addresses of Organizations

1. The Institute of Personnel Management,
   Central House, Upper Woburn Place, London, WC1H 0HX.

2. The Industrial Society,
   Robert Hyde House, 48 Bryanston Square, London, W1H 8AH.

3. The British Institute of Management,
   Management House, Parker Street, London, WC2B 5PT.

4. The British Association for Commercial and Industrial Education,
   16 Park Crescent, Regent's Park, London, W1N 4AP.

5. The Royal Society for the Prevention of Accidents,
   Industrial Safety Division, 52 Grosvenor Gardens, London, S.W.1.

6. The Tavistock Institute of Human Relations,
   Tavistock Centre, Belsize Lane, London, N.W.3.

7. The Manpower Society,
   1A Berners St., London, W.1.

The Bullock Committee Report on Industrial Democracy*

The main recommendations were these:

—Any firm with more than 2000 employees must introduce worker directors if 20 per cent of the workers request this.
—Equal numbers of union and shareholder representatives on a board (2x), plus a smaller group of co-opted directors (y) agreeable to both parties.
—Worker directors will be chosen only through union channels. They will serve for three years, and will be paid expenses but no fees.
—An Industrial Democracy Commission will be set up to watch over

* Report of the Committee of Inquiry on Industrial Democracy; Cmnd. 6706 (H.M.S.O., 1977).

the rules, encourage participation, and, if necessary, impose the 'y' group if unions and shareholders cannot agree.

—Subsidiaries may also ask for worker-boards if they employ more than 2000.

—£3 million will be made available for training trade union nominees in management practices, company law and finance.

A minority report was also published signed by three members (identified with the 'directors' side of the Committee). They were extremely concerned about the radical nature of the proposals and the effects which any legislation, forced through in the near future, could have in increasing conflict in industrial relations rather than encouraging cooperation, in damaging our industrial credibility abroad among people who invest in Britain and with our overseas customers and international bankers, and hence generally damaging confidence in the efficiency of British industry and commerce. Their view, in summary, was that there is no evidence whatsoever that the proposed changes would be beneficial and the risks are enormous. 'If ever there was a case for caution in an unknown, unassessable venture, it is this one' (Report, page 187).

The wide-ranging nature of the ensuing controversy, conducted at the time of writing in 1977 when the Labour Government's future was precarious to the point of almost certain defeat at the next general election, makes the prospect of legislation on the Committee's recommendations difficult to foresee. The 'Note of Dissent' (Report, page 166) written by Nicholas Wilson, a solicitor member of the Committee, therefore seems particularly relevant:

' "Industrial Democracy" is a phrase which at the time of the Committee's appointment was known to few and understood by fewer still. Since that time it has been thrust into the forefront of public debate more swiftly than any other concept of comparable importance in recent years. As a result, the Committee's recommendations, if they were to become "legislative opinion", would be far in advance of public opinion at large. This fact has overwhelming significance: recent history in the field of industrial relations illustrates more vividly than words the importance of social legislation keeping pace with public opinion. The lesson to be drawn is that there are limits to the rate at which legislation can successfully achieve "social engineering" in advance of social evolution. Despite the justification for employee representation—beyond challenge—one cannot ignore the genuine hostility to the concept on the part of a large section of middle and upper management, and the relative apathy on the part of many other employees. Such a setting is scarcely ideal for the introduction of radical legislation in an area of such importance. Inevitably any proposed legislation involves a balance between the group interests whose conflicts the legislation attempts to adjust.... Participation and influence in policy and decision-making can be readily and effectively achieved without the necessity of regulating the composition of boards and companies in a rigid and potentially divisive manner.'

Index

Absenteeism, 37, 301
Accidents, 54, 333
Accommodation (welfare), 321
Accountancy, and personnel management, 358
'Added value' concept, in pay settlements, 205
Adler, 32
Administrative Staff College, Henley, 181
Advertising for staff, 70
Advisory, Conciliation and Arbitration Service (A.C.A.S.), 7, 245, 251, 252, 253, 276, 277
Advisory nature of personnel management, 2, 12, 159
'Affirmative action' in race relations, 116
Age structure in an organization, 108
Agency shop agreements, 250
Agricultural Wages Act (1948), 194
Ambition, 32
Annual salaries for all workers, 324
Anxiety, cause of job frustration, 37
Appeals committees, 267
Applications for jobs, 61, 72, 353
Apprenticeships, 89, 134, 170
Apprentice supervisor, 171
Aptitude tests, 84
Arbitration, 245
Assessment centres, 143
Assessment of staff, 92, 120
Association of Salaried Staffs, Executives and Technicians, 226
Attendance money, 215
Attitudes, impact on personality, 47
Attitude surveys, 139
Auditing the personnel function, 22

B.A.C.I.E. (British Association for Commercial and Industrial Education), 351
Bargaining structure, 271
Barriers to effective communications, 280
Basic payments, 25

Behaviour
    at the workplace, 34, 266
    industrial, principles, 35
Behavioural sciences, 11, 15, 34, 40, 297
Birmingham's immigrants, 117
Blackburn Generating Station, absenteeism, 303
Blake–Mouton Grid, 16
Board of Directors, personnel manager on, 339
Bonuses, 216
Boredom, and its relief, 311
Box numbers in staff advertising, 71
Branches, trade union, 238
Branch meetings and shop stewards, 255
Bridlington Agreement, 241
Briefing groups, 287
British Council, 117
British Institute of Management
    activities, 351
    Management Consulting Services Information Bureau, 348
British Legion, 111
British Leyland Motor Co., procedural agreement, 272
British Steel Corporation, worker directors, 298
Brown, Wilfred, 35
Budget, personnel department, 340
Building industry, Joint Apprenticeship Board, 171
Bullock Committee Report, 375
Burlinghame, 32
Business Efficiency Exhibition, 354
Business Schools, London and Manchester, 181

Cadbury's immigrant workers, 118
Cannon, J., 363
Canteens, 320
Careers Advisory Officers, 68
Careers masters, 68
Central Training Council, 170

Change, 19, 36, 157, 272, 297
Chief Executive, 12
   attitude towards joint consultation, 265
Christian ideals, Sermon on the Mount, 21
Circuit scheme, aid to management training, 183
Circular letter, as source of labour supply, 70
Civil Service, 108, 122
   C.S. Department, 40, 137, 155
   Pay Research Unit, 192
   Selection Board, 86
Classical school of management theory, 8
Clocking-in systems, 324
Closed shop, 247, 249, 250
Coal Industry Nationalization Act (1946), provision for joint consultation, 263
Coal News, N.C.B. house journal, 287
Code of Industrial Relations Practice, 251, 256, 257, 265, 282
Collective bargaining, 190, 198
Colleges of Further Education, 166
Commission on Industrial Relations, 13, 250, 256
Committee on Dismissal Procedures, 94
Committee of Investigation, 245
Commonwealth Immigrants Act (1962), 114
Communications, 25, 36, 38, 155, 268, 279, 309
Companionship, 33
Comparability as factor in wage levels, 192
Competitions, 43
   supervisory management and, 179
Complaints
   race relations, 115
   symptoms of more deep-seated disturbances, 35
Computers, in P.E.R., 347
   and personnel records, 356
Conciliation, 252
   (see also A.C.A.S.)
Conciliation Act (1896), 245
Conciliation Committees (Race Relations Act), 115
Conciliation officers, 211, 251, 252
Conditions of work,
   cause of job frustration, 37
   concessions made to married women, 103
Confederation of British Industry, 55, 243
Conflict of management-worker interests, 10
Constitutional role of shop stewards, 259
Construction I.T.B., 162
Consultants, when to use their services, 348
Continental shift system, 317
Contract of employment, 61
Contracts of Employment Act (1972), 88
Convenor of shop stewards, 255

Cooling-off period, 250
Cooperation of management and workers: Mayo, 34
Cost of living, 191
Costs of labour turnover, 306
Court of Enquiry, 245
'Coventry, sending to', 48
Craft unions, 236
Critical incident analysis of training needs, 176

Day nurseries, 104
Day-release courses, 170
Decision time, in interviews, 81
Definitions of personnel management, 1
Delegation, 14, 44
Demarcation disputes, 247
Democracy in industry, 22, 256, 295
Demotivating factors, 38
Department of Employment, 7, 68, 113, 114, 160, 163, 165, 177, 196, 210, 270, 344
   Gazette, 345
Design of staff assessment forms, 126
Development of individuals, 121
Differentials, 25, 214
Diploma in Management Studies, 180
Disabled Persons Employment Act (1944), 110
Disabled workers, 110, 165
   mental illness, 113
Discharge, 93, 251, 277
Discipline, 176, 293
   joint committees, 267
   role of shop stewards, 259
Discrimination in employment, 115
   between men and women, 211
Discussion groups, in supervisory training, 179
Discussions, as part of staff assessment procedure, 127
Dismissal procedure, 94, 251, 277
Disputes machinery, 244, 272
Distillers Co. Ltd.
   breaks during working hours, 316
   pre-interview preparation form, 140
Donovan Commission Report, 201, 204, 243, 246
Drucker, Peter, 'Manager's Letter', 140

Earnings-related supplements, 53, 321
Education Act (1870), 5
Efficiency agreements, 232
Election of representatives to joint committees, 264
Electricity Act (1947), provision for joint consultation, 264
Employers' associations, 242, 260

Employment agencies, 68
  for older workers, 109
Employment and Training Act 1973, 160
Employment department, structure, 339
Employment function, 3, 52
Employment handbook, 89, 167, 285
Employment Medical Advisory Service, 333, 337
Employment offices, 68, 344
  planned improvements, 346
Employment policy, 23, 24
Employment Protection Bill, 276
Employment rehabilitation centres, 109, 112, 345
Employment Services Agency, 160, 345
Engineering and Allied Employers' Federation, 1922 agreement, 255
Engineering I.T.B., 162
English classes for immigrants, 117
Equal Opportunities Commission, 211
Equal Pay Act 1970, 210
Ergonomics, 312
Esso Petroleum Co.
  productivity agreement (Fawley), 229
  staff performance review form, 128
European Association of Personnel Management, 349
European Company Statute, 31
European Economic Community, 29
European Social Fund, 30
Evaluation
  of job analysis, 66
  of selection decisions, 87
  of training, 159, 188
'Exceptions' for wage increases above norm, 201
Exchange visits for supervisors, 179
Exit interviews, labour turnover, 95, 306
Ex-officers Association, 68
Export office procedure courses, 164

Factor comparisons in job evaluation, 218
Factories Act (1961), main provisions, 326
Factory Inspectors, powers, 327, 337
Fair Labor Standards Act (1938), 196
Fair Wages Resolutions, 197
Fatigue, and its remedies, 310
Fawley Agreement on productivity, 229
Federations of trade unions, 240
Fencing dangerous machinery, 326
Fire precautions in factories, 327
Firestone Tyre and Rubber Co., 267
'Flat' organization, effect on productivity, 36
Flexible working hours (Flexitime), 318
Follow-up,
  of induction courses, 168

of new employees, 87
of staff assessment recommendations, 124, 140
of staff transferred, 90
of supervisory training, 179
Forecasts, manpower, 56
Formal system of industrial relations, 248
'Formula for development', 152
Fox, Alan, 10, 15, 16
Fred Olsen Ltd., 299
Fringe benefits, 321
Frustration, job, 36, 297
Full employment
  effect on development of personnel management, 7
Functional leadership, 42
Functional management, 12

Geared incentive schemes, 215
General Council, T.U.C., 241
General Federation of Trade Unions, 240
General Practitioners, 302
General Secretary, the trade union, 239
General unions, 237
Glacier Metal Company, 35, 71
Good housekeeping, 310
Government
  as an employer, 197
  intervention in wage negotiations, 194
  sponsorship of personnel management, 6
Government contracts, employment of disabled workers, 111
Government Training Centres (Skillcentres), 53, 109, 164, 345
Graduated pension scheme, 322
Grievances
  policy statement, 25
  symptoms of more deep-seated disturbances, 35
Group apprenticeship schemes, 172
Group assessments, means of ensuring objectivity, 142
Group behaviour
  Mayo's findings, 34
  methods of encouraging efficiency, 47
  optimum size of groups, 35
Group bonus schemes, 216
Group dynamics, 50
Group selection techniques, 85
Guaranteed weekly payments, 276

Halo effect, in interviews, 80
Handbook for employees, 89, 167, 285
Harmonization policies (E.E.C.), 29
Hawthorne experiments, 34
Health of employees, 326

Health and Safety at Work Act 1974, 337
Herzberg, 38
High pay rates, 216
History of personnel management, 4
Holdsworth, Roger, 85
Horizontal communications, 283
Hours of work, 313
House journals, 285
Huddersfield, occupational health service, 331
Hull, survey of office conditions, 328
Human relations school of management theory, 9
Human resource audit, 363

I.C.I. Ltd., 298, 317, 324
Immigrant workers, 113
Incentives, 214
  link with motivation, 33
  non-financial, 38
Incomes norm as a factor in wage levels, 192
Indentures, apprentice, 89
Index of Retail Prices, 191, 209
Individual
  and personnel management, 3, 13
  his needs from his leader, 45
  role in the organization, 121, 153
Individual members, power of trade unions over, 247
Individual staff problems, 300
Induction training, 166
  policy statement, 24
Industrial Arbitration Board, 196, 245, 253
Industrial conferences (E.T.U.), 240
Industrial Courts Act (1919), 245
Industrial Development Councils, 163
Industrial Health and Safety Centre, 345
Industrial health service, 329
Industrial psychology, 6, 34
Industrial relations, 4, 233
  formal–informal systems, 248
  law in Europe, 30
Industrial Relations Act (1971), 94, 249
Industrial relations phase in personnel management, 6
Industrial Safety Advisory Council, 336
Industrial Society, The, 5, 287, 349
Industrial sociology, 34
Industrial Training Act (1964), 100, 159
Industrial Training Boards, 161
Industrial Training Research Unit, 161
Industrial Training Service, 164
Industrial Tribunals, 89, 100, 211, 251, 252, 277

Industrial unions, 237
Informal leader, his role and behaviour, 45
Informal system of industrial relations, 248, 268
Information, giving to T.U.s., 309
Inspectors, Factory, 327, 337, 338
  Wages, 195
Institute of Personnel Management, 1, 5, 348
  appointments service, 349
  definition of personnel management, 2
Institute of Supervisory Management, 177
Instructor training, 164, 177, 345
Instructor training colleges, 165
Intelligence, local labour markets, 58, 347
Intelligence tests, 83
International trade unionism, 242
Interviews, 61, 76
  appraisal, 127
  panel type, 82
  staff leaving, 95, 306
Intimidation of trade union members, 247
Iron and Steel I.T.B., 162

Jaques, Elliot, 35
Job analysis, 62
  and promotion, 92
Job centres, 68, 346
Job classification, 63, 218
Job definitions: superior-subordinate perception, 14
Job descriptions, 24, 54, 63, 77
  remedy for job frustration, 37
Job enlargement, 297
Job enrichment, 154, 158, 297
Job evaluation, 210, 215, 218
  L.A.M.S.A.C. procedure, 219
Job frustration, 36
Job preference, 32
Job ranking, 218
Job requisitions, 61
Job rotation, 90, 121, 180, 297
Job satisfaction, 36, 297
Job specification, 63
Job training, 168
Joint absentee committees, 267, 304
Joint Apprenticeship Board of the Building Industry, 171
Joint consultation, 260, 275
  and communications, 287
  industrial democracy, 295
  nationalized industries, 263
  on redundancy, 98
  policy statement, 25
  safety committees, 335, 337
Joint production committees, 262
Jung, 32

Justice,
  meaning in personnel management, 2
  principle of personnel policy, 22

Key result areas (MBO), 147

Labour market intelligence, 58, 347
Labour relations, 254
  initiative by management, 260, 275
  policy statements, 23, 25
Labour stability, measurement, 305
Labour turnover, 166, 304
  job satisfaction and morale, 77
Lay-off, 93
Leadership, 41
  by consent, 295
Leaving report, 95
Legally enforceable agreements, 250
Leisure from shorter working hours, 315
Letter of offer, 89
Letters of application, 72
Levy/grant/exemption criteria, 161
Lieu bonuses, 216
Line management, 12
Local Authorities Management Services
  Advisory Committee, job evaluation
  procedure, 219
Local Employment Committees, 344
Local Employment Offices, 68
Local unions, 237
London Gazette, publication of wage regula-
  tion proposals, 195
London Postal Schools, 173
London Transport Executive, recruitment
  arrangements with Barbados Govern-
  ment, 118
Long-service awards, 322
Long-term wage agreements, 207
Low pay problems, 203, 208
Lump-sum pay settlements, 209

Management,
  analysis into activities, 179
  line, staff, functional, 12
Management by objectives, 145
Management consultants, 348
Management development, 179
Management leadership, 275
Management sanctions, 48
Manpower forecasting, 56
Manpower planning, 52
  and working population, 101
  phase in personnel management, 7
  policy statement, 21
  strategies, 24
Manpower Services Commission, 160, 162,
  163

Manpower Society, 350
Married women, 102
Maternity, return to work, 276
Mayo, Elton, research, 34
McGregor, Douglas, 16, 17, 145
Measured day work, 216
  O.M.E. report, 217
Medical officers, 330
Medical records of employees, 331
Meday College of Technology, 77
Membership of trade unions, 236, 247, 250
Mental illness, disabled persons, 113
Mergers, effects on staff, 307
Merit-rating, 220
Minimum wages, 209
Misconduct committee, 267
Mobility of labour (EEC), 30
Modular training of personnel managers,
  185
Monotony, and its relief, 311
Morale, 37, 292
Motivation, 32, 38, 155
  of married women in taking jobs, 102
Multi-unionism, 242

National Advisory Committee on the Em-
  ployment of the older worker, 108
National Assistance Act (1948), 111
National Board for Prices and Incomes, 199,
  208, 231, 232
National conference, trade union, 239
National Economic Development Council,
  52, 199
National Examinations Board in Supervisory
  Studies, 177
National Executive Committee, trade union,
  239
National Health Service Act (1948), 111, 120
National Industrial Relations Court, 250
National Institute of Industrial Psychology,
  78n, 85
National Insurance Act (1946) 111; (1959)
  322; (1966) 99, 321
National Insurance (Industrial Injuries) Act,
  111, 335
National Joint Advisory Council, 243
  proposals on older workers, 119
National minimum wage, 209
National Plan, 52
National roll of employers, 111
National wages policy, 198
Nationalized industries,
  and joint consultation, 263
  redundancy policies, 99
News-sheets, 285
Noise, effects and prevention, 311

Norm for wage increases, 192, 200
Notice boards, 285
Notice, minimum period of, 88, 277
Nurseries for children of working mothers, 104

Objectives of the organization, 38, 55, 145
Objectivity in staff assessments, 122, 141
Occupational guidance service, 347
Occupational Health Services, 329
   policy statement, 25
Office of Manpower Economics, 202, 206
Office of Population Censuses and Surveys, 268
Offices, Shops and Railway Premises Act (1963), 328
Offices, conditions in, 329
Official Secrets Act, 89, 352
Official strikes, 248
Older workers, 53, 107
   and redundancy, 97
   training, 172
Olsen Ltd., Fred, 299
Operator training, 168
   policy statement, 24
Organization chart, in manpower planning, 54
Organizational behaviour, 19
Organizational Development, 19, 157
Organizational psychology, 35
Organizational theory, 8
Over Forty-Five's Association, 68, 109
Overtime, 313
Owen, Robert, 5

Panel interviews, 82
Participation by employees, 7, 31, 36, 38, 158, 296, 298, 299
   directors of British Steel Corporation, 298
Part-time workers, 106, 109
'Paternalism', 319
P.A.Y.E., 117
Pay relativities, 193
Pay review bodies, 202
Pension schemes, 322
   Royal warrants and grants, 111
Pareto's Law of salary levels, 228
Performance improvement guide, 147
Performance rating: methods of I.T.B. grants, 162
Personal problems, 321
   policy statement, 26
Personality, 46
   and leadership, 45
Personality tests, 84

Personnel management,
   and morale, 292
   advisory nature, 12
   introducing into an organization, 342
   measuring its success, 365
   routine and creative aspects, 8
   training in, 184
Personnel Management Advisory Service, 7
Personnel policy, 21
Personnel records, 353
Personnel specification, 63, 66
Persuasion, how to present a difficult case, 289
Physical surroundings, 310
Piece-rates advantage and drawbacks, 216
Plant bargaining, 256
Points rating in job evaluation, 218
Policy, personnel, 21
Population (working) forecast, 101
Pre-entry closed shops, 250
Prejudice against immigrants, 116
   in interviews, 80
President, trade union, 240
Prices and Incomes policy, 198
   Acts (1966, 1968), 201
Price Commission, 203
Price stability, 201
Primary groups, 36
Principles of personnel policy, 22
Procedural agreements, 272
Productivity and absenteeism, 302
Productivity bargains, 204, 229, 257
   restrictive practices, 269
Professional associations, 238, 274
   source of labour supply, 69
Professional and Executive Recruitment Service, 68, 344, 347
Proficiency tests, 84
Profit-sharing schemes, 215, 225
Programmed instruction, 169, 173
Projective type of personality test, 84
Promotion, 91
   of immigrant workers, 118
   to foreman, 49
   use of staff assessment, 122, 127
Promotion board, 92, 142, 143
Prosperity of an industry, factor in wage levels, 191
Protection against arbitrary dismissal, 93, 276
Protocol, managerial, 44
Public sector wages, 198, 202
   job evaluation in local government, 219
Publicity for suggestion schemes, 224
Publishing personnel policies, 26

Quality of life at work, 29, 296
Questionnaire type of personality test, 84

Race Relations Act (1968), 28, 115
    Board, 115
Rate-fixing, 215
Rates of pay, use of job analysis, 63
Reception, of new employee, 61
    of visitors, 351
Recommendations, personal, as source of
    labour supply, 69
Records of staff, 353
    medical, 331
Recruitment, 24, 60, 114
Reddin, W. J., 17
Redeployment, 52
Redundancy, 96, 278
    effect on motivation, 32
    human asset accounting, 362
    payments, 99
Redundancy Fund, 99
Redundancy Payments Act 1965, 99
Redundancy Rebates Act 1968, 99
References, 74
Regional Development Councils, 163
Regional employment premiums, 53
Regional organization of trade unions, 239
Registered disabled persons, 111
Registrar of Friendly Societies, 250, 253
Registration of trade unions, 250
Regular Forces Employment Association, 68,
    109
Rehabilitation, 111, 345
    Employment Rehabilitation Centres, 109
    112, 345
Relativities, pay, 193
Remploy Ltd., 111
Repetitive jobs, 311
Requisitions for staff, 61
Research
    accident prevention, 336
    occupational health, 311
Resettlement transfer scheme, 344
Resignations, 95
Rest-pauses at work, 312
Restrictive practices, 269
Retirement, 108
Review of salaries, 225
Robens Committee (Health and Safety), 337
Rodger, Professor Alec, 78n
Role expectations, 9
Role of individual in an organization, 120
Rorshach ink-blot test, 84
Rotation of jobs for training purposes, 90
Royal Commission on Incomes Distribu-
    tion, 202

Royal Commission on Trade Unions and
    Employers' Associations, 247
Royal Society for the Prevention of Accidents,
    336
Royal warrants, pensions, 111
Rules of behaviour, and joint consultation,
    266

Safety, 326, 330, 333, 364
    job analysis, 64
    policy statement, 26
Safety committee, 335
Safety officer, 335
Salaries, 225
    staff assessment, use in, 121
Sanctions, 47
Sandwich courses, 170
Scanlon plan, 218
Scholarships for apprentices, 171
School-leavers, induction, 168
Scientific management, 6, 93
Search, employer's right of, 352
Secretary of State for Employment (the
    Minister), 115, 195, 245, 250, 251, 252,
    277
Secrets, trade, 89
Security, motive for work, 33, 35
    of property, 352
Selection tests, 84
Self-discipline, 293
Self-realization, motive for work, 33
Seniority, 91, 96
Seven-point plan, 78
Sex Discrimination Act 1975, 210
Sheltered workshops, 111
Shifts, 316
Shop stewards, 239, 254
    and redundancy, 98
    influence on earnings, 200
Shop stewards' committee, 239
Short-listing, 61
Sickness and absenteeism, 303
Sickness benefits, 321
'Sitting-next-to-Nelly' in job training, 168
Skill dilution and wastage indices, 305
Slough, Industrial Health Service, 331
Small employers, provision of occupational
    health services, 331
Social activities, 323
Social contract, in pay policy, 202
Social status, 323
Sociology and personnel management, 29
Sources of labour supply, 67
Spearman's 'g' factor, 84
Sports clubs, 323
Staff assessment, 120

Staff associations, 238, 274
Staff requisition, 61
Staff-worker distinctions, 323
Stainer, Gareth, 56
State intervention in industrial disputes, 244
Statistical information about staff, 354
Status, staff-labour, 323
Status of the personnel manager, 354
Stereotypes, in interviews, 81
Stress at work, causes, 296
Strikes, 247, 248
Structure of industrial relations, 233
Structure of personnel departments, 339
Subordinate, positive role during performance assessment, 137, 138
Suggestion schemes, 221
Supervisors, 37
    absenteeism, 301
    administering incentives, 218
    and rehabilitation, 112
    assessment centres, 143
    changing role, 175
    communications, 284
    functions, 176
    married women, 104
    view of discipline, 294
Supervisory training, 175, 345
Suspension, 93
Sweden, works councils, 287
Systems theory, 9

Take-overs, 307
Targets in management by objectives, 147
Tavistock Institute of Human Relations, 351
Technical colleges, preparation-for-retirement courses, 110
Technology impact on human relations problems, 9
Termination of employment, 93
Terms and Conditions of Employment Act (1959), 196
Terms of employment in writing, 88
Testimonials, 74
Tests for selection, 83
T-groups, 51
Theories 'x' and 'y', 16, 145
Threshold agreements, 209
Time off with pay, 276
Toleration of breaches of disciplinary rules, 294
Trade tests, 84
Trade Union Act (1913), 234
Trade Union Amendment Act (1867), 233
Trade Union and Labour Relations Act 1974, 234, 250

Trade Union Congress, 55, 201, 239, 241, 298
    education of shop stewards, 257
Trade unions
    as sources of labour supply, 69
    definition and purposes, 234
    international, 30, 242
    sanctions, 48
    white-collar, 273
Trades councils, 239
Training, 3, 33, 159, 344, 362
    an 'on-the-job' function, 14
    European Social Fund, 30
    evaluation, 187
    for promotion, 92
    in labour relations, 275
    of personnel managers, 184
    of shop stewards, 257
    policy statement, 24
    worker representatives, 267
Training Opportunities Scheme (T.O.P.S.), 160, 165, 346
Training programmes, use of job analysis, 64
Training sections separate from production areas, 168
Training Services Agency, 160
Transfers of staff, 89
Transport, welfare provisions for, 321
T.G.W.U., 234, 237
T.W.I. (Training Within Industry), 177
    procedure for handling staff problems, 300

Unemployment benefits, 53, 99
Unfair dismissal, 94, 251, 277
Unfair industrial practices, 250
Uniformity in staff assessment, 122
Unit improvement plan (MBO), 151
University Appointments Officers, 68
Unofficial strikes, 247, 248

Validation of selection methods, 87
Verbal communications, 283
Vocational guidance, 113, 346, 347
Vocational training, 345
Voluntary acceptance of wages policy, 202
Voluntary principle of collective bargaining, 190
Volvo (Sweden), 50

Wages and Salaries, 190
    policy statement, 25
    use of job analysis, 63
Wages Council Act (1959), 194
Wages Councils, 194, 277
Wages drift, 200, 203, 248
Wages Inspectorate, 195
Wages regulation orders, 195

Welfare, 4, 106, 319, 327
  policy statement, 25
  provisions of Factories Act (1961), 326
Welfare phase in personnel management, 5
White-collar unions, 273
Whitley committee (1916), 260
Wireless and Telegraphy Act (1906), 27
Wool, Jute, and Flax I.T.B., 162
Woodward, Joan, 9
Work, a social obligation, 32
Working conditions, 37, 235, 310
Working groups, 2, 35, 47, 50

Works Committees, 260
  European, 31
Works Councils, Swedish, 287
Work-group sanctions, 47
Working population, 101
'Working-wife syndrome', 105
Work-measured incentive schemes, 215
Workshop rules, and shop stewards, 258
Written communications, 284

Youth Employment Service, 344